THE **BIG** BOOK OF
SOUPS

BEVERLY LEBLANC

THE **BIG** BOOK OF **SOUPS**

365 DELICIOUS RECIPES FOR ALL SEASONS

DUNCAN BAIRD PUBLISHERS

LONDON

The Big Book of Soups
Beverly LeBlanc

First published in the United Kingdom and Ireland in
 2011 by
Duncan Baird Publishers Ltd
Sixth Floor, Castle House
75–76 Wells Street
London W1T 3QH

Conceived, created and designed by
 Duncan Baird Publishers

Managing Editor: Grace Cheetham
Editors: Nicole Bator and Victoria Fernandez Salom
Managing Designer: Suzanne Tuhrim
Commissioned photography: William Lingwood
Food Stylist: Bridget Sargeson
Assistant Food Stylist: Jack Sargeson
Prop Stylist: Lucy Harvey

British Library Cataloguing-in-Publication Data:
A CIP record for this book is available from the
British Library

ISBN: 978-1-84483-977-3

10 9 8 7 6 5 4 3 2 1

Typeset in Univers
Colour reproduction by Colourscan, Singapore
Printed in China by Imago

Notes on the recipes

Unless otherwise stated:
Use medium fruit and vegetables
Use fresh ingredients, including herbs and spices
Do not mix metric and imperial measurements
1 tsp = 5ml 1 tbsp = 15ml 1 cup = 250ml

The recipes in this book make 4–6 servings.

To PMOB

Author's acknowledgments

*I would like to think this book is all my own work.
Many people, however, have contributed much
to the final product. First and foremost, I must thank
my husband Philip Back, who kept up with the
seemingly endless recipe testing and shopping. I also
want to thank my other recipe testers – Philip Clarke,
Henry Johnson, Moya Gibbon, Nicola Placidi and
Susanna Tee.*

*The team at Duncan Baird have been a pleasure
to work with, especially Nicole Bator with her endless
patience and encouragement. She's an editor's editor.
Thank you also to Grace Cheetham for commissioning
this book, to Victoria Fernandez Salom for her
attentive, careful editing and good suggestions, and
to designer Suzanne Tuhrim and her team for the
attractive, contemporary look of the book.*

*Some of the most enjoyable times while writing
this book were the masterclasses in Japanese,
Thai and Italian soups from Shirley Booth,
Amara Nondha-Asa and Nicola Placidi respectively.
Thank you all.*

*I am also especially appreciative to Paule Caillat
(promenadesgourmandes.com), Niru Gupta
(niruskitchen.com), Amelia Kay, and Susanna Tee
for their general help, and my cousin Kim Wright,
for ideas from her restaurant, Deli in the Rye,
in Jefferson, Ohio.*

*Big thank-yous also go to Rosemary Carr,
Bill Dean, David Healy, Jean Herbert, Victoria Keller,
Maggi McCormack, Norma MacMillan, Lee Rengos
(and her mom), Stefanie Roth and Floren Shivitz.*

Contents

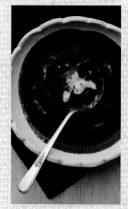

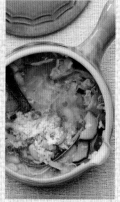

Introduction

It can be tempting to think of a book with three-hundred-and-sixty-five recipes as representing a recipe for every day of the year. Instead, I hope you will think of this collection as providing recipes for every occasion.

As I spent several cold, grey winter months totally immersed in reading about, thinking about, writing about, making and eating soups, I came to appreciate that the universal popularity of soups is due not only to their ability to satisfy, warm and comfort but also to their great versatility. The term 'soup' embraces many different liquid-based dishes, from thin, clear, delicately flavoured broths to big, substantial bowls of noodles, meat, poultry or vegetables. They can be righteously health conscious or indulgent, filling feasts-in-a-bowl. As you work your way through this book, you will soon appreciate how much soups have going for them. Regardless of how much cooking experience you have or how much time is available, you can make delicious soups.

Supermarkets and fast-food outlets provide plenty of prepared soup options – many of which are quite delicious and satisfying. But the case for making your own soups is unbeatable. From a financial perspective, you'll save lots of money. Many of the recipes in this book, for example, make four to six servings for less than the cost of a single pot of soup from my favourite sandwich shop. And even today with virtually all ingredients available year round, the old adage that cooking with the seasons saves you money still holds true. The vegetarian chapter offers plenty of scope for taking advantage of produce when it is most prolific and, therefore, least expensive. Soups can also transform leftovers into a second meal, cutting down on waste as well as your shopping bills. Making soups also gives you the opportunity to experiment with new ingredients. Galangal and hemp oil are two of the ingredients I hadn't used before, and they are now staples in my kitchen.

Somewhat ironically, it is the very versatility of soups that provided me with one of the biggest problems while planning this book: How much soup constitutes a serving? The different-sized appetites of adults and children was one obvious factor to consider, let alone the different-sized appetites of adults in different countries, as well as whether the soup is intended to be a meal in itself or just a light first course. I had many discussions with my editor about this, and the end result is that the recipes in this book 'make 4–6 servings'. This means you will get four adult-size bowls from a recipe with a little left for 'seconds', or six child-sized portions. After you've made a few recipes, you'll realize if you need to scale the quantities up or down for your requirements. The recipes in the Big Bowl Soups chapter, however, make soups that are meals in themselves, so when you make one of these recipes you won't have to do much other cooking.

I use the word 'satisfying' often when talking about soup. That is because soup-making is a satisfying experience both in the kitchen and at the table. With the majority of recipes in this book, very little effort and very little expense produce a satisfying result that gives more than just the nutrients you need to get through the day. A bowl of soup with a hunk of good bread is an enjoyable meal to share or savour on your own. When I was planning this book I looked North, South, East and West for inspiration. The result is a mix of international flavours that I hope you enjoy exploring and making at home as much as I have enjoyed writing about.

THE TECHNIQUES
PURÉEING & SIEVING SOUPS

Soups come in a variety of textures. Puréeing is a basic technique that gives many soups their smooth texture. Almost any soup can be puréed, but it is most suitable for vegetable, seafood and pulse and grain soups.

I've used a hand-held immersion blender for testing the recipes, but an upright blender, a food processor or a hand-turned mouli, or food mill, all do the job just as well. I choose the immersion blender for the simple reason it saves on washing up – you just put it in the saucepan and blend until the soup is the texture you desire and then wash the shaft and blade. If you are going to buy an immersion blender, choose a good quality one with a strong motor. It will be a false economy to buy a cheap one. The plus-point of using a mouli, however, is that it both purées and strains at the same time, which can save you time; the down side, is that it can require large storage space.

When you use an immersion blender, make sure the pan or bowl you are puréeing in is deep enough that the hot soup doesn't splash out and burn you. These blenders are usually sold with a beaker that is suitable to use when you are puréeing a small quantity but impractical for puréeing a whole soup. And when you are puréeing soups in a blender or food processor, use a folded tea towel to hold the lid in place, otherwise the hot steam could force the lid off and burn you.

Many soups are ready to serve immediately after puréeing, but some are sieved to obtain a smoother texture, or to remove small pieces of the ingredients, such as tomato skins and fennel fibres. Sometimes this is a matter of personal preference, but in some recipes it is essential, such as when the soup contains fish bones and scales.

I suggest a standard non-reactive metal sieve. Avoid using one with too fine a mesh; it simply takes too much time and elbow grease to work cooked vegetables through it. Instead, buy a less expensive one with larger holes in the mesh. If you prepare some of the fruit soups in the chilled soups chapter, or use any ingredient with a high acidic content, however, it is best to use a plastic mesh sieve so the acid doesn't react with metal and taint the flavour of your soup.

MAKING STOCK FOR SOUPS

Stock is the liquid that gives extra depth of flavour to many soups. It is perfectly possible to make delicious, satisfying bowls of soup without stock – the Italian Doctor's Bean & Spaghetti Soup and Aegean Red Mullet Soup are two great examples – but most soups rely on stock for their final taste.

The quality of the stock you use determines the quality of your soup, and deciding which stock to use in a recipe is arguably the most important step of the process. You have several options, ranging from homemade stock to prepared fresh stocks from the supermarket, concentrated liquid stocks to be diluted with water, concentrated gelled stocks and powders and, finally, the ubiquitous stock cube. The choice is personal, but least suitable is the stock cube, because of its high salt content and metallic taste from the additives and preservatives. Using homemade stock, on the other hand, gives you total control over the quality of all the ingredients that go into your soup, but it is the most time-consuming option. This is why most recipes in this book specify a homemade stock or a ready-made option – the choice is yours.

Homemade stock is easily made by simmering meat, poultry or seafood bones and trimmings, vegetables and other flavourings, such as herbs and spices. The process extracts the colours, flavours and nutrients from the ingredients, all of which are then transferred to your soup. Stock-making can be a very enjoyable time in the kitchen. It is an undemanding task, and the result is satisfying. Once you've made a large pot of stock, you can also use it to flavour sauces and stews.

The stock recipes in this book make larger quantities than specified in most recipes. This is because stock can easily be frozen in portions, and once I've decided to make a homemade stock, I might as well make enough to freeze several portions. If you don't have much freezer space, leave the stock to simmer, uncovered, for longer until half the quantity is left, which will have a concentrated flavour. Then leave this rich, intensely flavoured liquid to cool completely and freeze it in ice-cube trays. Use each cube straight from the freezer with enough cold water to complete 300ml/10½fl oz/scant 1¼ cups of the stock specified in the recipe.

Skimming soups and stocks – Stocks cook largely unattended, but your attention is most required towards the beginning of the process. As meat, seafood or poultry bones and trimmings are slowly heated to just below the boil, impurities are released and a grey scum appears on the surface. Use a large metal spoon, a slotted spoon or a round, perforated skimmer to remove this scum from the surface and discard it before adding the other flavouring ingredients. Take care not to remove too much of the liquid. Skimming can be a slow process, taking up to 30 minutes, but after you've finished this step you can leave the stock to gently simmer on its own. Pulses and vegetables also give off impurities while they simmer, but it isn't necessary to remove these. After you purée pulses, however, the thick layer of 'foam' that rises to the surface should be removed.

- 'Take stock and then make stock' is sage advice. Stock-making is a good way to utilize vegetables past their prime but not yet ready for the rubbish bin. Vegetable trimmings, such as mushrooms trimmings, tomato skins and onion skins (which give stock a richer, golden brown colour) are also excellent additions. Do not, however, include rotten or mouldy vegetables.
- Do not include potatoes in stocks because they make the liquid cloudy.
- Always break or chop bones before using them in stock. This gives the finished stock its slightly gelatinous texture that elevates soups made with homemade stock above ready-made versions.
- Trimmings from flat fish, such as plaice or sole, make excellent stock. Ask a fishmonger for these. They will likely be free or very inexpensive. Do not, however, include bones, heads or trimmings from oily fish in fish stocks.
- If you don't have time to make stock after roasting a chicken or large piece of beef on the bone, freeze the bones. Also freeze fish heads, bones and trimmings, and prawn shells.
- Never let a fish, meat or poultry stock boil, or it will turn cloudy.
- Take care not to overseason stocks or your soup will be too salty. Use only a small amount of salt at the beginning of cooking to draw out the flavour of the other ingredients. Do not season it again. This is especially important if you intend to reduce the stock before freezing.
- Add the flavouring ingredients, such as chopped vegetables, herbs and spices, after you have finished skimming the surface.

Storing Stocks – Stocks are ready to use immediately after cooking. Alternatively, leave them to cool completely, then cover and refrigerate for up to two days or freeze for up to six months.

COOKING DRIED PULSES FOR SOUPS

Pulses cover a broad category of ingredients that includes many dried beans, lentils and peas. (Peanuts are technically a pulse but because they can be eaten raw they are classed as nuts.) Pulses are an important source of vegetarian protein, they are inexpensive and add different textures to soups. Red split lentils and split peas, for example, cook to soft purées; rich butter beans and cannellini beans easily fall apart; chickpeas become soft and creamy but never loose their shape.

Pulses feature prominently in recipes from all over the world, including the Mediterranean, the Middle East, India and Southeast Asia. Dried pulses make useful ingredients to have in the cupboard. If you put them in an airtight container they will keep indefinitely; however, the older they are, the tougher their skins become and the longer they take to become tender.

Most pulses are available already cooked in tins, which saves time, but transforming the inedible dried pulse into a tender soup ingredient is a simple process. Lentils and split peas can be added straight to the pan to cook with the other ingredients, but most other pulses require overnight soaking in cold water. When you are ready to cook, drain and rinse the pulses, then put them in a saucepan with four times their volume of water, or the amount of liquid specified in a recipe. Cover and bring to the boil, then reduce the heat and simmer for the time specified in the recipe.

Dried mung, red kidney and soya beans, however, require an initial vigorous boiling for 10 minutes to destroy toxins they contain. Discard the soaking water, cover with fresh water and bring to the boil. Boil, uncovered, for 10 minutes, then follow the simmering time specified in the recipe.

Some recipes cook the soaked and drained pulses as part of the soup-making process, while others specify adding cooked pulses, in which case the tinned variety makes a suitable substitute.

Quick Cooking Technique – If you forget to soak dried pulses overnight, put them in a saucepan and cover with plenty of water. Cover and bring to the boil, boil for 10 minutes, then set aside, still covered, and leave to stand for 2 hours. Drain and rinse the pulses and continue with the recipe. (Soya beans, mung beans and red kidney beans do not need further cooking after this.)

OTHER SIMPLE TECHNIQUES FOR SOUP MAKERS

Adding flavour with cheese rinds and ham hocks – Take a tip from canny Italian cooks and use natural hard cheese rinds to add an intense but subtle flavour to slowly simmered soups. Simply scrub off any markings, wrap them in cling film and freeze them until you're ready to use them. Add a piece of rind to your soup and simmer for anywhere from 10 minutes to several hours – the longer the rind simmers the more likely it is to totally dissolve into the soup. When ready to serve the soup, use a slotted spoon to fish out the soft rind, and either discard it or cut it into small pieces to sprinkle over the soup. Parmesan, pecorino, mature Cheddar and any other hard cheese with a natural rind all work well. Do not use wax-covered rinds.

The end of a Parma or Serrano ham also contains lots of flavour, even if not enough meat for cooks to bother slicing. They can be used to add 'meatiness' to soups without the expense. You will find these at meat counters and delis, and often you will be given them for free. After gentle simmering, remove the meat from the rind and any bones and finely shred it over the soup.

One word of caution, however: most cheese rinds and ham heels are salty, so don't add extra salt until the end of the cooking process.

Making a bouquet garni – A bouquet garni is a bundle of fresh herbs, and often other ingredients, used to flavour soups. Tying the herbs together in a 'bouquet' with a piece of string makes it easier to remove them at the end of cooking. Always lightly crush the herb stalks with the back of a knife because they usually have more flavour than the leaves. If you don't have fresh herbs available, put dried herbs in a square of muslin and use a piece of string to secure it closed.

Chargrilling, roasting, and peeling peppers – To chargrill peppers, preheat the grill to high and lightly grease the grill rack. Halve the peppers lengthways and remove the cores and seeds. Put the peppers, cut-sides down, on the grill rack and grill until lightly charred. Transfer to a bowl, cover with a clean, folded tea towel and leave to cool, then peel.

To roast peppers, preheat the oven to 220°C/425°F/gas 7. Prepare the peppers as above, put them in a baking dish and roast for 40–45 minutes until lightly charred. Remove from the oven and peel as above.

Peeling, deseeding and grating tomatoes – Cut a small cross in the bottom of each tomato using a sharp knife, put them in a heatproof bowl and cover with boiling water. Leave to stand for 2–3 minutes, then drain. Use a small knife to peel off the skins and discard them. To deseed the tomato, cut it in half lengthways and use a small spoon to scoop out the core and seeds.

A quicker way to peel tomatoes is to grate them on the coarse side of a box grater, pressing firmly, and then discard the skin and core. The disadvantage, however, is that the tomato pulp will also include all the seeds.

Toasting nuts and seeds – Toasting gives nuts and seeds a deeper flavour. Heat a dry frying pan over a high heat until hot. Arrange the nuts or seeds in a single layer and dry-fry, stirring continuously, for about 2 minutes until they start turning golden and you can smell the aroma. Immediately transfer to a plate to prevent them from overbrowning or burning. Toasted nuts and seeds can be stored in airtight containers in a dark cupboard for up to 3 months.

Judicious seasoning – You can always add extra seasoning, but it's very difficult to mask the flavour of too much seasoning. Most of the recipes in this book season at an initial stage of cooking to draw out the flavours of the ingredients. Do this very lightly because you will adjust the salt and pepper again before serving. Always cook potatoes and rice in salted water, but season dried pulses after cooking so the salt doesn't draw out the moisture acquired during soaking.

If you accidentally over-season a soup, add a little sugar or, if suitable, boil a peeled and chopped floury potato in the soup. Taste soups before puréeing – you can always discard half the stock and replace it with fresh, unseasoned stock for a less salty taste, if necessary, at that point.

Basic Recipes

Beef Stock

MAKES about 2l/70fl oz/8 cups   **PREPARATION TIME** 5 minutes, plus overnight chilling (optional)   **COOKING TIME** 7 hours

2.5kg/5lb 8oz beef bones,
  chopped into large pieces
  (ask the butcher to do this)
3 large unpeeled onions, quartered
3 carrots, coarsely chopped
2 celery sticks, coarsely chopped
4 large garlic cloves, lightly crushed

1 bouquet garni made with 1 bay leaf
  and several parsley and thyme
  sprigs tied together
1 tbsp tomato purée
12 black peppercorns, lightly crushed
a small pinch of salt

1   Preheat the oven to 230°C/450°F/gas 8. Put the bones in a heavy-based roasting tin and roast for 50 minutes–1 hour until browned all over.
2   Stir in the onions, carrots and celery and roast for another 30–40 minutes until the vegetables are very tender and browned. Watch closely so they do not burn.
3   Transfer the bones and vegetables to a heavy-based stockpot and add 4.5l/157fl oz/4 quarts plus 1 cup water. Bring to the boil, uncovered, over a high heat, skimming the surface. This can take up to 20 minutes. When the foam stops rising, add the remaining ingredients, reduce the heat (use a heat diffuser if you have one) and simmer, covered, for 5 hours. Do not let the liquid boil. Skim the surface occasionally, if necessary.
4   Very carefully strain the stock through a muslin-lined colander into a large bowl and discard all the flavourings. Skim any fat from the surface and use immediately. Alternatively, leave the stock to cool completely, then cover and refrigerate overnight. The next day, use a large metal spoon to 'scrape' the congealed fat off the surface. Once cool, the stock will be lightly gelled. See page 8 for storage information.

Rich Chicken Stock

MAKES about 2l/70fl oz/8 cups   **PREPARATION TIME** 15 minutes, plus overnight chilling (optional)   **COOKING TIME** 2½ hours

2 celery sticks, with the leaves,
  coarsely chopped
1 large carrot, peeled and chopped
1 large onion, peeled but left whole
1 bouquet garni made with 2 bay
  leaves and several parsley and
  thyme sprigs tied together

1 chicken, about 1.5kg/3lb 5oz
6 black peppercorns, lightly crushed
a small pinch of salt

1   Put the celery, carrot, onion, bouquet garni and 1.5l/52fl oz/6 cups water in a saucepan. Cover and bring to the boil. Skim, then add the remaining ingredients and 1l/35fl oz/4 cups water, or enough to cover the chicken. Bring the liquid to just below the boil, skimming the surface as necessary. Do not let the liquid boil.
2   Reduce the heat to very low, cover and simmer for 1¾–2¼ hours until the meat almost falls off the bones.
3   Remove the chicken from the pot and set aside for another use. Strain the stock into a bowl and discard the flavourings. Skim the fat from the surface and use immediately. Alternatively, leave the stock to cool completely, then cover and refrigerate overnight. The next day, use a large metal spoon to 'scrape' the congealed fat off the surface. Once cooled, it will be slightly gelled. See page 8 for storage information.

Chicken Stock

MAKES about 2l/70fl oz/8 cups   **PREPARATION TIME** 10 minutes
COOKING TIME 3¼ hours

carcass and bones of 1 cooked
   chicken, or 900g/2lb mixed chicken
   bones, chopped
1 carrot, peeled and sliced
1 celery stick, with the leaves, sliced

1 bouquet garni made with 1 bay leaf
   and several parsley and thyme
   sprigs tied together
6 whole black peppercorns,
   slightly crushed
a small pinch of salt

1   Put the chicken and 2.4l/78fl oz/scant 9 cups water in a heavy-based stockpot.
    Bring to just below the boil, skimming the surface as necessary. When the foam
    has stopped rising, add the remaining ingredients, reduce the heat (use a heat
    diffuser if you have one) and simmer, covered, for 3 hours. Do not let the liquid boil.
    Skim the surface occasionally, if necessary.
2   Very carefully strain the stock into a bowl and discard the flavourings. Skim any fat
    from the surface and use immediately, or leave it to cool completely. Once cool
    it will be slightly gelled. See page 8 for storage information.

    GAME STOCK Prepare and store as Chicken Stock but use the bones from roast
    partridge, pheasant or other game birds, reduce the water to 1.5l/52fl oz/6 cups and
    reduce the simmering time to 1½ hours. Makes about 1.25l/44fl oz/5 cups.

    TURKEY STOCK Prepare and store as Chicken Stock but use broken turkey bones.

Fish Stock

MAKES about 2l/70fl oz/8 cups   **PREPARATION TIME** 10 minutes
COOKING TIME 30 minutes

1kg/2lb 4oz fish heads, bones and
   trimmings from white fish, such
   as hake, halibut, plaice or whiting,
   well rinsed to remove any blood
   and chopped
150ml/5fl oz/scant ⅔ cup dry
   white wine
1 carrot, peeled and thinly sliced
1 large leek, thinly sliced and rinsed

1 onion, thinly sliced
1 bouquet garni made with several
   parsley sprigs and 1 bay leaf tied
   together
½ lemon, thinly sliced
1 tsp black peppercorns,
   lightly crushed
a small pinch of salt

1   Put the fish heads, bones and trimmings in a large saucepan. Add the wine and
    2l/70fl oz/scant 8 cups water, cover and bring to just below the boil, skimming the
    surface as necessary. Add the remaining ingredients, reduce the heat to low and
    simmer, covered, for 20 minutes.
2   Very carefully strain the stock into a bowl and discard the flavourings. The stock
    is now ready to use. See page 8 for storage information.

Vegetable Stock

MAKES about 2l/70fl oz/8 cups   PREPARATION TIME 20 minutes
COOKING TIME 45 minutes

2 tbsp olive, hemp or sunflower oil
4 celery sticks, with the leaves,
   chopped
2 carrots, coarsely chopped
2 onions, finely chopped
1 leek, sliced and rinsed
6 garlic cloves

1 small tomato, chopped
1 bouquet garni made with 1 bay leaf
   and several parsley and thyme
   sprigs tied together
12 black peppercorns, lightly crushed
½ tsp salt
onion skins (optional)

1   Heat the oil in a saucepan over a medium heat. Stir in the celery, carrots, onions
   and leek, then reduce the heat to very low and cook, covered, for 10–15 minutes
   until very soft. Add the remaining ingredients and 2.2l/77fl oz/8¾ cups water, then
   cover and bring to the boil. Skim, then reduce the heat and simmer, partially
   covered, for 20 minutes.
2   Very carefully strain the stock into a bowl and discard all the flavourings. The stock
   is now ready to use. See page 8 for storage information.

Dashi

MAKES about 1.25l/44fl oz/5 cups   PREPARATION TIME 5 minutes, plus 30 minutes
soaking   COOKING TIME 20 minutes

25cm/10in piece of dried kombu

10g/¼oz/⅔ cup bonito flakes

1   Put the kombu and 1.4l/48fl oz/5½ cups water in a saucepan and leave to soak for
   30 minutes.
2   Bring to the boil, uncovered. As soon as it boils, skim the surface, then add the
   bonito flakes. Skim the surface again, if necessary. Reduce the heat and simmer,
   uncovered, for 10 minutes.
3   Strain the dashi into a large bowl and use immediately. Alternatively, leave to cool,
   then store in the fridge for up to 2 days. Freezing isn't recommended for more than
   2 weeks as it will lose much of its flavour.

VEGETARIAN DASHI Omit the bonito (fish) flakes in the above recipe. Instead soak
8 dried shiitake mushrooms in 1.4l/48fl oz/5½ cups hot water for at least 30 minutes.
Put the mushrooms and the soaking liquid in a saucepan. Add the kombu and leave
to soak for 30 minutes. Slowly bring to the boil, uncovered. As soon as it boils, skim the
surface, then reduce the heat and simmer, uncovered, for 10 minutes. Strain through
a muslin-lined sieve, and use the dashi as above.

INSTANT DASHI Many good-quality powdered dashi mixes are sold in Japanese food
shops, whole food shops and on the internet. Follow the instructions on the packet,
which is usually to dissolve 2 teaspoons powder in 1.25l/44fl oz/5 cups water. If you
are a vegetarian, check the labelling closely, or ask an assistant (it will be written
in Japanese), because instant dashi is made with and without bonito (fish flakes).

Beef Consommé

MAKES 1.25l/44fl oz/5 cups   PREPARATION TIME 15 minutes, plus 30 minutes chilling
and slow straining   COOKING TIME 50 minutes

280g/10oz boneless shin of beef,
   minced
1 carrot, peeled and diced
1 celery stick, finely chopped
1 leek, thinly sliced and rinsed

3 egg whites
1 tbsp tomato purée
1.5l/52fl oz/6 cups Beef Stock
   (see page 10) or ready-made stock
salt and freshly ground black pepper

1   Mix the minced beef, carrot, celery and leek together in a large bowl. Beat the egg
whites in another bowl until frothy, then add the tomato purée and mix together.
Add this mixture to the minced beef and stir together until well combined. Cover
and chill for 30 minutes.

2   Pour the stock into a saucepan, add the chilled egg-white mixture and season with
salt and pepper. Slowly bring to the boil, stirring. As soon as the liquid is frothy,
stop stirring. When the liquid comes to the boil, immediately reduce the heat
to very low (use a heat diffuser if you have one) and simmer, without stirring,
for 30–40 minutes until a solid crust forms.

3   Meanwhile, line a sieve with muslin and set over a large bowl. Gently poke a hole
in the centre of the crust to see if the stock is sparkling clear. When the stock
is clear, increase the hole in the crust and use a ladle to transfer the stock through
the muslin-lined sieve: do not push it through or squeeze the cloth. Once strained,
the consommé is ready to use. Alternatively, leave to cool completely, cover and
refrigerate for up to 2 days or freeze for up to 6 months.

CHICKEN CONSOMMÉ Make as above but replace the stock with Chicken Stock
(see page 11) and the meat with very finely chopped or minced boneless, skinless
chicken legs.

Parsley Dumplings

MAKES 12 or 24 dumplings   PREPARATION TIME 15 minutes
COOKING TIME 15 minutes

100g/3½oz/scant 2 cups panko
   (Japanese breadcrumbs), crushed,
   or fine dried breadcrumbs
55g/2oz/scant ½ cup self-raising flour,
   plus extra for shaping
½ tsp baking powder

3 tbsp finely chopped parsley or dill
¼ tsp salt
1 egg, beaten
3 tbsp milk
1 tbsp olive or hemp oil, plus extra
   if making the dumplings in advance

1   These can be shaped and cooked up to a day in advance. Mix the panko, flour,
baking powder, parsley and salt in a bowl. Make a well in the centre, add the egg,
milk and oil, then gradually beat together until a thick, crumbly dough forms. Lightly
flour your hands and divide the mixture into 12 or 24 equal pieces. Roll into balls,
taking care to smooth over all cracks and openings or the dumplings will become
soggy. Meanwhile, bring a large saucepan of water to the boil.

2   Reduce the heat so the water is just boiling. Add the dumplings and cook until they
rise to the surface, then cook for another 10 minutes.

3   Use a slotted spoon to transfer the dumplings to the soup and finish as instructed
in the recipe. If not using at once, transfer the dumplings to a plate and pour off any
excess water. Leave to cool, then very lightly coat with oil to prevent them from
sticking together, cover with cling film and refrigerate for up to 1 day. Reheat
in gently simmering soup.

POLENTA DUMPLINGS Make as above, but replace the panko or breadcrumbs with
300g/10½oz/2 cups medium polenta.

Croûtes

MAKES 4–6   PREPARATION TIME 5 minutes   COOKING TIME 6 minutes

4–6 slices of French bread, sliced on   olive or hemp oil (optional)
   the diagonal

1   Preheat the grill to high and position the grill rack 10cm/4in from the heat. Put the
bread slices on the rack and toast for 2–3 minutes on each side until golden brown
and crisp. Brush with oil, if desired, and serve warm or at room temperature.
The croûtes can be stored in an airtight container for up to 3 days.

GRUYÈRE OR CHEDDAR CROÛTES Follow the recipe as above. After brushing with oil,
sprinkle with grated cheese and grill until the cheese melts and is very lightly tinged.
Serve warm.

GOAT'S CHEESE CROÛTES Follow the recipe as above, but use a basil- or herb-flavoured
olive oil, if you like. After brushing with oil, sprinkle with crumbled or chopped rindless
goat's cheese and grill until the cheese melts. Serve warm.

Croûtons

MAKES 4–6 servings   PREPARATION TIME 5 minutes   COOKING TIME 4–6 minutes

15g/½oz butter
olive or hemp oil

2 slices of day-old sliced white
   or wholemeal bread, cut into
   0.5–1cm/¼–½in cubes with
   crusts removed

1   Croûtons are best made just before serving, so they are added to the soup hot.
Line a plate with several layers of kitchen paper and set aside. Melt the butter
with the oil in a large frying pan over a medium-high heat. Working in batches,
if necessary, add the bread cubes and fry, stirring, for 2–3 minutes until golden
brown and crisp.
2   Remove the croûtons from the pan and drain on the paper. If not using
immediately, leave to cool completely, then store in an airtight container and
reheat in a low oven before serving.

DILL CROÛTONS Prepare as above but toss with 2 tablespoons chopped dill while draining.

GARLIC CROÛTONS Use garlic-flavoured olive or sunflower oil in the recipe above.

Rouille

MAKES about 185ml/6fl oz/¾ cup; enough for 4–6 servings
PREPARATION TIME 10 minutes, plus chargrilling the pepper

55g/2oz/⅔ cup fresh breadcrumbs
2 large garlic cloves, chopped
1 large red pepper, chargrilled
   (see page 9), peeled, deseeded and
   chopped, or 1 roasted red pepper
   in oil, drained and chopped

125ml/4fl oz/½ cup extra-virgin olive
   oil, plus extra as needed
salt and cayenne pepper

1   Put the breadcrumbs, garlic and red pepper in a beaker or deep bowl and blend
until a thick paste forms. Add half the olive oil, season with salt and cayenne and
blend again. Slowly add the remaining oil, while blending, until a thick sauce forms.
Cover and refrigerate until required. Store in the fridge for up to 2 days.

Finishing Touches

Spiced Seeds – Heat a dry frying pan over a high heat. Add 30g/1oz/¼ cup each pumpkin and sunflower seeds, 3 tablespoons sesame seeds and 1 teaspoon fennel seeds, if desired, and cook, stirring, for 2–3 minutes until the seeds pop and start to colour. Immediately sprinkle over 1 tablespoon light soy sauce or tamari soy sauce and stir until evaporated. Transfer the seeds to a bowl and stir in ½ teaspoon celery seed. Store in an airtight container.

Dukkah – Heat a dry frying pan over a high heat until hot. Add 4 tablespoons blanched hazelnuts or shelled pistachios and dry-fry, stirring, for 2–3 minutes until golden brown. Immediately transfer to a mortar or mini food processor. Lightly crush the nuts, then put them in a bowl. Reheat the pan. One at a time dry-fry 2 teaspoons lightly crushed coriander seeds, 2 teaspoons sesame seeds and 1 teaspoon cumin seeds and add them to the nuts. Add ½ teaspoon dried thyme, season with salt and stir. Store in an airtight container for up to 1 week.

Roasted Pumpkin Seeds – Preheat the oven to 180°C/350°F/gas 4. Dissolve ½ tablespoon salt in 500ml/17fl oz/2 cups water in a saucepan over a high heat. Add 75g/2¾oz/½ cup pumpkin seeds and bring to the boil. Immediately reduce the heat and simmer for 10 minutes. Drain and pat completely dry. Toss the seeds with 1 teaspoon olive or hemp oil and spread out on a baking sheet. Roast for 10–20 minutes, stirring frequently, until golden brown. Meanwhile, line a plate with several layers of kitchen paper. Transfer the seeds onto the paper and leave to cool. Store in a sealed container in the fridge for up to 2 weeks.

Chilli Bon-Bon – This piquant sherry is great for adding to curried soups as an alternative to hot pepper sauce. Fill a jar with medium or dry sherry and add 2 or 3 slit bird's-eye chillies, deseeded. Seal the jar, shake and set aside for at least 5 days before using. This keeps indefinitely in the fridge or cupboard.

Crushed Herb Oils – Make this with basil, coriander or parsley leaves. Put a handful of leaves in a mortar with a pinch of salt and use a pestle to pound them to a paste. Slowly add olive or hemp oil, 1 tablespoon at a time, pounding until the oil is thick and fragrant. Adjust the salt and pepper, if necessary. These are best freshly made.

Chillies in Vinegar – This traditional accompaniment to Thai soups is usually made just before you start cooking the soup. Thickly slice long red chillies (not bird's-eye chillies unless you like very hot food), deseed if desired, and put them in a small bowl. Cover with distilled white vinegar and set aside until required.

Crisp-Fried Garlic – This is a traditional accompaniment to Thai soups that is usually prepared just before you start cooking the soup. Put 5 coarsely chopped garlic cloves in 5cm/2in olive, hemp or sunflower oil in a small saucepan over a high heat. Heat just until the garlic is golden brown and small bubbles appear around the edge, then immediately pour into a heatproof bowl and set aside to cool. Serve in little bowls for diners to add to their soup at the table, if they like.

Crisp-Fried Shallots – Cut 2 or 3 shallots in half lengthways, then thinly slice. Heat the oil and cook as above. If you remove the shallots and oil from the heat before they turn brown they will not over-cook in the residual heat and burn. When cool, use a slotted spoon to remove the shallots from the oil and drain on kitchen paper. Store in an airtight container for up to two days and use to sprinkle over soups.

Crunchy Mixed Seeds – Mix together 4 tablespoons each sunflower and pumpkin seeds, 2 tablespoons white sesame seeds, 1 tablespoon hemp seeds and 1 tablespoon lightly cracked flaxseed. Store covered in the fridge for up to 1 month.

Goji Berry & Seed Mix – Mix together 4 tablespoons goji berries, 2 tablespoons sunflower seeds, 1 tablespoon hemp seeds, 1 tablespoon sesame seeds and ½ teaspoon celery seeds. Store in an airtight container in the fridge for up to 2 weeks.

CHAPTER 1

VEGETARIAN SOUPS

This chapter is a cornucopia of recipes that celebrate the seasons. Brighten up the bleak winter months with hearty, colourful soups such as Golden Carrot & Sesame Soup and Thai-Style Pumpkin Soup. Usher in spring with Sorrel & Spinach Soup, which has an intense green colour and fresh flavour to help shake off the winter blues. Then, when warmer temperatures make you long for lighter choices, enjoy Summer Tomato Soup with Noodles and Rich Pepper & Orange Soup. You'll also find four seasonal farmers' market soups here, one for each season, designed to make the most of the produce that is at its best then.

Obviously, none of the soups in this chapter contain meat or meat stock, but many do contain dairy products. If you are following a vegan diet, though, you'll still find plenty of choices. Arame & Tofu Soup, Mushroom Miso Soup and Vegetable 'Spaghetti' Soup are just a few of the tempting options. See also the Pasta, Pulse & Grain and Chilled Soups chapters for more vegetarian and vegan recipes.

BEETROOT & APPLE SOUP (SEE PAGE 21)

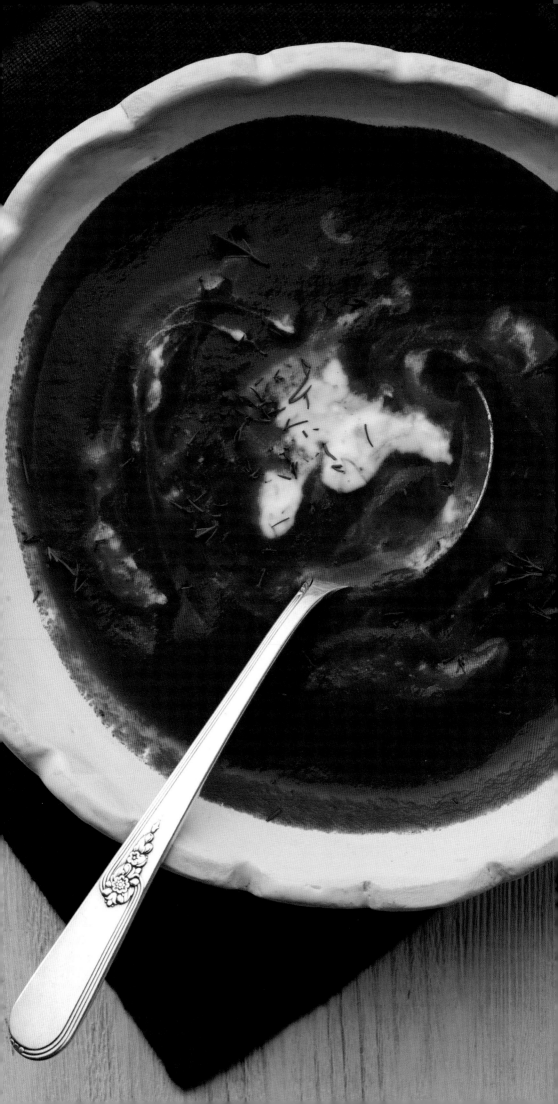

001   Artichoke Soup with Red Pepper Swirl

PREPARATION TIME 25 minutes, plus making the stock   COOKING TIME 1 hour

3 large globe artichokes, about
    500g/1lb 2oz, well rinsed between
    the leaves and stalks trimmed off
2 onions, coarsely chopped
4 large garlic cloves, halved
1 lemon, sliced
1.25l/44fl oz/5 cups Vegetable Stock
    (see page 12) or ready-made stock
4 tbsp crème fraîche or soured cream
salt and ground white pepper
chopped dill, to serve (optional)

RED PEPPER SWIRL
1 roasted red pepper in olive oil,
    drained and chopped
a pinch of salt
1 tbsp extra-virgin olive oil or hemp
    oil, or the oil from the bottled
    pepper, plus extra as needed
½ tsp balsamic vinegar

1   Put the artichokes, onions, garlic, lemon and stock in a large saucepan. Top up with
enough water to cover the artichokes, if necessary. Cover and bring to the boil,
then reduce the heat and simmer, partially covered, for 40–45 minutes until the
artichokes are tender and a leaf pulls out easily. Strain the artichokes, reserving
the cooking liquid, onions and garlic, and set aside until cool enough to handle.

2   Meanwhile, make the red pepper swirl. Blend the red pepper and salt until smooth.
Blend in the oil, then the vinegar and adjust the salt. Add extra oil for a smoother
purée, if you like, then set aside until required.

3   Pull away the leaves from the artichokes and set aside. Use a small spoon to scoop
out the hairy chokes from the base of the artichokes and discard, taking care not
to scoop into the heart. Chop the artichoke hearts and put them in a deep bowl
or blender. Use the spoon to scrape the flesh away from the leaves and add it to
the bowl. Add the onions, garlic and 500ml/17fl oz/2 cups of the cooking liquid and
blend until smooth.

4   Return the soup to the rinsed-out pan and slowly stir in enough of the remaining
cooking liquid to achieve the preferred consistency. (Any leftover cooking liquid can
be used in other recipes or frozen for up to 6 months.) Season with salt and white
pepper and reheat. Stir in the crème fraîche and adjust the salt and pepper,
if necessary. Heat the red pepper swirl in a separate pan over a low heat. Serve
immediately, drizzled with the red pepper swirl and sprinkled with dill, if using.

002   Annie's Herbed Peas-in-a-Pod Soup

PREPARATION TIME 15 minutes, plus making the stock   COOKING TIME 20 minutes

1.25l/44fl oz/5 cups Vegetable Stock
    (see page 12) or ready-made stock
400g/14oz peas in the pods, shelled
    with the pods reserved
15g/½oz butter
1½ tbsp olive or hemp oil
2 Little Gem lettuces, cored and
    leaves shredded

2 tbsp chopped chives
1 tbsp chopped mint leaves, plus
    extra, very finely chopped, to serve
125ml/4fl oz/½ cup crème fraîche
    or soured cream
salt and ground white pepper
borage or marigold petals, to serve
    (optional)

1   Put the stock and pea pods in a saucepan. Cover and bring to the boil, then reduce
the heat and simmer for 10 minutes until the pods are very tender. Blend until
smooth, then strain into a large bowl and work the pods through the sieve into the
bowl, rubbing back and forth with a spoon and scraping the bottom of the sieve.
Set the stock aside.

2   Wash and dry the pan, then melt the butter with the oil over a medium heat.
Add the peas, lettuce, chives and mint and reduce the heat to low. Cook, covered,
for 5 minutes. Slowly stir in the stock and season with salt and white pepper. Bring
to the boil, uncovered, then turn off the heat and blend until smooth. Stir in the
crème fraîche and adjust the salt and pepper, if necessary, then serve sprinkled
with extra mint and flower petals, if using.

003 Two-Bean Soup

PREPARATION TIME 15 minutes, plus soaking the beans overnight
COOKING TIME 1¾ hours

200g/7oz dried flageolet beans
1 garlic clove, chopped
1 bouquet garni made with the
  leaves from ½ celery stick, 1 bay
  leaf, 1 parsley sprig and 1 thyme
  sprig, tied together

½ onion, chopped
½ celery stick, left whole
450g/1lb green beans, chopped
salt and freshly ground black pepper
finely grated zest of 1 lemon, to serve
chopped dill, to serve

1   Put the dried beans in a bowl, cover with water and leave to soak overnight, then
    drain. Transfer to a saucepan, add 1.5l/53fl oz/6 cups water, cover and bring to the
    boil. Add the garlic, bouquet garni, celery and onion, reduce the heat and simmer,
    covered, for 1¼ hours.
2   Add the green beans and season with salt and pepper. Return to the boil, then
    reduce the heat and simmer, uncovered, for another 15–20 minutes until both
    beans are very tender. Strain the cooking liquid into a large bowl and reserve.
    Discard the bouquet garni and the celery and blend the beans until smooth.
3   Work the mixture through a sieve into the pan, rubbing back and forth with a spoon.
    Stir in 1.25l/44fl oz/5 cups of the reserved cooking liquid, or enough to achieve the
    preferred consistency, then reheat. (Any leftover stock can be used in other recipes
    or frozen for up to 6 months.) Adjust the salt and pepper, if necessary, and serve
    sprinkled with lemon zest and dill.

004 Aubergine & Mushroom Soup

PREPARATION TIME 20 minutes, plus 30 minutes resting and making the stock and
croûtes (optional)   COOKING TIME 1¾ hours

1 aubergine, about 350g/12oz,
  pricked all over with a fork
30g/1oz dried porcini mushrooms
3 tbsp olive oil
1 leek, halved lengthways,
  thinly sliced and rinsed
2 large garlic cloves, very
  finely chopped
250g/9 oz portobello or chestnut
  mushrooms, trimmed and sliced

600ml/21fl oz/scant 2½ cups
  Vegetable Stock (see page 12)
  or ready-made stock
250g/9oz sweet potatoes, peeled
  and chopped
1 rosemary sprig
salt and freshly ground black pepper
chopped chives, to serve
1 recipe quantity Goat's Cheese
  Croûtes (see page 14), to serve
  (optional)

1   Preheat the oven to 220°C/425°F/gas 7. Put the aubergine in a roasting pan and
    roast for 1–1¼ hours until very soft. Remove the pan from the oven, cover with
    a clean, thick towel or two clean tea towels and set aside for 30 minutes, then cut
    the aubergine in half and scoop the flesh into a bowl.
2   Meanwhile, put the dried mushrooms in a heatproof bowl and cover with
    750ml/26fl oz/3 cups hot water. Leave to soak for at least 30 minutes until tender,
    then strain the soaking liquid through a muslin-lined sieve, and set aside. Squeeze
    the mushrooms dry, trim off the base of each stalk and thinly slice the caps and
    stalks, then set aside.
3   Heat the oil in a saucepan over a medium heat. Add the leek and garlic and fry,
    stirring occasionally, for 2 minutes. Add the portobello mushrooms, season with
    salt and fry, stirring occasionally, for 5–8 minutes until the mushrooms give off their
    liquid. Stir in the stock and 600ml/21fl oz/scant 2½ cups of the reserved mushroom
    soaking liquid, then add the porcini mushrooms, sweet potatoes and rosemary.
    Cover and bring to the boil, then reduce the heat and simmer for 10 minutes. Stir in
    the aubergine flesh and simmer for 10 minutes. Discard the rosemary, then beat
    to blend the ingredients.
4   Discard the rosemary and adjust the salt and pepper, if necessary, then serve
    sprinkled with chives and with cheese croûtes on the side, if you like.

Egyptian Aubergine & Tomato Soup

PREPARATION TIME 20 minutes, plus making the stock and croûtons (optional)
COOKING TIME 35 minutes

125ml/4fl oz/½ cup olive oil,
  plus extra as needed
2 aubergines, about 700g/1lb 9oz
  total weight, peeled, cut into
  2.5cm/1in slices and patted dry
1 large onion, very finely chopped
2 garlic cloves, very finely chopped
½ tsp ground coriander
½ tsp ground cumin

600ml/21fl oz/scant 2½ cups tomato
  and vegetable juice
455ml/16fl oz/scant 2 cups Vegetable
  Stock (see page 12)
6 tbsp Greek yogurt
salt and freshly ground black pepper
chopped mint leaves, to serve
1 recipe quantity Garlic Croûtons
  (see page 14), to serve

1   Heat two large frying pans over a high heat until a splash of water 'dances' on the
    surface. Reduce the heat to medium and add a thin layer of oil to each. Add
    as many aubergine slices as will fit in a single layer and fry for 3–3½ minutes
    on each side until just beginning to brown. Do not overbrown or the soup will taste
    bitter. Transfer the slices to a large bowl or blender. Add extra oil to the pans
    between batches, if necessary.
2   Blend the aubergines until smooth, then set aside.
3   Heat 2 tablespoons of the oil in a saucepan over a medium heat. Add the onion
    and fry, stirring occasionally, for 10–12 minutes until golden brown. Stir in the garlic,
    coriander and cumin and fry, stirring continuously, for 30 seconds until aromatic.
    Add the tomato and vegetable juice and stock, stir in the aubergine purée and
    season with salt and pepper. Cover and bring to the boil, then reduce the heat
    and simmer, uncovered, for 5 minutes, stirring occasionally.
4   Stir in the yogurt and adjust the salt and pepper, if necessary. Serve sprinkled
    with mint and with the croûtons for adding at the table.

006 Asparagus & Pea Soup

PREPARATION TIME 15 minutes, plus making the stock   COOKING TIME 30 minutes

15g/½oz butter
1 tbsp olive or hemp oil
1 shallot, sliced
600g/1lb 5oz asparagus, chopped
1 floury potato, peeled and chopped

1l/35fl oz/4 cups Vegetable Stock
 (see page 12) or ready-made stock
40g/1½oz/¼ cup frozen peas
4 tbsp crème fraîche or sour cream
salt and freshly ground black pepper

1   Melt the butter with the oil in a saucepan over a medium heat. Add the shallot and fry, stirring, for 3–5 minutes until softened. Stir in the asparagus, potatoes and stock and season with salt and pepper.
2   Cover and bring to the boil, then reduce the heat and simmer, partially covered, for 10 minutes. Add the peas and simmer for 5–8 minutes until the potatoes are tender. Blend the soup until smooth, then stir in the crème fraîche, adjust the salt and pepper, if necessary, and serve.

007 Vegetarian Borscht

PREPARATION TIME 20 minutes, plus making the stock   COOKING TIME 40 minutes

1½ tbsp olive or hemp oil
1 onion, finely chopped
1 tsp caraway seeds
¼ tsp hot paprika, or to taste
1.25l/44fl oz/5 cups Vegetable Stock
 (see page 12) or ready-made stock
350g/12oz cooked beetroot, peeled
 and grated

1 bay leaf
1 waxy potato, peeled and diced
75g/2½oz white cabbage, shredded
75g/2½oz turnip, peeled and diced
2 tbsp red wine or cider vinegar
2 tbsp orange juice
salt and freshly ground black pepper
soured cream or smetana, to serve

1   Heat the oil in a saucepan over a medium heat. Add the onion and fry, stirring, for 3–5 minutes until softened. Add the caraway seeds and paprika and stir for 30 seconds until aromatic. Watch closely so the spices do not burn.
2   Immediately add the stock, beetroot, bay leaf, potato, cabbage, turnip, vinegar and juice. Season, cover and bring to the boil. Reduce the heat and simmer for 25 minutes until the vegetables are tender.
3   Discard the bay leaf. Blend about one-third of the vegetables until smooth. Return this mixture to the pan and adjust the salt and pepper, if necessary. Serve sprinkled with dill and topped with soured cream.

008 Beetroot & Apple Soup

PREPARATION TIME 15 minutes, plus making the stock   COOKING TIME 55 minutes

1 large cooking apple,
 peeled and chopped
1 tbsp lemon juice
1½ tbsp olive or hemp oil
1 onion, chopped
½ tbsp caraway seeds
800ml/28fl oz/scant 3½ cups
 Vegetable Stock (see page 12)

450g/1lb beetroot, peeled and diced
salt and freshly ground black pepper

HORSERADISH & DILL CREAM
5 tablespoons soured cream
1 tablespoon grated horseradish
½ tablespoon chopped dill
a pinch of salt

1   Toss the apple and lemon juice together in a bowl and set aside. Heat the oil in a saucepan over a medium heat. Add the onion and fry, stirring, for 3–5 minutes until softened. Add the caraway seeds and stir for 30 seconds until aromatic. Watch closely so they do not burn. Add the stock and beetroot, cover and bring to the boil. Reduce the heat and simmer for 30 minutes.
2   Meanwhile, make the horseradish and dill cream. Put all the ingredients in a bowl and stir, then cover and chill.
3   Add the apple and any remaining lemon juice to the pan and simmer for 10 minutes until the beetroots are tender. Blend the soup until smooth, then season with salt and pepper. Serve topped with the horseradish cream.

009 Broccoli & Parsley Soup

PREPARATION TIME 15 minutes, plus making the stock and pumpkin seeds
COOKING TIME 30 minutes

1 tbsp sunflower oil
2 shallots, chopped
2 large garlic cloves, finely chopped
1l/35fl oz/4 cups Vegetable Stock
    (see page 12) or ready-made stock
350g/12oz broccoli, cut into florets
    and the stalks sliced
1 bunch of curly parsley, about
    30g/1oz, leaves and stems
    chopped

a pinch of chilli flakes, or to taste
1 Parmesan or other cheese rind,
    about 7.5 x 5cm/3 x 2in
    (see page 9; optional)
salt and freshly ground black pepper
Roasted Pumpkin Seeds
    (see page 15), to serve
chopped chives, to serve (optional)

1   Heat the oil in a saucepan over a medium heat. Add the shallots and fry, stirring
    occasionally, for 2 minutes. Stir in the garlic and fry for another 1–3 minutes until
    the shallots are softened but not coloured.
2   Add the stock, broccoli, parsley, chilli flakes and cheese rind, if using, and season
    with salt and pepper, but remember the rind will be salty, if you are using it, so you
    might not need to add much salt. Cover and bring to the boil, then reduce the heat
    and simmer for 15–20 minutes until the broccoli stalks are very tender.
3   Discard the cheese rind, if used. Blend the soup, then adjust the salt and pepper,
    if necessary. Serve sprinkled with the seeds and chives, if you like.

010 Broccoli & Spinach Soup

PREPARATION TIME 15 minutes, plus making the stock   **COOKING TIME** 35 minutes

30g/1oz butter
1 tbsp olive or hemp oil
1 small leek, about 100g/3½oz,
   thinly sliced and rinsed
1 large garlic clove, crushed
1.25l/44fl oz/5 cups Vegetable Stock
   (see page 12) or ready-made stock

1 floury potato, peeled and diced
175g/6oz broccoli, chopped
85g/3oz baby spinach leaves
freshly grated nutmeg, to taste
salt and freshly ground black pepper
55–85g/2–3oz blue cheese, such
   as Roquefort, crumbled, to serve

1   Melt the butter with the olive oil in a saucepan over a medium heat. Stir in the leek
    and garlic, reduce the heat to low and cook, covered, for 10–12 minutes, stirring
    occasionally, until the leeks are softened. Add the stock, potato and broccoli.
2   Season with salt and pepper. Cover and bring to the boil, then reduce the heat and
    simmer, covered, for 15 to 20 minutes until the broccoli and potatoes are very
    tender. Add the spinach and stir until it wilts, then strain the soup into a large bowl.
3   Return the vegetables to the pan and blend until smooth. Stir in enough of the
    stock to achieve the preferred consistency. Reheat the soup and add the nutmeg.
    Adjust the salt and pepper, if necessary, then serve topped with the cheese.

011 Creamy Brussels Sprout Soup

PREPARATION TIME 15 minutes, plus making the stock   **COOKING TIME** 30 minutes

1½ tbsp garlic-flavoured olive oil
1 onion, chopped
600g/1lb 5oz Brussels sprouts,
   coarsely chopped
350g/12oz soft tofu, drained

1l/35fl oz/4 cups Vegetable Stock
   (see page 12) or ready-made stock
4 tbsp orange juice
salt and freshly ground black pepper
chopped parsley leaves, to serve

1   Heat the oil in a saucepan over a medium heat. Add the onion and fry, stirring
    occasionally, for 8–10 minutes until light golden brown. Add the Brussels sprouts
    and stir for 5–8 minutes until they wilt.
2   Add the tofu and 500ml/17fl oz/2 cups of the stock and season with salt and
    pepper. Bring to the boil, stirring occasionally, then reduce the heat and simmer,
    covered, for 5 minutes.
3   Blend the soup until smooth, then stir in enough of the remaining stock to achieve
    the preferred consistency. (Any leftover stock can be used in other recipes
    or frozen for up to 6 months.) Stir in the juice and reheat. Adjust the salt and
    pepper, if necessary, and serve sprinkled with parsley.

012 Basque-Style Cabbage & Bean Soup

PREPARATION TIME 10 minutes, plus making the stock   **COOKING TIME** 45 minutes

1.4l/48fl oz/5½ cups Vegetable Stock
   (see page 12) or ready-made stock
2 onions, sliced, skins reserved
3 tbsp olive oil
4 large garlic cloves, chopped

400g/14oz white cabbage, shredded
400g/14oz tinned pinto beans, rinsed
salt and freshly ground black pepper
sherry or red wine vinegar, to serve
smoked paprika, to serve

1   Put the stock and onion skins in a saucepan. Cover and bring to the boil over
    a high heat, then reduce the heat and simmer for 10 minutes.
2   Meanwhile, heat the oil in another saucepan over a medium heat. Add the onions
    and fry, stirring, for 7 minutes. Stir in the garlic and fry for 1–3 minutes until the
    onions are light brown. Stir in the cabbage. Strain the stock into the pan, discarding
    the onion skins. Season with salt and pepper, cover and bring to the boil. Reduce
    the heat and simmer for 10 minutes. Add the beans and simmer for 5 minutes
    to warm through. Adjust the salt and pepper, if necessary.
3   Put 1 tablespoon of sherry in each bowl and sprinkle with a little paprika. Ladle the
    soup into the bowls and serve.

013 Cabbage & Sauerkraut Soup

PREPARATION TIME 15 minutes, plus making the stock   COOKING TIME 45 minutes

1½ tbsp garlic-flavoured olive oil
1 large onion, chopped
1 tsp caraway seeds
1l/35fl oz/4 cups Vegetable Stock
    (see page 12) or ready-made stock
400g/14oz tinned chopped tomatoes
1 tbsp tomato purée
½ tsp soft light brown sugar
1 bay leaf

450g/1lb small waxy potatoes,
    cut into bite-sized pieces
280g/10oz savoy cabbage, cored and
    thinly sliced
140g/5oz/1 cup sauerkraut, drained
salt and freshly ground black pepper
chopped parsley leaves, to serve
soured cream (optional), to serve

1   Heat the oil in a large saucepan over a medium heat. Add the onion and fry, stirring
    occasionally, for 3–5 minutes until softened but not coloured. Add the caraway
    seeds and fry for 30 seconds until aromatic. Watch closely so they do not burn.
2   Stir in the stock, tomatoes, tomato purée, sugar and bay leaf and season with salt
    and pepper. Cover and bring to the boil, then reduce the heat and simmer for
    10 minutes.
3   Stir in the potatoes and cabbage and simmer, covered, for 10 minutes. Stir in
    the sauerkraut and simmer, covered, for another 10 minutes until the potatoes and
    cabbage are tender. Discard the bay leaf. Adjust the salt and pepper, if necessary,
    then serve sprinkled with parsley and topped with soured cream, if you like.

014 Thick Cabbage & Bread Soup

PREPARATION TIME 20 minutes, plus overnight soaking and cooking the beans (optional)
and making the stock   COOKING TIME 1½ hours

100g/3½oz/½ cup dried borlotti beans
    or 200g/7oz tinned borlotti beans,
    drained and rinsed
2 tbsp garlic-flavoured olive oil
2 celery sticks, finely chopped
2 carrots, peeled and finely chopped
1 onion, finely chopped
1 tsp celery seeds
1.25l/44fl oz/5 cups Vegetable Stock
    (see page 12) or ready-made stock,
    plus extra as needed
280g/10oz white cabbage, shredded
1 tbsp tomato purée

1 small handful of parsley, tied
    together with the stalks crushed
125g/4oz day-old country-style bread,
    crusts removed and the crumb
    torn into pieces
celery salt
freshly ground black pepper

PAPRIKA & LEMON OIL
3 tbsp olive or hemp oil
1½ tsp sweet, smoked or hot paprika
finely grated zest of 1 lemon

1   If using dried beans, put them in a bowl, cover with water and leave to soak
    overnight, then drain. Transfer to a saucepan, add 1.5l/53fl oz/6 cups water, cover
    and bring to the boil. Reduce the heat and simmer, covered, for 50 minutes–1 hour,
    then drain.
2   To make the paprika oil, put the oil and paprika in a small saucepan over a medium-
    high heat and heat just until bubbles appear around the edge. Do not boil.
    Immediately pour the oil into a heatproof bowl, add the lemon zest and set aside
    to cool completely.
3   Heat the garlic oil in a saucepan over a medium heat. Add the celery, carrots and
    onion, reduce the heat to low and cook, covered, for 8–10 minutes, stirring
    occasionally, until the onion is softened and just beginning to colour. Add the garlic,
    stir for 1 minute, then add the celery seeds and stir for 30 seconds. Watch closely
    so they do not burn. Add the stock, cabbage, tomato purée and parsley and season
    with celery salt and pepper. Cover and bring to the boil, then reduce the heat and
    simmer for 3–5 minutes until the cabbage is tender. Add the beans and simmer
    for another 3–5 minutes to warm through.
4   Discard the parsley and stir in the bread. Leave to stand, covered, for 5 minutes
    to thicken. If it becomes too thick, stir in a little extra stock and reheat. Adjust the
    celery salt and pepper, if necessary, then serve drizzled with the paprika oil.

015 Carrot & Roasted Pepper Broth

PREPARATION TIME 15 minutes, plus making the stock and pesto (optional)
COOKING TIME 35 minutes

1 tbsp olive or hemp oil
1 large leek, halved lengthways,
    sliced and rinsed
2 garlic cloves
1.25l/44fl oz/5 cups Vegetable Stock
    (see page 12) or ready-made stock
2 carrots, peeled and thinly sliced
1 bay leaf

2 roasted red peppers in olive oil,
    drained and chopped
2 tbsp chopped parsley leaves
salt and freshly ground black pepper
1 recipe quantity Pumpkin Seed
    Pesto (see page 33), to serve
    (optional)

1 Heat the oil in a saucepan over a medium heat. Add the leek and fry, stirring,
   for 2 minutes. Add the garlic and fry for 1–3 minutes until the leek is softened but
   not coloured. Add the stock, carrots and bay leaf and season with salt and pepper.
2 Cover and bring to the boil, then reduce the heat and simmer for 15–20 minutes
   until the carrot is very tender. Add the roasted peppers and parsley and warm
   through. Discard the bay leaf and adjust the salt and pepper, if necessary, then
   serve topped with the pesto, if you like.

016 Carrot & Parsnip Soup

PREPARATION TIME 15 minutes, plus making the stock   COOKING TIME 30 minutes

15g/½oz butter
1 tbsp sunflower or olive oil
350g/12oz carrots, peeled and
    chopped
140g/5oz parsnips, peeled and
    chopped
1 onion, chopped

1 large garlic clove, finely chopped
875ml/30fl oz/3½ cups Vegetable
    Stock (see page 12)
    or ready-made stock
salt and freshly ground black pepper
2–3 tbsp red wine vinegar, to serve
chopped parsley leaves, to serve

1 Melt the butter with the oil in a large saucepan over a medium heat. Add the
   carrots, parsnip and onion and cook, covered, for 7 minutes, stirring occasionally.
   Add the garlic and cook, stirring occasionally, for another 1–3 minutes until the
   vegetables are softened but not coloured.
2 Stir in the stock and season with salt and pepper. Cover and bring to the boil over
   a high heat, then reduce the heat and simmer for 10–15 minutes until the
   vegetables are very tender. Blend the soup until smooth, then adjust the salt and
   pepper, if necessary. Drizzle each portion with ½ tablespoon vinegar and serve
   sprinkled with parsley.

017 Parmesan Broth with Peas & Carrots

PREPARATION TIME 15 minutes, plus making the stock   COOKING TIME 35 minutes

1.4l/48fl oz/5½ cups Vegetable Stock
    (see page 12) or ready-made stock
1 onion, peeled and quartered
1 Parmesan cheese rind, about
    7.5 x 5cm/3 x 2in (see page 9)
100g/3½oz/⅔cup frozen peas

100g/3½oz carrot, diced to the same
    size as the peas
2 cos lettuce leaves, finely chopped
salt and freshly ground black pepper
extra-virgin olive oil, to serve
freshly grated Parmesan cheese,
    to serve

1 Put the stock, onion and cheese rind in a saucepan, cover and bring to the boil,
   then reduce the heat and simmer for 20 minutes.
2 Discard the onion. Return the stock to the boil, add the peas and carrots and boil,
   uncovered, for 3–5 minutes until they are tender. Stir in the lettuce and simmer for
   30 seconds until wilted. Season with salt and pepper, but remember the cheese
   rind will have been salty. Discard the rind. Serve drizzled with oil and with
   Parmesan cheese for adding at the table.

018 Golden Carrot & Sesame Soup

PREPARATION TIME 15 minutes, plus making the stock and toasted seeds
COOKING TIME 30 minutes

1½ tbsp olive or hemp oil, plus extra
  to serve
1 onion, chopped
2 large garlic cloves, chopped
½ tsp ground coriander
¼ tsp turmeric
a pinch of cayenne pepper,
  or to taste
950ml/32fl oz/scant 4 cups
  Vegetable Stock (see page 12)
  or ready-made stock

350g/12oz carrots, peeled and
  thinly sliced
2 tbsp tahini
lemon juice, to taste
salt and freshly ground black pepper
toasted white sesame seeds
  (see page 9), to serve
black sesame seeds, to serve
chopped coriander leaves, to serve

1   Heat the oil in a saucepan over a medium heat. Add the onion and fry, stirring
    occasionally, for 2 minutes. Add the garlic and fry for 1–3 minutes until the onion
    is softened but not coloured. Add the ground coriander, turmeric and cayenne
    pepper and stir for 30 seconds. Watch closely so the spices do not burn.
2   Add the stock and carrots and season with salt and pepper. Cover and bring to the
    boil, then reduce the heat and simmer for 12–15 minutes until the carrots are very
    tender. Add the tahini and stir until it dissolves.
3   Blend the soup to the preferred consistency, then add the lemon juice and
    adjust the salt and pepper, if necessary. Serve sprinkled with sesame seeds
    and coriander leaves and drizzled with oil.

019 Carrot & Coriander Soup

PREPARATION TIME 10 minutes, plus making the stock and dukkah
COOKING TIME 35 minutes

15g/½oz butter
1 tbsp olive or hemp oil
350g/12oz carrots, peeled and sliced
1 onion, sliced
½ tsp ground coriander
1 bunch of coriander, about 30g/1oz,
    stalks and leaves chopped

875ml/30fl oz/3½ cups
    Vegetable Stock (see page 12)
    or ready-made stock
½ tsp caster sugar
salt and freshly ground black pepper
natural yogurt, to serve (optional)
Dukkah (see page 15), to serve

1   Melt the butter with the oil in a saucepan over a medium heat. Add the carrots and
    onion and fry, stirring occasionally, for 3–5 minutes until the onion is softened but
    not browned. Add the ground coriander and stir for 30 seconds. Watch closely
    so it does not burn. Add the chopped coriander, stock and sugar and season with
    salt and pepper. Cover and bring to the boil, then reduce the heat and simmer for
    15–20 minutes until the carrots are very tender. Blend the soup until smooth.
2   Adjust the salt and pepper, if necessary. Swirl a little yogurt over each portion,
    if you like, sprinkle with the dukkah and serve.

020 Vegetable 'Spaghetti' Soup

PREPARATION TIME 15 minutes, plus making the stock   COOKING TIME 10 minutes

875ml/30fl oz/scant 3½ cups
    Vegetable Stock (see page 12)
    or ready-made stock
400ml/14fl oz/scant 1⅔ cups passata
6 garlic cloves, chopped

1 leek, sliced and rinsed
1 carrot, peeled
1 courgette
salt and freshly ground black pepper
basil leaves, torn, to serve

1   Put the stock, passata, garlic and leek in a saucepan. Cover and bring to the boil,
    then reduce the heat and simmer while you prepare the vegetables in step 2.
2   Use a julienne tool to cut the carrot and courgette into long, thin 'spaghetti' strands.
    Alternatively, use a vegetable peeler to cut wide, thin strips of the two vegetables,
    then stack the strips and cut into long, thin strips. Strain the stock.
3   Discard the garlic and leek. Return the stock to the pan, cover and bring to the boil.
    Add the carrot and boil for 30 seconds, then add the courgette and boil for another
    30 seconds–1 minute until tender. Season with salt and pepper, then transfer the
    vegetables to bowls. Ladle the soup over them and serve sprinkled with basil.

021 Cauliflower & Cheese Soup

PREPARATION TIME 10 minutes, plus making the stock and croûtons
COOKING TIME 15 minutes

600g/1lb 5oz small cauliflower florets
1 leek, sliced and rinsed
1 tbsp lemon juice
600ml/21fl oz/scant 2½ cups milk
2 tsp mustard powder

140g/5oz Cheddar cheese, grated
freshly grated nutmeg
salt and freshly ground black pepper
1 recipe quantity Garlic Croûtons
    (see page 14), hot, to serve

1   Put the cauliflower, leek, lemon juice and 1.5l/52fl oz/6 cups water in a saucepan,
    adding more water, if necessary, so the vegetables are covered. Season lightly with
    salt, then cover and bring to the boil. Reduce the heat and simmer for 5–8 minutes
    until the cauliflower is very tender. Drain and set aside.
2   Return the cauliflower and leek to the pan. Add the milk and mustard powder and
    simmer over a low heat for 5 minutes. Do not boil. Blend the soup until smooth,
    then stir in enough of the reserved stock to achieve the preferred consistency.
    Add the cheese and stir until it melts. Season with nutmeg and adjust the salt
    and pepper, if necessary. Serve sprinkled with the croûtons.

022 Celeriac & Pear Soup

PREPARATION TIME 20 minutes, plus making the stock and croûtes (optional)
COOKING TIME 25 minutes

400g/14oz celeriac, peeled
  and chopped
2 tbsp lemon juice
1 large pear, peeled and chopped
1 tbsp olive or hemp oil
1 onion, finely chopped
2 garlic cloves, finely chopped

1 floury potato, peeled and chopped
950ml/32fl oz/scant 4 cups
  Vegetable Stock (see page 12)
  or ready-made stock
salt and ground white pepper
Goat's Cheese Croûtes (see page 14),
  to serve (optional)

1 Toss the celeriac with half the lemon juice in a bowl. Toss the pear with the remaining lemon juice in another bowl and set both bowls aside.
2 Heat the oil in a saucepan over a medium heat. Add the onion and fry, stirring, for 2 minutes. Add the garlic and fry for 1–3 minutes until softened. Add the stock, celeriac and potato and season with salt and white pepper. Cover and bring to the boil, then reduce the heat and simmer for 10–15 minutes until the vegetables are tender. Add the pear and any remaining lemon juice. Blend the soup.
3 Adjust the salt and pepper, if necessary. Serve with croûtes on the side, if you like.

023 Curried Cauliflower & Potato Soup

PREPARATION TIME 15 minutes, plus making the stock   COOKING TIME 30 minutes

1½ tbsp sunflower or groundnut oil
2 large garlic cloves, crushed
1 green chilli, deseeded and chopped
1 tsp cumin seeds
1 tsp turmeric
1 large waxy potato, diced

1.25l/44fl oz/5 cups Vegetable Stock
  (see page 12) or ready-made stock
½ tsp salt, plus extra to season
750g/1lb 10oz cauliflower florets
2 handfuls of baby spinach leaves
a large pinch of garam masala
freshly ground black pepper

1 Heat the oil in a saucepan over a medium heat. Add the garlic, chilli, cumin seeds and turmeric and stir for 30 seconds. Watch closely so they do not burn. Add the potato and stir well. Add the stock and salt and season with pepper. Cover and bring to the boil, then reduce the heat and simmer for 5 minutes.
2 Add the cauliflower and simmer for 10–15 minutes until tender. Add the spinach and stir until it wilts. Adjust the salt and pepper, if necessary, and stir in the garam masala, then serve.

024 Roasted Cauliflower & Pepper Soup

PREPARATION TIME 15 minutes, plus making the stock   COOKING TIME 35 minutes

750g/1lb 10oz cauliflower florets
1 red pepper, halved and deseeded
1½ tbsp olive or hemp oil
1 large onion, finely chopped
2 large garlic cloves, chopped

1 tbsp plain white or wholemeal flour
400ml/14fl oz/scant 1¾ cups
  Vegetable Stock (see page 12)
  or ready-made stock
salt and freshly ground black pepper

1 Preheat the oven to 200°C/400°F/gas 6. Roast the cauliflower and pepper in a baking tray for 25–30 minutes, stirring twice, until softened but not charred.
2 Meanwhile, heat the oil in a saucepan over a medium heat. Add the onion and fry, stirring, for 2 minutes. Add the garlic and stir for 1–3 minutes until the onion is softened. Sprinkle in the flour and stir for 2 minutes. Slowly add the stock, stirring to prevent lumps from forming. Bring to the boil, then reduce the heat and simmer, partially covered, until the roasted vegetables are ready.
3 Remove the vegetables from the oven and coarsely chop. Add to the soup, season with salt and pepper and simmer for 5 minutes, then blend until smooth. Work the soup through a sieve into a large bowl, rubbing back and forth with a spoon and scraping the bottom of the sieve. Return the soup to the pan and reheat it. Adjust the salt and pepper, if necessary, and serve.

025 Mediterranean Fennel Soup

PREPARATION TIME 15 minutes, plus making the stock **COOKING TIME** 45 minutes

2 tbsp garlic-flavoured olive oil
2 large fennel bulbs, sliced, with the
   fronds reserved
2 shallots, sliced
1 tsp fennel seeds
125ml/4fl oz/½ cup dry white wine
680g/1lb 8oz tomatoes, chopped

1 tbsp tomato purée
1l/35fl oz/4 cups Vegetable Stock
   (see page 12) or ready-made stock
85g/3oz/heaped ⅔ cup large pitted
   black olives, sliced
salt and freshly ground black pepper
French bread, to serve

1   Heat the oil in a large saucepan over a medium heat. Add the fennel and shallots
    and fry, stirring occasionally, for 3–5 minutes until the shallots are softened but not
    coloured. Add the fennel seeds and stir for 30 seconds. Stir in the wine, increase
    the heat to high and cook for 5–6 minutes until almost evaporated.
2   Add the tomatoes, tomato purée, stock and olives and season with pepper. Do not
    add salt at this point because the olives will be salty. Cover and bring to the boil,
    then reduce the heat and simmer for 20–25 minutes. Adjust the salt and pepper,
    but remember salt might not be necessary. Serve sprinkled with the fennel fronds
    and with French bread on the side.

026 Fennel & Celeriac Soup

PREPARATION TIME 20 minutes, plus making the stock and seeds
COOKING TIME 35 minutes

200g/7oz celeriac, peeled and
  chopped
½ tbsp lemon juice
3 tbsp olive or hemp oil
2 fennel bulbs, with the fronds, sliced
1 shallot, sliced
1 small floury potato, peeled and
  chopped
2 tbsp aniseed-flavoured spirit,
  such as Pernod

800ml/28fl oz/scant 3½ cups
  Vegetable Stock (see page 12)
  or ready-made stock
1 bouquet garni made with 1 celery
  stick, 1 bay leaf, 1 parsley sprig
  and 1 thyme sprig tied together
400ml/14fl oz/scant 1¾ cups
  whole milk
celery salt
ground white pepper
Spiced Seeds (see page 15), to serve

1   Toss the celeriac with the lemon juice and set aside. Heat the oil in a saucepan
    over a medium heat. Stir in the celeriac, fennel, shallot and potato, then reduce the
    heat to low and cook, covered, for 10–12 minutes until softened but not coloured.
    Add the spirit and cook for 1–2 minutes until evaporated. Add the stock and
    bouquet garni and season with celery salt and white pepper.
2   Cover and bring to the boil, then reduce the heat to low. Simmer for 12–15 minutes
    until all the vegetables are very tender. Discard the bouquet garni and blend the
    soup until smooth.
3   Work the soup through a sieve into a large bowl, rubbing back and forth with
    a spoon and scraping the bottom of the sieve. Return the soup to the pan, add the
    milk and reheat. Do not boil. Adjust the salt and pepper, if necessary, then serve
    sprinkled with seeds. If you reheat the soup, do not boil it. You can also serve this
    soup chilled, adding a little extra stock to thin it and seasoning again with salt and
    pepper after chilling, if necessary.

027 Roasted Mediterranean Vegetable Soup

PREPARATION TIME 15 minutes, plus resting and making the stock and flavoured oil
COOKING TIME 1¾ hours

1 aubergine, about 350g/12oz,
  pricked all over with a fork
2 red peppers, left whole
2 garlic cloves, whole and unpeeled
2 red onions, halved and unpeeled
3 tbsp olive or hemp oil, plus extra
  to serve
2 large tomatoes, halved

2 oregano or marjoram sprigs
950ml/32fl oz/scant 4 cups
  Vegetable Stock (see page 12)
  or ready-made stock
salt and freshly ground black pepper
1 recipe quantity Crushed Basil Oil
  (see page 15), to serve

1   Preheat the oven to 220°C/425°F/gas 7. Put the aubergine, red peppers, garlic and
    onions in a large roasting pan. Drizzle with half the oil and toss to coat. Roast for
    55 minutes, then add the tomatoes, cut-sides down, and roast for a further
    20–30 minutes until the vegetables are very tender and the tomato skins have
    burst. Remove from the oven, cover with two clean tea towels and leave to rest
    for 20 minutes.
2   Cut the aubergine in half and scoop the flesh into a bowl. Working on a plate
    to collect the juices, peel off the pepper skins and discard the stalks, cores and
    seeds. Add the flesh and any juices to the bowl. Squeeze the garlic flesh into the
    bowl. Peel the onions and coarsely chop, then add them to the bowl. Peel, halve
    and deseed the tomatoes, then chop and add them to the bowl.
3   Heat the remaining oil in a saucepan over a medium heat. Add the vegetables and
    their juices to the pan along with the stock and oregano. Season with salt and
    pepper, cover and bring to the boil. Reduce the heat and simmer for 10 minutes.
    Discard the oregano sprigs and blend the soup until smooth. Adjust the salt and
    pepper, if necessary, then serve drizzled with basil oil.

028 Courgette & Dolcelatte Soup

PREPARATION TIME 15 minutes, plus making the stock and croûtes
COOKING TIME 30 minutes

1 tbsp olive or hemp oil, plus extra
  to serve
1 celery stick
1 leek, sliced and rinsed
2 courgettes, about 400g/14oz,
  chopped
1.4l/48fl oz/5½ cups Vegetable Stock
  (see page 12) or ready-made stock

1 bay leaf
100g/3½oz dolcelatte cheese,
  chopped, with rind discarded
salt and freshly ground black pepper
1 recipe quantity Garlic Croûtes
  (see page 14), to serve
chopped chives, to serve
flax seeds, lightly crushed, to serve

1 Heat the oil in a saucepan over a medium heat. Add the celery and leek and fry, stirring occasionally, for 8–10 minutes until light golden brown. Add the courgettes and fry for 2–3 minutes until the skins turn bright green.
2 Add the stock and bay leaf and season with salt and pepper, but remember the cheese added later will be salty. Cover and bring to the boil. Reduce the heat and simmer, covered, for 5–8 minutes until the courgettes are tender. Discard the bay leaf, then blend the soup to the preferred consistency. Add the cheese and stir until it melts and adjust the salt and pepper, if necessary.
3 Divide the croûtes into bowls and drizzle with oil. Ladle the soup over them, sprinkle with chives and seeds and serve. You can also serve this soup chilled, adding a little extra stock to thin it and seasoning again with salt and pepper after chilling, if necessary.

029 Vegetable Chowder

PREPARATION TIME 20 minutes, plus making the stock and seeds
COOKING TIME 35 minutes

2 tbsp rapeseed or sunflower oil
1 carrot, peeled and diced
1 celery stick, thinly sliced
1 onion, finely chopped
1 red pepper, deseeded and
  finely chopped
600ml/21fl oz/scant 2½ cups
  Vegetable Stock (see page 12)
  or ready-made stock
4 new potatoes, diced
200g/7oz/1⅓ cups frozen
  sweetcorn kernels

5 tbsp plain wholemeal or white flour
a pinch of cayenne pepper
600ml/21fl oz/scant 2½ cups
  whole milk
125g/4½oz mature Cheddar
  or Gruyère cheese, grated
salt and freshly ground black pepper
Roasted Pumpkin Seeds
  (see page 15), to serve
chopped parsley leaves, to serve

1 Heat the oil in a saucepan over a medium heat. Stir in the carrot, celery, onion and red pepper. Reduce the heat to low and cook, covered, for 10–12 minutes, stirring occasionally, until the vegetables are softened but not coloured. Add the stock, potatoes and sweetcorn and season with salt and pepper. Cover and bring to the boil. Reduce the heat and simmer for 10–12 minutes until the potatoes and carrots are tender.
2 Meanwhile, put the flour and cayenne pepper in a large bowl and make a well in the centre. Heat the milk in a small pan until simmering but not boiling, then slowly pour it into the flour, stirring continuously to prevent lumps from forming.
3 When the vegetables are tender, increase the heat to medium but do not let the soup boil. Add a ladleful of the hot soup to the milk mixture and stir together, then whisk the mixture into the soup. Add the cheese and simmer for 2 minutes, stirring continuously. Do not boil. Adjust the salt and pepper, if necessary, then serve sprinkled with the seeds and parsley. If you reheat the soup, do not boil it.

030 Scandinavian Vegetable Soup

PREPARATION TIME 15 minutes, plus making the stock   COOKING TIME 40 minutes

1.25l/44fl oz/5 cups Vegetable Stock
  (see page 12) or ready-made stock
140g/5oz green beans, chopped
3 new potatoes, thinly sliced
1 carrot, peeled and diced
350g/12oz small cauliflower florets
1 bay leaf
1 tsp ground coriander
a pinch of cayenne pepper,
  or to taste

200g/7oz/1¼ cups frozen peas
30g/1oz butter
1½ tsp plain white flour
200ml/7fl oz/scant 1 cup whole milk
1 large egg yolk
2 tbsp crème fraîche or soured cream
3 radishes, grated
salt and ground white pepper
finely chopped dill, to serve

1   Put the stock, green beans, potatoes, carrot, cauliflower, bay leaf, coriander and
    cayenne pepper in a large saucepan. Season with salt and white pepper, then cover
    and bring to the boil. Reduce the heat and simmer for 12 minutes, then add the
    peas and simmer for another 2–3 minutes until all the vegetables are tender.

2   Strain the stock into a bowl and reserve. Discard the bay leaf and set the
    vegetables aside and keep warm. Return the pan to a low heat and melt the butter.
    Sprinkle in the flour and stir for 2 minutes, then slowly stir in the reserved stock,
    stirring continuously to prevent lumps from forming. Cover and bring to the boil,
    then reduce the heat to low. Simmer, covered, for 5 minutes, then stir in the milk.

3   Beat the egg yolk and crème fraîche together in a bowl, then whisk in a ladleful
    of the hot soup. Remove the pan from the heat and whisk the egg mixture into the
    soup. Return the vegetables to the pan, add the radishes and reheat gently but
    do not boil. Adjust the salt and pepper, if necessary. Serve sprinkled with dill. If you
    reheat the soup, do not boil it.

031 Italian Bread & Tomato Soup

PREPARATION TIME 15 minutes, plus making the stock and 30 minutes standing
COOKING TIME 20 minutes

5 tbsp fruity extra-virgin olive oil,
  plus extra to serve
1 red onion, finely chopped
4 large garlic cloves, crushed
600g/1lb 5oz plum tomatoes,
  chopped
1 tbsp tomato purée
a small handful of basil leaves,
  plus extra to serve

½ tsp caster sugar
a pinch of dried chilli flakes,
  or to taste
1.4l/48fl oz/6 cups Vegetable Stock
  (see page 12) or ready-made stock
4 thick slices of day-old ciabatta
  or other country-style bread,
  torn into pieces
salt and freshly ground black pepper

1   Heat the oil in a large saucepan over a medium heat. Add the onion and fry, stirring
    occasionally, for 2 minutes. Add the garlic and fry for 1–2 minutes until the onion
    is softened but not coloured. Stir in the tomatoes, tomato purée, basil, caster sugar
    and chilli flakes and cook, stirring for 5–10 minutes until the tomatoes are softened
    and breaking down. Season with salt and pepper.

2   Add the stock, cover and bring to the boil, then stir in the bread and remove the
    pan from the heat. Leave to stand, covered, for at least 30 minutes.

3   Reheat the soup and adjust the salt and pepper, if necessary. Serve sprinkled
    with the basil and drizzled with extra oil.

032 Celery & Celeriac Soup

PREPARATION TIME 15 minutes, plus making the stock and seeds
COOKING TIME 30 minutes

15g/½oz butter
1 tbsp sunflower oil
½ onion, finely chopped
450g/1lb celery, stalks and leaves
   chopped
200g/7oz celeriac, peeled
   and chopped

875ml/28fl oz/3½ cups Vegetable
   Stock (see page 12) or ready-made
   stock, plus extra as needed
celery salt
freshly ground black pepper
Spiced Seeds (see page 15), to serve

1 Melt the butter with the oil in a saucepan over a medium heat. Add the onion and
   fry, stirring, for 3–5 minutes until softened but not coloured. Stir in the celery,
   celeriac and stock. Season with celery salt and pepper, cover and bring to the boil.
   Reduce the heat and simmer, uncovered, for 10–15 minutes until the vegetables
   are very tender.
2 Blend the soup, then, working in batches, strain it into a large bowl and work it
   through the sieve, rubbing back and forth with a spoon and scraping the bottom
   of the sieve. Return to the pan, reheat and adjust the salt and pepper, if necessary.
   Serve sprinkled with the seeds. You can also serve this soup chilled, adding a little
   extra stock to thin it, if necessary.

033 Winter Potage

PREPARATION TIME 20 minutes, plus making the stock   COOKING TIME 45 minutes

30g/1oz butter
1 tbsp olive or hemp oil
4 large garlic cloves, chopped
200g/7oz carrots, peeled and diced
200g/7oz celeriac, peeled and diced
1 parsnip, peeled and chopped
1 floury potato, peeled and diced
875ml/30fl oz/3½ cups
   Vegetable Stock (see page 12)
   or ready-made stock
1 Parmesan cheese rind, about
   7.5 x 5cm/3 x 2in (see page 9)
salt and freshly ground black pepper

PUMPKIN SEED PESTO
5 tbsp garlic-flavoured olive oil
40g/1½oz/heaped ⅓ cup unsalted
   hulled pumpkin seeds
3 tbsp flat-leaf parsley leaves
1 spring onion, finely chopped
1½ tsp lemon juice, or to taste

1 Melt the butter with the oil in a saucepan over a medium heat. Stir in the garlic,
   carrot, celeriac, parsnip and potato, then add 4 tablespoons of the stock and season
   very lightly with salt and pepper. Reduce the heat to low (use a heat diffuser if you
   have one) and cook, covered, for 20–25 minutes, stirring occasionally and adding
   extra stock, if necessary, until the vegetables are tender. (The longer the
   vegetables cook, the sweeter they will taste.)
2 Meanwhile, make the pesto. Line a plate with several layers of kitchen paper and
   set aside. Heat half the oil in a saucepan over a high heat until it shimmers. Add
   the seeds and fry for 30 seconds–1 minute until they start to pop and turn golden
   brown. Watch closely so they do not overbrown or burn. Immediately turn them
   out onto the paper and set aside to cool, then transfer to a mini food processor
   or blender. Add the parsley, spring onion and remaining oil and season with salt
   and pepper. Cover and blend until a thick paste forms, then add the lemon juice.
   Adjust the salt and pepper and add extra lemon juice, if necessary.
3 Stir the remaining stock into the soup, add the cheese rind and simmer, covered,
   for 15 minutes. Discard the cheese rind, then blend the soup until smooth. Adjust
   the salt and pepper, if necessary, but remember the cheese rind will have been
   salty. Serve topped with a dollop of pesto. Any leftover pesto can be stored
   in a covered container in the fridge for up to 2 days with an extra layer of olive oil
   on top, although the flavour does become a bit bitter.

Sunshine Winter Soup

PREPARATION TIME 15 minutes, plus making the stock and seeds
COOKING TIME 30 minutes

1½ tbsp olive or hemp oil
3 celery sticks, finely chopped,
  with the leaves reserved
2 large carrots, peeled and diced
2 shallots, finely chopped
1 tsp fennel seeds
a large pinch of saffron threads
1.4l/48fl oz/5½ cups Vegetable Stock
  (see page 12) or ready-made stock

400g/14oz pumpkin, peeled,
  deseeded and diced
1 bouquet garni made with the
  reserved celery leaves, 2 parsley
  sprigs, 1 bay leaf and 1 thyme
  sprig tied together
salt and freshly ground black pepper
toasted sunflower seeds
  (see page 9), to serve
chopped chives, to serve

1   Heat the oil in a saucepan over a medium heat. Add the celery, carrots and shallots
and stir for 3–5 minutes until the shallots are softened but not coloured. Add the
fennel seeds and saffron and stir for 30 seconds until aromatic. Watch closely
so they do not burn.

2   Add the stock, pumpkin and bouquet garni and season with salt and pepper.
Cover and bring to the boil, then reduce the heat and simmer, partially covered,
for 12–15 minutes until the vegetables are tender. Discard the bouquet garni and
adjust the salt and pepper, if necessary. Serve sprinkled with the seeds and chives.

035 Summer Farmers' Market Soup

PREPARATION TIME 15 minutes, plus making the stock and preparing the tomatoes
COOKING TIME 30 minutes

1.4l/48fl oz/5½ cups Vegetable Stock (see page 12) or ready-made stock
freshly cut kernels from 2 sweetcorn cobs, with the cobs reserved and cut in half
1½ tbsp sunflower, olive or hemp oil
1 onion, finely chopped
1 large garlic clove, finely chopped
3 large tomatoes, peeled (see page 9), deseeded and chopped
2 courgettes, diced
1½ tsp marjoram leaves, chopped
salt and freshly ground black pepper
basil leaves, torn, to serve

1 Put the stock and corn cobs in a saucepan, season with salt and then cover and bring to the boil. Reduce the heat and simmer for 10 minutes, then discard the corn cobs.
2 Meanwhile, heat the oil in another saucepan over a medium heat. Add the onion and garlic and fry, stirring occasionally, for 3–5 minutes until softened but not coloured. Add the tomatoes and courgettes and stir for 2 minutes.
3 Add the stock and marjoram to the vegetables, cover and bring to the boil. Reduce the heat and simmer for 3 minutes, then add the corn kernels and simmer for another 3–5 minutes until the kernels are tender. Adjust the salt and pepper, if necessary, and serve sprinkled with basil.

036 Autumn Farmers' Market Soup

PREPARATION TIME 15 minutes, plus making the stock and croûtes
COOKING TIME 40 minutes

1½ tbsp olive or hemp oil
200g/7oz butternut squash, deseeded, peeled and finely chopped
1 carrot, peeled and diced
2 garlic cloves, finely chopped
1 leek, halved lengthways, thinly sliced and rinsed
310ml/10¾fl oz/1¼ cups sweet or dry cider, to taste
950ml/32fl oz/scant 4 cups Vegetable Stock (see page 12) or ready-made stock
2 sage sprigs
2 tbsp crème fraîche or soured cream (optional)
salt and freshly ground black pepper
chopped parsley leaves, to serve
1 recipe quantity Cheddar Croûtes (see page 14), to serve

1 Heat the oil in a saucepan over a medium heat. Stir in the squash, carrot, garlic and leek, cover and reduce the heat to low. Cook for 10–12 minutes, stirring occasionally, until the vegetables begin to soften. Stir in the cider, stock and sage and season with salt and pepper, then cover again and bring to the boil.
2 Reduce the heat and simmer for 15–20 minutes until the vegetables are tender. Discard the sage sprigs, then stir in the crème fraîche, if using. Adjust the salt and pepper, if necessary, and serve sprinkled with parsley and with croûtes on the side.

037 Winter Farmers' Market Soup

PREPARATION TIME 20 minutes, plus making the stock and seeds
COOKING TIME 30 minutes

15g/½oz butter
1 tbsp olive or hemp oil
1 large carrot, peeled and diced
1 head of chicory, halved lengthways
and sliced
1 waxy potato, peeled and diced
1 large onion, finely chopped
1 shallot, finely chopped
200g/7oz celeriac, peeled and diced
1.25l/44fl oz/5 cups Vegetable Stock
(see page 12) or ready-made stock

1 bouquet garni made with 1 piece
of celery stick, 1 bay leaf and
several parsley and thyme sprigs
tied together
4 tbsp crème fraîche or soured cream
2 tbsp chopped chives
2 spring onions, thinly sliced
salt and freshly ground black pepper
Spiced Seeds (see page 15)
1 roasted red pepper in olive oil,
drained and diced, to serve

1   Melt the butter with the oil in a saucepan over a medium heat. Add the carrot,
chicory, potato, onion, shallot and celeriac and fry, stirring, for 3–5 minutes until the
onion is softened but not coloured. Add the stock and bouquet garni and season
with salt and pepper. Cover and bring to the boil, then reduce the heat and simmer
for 10–15 minutes until the vegetables are tender. Discard the bouquet garni.
2   Blend one-third of the soup until smooth, then return it to the pan. Add the crème
fraîche, chives and spring onions and reheat, then adjust the salt and pepper,
if necessary. Serve sprinkled with the seeds and red pepper.

038 Spring Farmers' Market Soup

PREPARATION TIME 15 minutes, plus making the stock   **COOKING TIME** 35 minutes

1.4l/48fl oz/5½ cups Vegetable Stock
(see page 12) or ready-made stock
4 large tomatoes, chopped
1 large shallot, sliced
2 large garlic cloves, chopped
1 bouquet garni made with 1 piece
of celery stick with leaves, 1 bay
leaf and several basil sprigs tied
together

1 tsp caster sugar
1 tsp dried mint
4 new potatoes, halved or quartered
6 baby carrots, halved lengthways
200g/7oz/1⅓ cups shelled peas
12 asparagus tips
salt and freshly ground black pepper
freshly grated Parmesan cheese,
to serve

1   Put the stock, tomatoes, shallot, garlic, bouquet garni and sugar in a saucepan over
a high heat. Cover and bring to the boil, then uncover and boil gently for 10 minutes
to reduce slightly. Strain the stock into a bowl, pressing down to extract as much
flavour as possible.
2   Return the stock to the pan, add the mint and return to the boil. Add the potatoes
and carrots and season with salt and pepper. Reduce the heat and simmer,
covered, for 8 minutes. Add the peas and simmer for another 3–5 minutes,
if frozen, or for 5–8 minutes, if fresh. Add the asparagus for the final 3 minutes and
simmer until all the vegetables are tender but still retain a little crispness. Adjust
the salt and pepper, if necessary, and serve with Parmesan cheese on the side.

039 Twice-Cooked Sweet Potato Soup

PREPARATION TIME 15 minutes, plus making the stock and berry and seed mix
COOKING TIME 50 minutes

350g/12oz sweet potatoes, pricked all
  over with a fork
15g/½oz butter
1 tbsp sunflower oil
1 shallot, finely chopped
1 large garlic clove, chopped
750–900ml/26–31fl oz/3–scant 4 cups
  Vegetable Stock (see page 12)
  or ready-made stock

4 tbsp crème fraîche or sour cream,
  plus extra to serve (optional)
freshly grated nutmeg, to taste
salt and freshly ground black pepper
Goji Berry & Seed Mix (see page 15),
  to serve
chopped chives, to serve

1   Preheat the oven to 220°C/425°F/gas 7. Put the sweet potatoes on the oven rack
    and roast for 30–40 minutes until very tender when pierced with a knife. Transfer
    them to a heatproof bowl, cover with a clean tea towel and set aside until cool
    enough to handle, then pull away and discard the skins. Set aside the potato flesh.
2   Melt the butter with the oil in a saucepan over a medium heat. Add the shallot and
    fry, stirring occasionally, for 2 minutes. Stir in the garlic and fry for 1–3 minutes until
    the shallot is softened but not coloured. Stir in the sweet potatoes, mashing them
    up with a wooden spoon. Slowly stir in 375ml/13fl oz/1½ cups of the stock, then
    season with salt and pepper and bring to the boil, stirring.
3   Remove from the heat and blend, then slowly stir in enough of the remaining stock
    to achieve the preferred consistency. (Any leftover stock can be used in other
    recipes or frozen for up to 6 months.) Reheat, then stir in the crème fraîche and
    nutmeg. Adjust the salt and pepper, if necessary, and serve topped with crème
    fraîche, if you like, and sprinkled with berry and seed mix and chives.

040 Gujarati Yogurt Soup

PREPARATION TIME 15 minutes   COOKING TIME 10 minutes

8 fresh curry leaves
1 green chilli, deseeded (optional)
  and chopped, or to taste
1cm/½in piece of root ginger,
  peeled and grated, or to taste
5mm/¼in piece of white turmeric
  (optional)
2.5cm/1in piece of cucumber,
  deseeded and chopped
2 tbsp chickpea flour

½ tsp ground coriander
600g/1lb 5oz/scant 2½ cups
  natural yogurt
30g/1oz ghee or 2 tbsp sunflower oil
1 tsp cumin seeds
1 tsp black mustard seeds
½ tsp fenugreek seeds
a pinch of ground asafoetida
salt
2 handfuls of coriander leaves, torn

1   Put half the curry leaves, the chilli, ginger and white turmeric, if using, in a small
    food processor and blend until very finely chopped (or use a mortar and pestle).
    Add the cucumber and blend again until the mixture forms a paste.
2   Put the chickpea flour and ground coriander in a bowl and season with salt, then
    add the yogurt and 600ml/21fl oz/2½ cups water and stir until smooth. Adjust the
    salt, if necessary, adding more chilli and ginger, if you like.
3   Melt the ghee in a saucepan over a medium heat. Add the cumin, mustard and
    fenugreek seeds and stir for 30 seconds until they crackle and pop. Watch closely
    so they do not burn. Stir in the asafoetida and remaining curry leaves and stir just
    until the leaves sizzle.
4   Reduce the heat to very low (use a heat diffuser if you have one) and add the
    yogurt mixture, stirring continuously to prevent it from separating. Watch closely
    because the mixture will splutter. Stir for 8–10 minutes until the soup thickens.
    Serve sprinkled with the coriander leaves.

Leek & Sweet Potato Herb Soup

PREPARATION TIME 15 minutes, plus making the stock   **COOKING TIME** 15 minutes

1 small handful of chervil
1 small handful of thyme
2 tarragon sprigs
1 large handful of curly-leaf parsley,
   leaves finely chopped and stalks
   reserved and lightly crushed
1 small handful of chives, half
   of them chopped and kept
   separate

1.5l/52fl oz/6 cups Vegetable Stock
   (see page 12) or ready-made stock
2 leeks, sliced in half lengthways,
   thinly sliced and rinsed
15g/½oz butter
1 tbsp sunflower, olive or hemp oil
280g/10oz sweet potatoes, peeled
   and cut into bite-sized pieces
salt and freshly ground black pepper

1   Strip the leaves from half the chervil, thyme and tarragon sprigs and mix them
    together with the chopped parsley and chopped chives, then set aside.
2   Put the parsley stalks, whole chives and whole chervil, thyme and tarragon sprigs
    in a saucepan. Add the stock and half the leeks and season lightly with salt. Cover
    and bring to the boil, then boil, uncovered, for 10 minutes.
3   Meanwhile, melt the butter with the oil in a saucepan over a medium heat. Stir in
    the sweet potatoes and remaining leek and reduce the heat to low. Cook, covered,
    for 8–10 minutes, stirring occasionally, until the leek is softened but not coloured.
4   Strain the stock into the pan with the sweet potatoes, pressing down to extract
    as much flavour as possible. Bring to the boil, uncovered, then reduce the heat and
    simmer for 2–3 minutes until the potatoes are tender. Adjust the salt and pepper,
    if necessary. Just before serving, stir in the chopped herbs and simmer for no more
    than 30 seconds, then serve.

042　Potato & Mixed Vegetable Soup

PREPARATION TIME 15 minutes, plus making the stock　COOKING TIME 35 minutes

15g/½oz butter
1 tbsp olive or hemp oil
1 carrot, peeled and diced
1 onion, finely chopped
1 red pepper, deseeded and chopped
1.25l/44fl oz/5 cups Vegetable Stock
　(see page 12) or ready-made stock

280g/10oz floury potatoes, peeled
　and cut into bite-sized pieces
1 bay leaf
4 tbsp chopped parsley leaves,
　plus extra to serve
salt and freshly ground black pepper
ground sumac, to serve

1　Melt the butter with the oil in a saucepan over a medium heat. Stir in the carrot,
　onion and pepper, reduce the heat to low and cook, covered, for 10–12 minutes,
　stirring occasionally, until softened but not coloured.
2　Add the stock, potatoes and bay leaf and season with salt and pepper. Cover and
　bring to the boil, then reduce the heat to low. Simmer for 10–12 minutes until
　the potatoes are tender. Discard the bay leaf, stir in the parsley and adjust the salt
　and pepper, if necessary. Serve sprinkled with parsley and ground sumac.

043　Curried Potato & Kale Soup

PREPARATION TIME 15 minutes, plus making the stock　COOKING TIME 30 minutes

1½ tbsp sunflower or groundnut oil
1 large onion, finely chopped
2 large garlic cloves, crushed
1 tsp ground coriander
1 tsp ground cumin
½ tsp chilli powder
½ tsp fenugreek seeds
½ tsp turmeric

1l/35fl oz/4 cups Vegetable Stock
　(see page 12) or ready-made stock
200g/7oz curly kale, stalks removed,
　leaves chopped and rinsed
280g/10oz floury potatoes, peeled
　and chopped
salt and freshly ground black pepper

1　Heat the oil in a saucepan over a medium heat. Add the onion and fry, stirring
　occasionally, for 2 minutes. Add the garlic and fry for another 1–3 minutes until
　the onion is softened. Add the coriander, cumin, chilli powder, fenugreek and
　turmeric and stir for 30 seconds. Watch closely so the spices do not burn.
2　Add the stock, kale and potatoes and season with salt and pepper. Cover and bring
　to the boil. Reduce the heat and simmer for 12–15 minutes until the potatoes are
　tender but still holding their shape.
3　Blend about one-third of the soup until smooth, then stir this mixture back into
　the soup. Adjust the salt and pepper, if necessary, and serve.

044　No-Fat Vegetable Pot

PREPARATION TIME 20 minutes, plus making the stock　COOKING TIME 40 minutes

1.5l/52fl oz/6 cups Vegetable Stock
　(see page 12) or ready-made stock
500ml/17fl oz/2 cups passata
4 garlic cloves, very finely chopped
1 bouquet garni made with the
　leaves of 1 celery stick, 1 bay leaf
　and a few parsley sprigs tied
　together

400g/14oz butternut squash, peeled,
　deseeded and chopped
1 onion, chopped
1 carrot, peeled and sliced
1 celery stick, thinly sliced
1 leek, sliced and rinsed
1 parsnip, peeled and sliced
a pinch of dried chilli flakes (optional)
salt and freshly ground black pepper

1　Put the stock, passata, garlic and bouquet garni in a saucepan and season with salt
　and pepper. Cover and bring to the boil, then uncover and boil for 10 minutes
　to reduce slightly. Add the squash, onion, carrot, celery, leek, parsnip and chilli
　flakes and return to the boil.
2　Reduce the heat and simmer, covered, for 15–20 minutes until all the vegetables
　are tender. Discard the bouquet garni and adjust the salt and pepper, if necessary,
　then serve. Any leftover soup can be blended and used as a pasta sauce.

045 Roasted Garlic & Tomato Soup

PREPARATION TIME 15 minutes, plus making the stock COOKING TIME 30 minutes

1 large garlic bulb, whole and
   unpeeled
2 tbsp fruity extra-virgin olive oil,
   plus extra for roasting the garlic
   and to serve
2 onions, finely chopped
2 large garlic cloves, finely chopped
670ml/23fl oz/2⅔ cups passata

455ml/16fl oz/scant 2 cups
   Vegetable Stock (see page 12)
   or ready-made stock
1 Parmesan cheese rind, about 7.5 x
   5cm/3 x 2in (see page 9; optional)
a pinch of chilli flakes (optional)
salt and freshly ground black pepper
a small handful of basil leaves,
   to serve

1 Preheat the oven to 200°C/400°F/gas 6. Rub the whole garlic with oil, put it directly
on the oven rack and roast for 25–30 minutes until very soft.

2 Meanwhile, heat the oil in a saucepan over a medium heat. Add the onion and fry,
stirring occasionally, for 2 minutes. Stir in the chopped garlic and fry for another
1–3 minutes until the onion is softened but not coloured. Stir in the passata and
stock and add the cheese rind and chilli flakes, if using. Season with salt and
pepper, but remember if you have used the cheese rind, it will be salty. Cover
and bring to the boil, then reduce the heat and leave to simmer until the garlic
finishes roasting.

3 When the roasted garlic is tender, transfer it to a work surface, using a clean tea
towel to protect your fingers. Set aside until cool enough to handle, then separate
it into cloves and squeeze the soft flesh directly into the soup. Use a wooden
spoon to mash the garlic against the side of the pan and stir until it 'dissolves'.
Discard the cheese rind. Adjust the salt and pepper, if necessary, then serve
topped with basil leaves and drizzled with olive oil.

046 Slow-Cooked Tomato & Orange Soup

PREPARATION TIME 15 minutes, plus making the stock and croûtes (optional)
COOKING TIME 1¼ hours

30g/1oz butter
1 tbsp olive or hemp oil
2 celery sticks, finely chopped
2 shallots, finely chopped
2 large garlic cloves, finely chopped
750g/1lb 10oz large juicy tomatoes,
   chopped
1l/35fl oz/4 cups Vegetable Stock
   (see page 12) or ready-made stock

a pinch of caster sugar
a pinch of cayenne pepper
finely grated zest of 1 orange
2–4 tbsp orange juice
salt and freshly ground black pepper
1 recipe quantity Goat's Cheese
   Croûtes (see page 14), to serve
   (optional)

1 Melt the butter with the oil in a saucepan over a medium heat. Add the celery and
shallots and fry, stirring occasionally, for 2 minutes. Stir in the garlic and fry for
another 1–3 minutes until the shallots are softened but not coloured. Add the
tomatoes and stir for 2 minutes, then stir in the stock, sugar and cayenne pepper,
and season with salt and pepper. Cover and bring to the boil, then reduce the heat
to low (use a heat diffuser if you have one) and simmer for 1 hour.

2 Strain the soup to remove the tomato seeds and skins, rubbing back and forth with
a spoon and scraping the bottom of the sieve. Return the soup to the pan and blot
with folded kitchen paper to remove the excess fat from the surface. Stir in the
orange zest and 2 tablespoons of the orange juice and reheat. Adjust the salt and
pepper, and add more orange juice, if you like. Serve with croûtes, if you like.

047 # Tomato & Thyme Soup
with Polenta Dumplings

PREPARATION TIME 15 minutes, plus making the stock and dumplings
COOKING TIME 45 minutes

30g/1oz butter
1 tbsp sunflower oil
1 large onion, thinly sliced
1 garlic clove, crushed
185ml/6fl oz/¾ cup dry white wine
3 tbsp plain white or wholemeal flour
a pinch of mustard powder
600ml/21fl oz/scant 2½ cups
   Vegetable Stock (see page 12)
   or ready-made stock

800g/1lb 5oz tinned chopped
   tomatoes
½ bunch of lemon thyme, about
   15g/½oz, tied together, plus extra
   leaves to serve
4 tbsp tomato purée
2 tsp caster sugar
250ml/9fl oz/1 cup single cream
1 recipe quantity Polenta Dumplings
   (see page 13)
salt and freshly ground black pepper

1. Melt the butter with the oil in a saucepan over a medium heat. Add the onion and fry, stirring occasionally, for 2 minutes. Add the garlic and fry for 1–3 minutes until the onion is softened. Stir in the wine, increase the heat to high and cook for 6–8 minutes until almost evaporated, then reduce the heat to low.

2. Sprinkle in the flour and mustard powder and stir for 2 minutes. Slowly add the stock, stirring to prevent lumps from forming, then stir in the tomatoes, thyme, tomato purée and sugar and season with salt and pepper. Cover and bring to the boil, then reduce the heat and simmer for 15 minutes.

3. Discard the thyme sprigs and blend the soup. Strain the soup into a large bowl and work it through the sieve, rubbing back and forth with a spoon and scraping the bottom of the sieve. Return the soup to the pan, stir in the cream and reheat without boiling. Add the dumplings and simmer to reheat. Adjust the salt and pepper, if necessary, then serve sprinkled with extra thyme leaves. If you reheat the soup, do not boil it.

048 Chargrilled Pepper & Sun-Dried Tomato Soup

PREPARATION TIME 10 minutes, plus making the chargrilled peppers and stock
COOKING TIME 35 minutes

8 sun-dried tomatoes in oil,
    drained, with 1½ tbsp of the
    oil reserved
1 large shallot, sliced
2 large garlic cloves, crushed
3 large red peppers, chargrilled
    (see page 9), peeled, deseeded
    and sliced

950ml/32fl oz/scant 4 cups
    Vegetable Stock (see page 12)
    or ready-made stock
½ tsp caster sugar
salt and freshly ground black pepper
chopped chives or torn basil leaves,
    to serve

1   Heat the reserved oil in a saucepan over a medium heat. Add the shallot and fry,
    stirring occasionally, for 2 minutes. Stir in the garlic and fry for 1–3 minutes until the
    shallot is softened but not coloured, then stir in the tomatoes and red peppers.
    Add the stock and sugar and season with salt and pepper. Cover and bring to the
    boil, then reduce the heat and simmer for 20 minutes.
2   Blend until smooth, then, working in batches, strain the soup into a large bowl
    and work it through the sieve, rubbing back and forth with a spoon and scraping
    the bottom of the sieve. Return it to the pan and adjust the salt and pepper,
    if necessary. Serve sprinkled with chives. You can also serve this soup chilled,
    adding a little extra stock to thin it and seasoning again with salt and pepper
    after chilling, if necessary.

049 Summer Tomato Soup with Noodles

PREPARATION TIME 15 minutes, plus making the stock and flavoured oil
COOKING TIME 1½ hours

30g/1oz butter
½ tbsp olive or hemp oil
1 celery stick, finely chopped
1 onion, finely chopped
4 large garlic cloves, finely chopped
750g/1lb 10oz juicy tomatoes,
    chopped
750ml/26fl oz/3 cups Vegetable Stock
    (see page 12) or ready-made stock
¼ tsp chilli flakes, or to taste

¼ tsp dried oregano
100g/3½oz angel hair pasta
    or spaghetti, broken into
    bite-sized pieces
salt and freshly ground black pepper
1 recipe quantity Crushed Basil Oil
    (see page 15), to serve
freshly grated Parmesan or pecorino
    cheese, to serve

1   Melt the butter with the oil in a saucepan over a medium heat. Add the celery
    and onion and fry, stirring occasionally, for 2 minutes. Stir in the garlic and fry for
    another 1–3 minutes until the onion is softened but not coloured. Add the tomatoes
    and stir for 2 minutes, then stir in the stock, chilli flakes and oregano and season
    with salt and pepper. Cover and bring to the boil, then reduce the heat to very low
    (use a heat diffuser if you have one) and simmer for 1 hour.
2   Strain the soup into a large bowl and work it through the sieve to remove the
    tomato seeds and skins, rubbing back and forth with a spoon and scraping the
    bottom of the sieve. Return the soup to the pan, cover and bring to the boil.
    Add the pasta and boil, uncovered, for 6–10 minutes, or according to the packet
    instructions, until al dente. Adjust the salt and pepper, if necessary, then serve
    drizzled with basil oil and with Parmesan cheese on the side.

050 Edamame & Mushroom Soup

PREPARATION TIME 15 minutes, plus making the dashi, and 30 minutes soaking the mushrooms **COOKING TIME** 30 minutes

5 dried shiitake mushrooms
100g/3½oz frozen shelled edamame
  soya beans
100g/3½oz enoki mushrooms,
  ends trimmed
600ml/21fl oz/scant 2½ cups
  Vegetarian Dashi (see page 12)
  or instant vegetarian dashi

soy sauce, to taste
140g/5oz firm tofu, drained and diced
salt
shiso or coriander leaves, to serve
yuzu powder or grated lemon
  or tangerine zest, to serve

1 Put the shiitake mushrooms and 750ml/26fl oz/3 cups boiling water in a heatproof bowl and leave to soak for 30 minutes until tender.
2 Meanwhile, bring a saucepan of salted water to the boil. Add the edamame and boil for 5 minutes until tender. Drain and immediately rinse under cold running water. Drain again and set aside.
3 Strain the mushrooms through a muslin-lined sieve. Put 600ml/21fl oz/2½ cups of the soaking liquid in a saucepan, add the dashi and bring to the boil, covered, over a high heat. Meanwhile, squeeze the mushrooms dry, cut off the stalks and slice the caps. Add the shiitake mushrooms and edamame to the dashi mixture, reduce the heat and simmer, covered, for 5 minutes, then season with soy sauce.
4 Divide the tofu into bowls. Divide the edamame and mushrooms into the bowls and ladle the soup over them. Serve sprinkled with shiso and yuzu.

051 Hot Tomato & Yogurt Soup

PREPARATION TIME 15 minutes, plus making the stock and preparing the tomatoes **COOKING TIME** 20 minutes

4 tbsp chickpea flour
½ tsp cayenne pepper, or to taste
½ tsp salt, plus extra to season
455ml/16fl oz/scant 2 cups
  natural yogurt
5 large tomatoes, grated (see page 9)
30g/1oz ghee or 2 tbsp sunflower oil
2 garlic cloves, crushed

900ml/31fl oz/3¾ cups
  Vegetable Stock (see page 12),
  ready-made stock or water,
  plus extra as needed
freshly ground black pepper
Spiced Seeds (see page 15), to serve
chopped coriander leaves, to serve

1 Mix the chickpea flour, cayenne pepper and salt together in a large bowl and make a well in the centre. Add the yogurt, whisking to prevent lumps from forming, then stir in the tomatoes and set aside.
2 Melt the ghee in a saucepan over a medium heat. Add the garlic and stir for 30 seconds until very lightly coloured. Watch closely so it does not burn. Remove the pan from the heat and slowly stir in the yogurt mixture, then stir in the stock.
3 Return the pan to the heat and bring to the boil, whisking continuously. Reduce the heat to very low (use a heat diffuser if you have one) and simmer for 6–8 minutes, whisking occasionally, until the soup thickens and the raw flavour of the flour has cooked out. If it thickens too much, stir in a little extra stock or water. Season with pepper and adjust the salt, if necessary. Serve sprinkled with seeds and coriander leaves.

052 Mushroom Miso Soup

PREPARATION TIME 10 minutes, plus making the dashi   COOKING TIME 15 minutes

1 recipe quantity Vegetarian Dashi
(see page 12) or 1.25ml/44fl oz/
5 cups instant vegetarian dashi
4 tbsp dark miso paste
5 shiitake mushroom caps,
thinly sliced

140g/5oz shimeji or enoki
mushrooms, ends trimmed
2 spring onions, finely chopped
140g/5oz tofu, drained and diced
1 coriander leaf for each bowl,
to serve

1   Put the dashi in a saucepan, cover and bring to the boil, then reduce the heat
and leave to simmer. Put the miso paste in a heatproof bowl and slowly stir in
1–2 ladlefuls of the dashi to make a thin paste, then stir it into the dashi. Do not
boil. Add the mushrooms and spring onions and simmer for 1–2 minutes until the
mushrooms are tender.
2   Divide the tofu into bowls. Divide the mushrooms and spring onions into the bowls,
then ladle the soup over them. Top with 1 coriander leaf and serve.

053 Wakame Miso Soup

PREPARATION TIME 5 minutes, plus making the dashi   COOKING TIME 15 minutes

1 recipe quantity Vegetarian Dashi
(see page 12) or 1.25l/44fl oz/
5 cups prepared instant vegetarian
dashi
4 tbsp light miso paste

1 handful of bean sprouts, rinsed
2 tbsp dried wakame flakes
140g/5oz tofu, drained and diced
2 spring onions, very finely chopped,
to serve

1   Put the dashi in a saucepan, cover and bring to the boil, then reduce the heat to
low and leave to simmer. Put the miso paste in an heatproof bowl and slowly stir in
1–2 ladlefuls of the hot dashi to form a thin paste. Stir this into the dashi and add
the bean sprouts. Do not boil. Stir in the wakame, which will immediately soften.
2   Divide the tofu into bowls, then add the bean sprouts. Ladle the soup into the
bowls and serve sprinkled with spring onions.

054 Hot & Sour Vegetable Soup with Tofu

PREPARATION TIME 10 minutes, plus at least 30 minutes soaking the mushrooms and
making the stock   COOKING TIME 15 minutes

2 handfuls of bean sprouts
8 dried Chinese mushrooms
1.25l/44fl oz/5 cups Vegetable Stock
(see page 12) or ready-made stock
3 tbsp Chinese rice vinegar
1 tbsp light soy sauce
140g/5oz tinned bamboo shoots,
drained and very thinly sliced
4 baby corn cobs, halved lengthways
2 large garlic cloves, finely chopped

4 mangetout, very thinly sliced
lengthways
1–2 bird's-eye chillies, deseeded
(optional) and sliced
1 carrot, peeled and grated
lengthways
2 tbsp arrowroot
250g/9 oz firm tofu, drained
and diced
shiso or coriander leaves, to serve

1   Put the bean sprouts in a bowl, cover with cold water and set aside. Put the
mushrooms in a heatproof bowl, cover with boiling water and leave to soak for
30 minutes until tender. Drain, rinse under cold water and squeeze dry. Trim the
base off the stalks, if necessary, slice the caps and stalks and set aside.
2   Put the stock, vinegar and soy sauce in a saucepan. Cover and bring to the boil,
then reduce the heat to medium and add the bamboo shoots, corn cobs, garlic,
mangetout, chillies, carrot and mushrooms. Cover and boil for 2 minutes.
3   Put the arrowroot and 3 tablespoons cold water in a small heatproof bowl and mix
until smooth, then stir in a ladleful of the hot stock. Stir this mixture into the soup
and simmer for 2–3 minutes until it thickens slightly. Drain the bean sprouts,
then add them and the tofu to the pan. Warm through, then serve sprinkled
with shiso leaves.

055 Cream of Mushroom Soup

PREPARATION TIME 15 minutes, plus 30 minutes soaking the mushrooms and making the stock   **COOKING TIME** 25 minutes

30g/1oz dried porcini mushrooms
30g/1oz butter
1 tbsp olive or hemp oil
1 shallot, finely chopped
600g/1lb 5oz chestnut and/
   or portobello mushrooms,
   trimmed and sliced
2 tbsp plain white or wholemeal flour

1.4l/48fl oz/5½ cups Vegetable Stock
   (see page 12) or ready-made stock
1 tsp dried thyme
250ml/9fl oz/1 cup double cream
1 tbsp Marsala wine, or to taste
salt and freshly ground black pepper
finely chopped parsley leaves,
   to serve

1   Put the porcini mushrooms and 250ml/9fl oz/1 cup boiling water in a heatproof bowl and leave to soak for 30 minutes until tender. Strain through a muslin-lined sieve and set the liquid aside. Squeeze the mushrooms, then trim the stalks, if necessary, and thinly slice the caps and stalks, then set aside.
2   Melt the butter with the oil in a saucepan over a medium heat. Add the shallot and fry, stirring occasionally, for 2 minutes. Add all the mushrooms, season with salt and cook, stirring occasionally, for 4–5 minutes until the mushrooms soften and give off their liquid. Sprinkle in the flour and stir for 2 minutes.
3   Remove the pan from the heat and slowly add the stock, stirring continuously to prevent lumps from forming. Return the pan to the heat, add the thyme and season with pepper. Cover and bring to the boil, then boil, uncovered, for 5 minutes until the liquid is reduced by about half. Stir in the cream, wine and 200ml/9fl oz/1 cup of the reserved soaking liquid and return to the boil, stirring. Adjust the salt and pepper, if necessary, and serve sprinkled with parsley.

056 Tuscan 'Cooked Water' Soup

PREPARATION TIME 15 minutes, plus preparing the tomatoes
COOKING TIME 50 minutes

3 tbsp fruity extra-virgin olive oil,
   plus extra to serve
2 celery sticks, finely chopped
1 carrot, peeled and diced
1 large red onion, diced
1 red pepper, deseeded and diced
3 large plum tomatoes, peeled
   (see page 9), deseeded and diced

1 Parmesan, pecorino or Gruyère
   cheese rind, about 7.5 x 5cm/
   3 x 2in (see page 9; optional)
1 large egg for each bowl
1 slice of day-old ciabatta bread
   for each bowl
2–3 large garlic cloves, halved
freshly grated pecorino cheese,
   to serve

1   Heat the oil in a saucepan over a medium heat. Add the celery, carrot, onion and pepper and fry, stirring, for 3–5 minutes until the onion is softened but not browned. Add the tomatoes, cheese rind, if using, and 1.25l/44fl oz/5 cups water. Season with salt and pepper. Cover and bring to the boil, then reduce the heat and simmer for 30 minutes.
2   Preheat the grill to high. Uncover the pan and reduce the heat so the soup is just simmering. Remove the cheese rind from the soup; depending on how much it has dissolved, you can either discard it or finely chop and set it aside.
3   Break the eggs, one by one, into a cup and then gently lower them into the simmering soup. Use a large metal spoon to spoon some of the liquid over each egg and poach for 3 minutes for soft-set yolks and up to 5 minutes for firmer yolks. Adjust the salt and pepper, if necessary.
4   Meanwhile, toast the bread under the grill for 1–2 minutes on each side until crisp and golden brown. Rub one side of each slice with half a garlic clove, pressing down firmly, then set aside and keep warm while the eggs poach.
5   Divide the toast into bowls and drizzle generously with olive oil. Transfer 1 egg to each bowl and sprinkle with cheese and chopped rind, if using. Ladle the soup into the bowls and serve with olive oil for adding at the table.

057   Mixed Mushroom Broth

PREPARATION TIME 15 minutes, plus 30 minutes soaking the mushrooms and making the stock   COOKING TIME 20 minutes

15g/½oz dried porcini mushrooms
3 tbsp olive or hemp oil
1 large leek, halved lengthways,
   thinly sliced and rinsed
2 large garlic cloves, finely chopped
600g/1lb 5oz mixed mushrooms,
   coarsely chopped

1.25l/44fl oz/5 cups Vegetable Stock
   (see page 12) or ready-made stock
5cm/2in rosemary sprig
2 tbsp sweet sherry
salt and freshly ground black pepper

1 Put the porcini mushrooms and 250ml/9fl oz/1 cup boiling water in a heatproof bowl and leave to soak for 30 minutes until tender. Strain through a muslin-lined sieve and reserve the liquid. Squeeze the mushrooms, then trim the stalks, if necessary, and thinly slice the caps and stalks, then set aside.
2 Heat the oil in a saucepan over a medium heat. Add the leek and garlic and fry, stirring occasionally, for 2 minutes. Add the mushrooms, season with salt and cook for 5–8 minutes, stirring, until the mushrooms give off their liquid. Stir in the stock, rosemary, porcini mushrooms and reserved liquid and season with salt and pepper.
3 Cover and bring to the boil, then reduce the heat and simmer for 8–10 minutes until the mushrooms are tender. Discard the rosemary sprig, stir in the sherry and adjust the salt and pepper, if necessary, then serve.

058   Shiitake & Chinese Cabbage Soup

PREPARATION TIME 10 minutes, plus making the stock   COOKING TIME 45 minutes

1.25l/44fl oz/5 cups Vegetable Stock
   (see page 12) or ready-made stock
2.5cm/1in piece of root ginger,
   peeled and smashed in one piece

1cm/½in piece of galangal, peeled
   and smashed in one piece
30g/1oz dried shiitake mushrooms
light soy sauce, to taste
300g/10½oz Chinese cabbage, sliced

1 Put the stock, ginger and galangal in a saucepan. Cover and bring to the boil, then reduce the heat and simmer for 30 minutes. Meanwhile, put the shiitake mushrooms and 250ml/9fl oz/1 cup boiling water in a heatproof bowl and leave to soak for 30 minutes until tender. Strain through a muslin-lined sieve and set the liquid aside. Squeeze the mushrooms dry, cut off the stalks and slice the caps.
2 Stir the reserved liquid into the stock and season with soy sauce. Add the mushrooms and cabbage and simmer for 5–8 minutes until the mushrooms are tender, then discard the ginger and galangal and serve.

059   Mushroom & Coconut Soup

PREPARATION TIME 15 minutes, plus making the stock and chillies
COOKING TIME 20 minutes

1 small handful of bean sprouts
700ml/26fl oz/3 cups coconut milk
500ml/17fl oz/2 cups Vegetable Stock
   (see page 12) or ready-made stock
½ lemongrass stalk, crushed
2 tbsp lime juice, or to taste
5 kaffir lime leaves

400g/14oz chestnut mushrooms,
   trimmed and sliced
200g/7oz oyster mushrooms,
   trimmed and sliced
salt and freshly ground black pepper
Chillies in Vinegar (see page 15),
   to serve

1 Put the bean sprouts in a bowl, cover with cold water and set aside.
2 Put the coconut milk, stock, lemongrass, lime juice and lime leaves in a saucepan. Season with salt and pepper, cover and bring to the boil. Add all the mushrooms, reduce the heat and simmer, covered, for 6–8 minutes until the mushrooms are tender. Discard the lime leaves and lemongrass.
3 Drain the bean sprouts and add them to the soup. Adjust the salt and pepper, if necessary, and add extra lime juice to taste. Serve with the chillies on the side.

060 Arame & Tofu Soup

PREPARATION TIME 25 minutes, plus making the dashi and seeds
COOKING TIME 15 minutes

20g/¾oz dried arame
1l/35fl oz/4 cups Vegetarian Dashi
  (see page 12) or prepared instant
  vegetarian dashi
2 radishes, thinly sliced
1 carrot, peeled and coarsely grated
1 red chilli, deseeded and thinly
  chopped

1 courgette, coarsely grated
1 tbsp light soy sauce
1 tbsp rice wine
400g/14oz fried tofu, cut into
  1cm/½in cubes
toasted sesame seeds (see page 9),
  to serve

1 Put the arame in a bowl, cover with cold water and leave to soak for 15 minutes
   until doubled in volume, then drain.
2 Put the dashi in a saucepan over a high heat, cover and bring to the boil. Add the
   arame and boil, covered, for 3–5 minutes until tender. Add the radishes, carrot, chilli
   and courgette and boil, uncovered, for 30 seconds–1½ minutes until the vegetables
   are tender. Stir in the soy sauce and rice wine. Divide the tofu into bowls and ladle
   the arame and soup over it. Serve sprinkled with sesame seeds.

061 Welsh Leek & Parsley Soup with Rarebit 'Soldiers'

PREPARATION TIME 20 minutes, plus making the stock   COOKING TIME 25 minutes

15g/½oz butter
1 tbsp sunflower, olive or hemp oil
1 leek, sliced and rinsed
1 large garlic clove, chopped
750ml/26fl oz/3 cups Vegetable Stock
    (see page 12) or ready-made stock
400g/14oz floury potatoes, peeled
    and chopped
330ml/10¼fl oz/1⅓ cups whole milk
140g/5oz curly parsley, leaves and
    stalks chopped, with 2 tbsp leaves
    reserved to serve
salt and ground white pepper

RAREBIT SOLDIERS
3 slices of white or wholemeal bread
200g/7oz mature Cheddar cheese
    or Caerphilly cheese, grated
    or crumbled
1½ tsp mustard powder
1 tbsp brown ale, cider or dry white
    wine
vegetarian Worcestershire sauce,
    to taste

1   Preheat the grill to high and line a baking sheet with foil. Melt the butter with the oil in a saucepan over a medium heat. Add the leek and fry, stirring, for 2 minutes. Stir in the garlic and fry for 1–3 minutes until the leek is softened but not coloured. Add the stock and potatoes and season well with salt. Cover and bring to the boil, then reduce the heat and simmer for 10–12 minutes until the potatoes are very tender.

2   Meanwhile, to make the soldiers, toast the bread on one side under the grill for 1–2 minutes until golden brown. Put the bread on the baking sheet, toasted-side down, and set aside. Put the cheese, mustard powder and ale in a small saucepan over a medium heat and beat until the cheese melts and a thick paste forms. Spread the paste over the bread and splash with a few drops of Worcestershire sauce. Grill for 2 minutes until the cheese mixture bubbles. Cut the crusts off the toast, then cut each slice into 4 'soldiers'. Set aside and keep warm.

3   Add the milk to the soup and return to just below the boil. As it starts to bubble, stir in the parsley, then immediately turn off the heat. Leave to stand, uncovered, for about 30 seconds to soften the parsley, then blend the soup until smooth. Adjust the salt and white pepper, if necessary, and serve sprinkled with parsley and with the 'soldiers' on the side. If you reheat the soup, do not boil it.

062 Forager's Nettle & Wild Garlic Soup

PREPARATION TIME 25 minutes, plus making the stock   COOKING TIME 35 minutes

250g/9oz young stinging nettle tops
    (use only the top 5–6cm/2–2½in)
30g/1oz butter
1 tbsp olive or hemp oil
1 large onion
1 tsp caster sugar
5 stalks of wild garlic, chopped,
    with the flowery tops reserved,
    if available, to serve

1 floury potato, peeled and chopped
1.4l/48fl oz/5½ cups Vegetable Stock
    (see page 12) or ready-made stock
salt and freshly ground black pepper
wild garlic flowers or chopped
    chives, to serve (optional)
soured cream, to serve (optional)

1   Wearing rubber gloves, remove the nettle leaves from the stems. Tie the stems together with kitchen string and lightly crush, then set aside. Wash the leaves well in several changes of cold water, then transfer to a colander and set aside to drain.

2   Melt the butter with the oil in a saucepan over a medium heat. Add the onion and sugar and fry, stirring, for 10–12 minutes until the onions are starting to caramelize. Stir in the wild garlic and potatoes and fry for 2 minutes. Add the stock and nettle leaves and stalks and season with salt and pepper.

3   Cover and bring to the boil, then reduce the heat and simmer, uncovered, for 12–15 minutes until the potato is tender. Remove the nettle stalks, then blend the soup until smooth, stopping to unclog the blender blades if necessary. Adjust the salt and pepper, if necessary, and serve sprinkled with wild garlic flowers and with soured cream on the side, if you like.

063 Rich Orange-Scented Chestnut Soup

PREPARATION TIME 25 minutes, plus making the stock   COOKING TIME 55 minutes

2 sweet cooking apples,
  peeled and chopped
1 tbsp lemon juice
2 tbsp sunflower, olive or hemp oil
140g/5oz celeriac, peeled and
  chopped
1 onion, chopped
1 leek, chopped and rinsed
1 bay leaf
1 thyme sprig

a pinch of freshly grated nutmeg
250g/9oz tinned or vacuum-packed
  chestnuts, drained and chopped
1l/35fl oz/4 cups Vegetable Stock
  (see page 12) or ready-made stock
2 tbsp orange juice
4 tbsp double cream
salt and freshly ground black pepper
grated zest of 2 oranges, to serve

1   Put the apples in a bowl, add the lemon juice and toss together, then set aside.
2   Heat the oil in a large saucepan over a medium heat. Add the celeriac, onion, leek,
    bay leaf, thyme and nutmeg and season with salt and pepper. Cook, covered,
    for 8–10 minutes, stirring. Stir in the apples, chestnuts, stock and orange juice.
3   Cover and bring to the boil, then reduce the heat and simmer for 30–35 minutes
    until the chestnuts are tender enough to be mashed against the side of the pan.
    Discard the bay leaf and thyme. Blend the soup until smooth, then stir in the cream
    and adjust the salt and pepper, if necessary. Serve sprinkled with orange zest.

064 Creamy Peanut & Chilli Soup

PREPARATION TIME 10 minutes, plus making the stock   COOKING TIME 35 minutes

2 tbsp sunflower oil
1 celery stick, thinly sliced
1 small onion, very finely chopped
1½ tbsp plain flour
750ml/26fl oz/3 cups Vegetable Stock
  (see page 12) or ready-made stock

a pinch of chilli flakes, or to taste
175g/6oz/¾ cup natural smooth
  peanut butter
185ml/6fl oz/¾ cup single cream
salt and freshly ground black pepper

1   Heat the oil in a saucepan. Add the celery and onion and fry, stirring, for 3–5
    minutes until softened. Sprinkle in the flour and stir for 2 minutes, then slowly stir
    in the stock and chilli flakes and season with salt and pepper, stirring continuously.
2   Bring to the boil, then add the peanut butter and stir until it dissolves. Reduce
    the heat and simmer, covered, for 15 minutes. Stir in the cream and simmer for
    2 minutes. Do not boil. Adjust the salt and pepper, if necessary, and serve.

065 Plantain & Sweetcorn Soup

PREPARATION TIME 10 minutes, plus 30 minutes soaking the chilli and making the stock
COOKING TIME 40 minutes

1 dried ancho chilli pepper
1l/35fl oz/4 cups Vegetable Stock
  (see page 12) or ready-made stock
15g/½oz butter
2 tbsp sunflower oil
1 onion, chopped

1 green pepper, deseeded
  and chopped
2 large garlic cloves, crushed
2 green plantains, coarsely grated
400g/14oz/2⅔ cups frozen
  sweetcorn kernels
salt and freshly ground black pepper

1   Put the ancho chilli in a heatproof bowl, cover with hot water and leave to soak for
    30 minutes, then drain and finely chop. Pound the chilli to form a paste, adding
    a little of the stock, if necessary, then set aside.
2   Melt the butter with the oil in a saucepan over a medium heat. Add the onion and
    pepper and fry, stirring, for 2 minutes. Add the garlic and chilli paste and fry for
    another 1–3 minutes until the onion is softened. Add the plantain and remaining
    stock and season with salt and pepper. Cover and bring to the boil, then reduce
    the heat and simmer, covered, for 15 minutes, stirring occasionally. Stir in the
    sweetcorn and simmer for 10 minutes. Adjust the salt and pepper and serve.

Okra & Sweetcorn Soup

PREPARATION TIME 15 minutes, plus 30 minutes soaking the okra, making the stock and chilli bon-bon and preparing the tomatoes   **COOKING TIME** 30 minutes

100g/3½oz okra, sliced
1 tbsp white wine vinegar
½ tsp salt, plus extra to season
1 tbsp sunflower oil
1 onion, finely chopped
2 garlic cloves, chopped
1.25l/44fl oz/5 cups Vegetable Stock
 (see page 12) or ready-made stock
a pinch of chilli flakes (optional)

4 large tomatoes, peeled (see
 page 9), deseeded and chopped
400g/14oz/2⅔ cups frozen
 sweetcorn kernels
1 tbsp tomato purée
2 tbsp chopped curly parsley leaves
freshly ground black pepper
Chilli Bon-Bon (see page 15) or hot
 pepper sauce, to serve

1   Put the okra, vinegar and salt in a large bowl. Cover with water and leave to soak for 30 minutes, then drain, rinse, drain again and set aside. This helps to reduce the okra's sliminess while it cooks.
2   Heat the oil in a saucepan over a medium heat. Add the onion and fry, stirring occasionally, for 2 minutes. Add the garlic and okra and fry, stirring continuously, for 3–6 minutes until the onion is softened and light golden brown. Add the stock and chilli flakes, if using, and season with salt and pepper. Cover and bring to the boil, then reduce the heat and simmer for 5 minutes.
3   Stir in the tomatoes, sweetcorn and tomato purée and simmer for 5–10 minutes until the okra is tender. Stir in the parsley and adjust the salt and pepper, if necessary. Serve with chilli bon-bon for adding at the table.

067 Cream of Sweetcorn Soup

PREPARATION TIME 10 minutes, plus making the stock   COOKING TIME 35 minutes

800ml/28fl oz/scant 3¼ cups
   Vegetable Stock (see page 12)
   or ready-made stock
freshly cut kernels from 2 corn cobs,
   about 350g/12oz, with the cobs
   reserved and cut in half
30g/1oz butter
3 tbsp plain white flour

455ml/16fl oz/scant 2 cups
   whole milk
1 roasted red pepper in olive oil,
   drained and finely chopped
2 spring onions, very thinly sliced
cayenne pepper (optional)
salt and freshly ground black pepper
chopped parsley leaves, to serve

1   Put the stock and corn cobs in a large saucepan and season with salt. Cover and bring to the boil, then reduce the heat and simmer for at least 10 minutes.
2   Meanwhile, melt the butter in a large saucepan over a medium heat. Sprinkle in the flour and stir for 2 minutes, then remove the pan from the heat and slowly stir in the milk, stirring continuously to prevent lumps from forming.
3   Remove the corn cobs from the stock. Slowly stir 600ml/21fl oz/scant 2½ cups of the stock into the white sauce and simmer for 5 minutes, stirring occasionally, until the sauce is thickened and smooth.
4   Stir in the corn kernels and simmer for 5 minutes. Add the red pepper and spring onions and season with cayenne pepper, if using. Season with salt and pepper, but remember the stock has been salted. Simmer for 3–5 minutes until the corn and pepper are tender. Serve sprinkled with parsley.

068 Onion & Mustard Soup

PREPARATION TIME 15 minutes, plus making the stock and crisps
COOKING TIME 35 minutes

40g/1½oz butter
½ tbsp sunflower oil
500g/1lb 2oz onions, finely chopped
1 leek, white part only, thinly sliced
   and rinsed
⅓ fennel bulb, chopped
1l/35fl oz/4 cups Vegetable Stock
   (see page 12) or ready-made stock
1 tbsp wholegrain mustard

salt and freshly ground black pepper
alfalfa sprouts, to serve
chopped chives, to serve

PARMESAN CRISPS
75g/2½oz Parmesan cheese,
   finely grated
1 tsp plain white or wholemeal flour

1   Melt the butter with the oil in a saucepan over a medium heat. Add the onions, leek and fennel and fry, stirring occasionally, for 3–5 minutes until the vegetables are softened but not coloured. Stir in the stock and season with salt and pepper. Cover and bring to the boil, then reduce the heat and simmer for 25–30 minutes until the vegetables are very tender.
2   Meanwhile, make the Parmesan crisps. Preheat the oven to 190°C/375°F/gas 5 and line a baking sheet with baking parchment. Mix the cheese and flour together in a bowl, then divide the mixture into 12 equal portions and space them out on the baking sheet. Bake for 10–15 minutes until they spread and become golden brown. Use a spatula to transfer the crisps to a wire rack and leave to cool completely.
3   Blend the soup until smooth. Working in batches, strain the soup through a fine sieve back into the pan, rubbing back and forth with a spoon and scraping the bottom of the sieve. Stir in the mustard and reheat. Adjust the salt and pepper, if necessary, then serve sprinkled with alfalfa sprouts and chives and with the cheese crisps on the side.

069 Curried Parsnip Soup

PREPARATION TIME 15 minutes, plus making the stock   COOKING TIME 30 minutes

2 tbsp sunflower oil
1 large onion, chopped
2 garlic cloves, chopped
1 tbsp Madras or other curry paste
½ tsp turmeric
350g/12oz parsnips, peeled and
   chopped
1 large sweet cooking apple, peeled,
   cored and chopped

600ml/2½fl oz/scant 2½ cups
   Vegetable Stock (see page 12)
   or ready-made stock
600ml/2½fl oz/scant 2½ cups
   whole milk
salt and freshly ground black pepper
natural yogurt, to serve
shredded coriander leaves, to serve

1   Heat the oil in a saucepan over a medium heat. Add the onion and fry, stirring,
    for 2 minutes. Add the garlic and fry for 1–3 minutes until the onion is softened.
    Stir in the curry paste and turmeric and fry, stirring, for 30 seconds. Watch closely
    so the spices do not burn. Stir in the parsnips and apple, then add the stock and
    season with salt and pepper. Cover and bring to the boil.
2   Reduce the heat and simmer for 12–15 minutes until the parsnips are tender.
    Stir in the milk and simmer for another 5 minutes. Do not boil. Blend the soup
    until smooth, adjust the salt and pepper, if necessary, and serve topped with a
    swirl of yogurt and sprinkled with coriander. If you reheat the soup, do not boil it.

070 Parsnip & Orange Soup

PREPARATION TIME 20 minutes, plus making the stock   COOKING TIME 35 minutes

30g/1oz butter
1 tbsp sunflower oil
1 large onion, chopped
1 large garlic clove, chopped
2 tbsp plain white or wholemeal flour
950ml/32fl oz/scant 4 cups
   Vegetable Stock (see page 12)
   or ready-made stock

400g/14oz parsnips, peeled
   and chopped
1 floury potato, peeled and chopped
125ml/4fl oz/½ cup orange juice
salt and freshly ground black pepper
grated zest of 2 oranges, to serve
black sesame seeds, to serve

1   Melt the butter with the oil in a saucepan over a medium heat. Add the onion and
    fry, stirring occasionally, for 2 minutes. Stir in the garlic and fry for 1–3 minutes
    until the onion is softened. Sprinkle in the flour and cook, stirring, for 2 minutes,
    then slowly pour in the stock, stirring continuously to prevent lumps from forming.
    Add the parsnips and potatoes and season with salt and pepper.
2   Cover and bring to the boil, then reduce the heat and simmer for 15–20 minutes
    until the parsnips are very tender. Stir in the orange juice, then blend the soup until
    smooth. Adjust the salt and pepper, if necessary, and serve sprinkled with the
    orange zest and sesame seeds.

071 Red-Hot Red Pepper Soup

PREPARATION TIME 15 minutes, plus making the stock   COOKING TIME 30 minutes

30g/1oz butter
2 tbsp olive or hemp oil
1 shallot, chopped
5 roasted red peppers in olive oil,
   drained and chopped
1 floury potato, peeled and chopped

1 red chilli, sliced
1.25l/44fl oz/5 cups Vegetable Stock
   (see page 12) or ready-made stock
salt and freshly ground black pepper
hot pepper sauce, to serve

1   Melt the butter with the oil in a saucepan over a medium heat. Add the shallot and
    fry, stirring, for 3–5 minutes until softened. Stir in the peppers, potato and chilli
    and fry, stirring, for 5 minutes. Add the stock and season with salt and pepper.
2   Cover and bring to the boil, then reduce the heat and simmer for 10 minutes until
    the potato is tender. Blend until smooth, reheat and adjust the salt and pepper,
    if necessary. Serve with hot pepper sauce.

072 Rich Pepper & Orange Soup

PREPARATION TIME 15 minutes   **COOKING TIME** 25 minutes

3 tbsp olive or hemp oil
8 large red peppers, or a mix of red,
   orange and yellow peppers,
   deseeded and sliced
4–6 tbsp lemon juice
finely grated zest of 2 large oranges

290ml/10fl oz/1 cup plus 2 tbsp blood
   orange juice
salt and freshly ground black pepper
thinly sliced mint leaves, to serve
hot pepper sauce, to serve (optional)

1   Heat the oil in a saucepan over a medium heat. Add the red peppers, 2 tablespoons
    of the lemon juice and half the orange zest and season with salt and pepper. Cook,
    covered, for 20–25 minutes, stirring frequently, until the peppers are very tender.
    Watch closely so they do not burn.
2   Remove the pan from the heat and stir in the orange juice and 2 tablespoons of the
    remaining lemon juice. Blend until smooth, then strain the soup into a large bowl
    and work it through the sieve, rubbing back and forth with a spoon and scraping
    the bottom of the sieve. Gradually stir in enough of the remaining lemon juice
    to sharpen the flavour, if necessary, tasting as you go. Adjust the salt and pepper,
    if necessary, then serve sprinkled with the orange zest and mint and with hot
    pepper sauce, if you like. You can also serve this soup chilled, adding a little extra
    stock to thin it and seasoning again with salt and pepper after chilling, if necessary.

073 Watercress Soup

PREPARATION TIME 15 minutes, plus making the stock   **COOKING TIME** 30 minutes

30g/1oz butter
1 tbsp sunflower oil
1 shallot, finely chopped
1 large floury potato, peeled
   and diced
1.25l/44fl oz/5 cups Vegetable Stock
   (see page 12) or ready-made stock

400g/14oz watercress, trimmed
   and chopped
4 tbsp crème fraîche or soured cream
4 tbsp whole milk
freshly grated nutmeg, to taste
salt and freshly ground black pepper

1   Melt the butter with the oil in a saucepan over a medium heat. Add the shallot and
    fry, stirring, for 3–5 minutes until softened. Stir in the potato, then add the stock
    and season with salt and pepper. Cover and bring to the boil. Reduce the heat and
    simmer for 10–12 minutes until the potato is tender. Uncover, add the watercress
    and simmer for 1 minute, then blend the soup until smooth.
2   Bring to just below the boil and stir in the crème fraîche and milk. Add the nutmeg
    and adjust the salt and pepper, if necessary, and serve. You can also serve this
    soup chilled, adding a little extra stock to thin it and seasoning again with salt and
    pepper after chilling, if necessary.

074 Spinach & Buttermilk Soup

PREPARATION TIME 10 minutes, plus making the stock   **COOKING TIME** 25 minutes

875ml/30fl oz/3½ cups
   Vegetable Stock (see page 12)
   or ready-made stock
450g/1lb spinach, any thick stalks
   removed, and leaves chopped

½–1 tbsp lemon juice
290ml/10fl oz/1¼ cups buttermilk,
   plus extra to serve
freshly grated nutmeg, to taste
salt and freshly ground black pepper

1   Put the stock and spinach in a saucepan, add ½ tablespoon of the lemon juice and
    season with salt and pepper. Cover and bring to the boil, then reduce the heat
    and simmer for 10–12 minutes until tender.
2   Blend the soup until smooth, then strain it into a bowl and work it through the
    sieve, rubbing back and forth with a spoon and scraping the bottom of the sieve.
    Return the soup to the pan, stir in the buttermilk and season with nutmeg. Reheat,
    but do not boil it. Adjust the salt and pepper, if necessary, then add extra lemon
    juice or nutmeg, if you like. Serve with a little extra buttermilk swirled in.

075 Curried Spinach & Coconut Soup

PREPARATION TIME 15 minutes, plus making the stock   COOKING TIME 25 minutes

15g/½oz butter
1½ tbsp sunflower or groundnut oil
1 leek, halved lengthways, thinly
   sliced and rinsed
2 garlic cloves, finely chopped
2.5cm/1in piece of root ginger,
   peeled and grated
1 tbsp korma or other curry powder
1 tsp ground coriander
1 tsp cumin seeds, lightly crushed

200g/7oz spinach, any thick stalks
   removed, and leaves chopped
750ml/26fl oz/scant 3 cups
   Vegetable Stock (see page 12)
   or ready-made stock
400ml/14fl oz/scant 1⅔ cup
   coconut milk
55g/2oz silken tofu
lime juice, to taste
sesame seeds, to serve

1   Melt the butter with the oil in a saucepan over a medium heat. Add the leek and
    fry, stirring occasionally, for 2 minutes. Stir in the garlic and ginger and fry for
    1–3 minutes until the leek is softened but not coloured. Stir in the curry powder,
    coriander and cumin seeds and stir for 30 seconds. Watch closely so the spices
    do not burn. Add the spinach and stir for 3–5 minutes until wilted.
2   Stir in the stock, coconut milk and tofu. Cover and bring to just below the boil.
    Reduce the heat and simmer for 5 minutes, then blend until smooth. Season
    with lime juice and serve sprinkled with sesame seeds.

076 Spinach & Mung Bean Soup

PREPARATION TIME 10 minutes, plus making the stock   COOKING TIME 25 minutes

1.25l/35fl oz/4 cups Vegetable Stock
   (see page 12) or ready-made stock
140g/5oz turnips, peeled and
   coarsely grated
1 tbsp dried mint leaves
½ tsp ground fenugreek

a pinch of turmeric
400g/14oz baby spinach leaves,
   chopped
200g/7oz tinned mung beans,
   drained and rinsed
salt and freshly ground black pepper

1   Put the stock, turnips, mint, fenugreek and turmeric in a saucepan. Stir in the
    spinach and season with salt and pepper. Cover and bring to the boil, then reduce
    the heat to low. Simmer for 10–12 minutes until the vegetables are very tender.
2   Blend the soup, then stir in the mung beans and simmer for 4–5 minutes to warm
    through. Adjust the salt and pepper, if necessary, and serve.

077 Courgette & Rocket Soup with Croûtes

PREPARATION TIME 15 minutes, plus making the stock, berry and seed mix, and croûtes
COOKING TIME 20 minutes

30g/1oz butter
1 tbsp olive or hemp oil
2 onions, finely chopped
2 large garlic cloves, crushed
2 large courgettes, sliced
55g/2oz rocket leaves, chopped
1.4l/48fl oz/5½ cups Vegetable Stock
   (see page 12) or ready-made stock

2–3 tbsp lemon juice
salt and freshly ground black pepper
Goji Berry & Seed Mix (see page 15),
   to serve
1 recipe quantity Goat's Cheese
   Croûtes (see page 14), to serve

1   Melt the butter with the oil in a saucepan over a medium heat. Add the onion and
    fry, stirring, for 2 minutes. Add the garlic and fry for 1–3 minutes until the onion is
    softened. Add the courgettes and fry, stirring, for 2–3 minutes until the skins turn
    bright green. Stir in the rocket and stock, then cover and bring to the boil.
2   Reduce the heat and simmer, covered, for 2–3 minutes until the courgettes are
    tender. Stir in the lemon juice to taste and season with salt and pepper. Blend the
    soup until smooth, then serve sprinkled with the berry and seed mix and with
    the croûtes on the side.

078

Spring Sorrel & Spinach Soup
with Egg Butterballs

PREPARATION TIME 25 minutes, plus making the stock and cooking the eggs
COOKING TIME 40 minutes

30g/1oz butter
1 tbsp olive or hemp oil
1 large onion, chopped
4 large garlic cloves, chopped
100g/3½oz young sorrel leaves,
    stalks crushed
2 handfuls of baby spinach leaves
1.25l/44fl oz/5 cups Vegetable Stock
    (see page 12) or ready-made stock
2 tbsp chopped parsley leaves
salt and freshly ground black pepper

EGG BUTTERBALLS
100g/3½oz butter, at room
    temperature
2 large hard-boiled egg yolks,
    chopped
a pinch of turmeric
a pinch of cayenne pepper (optional)

1   Melt the butter with the oil in a saucepan over a medium heat. Add the onion and garlic, reduce the heat to low and cook, covered, for 10–12 minutes until very tender and just starting to turn golden. Add the sorrel and spinach and stir for 3–5 minutes until wilted. Add the stock and parsley and season with salt and pepper.

2   Bring to the boil, partially covered. Reduce the heat and simmer, partially covered, for 10–15 minutes until the leaves are very tender.

3   Meanwhile, make the butterballs. Put the butter, egg yolks, turmeric and cayenne pepper, if using, in a bowl and beat together. Season with salt and pepper, then divide the mixture into 12 equal portions and roll into balls. (The butterballs can be made up to 1 day in advance and chilled until required.)

4   Blend the soup until smooth, then work it through a sieve into a bowl, rubbing back and forth with a spoon and scraping the bottom of the sieve. Return to the pan, adjust the salt and pepper, if necessary, and reheat. Add the butterballs and serve.

079 Butternut Squash & Chestnut Soup

PREPARATION TIME 15 minutes, plus making the stock   COOKING TIME 40 minutes

1 tbsp olive or hemp oil
1 red onion, chopped
2 large garlic cloves, finely chopped
600g/1lb 5oz butternut squash,
    peeled, deseeded and chopped
875ml/30fl oz/3½ cups Vegetable
    Stock (see page 12)

1 bay leaf
250g/9oz/scant 1 cup tinned chestnut
    purée
salt and freshly ground black pepper
Greek-style yogurt, to serve
flax seeds, lightly crushed, to serve

1   Heat the oil in a saucepan over a medium heat. Add the onion and fry, stirring occasionally, for 2 minutes. Add the garlic and fry for 1–3 minutes until the onion is softened but not coloured, then stir in the squash. Add the stock and bay leaf and season with salt and pepper. Cover and bring to the boil, then reduce the heat and simmer for 20–25 minutes until the squash is very tender.
2   Strain the stock and discard the bay leaf. Return the squash and onion to the pan and stir in the chestnut purée. Gradually stir in enough of the stock to achieve the preferred consistency. Reheat, adjust the salt and pepper, if necessary, then serve topped with yogurt and sprinkled with flax seeds.

080 Thai-Style Pumpkin Soup

PREPARATION TIME 25 minutes, plus making the stock   COOKING TIME 45 minutes

900g/2lb pumpkin, cut into wedges
    and deseeded
3 tbsp olive or hemp oil
2 shallots, chopped
2 garlic cloves, chopped
2 tbsp peeled and grated root ginger
500ml/17fl oz/2 cups Vegetable Stock
    (see page 12) or ready-made stock

1 bird's-eye chilli, deseeded
    (optional) and chopped
1 lemongrass stalk, finely chopped,
    with outer layer removed
500ml/17fl oz/2 cups coconut milk
salt and freshly ground black pepper
chopped coriander leaves, to serve
chopped roasted peanuts, to serve
lime wedges, to serve

1   Preheat the oven to 220°C/425°F/gas 7. Put the pumpkin in a baking tray, drizzle with 1 tablespoon of the oil and season with salt. Toss well to coat and roast for 40–50 minutes, stirring once or twice, until the pumpkin is tender. Remove from the oven and set aside until cool enough to handle.
2   Meanwhile, heat the remaining oil in a saucepan over a medium heat. Stir in the shallots and fry, stirring occasionally, for 2 minutes. Add the garlic and ginger and fry for 1–3 minutes until the shallots are softened but not coloured. Add the stock, chilli and lemongrass and season with salt and pepper. Cover and bring to the boil, then reduce the heat and simmer for 15 minutes.
3   Scrape the pumpkin flesh from the skin and add it to the soup, then blend until smooth. Stir in the coconut milk, reheat and adjust the salt and pepper, if necessary. Serve sprinkled with coriander and peanuts and with lemon wedges for squeezing over.

081 Breakfast Tea Soup

PREPARATION TIME 10 minutes, plus making the tea   COOKING TIME 2 minutes

750ml/26fl oz/scant 3 cups
    whole milk
4–6 slices of white bread, buttered
    with crusts cut off
4–6 tbsp caster sugar, or to taste

ground clove, to taste
cinnamon, to taste
500ml/17fl oz/2 cups freshly
    brewed tea

1   Heat the milk to just below the boil. Meanwhile, divide the bread into four bowls and sprinkle each portion with 1 tablespoon of the sugar and a little ground clove and cinnamon. Pour the tea over the bread.
2   Add the milk, stir well and serve, sprinkling with extra sugar, if you like.

082 Roasted Squash & Tomato Soup

PREPARATION TIME 20 minutes, plus making the stock　**COOKING TIME** 25 minutes

3 large tomatoes, halved
600g/1lb 5oz butternut squash
6 large whole garlic cloves, peeled
1 red onion, quartered
1cm/½in piece of root ginger, peeled
　and thinly sliced
2½ tbsp olive or hemp oil, plus extra
　for frying the seeds

½ tsp ground coriander
½ tsp ground cumin
½ tsp hot paprika, or to taste
750ml/26fl oz/3 cups Vegetable Stock
　(see page 12) or ready-made stock
salt and freshly ground black pepper
chopped parsley leaves, to serve

1　Preheat the oven to 220°C/425°F/gas 7. Put the tomatoes, cut-sides down,
　in a baking tray. Cut the squash in half, scoop out the seeds and set them aside.
　Coarsely chop the squash into 5cm/2in pieces – there's no need to peel it – and add
　it to the baking tray, along with the garlic, onion and ginger. Add the oil, coriander,
　cumin and paprika and season with salt and pepper. Toss well to coat, then roast
　for 20 minutes, stirring once or twice, until the squash and onion are tender and
　the tomato skins have burst.

2　Meanwhile, put several layers of kitchen paper on a plate and set aside. Rinse the
　squash seeds well and use your fingers to remove the fibres, then pat dry with
　kitchen paper. Heat a thin layer of the oil in a frying pan over a high heat. Add the
　seeds and stir for 30 seconds–1 minute until they start to pop and turn golden
　brown. Watch closely so they do not burn. Immediately turn them out of the pan
　onto the prepared plate and set aside.

3　Transfer the vegetables from the baking tray to a large heatproof bowl or blender
　and add half the stock. Blend until smooth. Working in batches, strain the soup into
　a saucepan and work it through the sieve, rubbing back and forth with a spoon and
　scraping the bottom of the sieve. Stir in enough of the remaining stock to achieve
　the preferred consistency and reheat. (Any leftover stock can be used in other
　recipes or frozen for up to 6 months.) Adjust the salt and pepper, if necessary,
　then serve, sprinkled with the seeds and parsley.

083 Spiced Pumpkin & Apple Soup

PREPARATION TIME 15 minutes, plus making the stock and toasting the almonds
COOKING TIME 30 minutes

15g/½oz butter
1 tbsp olive or hemp oil
1 small onion, finely chopped
2 garlic cloves, very finely chopped
½ tbsp peeled and chopped root
   ginger
½ tsp cinnamon
cayenne pepper, to taste
1.25l/44fl oz/5 cups Vegetable Stock
   (see page 12) or ready-made stock

425g/15oz/heaped 1¾ cups tinned
   pumpkin purée
1 apple, such as Granny Smith,
   peeled, cored and chopped
½ tsp dried thyme leaves
1 bay leaf
4 tbsp dry sherry
4 tbsp Greek-style yogurt
salt and freshly ground black pepper
toasted flaked almonds (see page 9),
   to serve

1   Heat the butter and oil in a saucepan over a medium heat. Add the onion and fry, stirring, for 2 minutes. Add the garlic and ginger and fry for 1–3 minutes until the onion is softened. Add the cinnamon and cayenne pepper and stir for 30 seconds. Watch closely so the spices do not burn. Stir in the stock, pumpkin purée, apple, thyme and bay leaf and season with salt and pepper. Cover and bring to the boil, then reduce the heat and simmer for 15 minutes. Discard the bay leaf.

2   Blend the soup until smooth. Stir in the sherry and yogurt and reheat but do not boil. Adjust the salt and pepper, if necessary, then serve sprinkled with almonds.

084 Swiss Chard & Garlic Broth

PREPARATION TIME 15 minutes, plus making the stock   COOKING TIME 35 minutes

1.5l/52fl oz/6 cups Vegetable Stock
   (see page 12) or ready-made stock
1 large garlic bulb, separated into
   cloves, peeled and lightly crushed
1 onion, unpeeled and cut in half
1 floury potato, peeled and chopped
1 bay leaf

a large pinch of saffron threads
a pinch of dried chilli flakes
½ tsp salt, plus extra to season
450g/1lb Swiss chard leaves, thick
   stalks removed, leaves thinly sliced
freshly ground black pepper

1   Put the stock, garlic, onion, potato, bay leaf, saffron, chilli flakes and salt in a large saucepan over a high heat. Cover and bring to the boil, then reduce the heat and simmer, partially covered, for 20 minutes to reduce slightly. Strain the stock into a bowl. Discard the onion and bay leaf, then press down on the garlic and potato to extract as much flavour and texture as possible.

2   Return 1.25l/44fl oz/5 cups of the stock to the pan and bring to the boil. Add the Swiss chard, reduce the heat and simmer for 3–5 minutes until wilted. Adjust the salt and pepper, if necessary, and serve.

085 Yogurt & Coriander Soup

PREPARATION TIME 15 minutes, plus making the stock   COOKING TIME 45 minutes

1l/35fl oz/4 cups Vegetable Stock
   (see page 12) or ready-made stock
3 large garlic cloves, chopped
1 large onion, chopped
1 large handful of coriander, leaves
   chopped and stalks separated

1 tsp coriander seeds, lightly crushed
finely grated zest of 2 limes
2–4 tbsp lime juice
400g/14oz/scant 1¾ cups Greek-style
   yogurt, whisked
salt and freshly ground black pepper

1   Put the stock, garlic, onion, coriander stalks and seeds, and lime zest in a saucepan. Season with salt and pepper, cover and bring to the boil, then reduce the heat and simmer for 35 minutes. Strain the stock, then return it to the pan.

2   Whisk the yogurt in a bowl with a ladleful of the hot stock, then stir back into the soup and reheat. Do not boil. Stir in the coriander leaves and lime juice to taste, adjust the salt and pepper, if necessary, then serve.

086 Amish Potato Soup with Rivvels

PREPARATION TIME 15 minutes   COOKING TIME 25 minutes

300g/10½oz waxy potatoes,
   peeled and diced
1 celery stick, finely chopped
1 onion, finely chopped
500ml/17fl oz/2 cups whole milk
15g/½oz butter
salt and freshly ground black pepper
chopped parsley leaves, to serve

RIVVELS
75g/2½oz/heaped ½ cup plain flour,
   plus extra as needed
¼ teaspoon salt
1 small egg, beaten

1   Put the potatoes, celery, onion and 700ml/24fl oz/scant 3 cups water in a saucepan
    and season lightly with salt. Cover and bring to the boil, then reduce the heat and
    simmer for 10–15 minutes until the potatoes are tender.
2   Meanwhile, to make the rivvels, put the flour and salt in a bowl and make a well
    in the centre. Add the egg and beat it into the flour until the mixture begins to flake
    like pastry. Add extra flour, 1 tablespoon at a time, if necessary, until the mixture
    flakes. Press the mixture between your thumb and fingers to make flakes slightly
    less than 1cm/½in in size. Put the flakes in a sieve and gently shake to get rid
    of any excess flour.
3   When the potatoes are tender, stir in the milk and butter and bring to just below
    the boil. Drop the rivvels into the pan and cook for 3 minutes until the soup thickens
    and the rivvels form dumpling-like lumps. Season with salt and pepper and serve
    sprinkled with parsley.

087 Rosemary-Scented Pea & Lentil Soup

PREPARATION TIME 10 minutes, plus making the stock   COOKING TIME 1 hour

1 tbsp olive or hemp oil
1 shallot, chopped
seeds from 1 green cardamom pod
1.4l/48fl oz/5½ cups Vegetable Stock
   (see page 12) or ready-made stock

100g/3½oz/heaped ½ cup dried green
   lentils, picked over and rinsed
2 tbsp chopped rosemary leaves
100g/3½oz/⅔ cup frozen peas
salt and freshly ground black pepper
Greek yogurt, to serve

1   Heat the oil in a saucepan over a medium heat. Add the shallot and fry for
    3–5 minutes until softened. Add the cardamom seeds and stir for 30 seconds until
    aromatic. Watch closely so they do not burn. Add the stock, lentils and rosemary
    and season with salt and pepper. Cover and bring to the boil, then reduce the heat
    and simmer for 30–40 minutes until the lentils are tender.
2   Add the peas and simmer, uncovered, for 3–5 minutes until tender, then blend
    until smooth. Adjust the salt and pepper, if necessary, and serve with yogurt.

088 Corn & Bean Broth

PREPARATION TIME 5 minutes, plus making the stock   COOKING TIME 35 minutes

1.5l/52fl oz/6 cups Vegetable Stock
   (see page 12) or ready-made stock
4 garlic cloves, chopped
2 leeks, trimmed, chopped and
   rinsed
1 bay leaf

400g/14oz tinned cannellini or red
   kidney beans, drained and rinsed
140g/5oz/1 cup frozen corn kernels
salt and freshly ground black pepper
chopped chives, to serve
chopped parsley leaves, to serve

1   Put the stock, garlic, leeks and bay leaf in a saucepan over a high heat and season
    with salt and pepper. Cover and bring to the boil, then reduce the heat and simmer,
    partially covered, for 20 minutes to reduce slightly and flavour the stock.
2   Strain the stock into a bowl. Return 1.25l/44fl oz/5 cups of the stock to the pan
    and bring to the boil. Add the beans and corn and simmer over a medium heat for
    5–8 minutes until the corn is tender. Adjust the salt and pepper, if necessary, then
    serve sprinkled with chives and parsley.

CHAPTER 2

MEAT SOUPS

It's easy to think of meat soups as substantial winter meals, but light, spiced soups imbued with traditional flavourings from Southeast Asia give this chapter a year-round appeal. The recipes here include quick-cooking Asian soups, such as Thai-inspired Beef & Coconut Soup with Pea Aubergines and Bangkok Pork & Prawn Soup, as well as slow-simmered, more filling soups such as Hearty Beef & Stout Soup and Cardamom-Scented Lamb Soup with Couscous. Substantial soups like these will not only warm and satisfy you on cold days but fill your kitchen with inviting aromas as well. And, like most stews and casseroles, slow-cooked meat soups benefit from being made a day in advance and reheated, making them an ideal choice when friends are coming round for a meal.

Rich meat soups can be surprisingly economical, too. Portuguese Caldo Verde, German Liver Dumpling Soup and Oxtail Soup with Barley make filling soups that won't cost a lot.

If the choices here leave you craving more, see the Big Bowl Soups chapter for more meaty inspiration.

HAM & CHEESE CHICORY SOUP (SEE PAGE 80)

089 Curried Beef & Potato Soup

PREPARATION TIME 20 minutes, plus making the stock   COOKING TIME 40 minutes

3 garlic cloves, finely chopped
1cm/½in piece of root ginger,
   peeled and very finely chopped
2 tbsp groundnut or sunflower oil
2 onions, chopped
1 tbsp chopped coriander leaves
1 tsp turmeric

½ tsp cayenne pepper, or to taste
400g/14oz minced beef
875ml/30fl oz/3½ cups Beef Stock
   (see page 10) or ready-made stock
400g/14oz tinned chopped tomatoes
4 waxy new potatoes, diced
salt and freshly ground black pepper

1   Put the garlic and ginger in a small food processor, or use a mortar and pestle. Season with salt and grind together to form a paste, then set aside.
2   Heat the oil in a saucepan over a medium heat. Add the onions and fry, stirring occasionally, for 2 minutes. Stir in the garlic paste, coriander leaves, turmeric and cayenne and fry, stirring, for 1–3 minutes until the onions are softened. Stir in the beef and fry, breaking up the meat, for 2–3 minutes until it changes colour. Pour off the excess fat, then stir in the stock and tomatoes. Season with salt and pepper.
3   Bring to the boil. Skim, then simmer, covered, for 10 minutes. Stir in the potatoes and add water if the soup is too thick. Simmer, covered, for 10–12 minutes until they are tender. Skim and adjust the salt and pepper, if necessary, then serve.

090 Quick Tex-Mex Chilli Soup

PREPARATION TIME 10 minutes, plus making the stock   COOKING TIME 35 minutes

2 tbsp garlic-flavoured sunflower oil
1 large onion, finely chopped
200g/7oz minced beef
400g/14oz tinned kidney beans,
   drained and rinsed
400g/14oz tinned chopped tomatoes
4 tsp chilli con carne seasoning mix

½ teaspoon caster sugar
500ml/17fl oz/2 cups Beef Stock
   (see page 10) or ready-made stock
salt and freshly ground black pepper
soured cream, to serve
tortilla chips, to serve

1   Heat the oil in a saucepan over a medium heat. Add the onion and fry, stirring, for 3 minutes. Add the beef and fry for 5–8 minutes, breaking up the meat, until browned. Pour off the excess fat.
2   Stir in the beans, tomatoes, chilli seasoning and sugar. Add the stock and bring to the boil, stirring occasionally. Skim, if necessary, then reduce the heat and simmer, covered, for 15 minutes. Season with salt and pepper, if necessary, but remember the chilli seasoning contains both. Serve with soured cream and tortilla chips.

091 Stuffed-Pepper-in-a-Bowl Soup

PREPARATION TIME 15 minutes, plus making the stock and rice
COOKING TIME 45 minutes

1 tbsp garlic-flavoured olive oil
1 onion, finely chopped
200g/7oz minced beef
500ml/17fl oz/2 cups Beef Stock
   (see page 10) or ready-made stock
400g/14oz tinned chopped tomatoes
375ml/13fl oz/1½ cups passata
½ green pepper, deseeded and
   chopped

½ red pepper, deseeded
   and chopped
2 tbsp soft light brown sugar
1½ tsp dried thyme leaves
a pinch of ground allspice
a pinch of chilli flakes, or to taste
salt and freshly ground black pepper
100g/3½oz/½ cup cooked rice
2 tbsp chopped parsley leaves

1   Heat the oil in a saucepan over a medium heat. Add the onion and fry, stirring, for 3 minutes. Stir in the beef and fry, breaking up the meat, for 5–8 minutes until browned. Pour off the excess fat, then stir in the stock, tomatoes, passata, peppers, sugar, thyme, allspice and chilli flakes and season with salt and pepper.
2   Bring to the boil, then simmer for 25 minutes. Skim and stir in the rice. Heat through, adjust the salt and pepper, if necessary, and serve sprinkled with parsley.

092 Red Wine Soup

PREPARATION TIME 20 minutes, plus making the stock and croûtes
COOKING TIME 45 minutes

15g/½oz butter
2 tbsp garlic-flavoured olive oil
600g/1lb 5oz chestnut mushrooms, trimmed and thinly sliced
1 onion, finely chopped
2 carrots, peeled and sliced
2 celery sticks, thinly sliced
3 new potatoes, peeled and diced

250ml/9fl oz/1 cup dry red wine
1l/35fl oz/4 cups Beef Stock (see page 10) or ready-made stock
1 tbsp cornflour
salt and freshly ground black pepper
chopped parsley leaves, to serve
1 recipe quantity Gruyère Croûtes (see page 14), to serve

1   Melt the butter with half the oil in a saucepan over a medium heat. Add the mushrooms, season with salt and fry, stirring, for 5–8 minutes until they release their juices. Remove them from the pan and set aside.
2   Add the remaining oil to the fat remaining in the pan. Add the onion, reduce the heat and cook, covered, for 10–12 minutes until softened and just starting to colour. Add the carrots, celery and potatoes and stir for 2 minutes. Stir in the wine, increase the heat to high and cook for 8 minutes until reduced to about 4 tablespoons. Add the stock and mushrooms and season with salt and pepper. Cover and bring to the boil, then reduce the heat and simmer for 5 minutes.
3   Put the cornflour and 125ml/4fl oz/½ cup cold water in a medium heatproof bowl and mix until dissolved. Stir a ladleful of the stock into the cornstarch mixture, then stir this into the soup. Bring to the boil, stirring until the soup thickens and the vegetables are tender. Adjust the salt and pepper, if necessary, then serve sprinkled with parsley and with croûtes on the side.

093 Hearty Beef & Stout Soup

PREPARATION TIME 20 minutes, plus making the stock   COOKING TIME 2 hours

600g/1lb 5oz boneless beef silverside or chuck, in one piece
1 tbsp plain white or wholemeal flour
3 tbsp sunflower oil
2 carrots, peeled and sliced
1 leek, halved lengthways, thinly sliced and rinsed
4 large garlic cloves, chopped
350g/12oz chestnut mushrooms, trimmed and thinly sliced

625ml/21½fl oz/2½ cups Beef Stock (see page 10) or ready-made stock
600ml/21fl oz/scant 2½ cups stout, such as Guinness
1 bouquet garni made with 1 piece of celery stick, 1 bay leaf and several parsley and thyme sprigs tied together
salt and freshly ground black pepper
chopped parsley leaves, to serve

1   Put the beef in a plastic bag, add the flour and season with salt and pepper. Hold the top of the bag closed and shake well to coat the beef. Transfer the beef to a plate, shaking off any excess flour. Heat half the oil in a large saucepan over a medium heat. Add the beef and fry for 3–5 minutes until browned on both sides, then remove the beef from the pan and set aside.
2   Add the remaining oil to the pan and heat. Stir the carrots and leek into the pan, reduce the heat to very low (use a heat diffuser if you have one) and cook, covered, for 8–10 minutes until the carrot is softened and just starting to colour. Add the garlic and fry for another 30 seconds. Add the mushrooms, season with salt and fry for 5–8 minutes until the mushrooms release their juices.
3   Add the stock, scrape the base of the pan, using a spoon, and stir well. Return the beef to the pan, cover and bring to the boil. Skim, then add the stout and bouquet garni. Season with salt and pepper, but remember the beef has already been seasoned. Reduce the heat and simmer, covered, for 1½–1¾ hours until the beef is very tender. Remove the beef and set aside until cool enough to handle. Discard the bouquet garni.
4   Cut the beef into fine shreds, return it to the soup and warm through. Adjust the salt and pepper, if necessary, and serve sprinkled with parsley.

094 French Onion Soup

PREPARATION TIME 10 minutes, plus making the stock and croûtes
COOKING TIME 40 minutes

30g/1oz butter
2 tbsp olive oil
4 large onions, thinly sliced
4 garlic cloves, crushed
1 tsp caster sugar
1.25l/44fl oz/5 cups Beef Stock
  (see page 10) or ready-made stock
6 tbsp brandy

1 bouquet garni made with 1 piece
  of celery stick, 1 bay leaf, 4 parsley
  sprigs and 4 thyme sprigs tied
  together
salt and freshly ground black pepper
1 Croûte (see page 14) for each bowl,
  to serve
250g/9oz Gruyère cheese, grated,
  to serve

1 Melt the butter with the oil in a saucepan over a medium heat. Add the onions and
   fry, stirring, for 3–5 minutes until softened. Reduce the heat to very low (use a heat
   diffuser if you have one), stir in the garlic and sugar and fry, stirring frequently,
   for another 5–8 minutes until the onions are golden brown and caramelized.
   Add the stock, brandy and bouquet garni and season with salt and pepper. Cover
   and bring to the boil, then reduce the heat and simmer for 15 minutes.
2 Meanwhile, preheat the grill to high. Arrange four or six flameproof soup bowls
   on a baking sheet and put 1 croûte in each.
3 Discard the bouquet garni. Ladle the soup into the bowls and divide the cheese
   over the tops. Grill for 2–3 minutes until the cheese has melted and is bubbling.
   Serve immediately.

095 Thai Beef & Cabbage Soup

PREPARATION TIME 20 minutes, plus making the stock, garlic and chillies
COOKING TIME 2 hours

1.4l/48fl oz/5½ cups Beef Stock
  (see page 10) or ready-made stock
600g/1lb 5oz boneless beef silverside
  or chuck, in one piece, trimmed
4cm/1½in piece of galangal,
  peeled and sliced
1cm/½in piece of root ginger,
  peeled and sliced
2 tbsp light soy sauce, or to taste
1 kaffir lime leaf
1 cinnamon stick

85g/3oz green beans, cut into
  bite-sized pieces
3 celery sticks, thinly sliced
85g/3oz Chinese cabbage, shredded
freshly ground black pepper
chopped coriander leaves, to serve
Crisp-Fried Garlic (see page 15),
  to serve
Chillies in Vinegar (see page 15),
  to serve

1   Put the stock and beef in a saucepan. Season with pepper, cover and bring to the boil. Skim, then add the galangal, ginger, soy sauce, lime leaf and cinnamon stick. Reduce the heat and simmer, covered, for 1½–1¾ hours until the beef is tender. Remove the beef from the pan and set aside until cool enough to handle. Discard the galangal, ginger, lime leaf and cinnamon stick.
2   Stir the beans and celery into the stock and simmer for 10 minutes. Add the cabbage and simmer for 3–5 minutes until the vegetables are tender. Remove any sinew from the beef and cut the flesh into bite-sized pieces, then return it to the soup. Reheat, adjust the salt and pepper, if necessary, and serve sprinkled with coriander and with the garlic and chillies on the side.

096 Beef Soup with Mushrooms & Peas

PREPARATION TIME 10 minutes, plus making the stock   COOKING TIME 2¼ hours

450g/1lb boneless beef silverside
  or chuck, in one piece, trimmed
1 tbsp plain white or wholemeal flour
½ tsp hot paprika
3 tbsp sunflower oil
1 large leek, sliced and rinsed
2 large garlic cloves, chopped
400g/14oz chestnut mushrooms,
  trimmed and thinly sliced

1.25l/44fl oz/5 cups Beef Stock
  (see page 10) or ready-made stock
1 bouquet garni made with 1 piece
  of celery stick, 1 bay leaf and
  several parsley and thyme sprigs
  tied together
100g/3½oz/scant ⅔ cup frozen peas
Worcestershire Sauce, to taste
salt and freshly ground black pepper
chopped parsley leaves, to serve

1   Put the beef in a plastic bag, add the flour and paprika and season with salt and pepper. Hold the top of the bag closed and shake well to coat the beef. Transfer the beef to a plate, shaking off any excess flour. Heat 2 tablespoons of the oil in a saucepan over a medium heat. Add the beef and fry for 3–5 minutes until browned on both sides. Remove it from the pan and set aside.
2   Add the remaining oil to the fat remaining in the pan and heat over a medium heat. Add the leek and fry, stirring occasionally, for 2 minutes. Add the garlic and fry for 1–3 minutes until the leek is softened but not coloured. Add the mushrooms, season with salt and fry for 5–8 minutes until the mushrooms give off their juices. Add the stock and use a spoon to scrape the base of the pan.
3   Return the beef to the pan with any accumulated juices and season with salt and pepper – but remember that the mushrooms and beef have already been salted. Cover and bring to the boil. Skim, then add the bouquet garni. Reduce the heat and simmer, covered, for 1½–1¾ hours until the beef is tender. Remove the beef and set aside until cool enough to handle. Discard the bouquet garni.
4   Add the peas to the soup, bring to the boil and boil for 3–5 minutes until tender. Remove any sinew from the beef and cut the flesh into fine shreds, then return it to the soup and warm through. Add the Worcestershire sauce and adjust the salt and pepper, if necessary. Serve sprinkled with parsley.

097 Beef & Celeriac Soup

PREPARATION TIME 20 minutes, plus making the stock   COOKING TIME 2 hours

1½ tbsp olive or hemp oil
1 small leek, sliced in half
   lengthways, thinly sliced
   and rinsed
200g/7oz fennel, thinly sliced
2 large garlic cloves, chopped
600g/1lb 5oz boneless beef silverside
   or chuck, in one piece, trimmed

750ml/26fl oz/3 cups Beef Stock
   (see page 10) or ready-made stock
400g/14oz tinned chopped tomatoes
2 thyme sprigs
200g/7oz celeriac, peeled and cut into
   bite-sized pieces
salt and freshly ground black pepper
chopped parsley leaves, to serve

1   Heat the oil in a saucepan over a medium heat. Add the leek and fennel and fry,
    stirring occasionally, for 2 minutes. Stir in the garlic and fry for 1–3 minutes until
    the leek is softened but not coloured. Add the beef, stock, tomatoes and thyme
    and season with salt and pepper. Cover and bring to the boil. Skim, then reduce
    the heat and simmer, covered, for 1¼ hours, stirring occasionally.
2   Add the celeriac and simmer for 15–30 minutes until the beef and celeriac are
    tender. Remove the beef and set aside until cool enough to handle. Discard the
    thyme sprigs. Remove any sinew from the beef and cut the flesh into bite-sized
    pieces, then return it to the soup. Adjust the salt and pepper, if necessary,
    and serve sprinkled with parsley.

098 Beef & Bulgar Wheat Soup

PREPARATION TIME 10 minutes, plus making the stock and chilli bon-bon (optional)
COOKING TIME 2¼ hours

1½ tbsp olive or hemp oil
2 onions, chopped
2 large garlic cloves
600g/1lb 5oz boneless beef silverside
   or chuck, in one piece, trimmed
1.25l/44fl oz/5 cups Beef Stock
   (see page 10) or ready-made stock
400g/14oz tinned chopped tomatoes
1 cinnamon stick
2 tbsp tomato purée

a pinch of caster sugar
several coriander sprigs, tied
   together with the stalks crushed,
   plus extra chopped leaves to serve
1 carrot, peeled and sliced
2 tbsp toasted or plain bulgar wheat
salt and freshly ground black pepper
Greek-style yogurt, to serve (optional)
Chilli Bon-Bon (see page 15) or hot
   pepper sauce, to serve (optional)

1   Heat the oil in a saucepan over a medium-high heat. Add the onions and fry, stirring,
    for 7 minutes. Add the garlic and fry for 1–3 minutes until the onions start to colour.
    Add the beef and stock, then cover and bring to the boil. Skim. Add the tomatoes,
    cinnamon stick, tomato purée, sugar and coriander sprigs and season with salt and
    pepper. Reduce the heat and simmer, covered, for 1½ hours.
2   Stir in the carrot and bulgar wheat and simmer, covered, for 20–25 minutes until
    the bulgar and beef are both tender. Remove the beef from the pan and set aside
    until cool enough to handle. Discard the coriander sprigs and cinnamon stick.
3   Remove any sinew from the beef and cut the meat into bite-sized pieces, then
    return it to the soup. Reheat and adjust the salt and pepper, if necessary. Serve
    topped with yogurt and coriander leaves and with chilli bon-bon on the side, if using.

099 Beef Consommé with Porcini Mushrooms

PREPARATION TIME 15 minutes, plus making the consommé and 30 minutes soaking the mushrooms   COOKING TIME 5 minutes

30g/1oz dried porcini mushrooms
1.25l/44fl oz/5 cups Beef Consommé
  (see page 13)

1 tbsp dry sherry (optional)
salt (optional)
chopped parsley leaves, to serve

1 Put the mushrooms in a heatproof bowl, cover with boiling water and leave to soak for 30 minutes until tender. Strain through a muslin-lined sieve. (The soaking liquid can be used in another recipe or frozen until required.) Squeeze the mushrooms, trim the bases of the stalks, if necessary, then thinly slice the caps and stalks and divide them into serving bowls.
2 Put the consommé in a saucepan over a high heat and heat to just below the boil. Stir in the sherry, if using, and season with salt, if required. Ladle the consommé over the mushrooms, sprinkle with parsley and serve immediately.

100 Chinese Beef & Greens Soup

PREPARATION TIME 15 minutes, plus making the stock   COOKING TIME 25 minutes

1.25l/44fl oz/5 cups Beef Stock
  (see page 10) or ready-made stock
2 large garlic cloves, cut in half
1 handful of watercress, leaves and
  stalks separated
1cm/½in piece of root ginger, peeled
  and sliced

1 thin slice of galangal, peeled
½ tbsp light soy sauce, or to taste
2 or 3 pak choi, halved or quartered
400g/14oz sirloin, rump or top side
  steak, thinly sliced across the grain
freshly ground black pepper
toasted sesame oil, to serve

1 Put the stock, garlic, watercress stalks, ginger, galangal and soy sauce in a saucepan. Cover and bring to the boil, then boil for 10 minutes. Strain, then return the stock to the pan. Bring to a slow boil, add the pak choi and boil for 3–5 minutes until tender.
2 Stir in the steak, reduce the heat and simmer for 30 seconds or until cooked to your liking. Stir in the watercress leaves and season with pepper. Add extra soy sauce, if necessary, then serve sprinkled with sesame oil.

101 Beef & Coconut Soup with Pea Aubergines

PREPARATION TIME 15 minutes, plus making the stock   COOKING TIME 20 minutes

1 small handful of bean sprouts
2 tbsp sunflower oil
1 red onion, chopped
2 red peppers, deseeded and halved
1 tbsp red curry paste
350g/12oz rump, sirloin or topside
  steak, thinly sliced across the grain
75g/2½oz/½ cup pea aubergines

200ml/7fl oz/ scant 1 cup coconut milk
2 kaffir lime leaves
½ tsp salt
lime juice, to taste (optional)
palm sugar or soft light brown sugar,
  to taste (optional)
coriander leaves, to serve
lime wedges, to serve

1 Put the bean sprouts in a bowl, cover with cold water and set aside. Put 1l/35fl oz/ 4 cups water in a measuring jug and set aside.
2 Heat the oil in a large wok with a lid or a saucepan over a high heat. Add the onion, peppers and curry paste, reduce the heat to medium and stir-fry for 2 minutes. Very slowly add 200ml/7fl oz/scant 1 cup of the water and stir until the fat forms bubbles on the surface. Add the beef and pea aubergines and stir-fry for 2 minutes, stirring in a little more of the water if the curry paste looks like it will burn. Slowly stir in the coconut milk, lime leaves, salt and the remaining water and bring to the boil. Reduce the heat and simmer, covered, for 5–7 minutes until the beef, peppers and pea aubergines are tender.
3 Drain the bean sprouts, add them to the soup and cook for 30 seconds to warm through. Stir in the lime juice and palm sugar, if using. Serve immediately, sprinkled with coriander leaves and with lime wedges for squeezing over.

102 Mrs Schultz's Beef & Vegetable Soup

PREPARATION TIME 15 minutes, plus making the stock   COOKING TIME 2 hours

2 tbsp garlic-flavoured sunflower oil,
   plus extra as needed
450g/1lb stewing steak, cut into
   bite-sized pieces and patted dry
1 onion, finely chopped
¼ tsp paprika
125ml/4fl oz/½ cup dry red wine
750ml/26fl oz/3 cups Beef Stock
   (see page 10) or ready-made stock

400g/14oz tinned chopped tomatoes
2 bay leaves
1 carrot, peeled, halved lengthways
   and thickly sliced
1 floury potato, peeled and diced
½ celery stick, finely chopped
salt and freshly ground black pepper
chopped parsley leaves, to serve

1   Heat 1½ tablespoons of the oil in a saucepan over a medium-high heat. Working
    in batches, if necessary, to avoid overcrowding the pan, fry the beef for
    2–3 minutes until browned on all sides, then transfer to a plate and set aside.
    Add more oil between batches, if necessary.

2   Add the remaining oil to the pan and heat. Add the onion and fry, stirring
    occasionally, for 3–5 minutes until softened but not coloured. Return the beef and
    any accumulated juices to the pan, and add the paprika. Stir in the wine and cook
    for 5–6 minutes until almost evaporated.

3   Add the stock, then cover and bring to the boil. Skim, then add the tomatoes and
    bay leaves and season with salt and pepper. Cover and return to the boil, then
    reduce the heat to very low (use a heat diffuser if you have one) and simmer
    for 1 hour.

4   Stir in the carrot, potato and celery and simmer, covered, for 30–45 minutes until
    the beef and vegetables are tender. Discard the bay leaves, then adjust the salt
    and pepper, if necessary. Serve immediately, sprinkled with parsley.

103 Beef & Wild Rice Soup

PREPARATION TIME 10 minutes, plus making the stock COOKING TIME 2 hours

1½ tbsp olive oil
1 red onion, finely chopped
2 large garlic cloves, finely chopped
1.25l/44fl oz/5 cups Beef Stock
 (see page 10) or ready-made stock
600g/1lb 5oz stewing beef silverside
 or chuck, in one piece, trimmed

1 bay leaf
100g/3½oz/½ cup wild rice
1 roasted red pepper in olive oil,
 drained and diced
1½ tsp Worcestershire sauce
salt and freshly ground black pepper
chopped parsley leaves, to serve

1 Heat the oil in a saucepan over a medium heat. Add the onion and fry, stirring occasionally, for 2 minutes. Stir in the garlic and fry for 1–3 minutes until the onion is softened but not browned. Add the stock and beef and season with salt and pepper. Cover and bring to the boil. Skim, then add the bay leaf. Reduce the heat and simmer, covered, for 1 hour.
2 Stir in the wild rice and simmer, covered, for another 35–40 minutes until the beef is tender and the wild rice grains are fluffy. Remove the beef and set aside until it is cool enough to handle.
3 Remove the sinew and cut the beef into bite-sized pieces. Return it to the soup. Stir in the roasted pepper and Worcestershire sauce and heat through. Discard the bay leaf and adjust the salt and pepper, if necessary. Serve sprinkled with parsley.

104 Osso Buco Soup with Gremolata

PREPARATION TIME 15 minutes, plus making the stock and gremolata
COOKING TIME 2 hours

2–3 tbsp olive oil, plus extra
 as needed
600g/1lb 5oz bone-in osso buco
 or veal shin, about 3 thick pieces
2 shallots, finely chopped
1 carrot, peeled and diced
1 celery stick, thinly chopped
4 large garlic cloves, very finely
 chopped
1.5l/48fl oz/5½ cups Beef Stock
 (see page 10) or ready-made stock

125ml/4fl oz/½ cup dry vermouth
500ml/17fl oz/2 cups passata
1 bay leaf
1 tbsp tomato purée
½ tsp caster sugar
a pinch of saffron threads
salt and freshly ground black pepper
1 recipe quantity Gremolata
 (see page 198), to serve

1 Heat 2 tablespoons of the oil in a saucepan over a medium heat. Working in batches, if necessary, to avoid overcrowding the pan, fry the osso buco for 2–3 minutes, turning occasionally, until browned on all sides. Remove from the pan and set aside. Add more oil between batches, if necessary.
2 Add the shallots, carrot and celery and fry, stirring occasionally, for 2 minutes. Add the garlic and fry for 1–3 minutes until the onion is softened but not coloured. Return the meat and any accumulated juices to the pan, add the stock and vermouth and season with salt and pepper. Cover and bring to the boil.
3 Skim, then add the passata, bay leaf, tomato purée, sugar and saffron and season again with salt and pepper. Reduce the heat to very low (use a heat diffuser if you have one) and simmer, covered, for 1½–1¾ hours until the meat is very tender. Remove the meat from the soup and set aside until cool enough to handle.
4 Remove the meat from the bones, finely shred it and return it to the soup. Use a small spoon or knife to push the marrow out of the centre of the bones and stir it into the soup, if you like. Adjust the salt and pepper, if necessary, then skim. Serve sprinkled with the gremolata.

105 Welsh Mountain Lamb & Leek Soup

PREPARATION TIME 20 minutes, plus making the seeds   COOKING TIME 1¾ hours

600g/1lb 5oz boneless shoulder
  of lamb, in one piece, trimmed
4 large garlic cloves, crushed
3 carrots, 2 coarsely chopped and
  1 sliced
3 celery sticks
3 large leeks, 2 thickly sliced and
  1 thinly sliced, all rinsed and kept
  separate

1 bouquet garni made with 2 bay
  leaves and several parsley and
  rosemary sprigs tied together
350g/12oz floury potatoes, peeled
  and chopped
salt and freshly ground black pepper
Spiced Seeds (see page 15), to serve

1   Put the lamb and 1.25l/44fl oz/5 cups water in a saucepan. Cover and bring to the
    boil. Skim, then add the garlic, chopped carrots, celery, thickly sliced leeks and
    bouquet garni. Season with salt and pepper, then reduce the heat and simmer,
    covered, for 1 hour.
2   Strain the stock and discard the vegetables and bouquet garni. Return the lamb
    and stock to the pan, then skim the fat from the surface. Add the sliced carrots,
    thinly sliced leeks and potatoes. Cover and bring to the boil, then reduce the heat
    and simmer for 30–45 minutes until the meat is meltingly tender and the potatoes
    are falling apart. Skim again, if necessary, then remove the lamb and set aside until
    cool enough to handle.
3   Cut the lamb into bite-sized pieces, return it to the soup and reheat. Adjust the
    salt and pepper, if necessary, and serve sprinkled with the seeds.

106 Lamb Vindaloo Soup

PREPARATION TIME 25 minutes, plus at least 1 hour marinating and making the stock
COOKING TIME 2¼ hours

600g/1lb 5oz boneless leg
   or shoulder of lamb or mutton,
   trimmed and cut into large chunks
   with any bones reserved
2 tbsp groundnut or sunflower oil
2 onions, sliced
4 green cardamom pods,
   lightly crushed
3 cloves
2 cinnamon sticks
1 tsp cumin seeds
1.25l/44fl oz/5 cups Vegetable Stock
   (see page 12) or ready-made stock
2 bay leaves

1 dried red chilli, deseeded
   (optional) and sliced
2 potatoes, chopped
salt and freshly ground black pepper
chopped coriander leaves, to serve

VINDALOO MARINADE
5 tbsp distilled white vinegar
1 tbsp tomato purée
2 onions, grated
2.5cm/1in piece of root ginger,
   peeled and chopped
1 large garlic clove, finely chopped
½ tsp turmeric

1   Mix all the ingredients for the marinade together in a large non-reactive bowl. Add the lamb and use your hands to rub in the marinade, then cover and chill for at least 1 hour to marinate.

2   When ready to cook, heat the oil in a large saucepan over a medium heat. Add the onions and fry, stirring, for 10–12 minutes until golden brown. Add the cardamom pods, cloves, cinnamon sticks and cumin seeds and stir for 30 seconds. Watch closely so the spices do not burn.

3   Stir in the lamb, marinade and any reserved bones. Add the stock and season with salt and pepper. Cover and bring to the boil. Skim, then add the bay leaves and chilli. Reduce the heat to very low (use a heat diffuser if you have one) and simmer, covered, for 1½–1¾ hours until the meat is very tender.

4   Remove the meat and bones and set the meat aside until cool enough to handle. Discard the bones. Add the potatoes to the soup and simmer, covered, for 12–15 minutes until they are tender. Shred the meat into bite-sized pieces and return it to the soup. Adjust the salt and pepper, if necessary, then serve sprinkled with coriander. Remember to remind your guests about the loose spices.

107 Scotch Broth

PREPARATION TIME 15 minutes   COOKING TIME 1¾ hours

1kg/2lb 4oz neck of lamb on the
   bone, trimmed and chopped into
   pieces (ask the butcher to do this)
1 bouquet garni made with 1 piece
   of celery stick, 1 bay leaf and
   several parsley and thyme sprigs
   tied together

55g/2oz/¼ cup pearl barley
2 leeks, thinly sliced and rinsed
1 carrot, peeled and diced
1 onion, finely chopped
1 turnip, peeled and diced
2 tbsp chopped parsley leaves
salt and freshly ground black pepper

1   Put the lamb and 1.75l/60fl oz/6⅔ cups water in a saucepan. Cover and slowly bring to just below the boil. Skim, then add the bouquet garni. Reduce the heat and simmer, covered, for 1 hour.

2   Stir in the barley, leeks, carrot, onion and turnip and return to just below the boil. Reduce the heat and simmer, covered, for 30–40 minutes until the meat and barley are tender. Remove the meat from the soup and set aside until cool enough to handle. Discard the bouquet garni.

3   Pull the meat away from the bones, cut it into small pieces and return it to the soup. Reheat, if necessary, then stir in the parsley. Season with salt and pepper and serve.

108 Spiced Lamb & Chickpea Soup

PREPARATION TIME 15 minutes, plus overnight soaking and cooking the chickpeas and making the stock and shallots **COOKING TIME** 2 hours

100g/3½oz/½ cup dried chickpeas
875ml/30fl oz/3½ cups Beef Stock
   (see page 10) or ready-made stock
600g/1lb 5oz boneless shoulder
   of lamb, in one piece, trimmed
2 large garlic cloves, chopped
1 bay leaf
1 large onion, chopped
2 tbsp lemon juice
1 tbsp tomato purée

1 tsp turmeric
1½ tsp cinnamon
a small pinch of ground cloves
a pinch of dried chilli flakes,
   or to taste
salt and freshly ground black pepper
chopped coriander leaves, to serve
Crisp-Fried Shallots (see page 15),
   to serve
hot pepper sauce, to serve (optional)

1   Put the chickpeas in a bowl, cover with water and leave to soak overnight, then drain.

2   Put the stock, lamb and chickpeas in another saucepan. Cover and bring to the boil. Skim, then add the garlic, bay leaf, onion, lemon juice, tomato purée, turmeric, cinnamon, cloves and chilli flakes. Season with salt and pepper, then reduce the heat to very low (use a heat diffuser if you have one) and simmer, covered, for 1½ hours until the lamb and chickpeas are tender. Skim the excess fat off the surface, remove the lamb and set aside until cool enough to handle. Discard the bouquet garni.

3   Chop the lamb into small pieces and return it to the soup. Adjust the salt and pepper, if necessary, and serve sprinkled with the coriander and shallots and with hot pepper sauce, if you like.

109 Winter Lamb & Onion Soup

PREPARATION TIME 10 minutes, plus making the stock **COOKING TIME** 55 minutes

3 tbsp olive or hemp oil
400g/14oz boneless lamb neck fillet,
   membrane removed and meat
   patted dry
4 large onions, thinly sliced
1 tsp dried mint leaves
½ tsp ground cumin
½ tsp fenugreek seeds, lightly
   crushed
½ tsp turmeric

2 tbsp plain white or wholemeal flour
1l/35fl oz/4 cups Chicken Stock
   (see page 11) or ready-made stock
1 cinnamon stick, broken in half
2 tbsp lemon juice
1 tsp caster sugar
salt and freshly ground black pepper
1 small handful of coriander leaves,
   to serve

1   Heat 2 tablespoons of the oil in a saucepan over a medium heat. Add the lamb and fry, turning often, for 4 minutes until browned all over. Remove from the pan and set aside.

2   Add the remaining oil to the pan and heat. Add the onions and season with salt and pepper. Reduce the heat to low and cook, covered, for 10–12 minutes, stirring occasionally, until very soft and just starting to colour. Add the mint, cumin, fenugreek seeds and turmeric and stir for 30 seconds. Sprinkle in the flour and cook, stirring, for another 2 minutes. Remove the pan from the heat and slowly pour in the stock, stirring continuously, then add the cinnamon stick.

3   Bring to the boil, then reduce the heat to very low and simmer, partially covered, for 15 minutes. Meanwhile, cut the lamb across the grain into very thin slices, then cut any large slices in half.

4   Add the lamb to the soup and simmer for another 10 minutes or until the lamb is cooked to your liking. Discard the cinnamon stick and stir in the lemon juice and sugar. Adjust the salt and pepper, if necessary, then serve sprinkled with coriander.

110 Lamb Meatball & Kale Soup

PREPARATION TIME 30 minutes, plus making the stock   **COOKING TIME** 35 minutes

30g/1oz/heaped ¼ cup dried
 breadcrumbs
2 tbsp milk
400g/14oz minced lamb
3 spring onions, very finely chopped
4 tbsp very finely chopped flat-leaf
 parsley leaves, plus extra to serve
1 tbsp finely chopped mint leaves
a pinch of cayenne pepper
4 garlic cloves, finely chopped

1 egg, beaten
2 tbsp olive or hemp oil, plus extra
 for frying the meatballs
2 large shallots
1.25l/44fl oz/5 cups Vegetable Stock
 (see page 12) or ready-made stock
100g/3½oz curly kale, stalks removed
 and leaves chopped
salt and freshly ground black pepper

1 Put the breadcrumbs in a large bowl, sprinkle with the milk and leave to soak for at least 10 minutes. Add the lamb, spring onions, parsley, mint, cayenne pepper and half the garlic and season with salt and pepper. Wet your hands and mix together. Work the egg, little by little, into the mixture. Divide the mixture into 6 equal portions, then divide each one into 6 portions to make a total of 36. Roll into meatballs and set aside. (At this point the meatballs can be chilled for up to 1 day.)

2 To fry the meatballs, heat a large frying pan over a high heat. When a splash of water 'dances' on the surface, add a thin layer of oil and reduce the heat to medium-low. Working in batches, if necessary, to avoid overcrowding the pan, fry the meatballs for 5–8 minutes, turning gently, until golden brown. Drain on kitchen paper and set aside until required.

3 Heat the oil in a saucepan over a medium heat. Add the shallots and fry, stirring occasionally, for 2 minutes. Add the remaining garlic and fry for 1–3 minutes until the shallots are softened but not coloured. Add the stock, cover and bring to the boil. Add the kale, reduce the heat and simmer, uncovered, for 5 minutes. Add the meatballs and season with salt and pepper, then simmer for 5 minutes to warm them through and until the kale is tender. Adjust the salt and pepper, if necessary. Divide the meatballs and kale into bowls, ladle the soup over them and serve immediately, sprinkled with parsley.

111 Spring Lamb Soup

PREPARATION TIME 15 minutes, plus making the stock   **COOKING TIME** 1¾ hours

2 tbsp olive or hemp oil
1 leek, sliced and rinsed
2 garlic cloves, sliced
650g/1lb 7oz lamb shoulder chops,
 trimmed
1.25l/44fl oz/5 cups Vegetable Stock
 (see page 12) or ready-made stock
400g/14oz tinned chopped tomatoes
2 tbsp lemon juice
1 tsp ground fenugreek

½ tsp ground coriander
2 rosemary sprigs
1 bay leaf
1 tbsp tomato purée
½ tsp soft light brown sugar
1 turnip, peeled and chopped
2 tbsp capers in brine, drained
 and rinsed
4 tbsp chopped parsley leaves
salt and freshly ground black pepper

1 Heat the oil in a saucepan over a medium heat. Add the leek and garlic, cover and reduce the heat to low. Cook for 10–12 minutes, stirring occasionally, until softened but not coloured. Stir in the lamb and stock and season with salt and pepper, then cover and bring to the boil. Skim, then add the tomatoes, lemon juice, fenugreek, coriander, rosemary, bay leaf, tomato purée and sugar. Season with salt and pepper, reduce the heat and simmer, covered, for 1 hour.

2 Stir in the turnip, capers and half the parsley and simmer, covered, for 20–25 minutes until the lamb and turnip are both tender. Remove the lamb, bones and rosemary. Discard the bones and rosemary and set the lamb aside until cool enough handle.

3 Cut the lamb into bite-sized pieces, return it to the soup and warm through. Adjust the salt and pepper, if necessary, and serve sprinkled with the remaining parsley.

112 Curried Lamb & Squash Soup

PREPARATION TIME 25 minutes, plus making the stock   **COOKING TIME** 2¼ hours

2–3 tbsp olive or hemp oil
600g/1lb 5oz boneless lamb
 shoulder, in one piece, trimmed
1 large onion, chopped
1 tsp curry powder
1 tsp ground coriander
1 tsp ground cumin
2 fresh curry leaves or 1 dried
1.4l/48fl oz/5½ cups Vegetable Stock
 (see page 12) or ready-made stock
2 bay leaves
1 tbsp lemon juice

1 bird's-eye chilli, deseeded
 (optional) and finely chopped
finely grated zest of 2 tangerines
 or 1 orange
200g/7oz butternut squash, peeled,
 deseeded and diced
2 large garlic cloves, chopped
2 waxy new potatoes, peeled
 and diced
1 carrot, peeled and diced
1 handful of baby spinach leaves
salt and freshly ground black pepper

1   Heat 2 tablespoons of the oil in a saucepan over a medium heat. Add the lamb and fry for 2–3 minutes until browned on both sides. Remove the lamb from the pan and set aside.
2   Add the remaining oil to the pan, if necessary, and heat. Add the onion and fry, stirring occasionally, for 8–10 minutes until golden brown. Add the curry powder, coriander, cumin and curry leaves and stir for 30 seconds. Watch closely so the spices and curry leaves do not burn. Return the lamb with any accumulated juices to the pan. Add the stock and season with salt and pepper, then cover and bring to the boil. Skim, then stir in the bay leaves, lemon juice, chilli and zest. Cover, reduce the heat to very low (use a heat diffuser if you have one) and simmer for 1½ hours.
3   Stir in the squash, garlic, potatoes and carrot and simmer for 25–30 minutes until the lamb is very tender. Add the spinach for the last 2–3 minutes and simmer until it wilts. Discard the bay and curry leaves. Adjust the salt and pepper, if necessary, then serve.

113 Cardamom-Scented Lamb Soup with Couscous

PREPARATION TIME 20 minutes, plus making the stock   **COOKING TIME** 2¼ hours

1½ tbsp olive or hemp oil
140g/5oz fennel, quartered and thinly
 sliced
2 garlic cloves, crushed
1cm/½in piece of root ginger, peeled
 and grated
2 green chillies, deseeded and
 chopped
1l/35fl oz/4 cups Vegetable Stock
 (see page 12) or ready-made stock

600g/1lb 5oz boneless, skinless lamb
 shoulder, in one piece, trimmed
2 bay leaves
1 carrot, peeled and sliced
seeds from 8 green cardamom pods,
 wrapped in a piece of muslin
¼ tsp turmeric
140g/5oz/¾ cup couscous
salt and freshly ground black pepper
chopped coriander leaves, to serve

1   Heat the oil in a saucepan over a medium heat. Add the fennel and fry, stirring occasionally, for 8–10 minutes until light golden brown. Add the garlic, ginger and chillies and stir for another 30 seconds. Watch closely so they do not burn.
2   Add the stock and lamb, season with salt and pepper, cover and bring to the boil. Skim, then stir in the bay leaves, carrot, cardamom seeds and turmeric. Reduce the heat and simmer, covered, for 1½–1¾ hours until the lamb is very tender. Remove the lamb from the soup and set aside until cool enough to handle.
3   Stir the couscous into the soup, cover and return the soup to the boil. Reduce the heat and simmer for 10 minutes until the couscous is tender.
4   Shred the lamb into bite-sized pieces and return it to the soup. Discard the seed bundle and bay leaves and adjust the salt and pepper, if necessary. Serve sprinkled with coriander.

114 Roast Lamb & Bean Soup

PREPARATION TIME 15 minutes, plus making the stock and cooking the lamb
COOKING TIME 40 minutes

1 tbsp olive or hemp oil
1 red onion, finely chopped
3 garlic cloves, finely chopped
1 tsp ground coriander
½ tsp ground cumin
½ tsp turmeric
1l/35fl oz/4 cups Beef Stock
    (see page 10) or ready-made stock
400g/14oz tinned chopped tomatoes
1 tbsp tomato purée
½ tbsp dried mint leaves or dill

1 tsp harissa, or to taste
½ tsp caster sugar
1 lamb bone, all fat removed
    (optional)
400g/14oz boneless, skinless cooked
    lamb, shredded with all fat
    removed
400g/14oz tinned cannellini beans
    or chickpeas, drained and rinsed
salt and freshly ground black pepper
chopped coriander leaves, to serve

1   Heat the oil in a saucepan over a medium heat. Add the onion and fry, stirring
    occasionally, for 2 minutes. Add the garlic and fry for 1–3 minutes until the onion
    is softened but not coloured. Add the ground coriander, cumin and turmeric and
    stir for 30 seconds until aromatic. Watch closely so the spices do not burn.

2   Add the stock, tomatoes, tomato purée, mint, harissa, sugar and lamb bone,
    if using. Season with salt and pepper, cover and bring to the boil over a high heat.
    Reduce the heat and simmer for 20 minutes, stirring once or twice to break up the
    tomatoes. Add the lamb and beans and simmer for 5 minutes to heat through.
    Discard the lamb bone, if used, then adjust the salt and pepper, if necessary,
    and add more harissa, if you like. Serve sprinkled with coriander leaves.

115 Pork, Mushroom & Tofu Soup

PREPARATION TIME 25 minutes, plus 30 minutes soaking the mushrooms and making the stock   COOKING TIME 45 minutes

2 dried shiitake mushrooms
30g/1oz dried cloud ear mushrooms
1.4l/48fl oz/5½ cups Chicken Stock
  (see page 11) or ready-made stock
5cm/2in piece of root ginger,
  peeled and sliced
3 tbsp light soy sauce
2 tbsp rice vinegar
1 carrot, peeled and cut into
  matchsticks

4 leaves Chinese cabbage, shredded
55g/2oz pickled preserved bamboo
  shoots, drained and chopped
2½ tbsp cornflour
400g/14oz pork fillet, trimmed,
  cut into 5cm/2in matchsticks
200g/7oz firm tofu, drained and
  finely chopped
85g/3oz/½ cup frozen peas
chopped coriander leaves, to serve

1   Put the shiitake and cloud ear mushrooms in separate heatproof bowls, cover each with 150ml/5fl oz/scant ⅔ cup warm water and leave to soak for at least 30 minutes. Meanwhile, put the stock, ginger, soy sauce and vinegar in a saucepan, cover and bring to the boil. Reduce the heat and simmer for 15 minutes. Strain the stock into a clean pan, discarding the ginger, and set aside.

2   Strain the shiitake mushrooms through a muslin-lined sieve into a clean bowl and reserve the soaking liquid. Squeeze the mushrooms, cut off the stalks and slice the caps, then set aside. Drain the cloud ear mushrooms, discarding the soaking liquid, then trim the base of the stalks, if necessary, and slice thinly.

3   Put 1l/35fl oz/4 cups of the stock and 125ml/4fl oz/½ cup of the shiitake soaking liquid in the saucepan. Add the mushrooms, carrot, cabbage and bamboo shoots. Put the cornflour in a heatproof bowl, add a ladleful of the stock and stir until a thin, smooth paste forms. Stir this mixture into the stock and bring to the boil, stirring, then reduce the heat and simmer for 5 minutes or just until slightly thickened. Reduce the heat to low and add the pork, tofu and peas, stirring gently so you don't break up the tofu. Simmer for 3–5 minutes until the pork is cooked through and the peas are tender. Serve sprinkled with coriander.

116 Pork, Mushroom & Mangetout Soup

PREPARATION TIME 20 minutes, plus making the stock   COOKING TIME 25 minutes

1 tbsp groundnut or sunflower oil
5 shiitake mushroom caps, sliced
1 large garlic clove, chopped
1cm/½in piece of root ginger, peeled
  and grated
1.25l/44fl oz/5 cups Chicken Stock
  (see page 11) or ready-made stock
400g/14oz pork fillet, trimmed, cut
  in half lengthways and thinly sliced
1 tbsp rice wine vinegar
2 tsp light soy sauce, or to taste

1 tbsp arrowroot
55g/2oz mangetout
2 spring onions, thinly sliced
  on the diagonal
1 roasted red pepper in olive oil,
  drained and thinly sliced
Chinese five-spice powder, to taste
salt
chopped Chinese chives or chopped
  chives, to serve

1   Heat the oil in a saucepan over a medium heat. Add the mushrooms, season with salt and fry, stirring, for 5–8 minutes until they are softened and give off their juices. Add the garlic and ginger and stir for 30 seconds until aromatic. Watch closely so they do not burn.

2   Add the stock, pork, vinegar and soy sauce and bring to just below the boil. Skim, if necessary, then reduce the heat and simmer for 2 minutes. Meanwhile, put the arrowroot and 3 tablespoons cold water in a small bowl and mix until smooth, then set aside.

3   Add the mangetout, spring onions, roasted pepper and arrowroot mixture to the saucepan and simmer for 2–3 minutes until the pork is cooked through, the vegetables are tender but still with bite and the soup is slightly thickened. Season with five-spice powder and salt or extra soy sauce to taste. Serve sprinkled with chives.

117 Bangkok Pork & Prawn Soup

PREPARATION TIME 20 minutes, plus making the stock **COOKING TIME** 25 minutes

2 tbsp sunflower oil
2 large garlic cloves, finely chopped
2 tsp ground coriander
400g/14oz boneless pork, such
as shoulder chops, cut into very
fine matchstick pieces
1l/35fl oz/4 cups Chicken Stock
(see page 11) or ready-made stock
5 shiitake mushroom caps,
thinly sliced
4 coriander roots, crushed

1 lemongrass stalk, cut into thirds,
with outer leaves removed
1 tbsp soy sauce, or to taste
1½ tsp fish sauce, or to taste
1 bird's-eye chilli, deseeded
(optional) and sliced
250g/9oz large prawns, peeled,
deveined and cut into thirds
4 spring onions, thinly sliced
on the diagonal
salt and freshly ground black pepper
coriander leaves, to serve

1   Heat the oil in a large saucepan over a medium heat. Add the garlic and ground
coriander and fry, stirring, for 1–2 minutes until the garlic is softened but not
coloured. Add the pork and fry for another 2 minutes, then add the stock. Cover
and bring to the boil, then skim the surface. Add the mushrooms, coriander roots,
lemongrass, soy sauce, fish sauce and chilli and season with salt and pepper.
Reduce the heat and simmer for 5 minutes.
2   Stir in the prawns and spring onions. Season again with pepper and simmer for
2–3 minutes until the prawns and pork are cooked through. Discard the coriander
roots and lemongrass. Adjust the salt and pepper, adding extra soy sauce and fish
sauce, if necessary. Serve sprinkled with coriander leaves.

118 Thai Meatball & Coconut Soup

PREPARATION TIME 25 minutes, plus making the stock, chillies and garlic
COOKING TIME 20 minutes

400g/14oz minced pork
2 coriander sprigs, leaves and stalks
very finely chopped, plus an extra
handful of leaves, chopped
2.5cm/1in piece of root ginger,
peeled and very finely chopped
1½ tbsp cornflour
1 tbsp sesame oil
1 tbsp light soy sauce
1l/35fl oz/4 cups Vegetable Stock
(see page 12) or ready-made stock

400ml/14fl oz/scant 1⅔ cups
coconut milk
1½ tbsp fish sauce, or to taste
salt and freshly ground black pepper
finely grated zest of 1 lime, to serve
Crisp-Fried Garlic (see page 15),
to serve
Chillies in Vinegar (see page 15),
to serve

1   Put the pork, finely chopped coriander, ginger, cornflour, sesame oil and soy sauce
in a large bowl and season with salt and pepper. Use your hands to mix together
and divide the mixture into 6 equal portions, then divide each one into 6 portions
to make a total of 36. Roll into meatballs and set aside.
2   Put the stock in a saucepan, cover and bring to the boil, then reduce the heat
so the liquid boils only very lightly. Working in batches, if necessary, to avoid
overcrowding the pan, add the meatballs and cook, uncovered, for 3–5 minutes
until they pop to the surface and are cooked though if you cut one open. Remove
the cooked meatballs from the pan and set aside.
3   Put the coconut milk and fish sauce in another saucepan and bring to just below
the boil. Season with salt and pepper, add the meatballs and slowly stir in enough
of the meatball cooking liquid to achieve the preferred consistency. Stir in the
chopped coriander leaves, adjust the salt and pepper, if necessary, and add more
fish sauce, if you like. Divide the meatballs and soup into bowls and sprinkle with
the lime zest. Serve with the garlic and chillies on the side.

119 Gammon & Pepper Soup

PREPARATION TIME 20 minutes, plus at least 2 hours soaking and making the stock
COOKING TIME 1½ hours

1 smoked gammon knuckle,
  about 1.3kg/3lb
2 carrots, coarsely chopped
3 celery sticks, coarsely chopped
2 onions, 1 quartered and 1 diced
4 bay leaves
1 tbsp black peppercorns, crushed
½ tsp coriander seeds, crushed
½ tsp salt, plus extra to season

2 tbsp olive or hemp oil
3 red peppers, deseeded and chopped
400g/14oz tinned chopped tomatoes
1 tbsp tomato purée
½ tsp soft light brown sugar
600ml/21fl oz/scant 2½ cups
  Vegetable Stock (see page 12)
  or ready-made stock
freshly ground black pepper

1 Put the gammon knuckle in a large bowl, cover with water and leave to soak for
   at least 2 hours, then drain. Change the water at least twice during soaking.
2 Put the knuckle in a large saucepan, cover with water and bring to the boil. Skim,
   then add the carrots, celery, quartered onion, bay leaves, peppercorns, coriander
   seeds and salt. Reduce the heat to very low (use a heat diffuser if you have one)
   and simmer, covered, for 1¼–1½ hours until the meat is tender.
3 About 20 minutes before the end of the simmering time, heat the oil in another
   saucepan over a medium heat. Add the red peppers and diced onion and fry,
   stirring occasionally, for 8–10 minutes until the onion has softened and turned
   a light golden brown. Stir in the tomatoes, tomato purée, brown sugar and
   600ml/21fl oz/scant 2½ cups of the simmering cooking liquid. Cover and bring
   to the boil, then reduce the heat and simmer for 10 minutes. Blend the soup until
   smooth. Strain the mixture into a bowl, rubbing back and forth with a spoon and
   scraping the bottom of the sieve. Return it to the pan, stir in the vegetable stock
   and reheat. If it is too thick, add a ladleful of the simmering cooking liquid.
4 Remove the knuckle from the pan and set aside until cool enough to handle. Strain
   the cooking liquid into a bowl and discard the flavourings. (The leftover cooking
   liquid can be cooled and refrigerated for up to 3 days or frozen for use in other
   recipes, and the bone can be used in Split Pea & Ham Soup (see page 159).)
5 Cut the gammon from the bone into bite-sized pieces, add it to the soup and heat
   through. Season with pepper and adjust the salt, if necessary, but remember that
   the cooking liquid will have been salty. Serve.

120 Bacon & Sweetcorn Chowder

PREPARATION TIME 15 minutes   COOKING TIME 35 minutes

5 unsmoked streaky bacon rashers,
  rinds removed, if necessary
1 tbsp sunflower oil
1 celery stick, finely chopped
1 onion, finely chopped
1 green pepper, deseeded and diced
3 tbsp plain white flour
800ml/28fl oz/3 cups whole milk

1 bay leaf
1 floury potato, peeled and diced
1 tsp dried thyme leaves
freshly grated nutmeg, to taste
400g/14oz/2⅔ cups frozen
  sweetcorn kernels
salt and freshly ground black pepper
chopped chives, to serve

1 Put the bacon rashers in a saucepan and fry over a high heat, turning occasionally,
   for 5–7 minutes until they brown and give off their fat. Remove the bacon from
   the pan and drain on kitchen paper, then cut into small pieces and set aside.
2 Add the oil to the fat remaining in the pan and reduce the heat to medium. Add the
   celery, onion and green pepper and fry, stirring occasionally, for 3–5 minutes until
   the onion is softened. Sprinkle in the flour and cook, stirring, for 2 minutes. Remove
   the pan from the heat and slowly add the milk, stirring continuously until smooth
   to prevent lumps from forming.
3 Return to the heat, add the bay leaf, potato and thyme and season with nutmeg,
   salt and pepper. Bring to just below the boil, stirring occasionally, then reduce the
   heat and simmer, covered, for 12 minutes, stirring occasionally. Add the bacon and
   sweetcorn and simmer for 3–5 minutes until both are tender. Adjust the nutmeg,
   salt and pepper, if necessary, then serve sprinkled with chives.

121 Portuguese Caldo Verde

PREPARATION TIME 10 minutes **COOKING TIME** 30 minutes

500g/1lb 2oz floury potatoes, peeled and chopped
2 large garlic cloves, chopped
250g/9oz curly kale or savoy cabbage, thick stalks removed, leaves shredded and rinsed

1 tsp dried dill or thyme leaves
100g/3½oz chorizo, casing removed and meat thinly sliced
salt and freshly ground black pepper
fruity extra-virgin olive oil, to serve
crusty country-style bread, to serve

1 Put the potatoes, garlic and 1.25l/44fl oz/5 cups water in a saucepan and season with salt and pepper. Cover and bring to the boil. Reduce the heat and simmer, covered, 10–15 minutes until the potatoes are very tender.

2 Use a potato masher or large metal spoon to coarsely mash the potatoes into the water. Add the kale and dill and simmer, uncovered, for 5–10 minutes until the kale wilts. Stir in the chorizo and warm through, then adjust the salt and pepper, if necessary. Serve with bread and olive oil for adding at the table.

122 Chorizo & Chestnut Soup

PREPARATION TIME 20 minutes, plus making the stock   COOKING TIME 40 minutes

115g/4oz chorizo, casing removed
   and chopped
½ tbsp olive or hemp oil (optional)
2 carrots, peeled and thinly sliced
1 celery stick, chopped
1 onion, finely chopped
1 tsp ground cumin
½ tsp ground coriander

a pinch of chilli flakes, or to taste
1.25l/44fl oz/5 cups Vegetable Stock
   (see page 12) or ready-made stock
200g/7oz tinned or vacuum-packed
   chestnuts, drained and chopped
salt and freshly ground black pepper
chopped parsley leaves, to serve

1   Fry the chorizo in a saucepan over a high heat, stirring, for 3–5 minutes until slightly
    crisp. Remove it from the pan and set aside. Reduce the heat to low and add the oil
    to the pan, if necessary. Stir in the carrots, celery and onion and cook, covered,
    for 10–12 minutes, stirring occasionally, until the vegetables are beginning to soften
    but not colour. Add the cumin, coriander and chilli flakes and stir for 30 seconds
    until aromatic. Watch closely so the spices do not burn.

2   Add the stock and chestnuts and season with salt and pepper. Cover and bring
    to the boil. Skim, then reduce the heat and simmer, covered, for 10–15 minutes
    until the vegetables and chestnuts are very tender. Blend until smooth, then adjust
    the salt and pepper, if necessary. Serve sprinkled with the parsley and fried chorizo.

123 Pea Green Soup with Ham & Blue Cheese

PREPARATION TIME 10 minutes, plus making the stock and flavoured oil
COOKING TIME 20 minutes

875ml/30fl oz/3½ cups
   Vegetable Stock (see page 12)
   or ready-made stock
400g/14oz/heaped 2½ cups
   frozen peas

55-80g/2–3oz blue cheese, crumbled
100g/3½oz cooked ham, diced
salt and freshly ground black pepper
1 recipe quantity Crushed Basil
   or Mint Oil (see page 15), to serve

1   Put the stock in a saucepan. Cover and bring to the boil, then stir in the peas.
    Reduce the heat and simmer, uncovered, for 5–8 minutes until the peas are tender,
    then remove about one-third of the peas and set aside.

2   Blend the soup to the preferred consistency. Strain the soup for an even smoother
    texture, if you like. Return the soup to the pan. Return the reserved peas to the
    soup and add the cheese and ham. Reheat, stirring until the cheese melts into the
    soup. Season with salt and pepper, if necessary, but remember the cheese and
    ham will be salty. Drizzle with the oil and serve.

124 Ham & Cheese Chicory Soup

PREPARATION TIME 15 minutes, plus making the stock   COOKING TIME 30 minutes

30g/1oz butter
1 tbsp olive oil
leaves from 4 heads of chicory,
   coarsely chopped
1 floury potato, peeled and diced
625ml/21½fl oz/2½ cups Vegetable
   Stock (see page 12) or ready-made
   stock

1 Parmesan cheese rind, about 7.5 x
   5cm/3 x 2in (see page 9; optional)
5 tbsp double cream
salt and ground white pepper
40g/1½oz thinly sliced Parma ham,
   to serve
freshly grated Gruyère cheese,
   to serve

1   Melt the butter with the oil in a saucepan over a medium heat. Add the chicory and
    potato and fry, stirring, for 3–5 minutes until the chicory wilts but does not brown.
    Add the stock, 600ml/21fl oz/scant 2½ cups water and the cheese rind, if using.

2   Cover and bring to the boil, then reduce the heat and simmer for 10–12 minutes
    until the potato is very tender. Discard the cheese rind, if used, add the cream
    and blend the soup until smooth. Season with salt and white pepper, and serve
    sprinkled with Parma ham and grated cheese.

125 Smoked Ham & Celery Chowder

PREPARATION TIME 20 minutes, plus making the stock   **COOKING TIME** 35 minutes

15g/½oz butter
1½ tbsp sunflower oil
400g/14oz smoked ham, rind and any
    fat removed and meat diced
2 celery sticks, finely chopped, with
    the leaves reserved to serve
1 leek, halved lengthways, sliced
    and rinsed
1 large floury potato, peeled
    and diced
2 tbsp plain white or wholemeal flour

500ml/17fl oz/2 cups Chicken Stock
    (see page 11) or ready-made stock
700ml/24fl oz/scant 3 cups milk
2 tbsp chopped parsley leaves
1 bay leaf
finely grated zest of 1 lemon
4 tbsp soured cream
celery salt
freshly ground black pepper
celery seeds, to serve

1   Melt the butter with 1 tablespoon of the oil in a saucepan over a medium heat.
    Add the ham and fry, stirring, for 2–3 minutes until just starting to crisp on the
    edges. Remove it from the pan and set aside.
2   Add the remaining oil to the pan. Add the celery and leek and fry, stirring
    occasionally, for 3–5 minutes until the leek is softened but not coloured. Stir in
    the potato and return the ham to the pan, then sprinkle in the flour and stir for
    2 minutes. Slowly add half the stock, scraping the base of the pan and stirring
    continuously to prevent lumps from forming.
3   Stir in the remaining stock, cover and bring to the boil, then skim. Reduce the heat
    to low and stir in the milk, parsley, bay leaf and lemon zest. Simmer, covered,
    for 15–18 minutes until the potato is starting to fall apart. Do not allow the soup
    to boil. Meanwhile, finely shred the reserved celery leaves.
4   Discard the bay leaf, stir in the soured cream and warm through. Season with
    celery salt and pepper, but remember the ham is salty. Serve sprinkled with celery
    leaves and seeds.

126 Smoked Sausage & Red Cabbage Soup

PREPARATION TIME 20 minutes, plus making the stock   **COOKING TIME** 35 minutes

1½ tbsp olive or hemp oil
1 onion, finely chopped
1 large garlic clove, finely chopped
200g/7oz smoked sausage, casing
    removed and sliced
1 floury potato, peeled and chopped
1l/35fl oz/4 cups Vegetable Stock
    (see page 12) or ready-made stock

100g/3½oz red cabbage, cored
    and shredded
1 sweet cooking apple, peeled,
    cored and chopped
lemon juice, to taste (optional)
salt and freshly ground black pepper
paprika, to serve
chopped parsley leaves, to serve

1   Heat the oil in a saucepan over a medium heat. Add the onion and fry, stirring
    occasionally, for 2 minutes. Add the garlic and fry for 1–3 minutes until the onion
    is softened but not coloured. Stir in the sausage and potato, then add the stock
    and season with salt and pepper.
2   Cover and bring to the boil, then reduce the heat and simmer for 12–15 minutes,
    stirring occasionally, until the potato is falling apart. Stir in the cabbage and apple
    and simmer for another 5–10 minutes until the cabbage is tender and the apple
    is dissolving. Stir well and adjust the salt and pepper, adding lemon juice,
    if necessary. Serve immediately, sprinkled with paprika and parsley.

127 Sausage, Fennel & Bean Soup

PREPARATION TIME 15 minutes, plus overnight soaking and cooking the beans (optional) and making the stock   COOKING TIME 30 minutes

200g/7oz/1 cup dried cannellini beans
   or 400g/14oz tinned cannellini
   beans, drained and rinsed
1½ tbsp garlic-flavoured olive oil
400g/14oz spicy Italian sausages,
   casings removed
1 celery stick, finely chopped

1 bulb fennel, thinly sliced
1.25l/44fl oz/5 cups Beef Stock
   (see page 10) or ready-made stock
2 carrots, peeled and diced
2 bay leaves
salt and freshly ground black pepper
chopped parsley leaves, to serve

1   If using dried beans, put them in a bowl, cover with water and leave to soak overnight, then drain. Transfer to a saucepan, add 1.5l/53fl oz/6 cups water, cover and bring to the boil. Reduce the heat and simmer, covered, for 50 minutes–1 hour until tender, then drain.

2   Heat the oil in a saucepan over a medium heat. Add the sausage meat and fry for 2–3 minutes, breaking up the meat, until browned all over. Remove the meat from the pan and set aside to drain on kitchen paper. Spoon off all but 1 tablespoon of the oil remaining in the pan. Add the celery and fennel and fry, stirring occasionally, for 8–10 minutes until light golden brown. Add the stock, carrots and bay leaves and season with salt and pepper.

3   Cover and bring to the boil. Skim, if necessary, then reduce the heat and simmer for 5 minutes. Return the sausage meat to the pan, add the beans and simmer for 2–3 minutes to warm through. Discard the bay leaves and skim again. Adjust the salt and pepper, if necessary, then serve sprinkled with parsley.

128 Venison & Chestnut Soup

PREPARATION TIME 25 minutes, plus at least 4 hours marinating and making the stock
COOKING TIME 1¾ hours

600g/1lb 5oz boneless venison
   shoulder, trimmed and cut into
   large chunks
250ml/9fl oz/1 cup full-flavoured dry
   red wine, such as Burgundy
1 shallot, sliced
1 tsp juniper berries, lightly crushed
4 large garlic cloves, chopped
1 tbsp olive oil
1 carrot, peeled and diced
1 celery stick, chopped
½ leek, halved lengthways, thinly
   sliced and rinsed

1.5l/48fl oz/5½ cups Beef Stock
   (see page 10) or ready-made stock
1 bouquet garni made with 1 piece
   of celery stick, 1 bay leaf, several
   parsley sprigs and 2 sage sprigs
   tied together
½–1 tbsp redcurrant jelly (optional)
6 peeled tinned or vacuum-packed
   chestnuts, drained and chopped
salt and freshly ground black pepper
chopped parsley leaves, to serve

1   Mix the venison, wine, shallot, juniper berries and half the garlic together in a non-reactive bowl. Cover and chill for at least 4 hours or up to 24.

2   Remove the venison from the marinade and set aside. Strain the marinade into a clean bowl and reserve.

3   Heat the oil in a saucepan over a medium heat. Add the carrot, celery and leek and fry, stirring occasionally, for 2 minutes. Add the remaining garlic and fry for 1–3 minutes until the leek is softened. Add the reserved marinade and cook for 8 minutes until almost evaporated. Add the stock and venison and season with salt and pepper.

4   Cover and bring to the boil, then skim and add the bouquet garni. Reduce the heat to very low (use a heat diffuser if you have one) and simmer, covered, for 1¼–1½ hours until the meat is very tender. Remove the venison from the soup and set aside. Discard the bouquet garni.

5   Stir in ½ tablespoon of the jelly, if using, then blend the soup until smooth. Return the venison to the pan, add the chestnuts and warm through. Adjust the salt and pepper, if necessary, and add more jelly, if you like. Serve sprinkled with parsley.

129 Haggis Soup

PREPARATION TIME 20 minutes, plus making the stock   COOKING TIME 35 minutes

1 tbsp olive or hemp oil
2 unsmoked streaky bacon rashers,
   rind removed, if necessary,
   and meat chopped
1 onion, chopped
2 large garlic cloves, finely chopped
250g/9oz haggis, casing removed

950ml/32fl oz/scant 4 cups Beef Stock
   (see page 10) or ready-made stock
100g/3½oz swede, peeled and diced
1 bay leaf
1 carrot, peeled and diced
1 turnip, peeled and diced
salt and freshly ground black pepper
chopped parsley leaves, to serve

1   Heat the oil in a saucepan over a medium heat. Add the bacon and fry, stirring occasionally, for 5–8 minutes until it is cooked and gives off its fat. Remove the bacon from the pan and set aside to drain on kitchen paper.
2   Add the onion to the fat remaining in the pan and fry, stirring occasionally, for 2 minutes. Add the garlic and fry for 1–3 minutes until the onion is softened but not coloured. Crumble in the haggis and stir well. Add the stock and season with salt and pepper. Cover and bring to the boil. Skim, then add the swede, bay leaf, carrot and turnip. Reduce the heat and simmer, covered, for 10–15 minutes until the vegetables are tender. Meanwhile, finely chop the bacon.
3   Discard the bay leaf and adjust the salt and pepper, if necessary. Serve sprinkled with the bacon and parsley.

130 German Liver Dumpling Soup

PREPARATION TIME 25 minutes, plus 30 minutes chilling and making the stock
COOKING TIME 25 minutes

1.4l/44fl oz/5 cups Beef Stock
   (see page 10), Beef Consommé
   (see page 13) or ready-made stock
200g/7oz/1¼ cups frozen peas
salt and freshly ground black pepper
chopped parsley leaves, to serve

LIVER DUMPLINGS
1 tbsp sunflower oil
1 large onion, grated

250g/9oz day-old bread, grated,
   or 250g/9oz/2½ cups dried
   bread crumbs
6 tbsp milk
140g/5oz calf's liver,
   membrane removed
1 egg beaten with 1 extra yolk
1 tbsp dried marjoram leaves
1 tbsp chopped parsley leaves
1 tsp sweet or wholegrain mustard

1   To make the dumplings, heat the oil in a saucepan over a medium heat. Add the onion and fry, stirring occasionally, for 8–10 minutes until golden brown. Transfer to a plate and set aside to cool. Meanwhile, put the bread and milk in a small bowl and leave to soak for 10 minutes. Finely chop the calf's liver in a blender or food processor and set aside. Put the bread with any leftover milk, onion, liver and eggs in a bowl and mix together. Add the marjoram, parsley and mustard and season with salt and pepper. (Fry a small amount in a frying pan to test for seasoning, if you like.) Using a wet spoon, divide the mixture into 12 or 24 equal portions, then use wet hands to roll each portion into a ball. Cover and refrigerate for at least 30 minutes.
2   Put the stock in a saucepan and season with salt and pepper. Cover and bring to the boil. Add the dumplings, then reduce the heat and simmer, covered, for 3 minutes. Add the peas and increase the heat to a slow boil. Boil for 3–5 minutes until the dumplings are cooked through and the peas are tender. Adjust the salt and pepper, if necessary, then serve sprinkled with parsley.

131 Game & Barley Broth

PREPARATION TIME 20 minutes, plus making the stock and cooking the pheasant
COOKING TIME 1½ hours

100g/3½oz lightly smoked lardons
1½ tbsp olive or hemp oil
1 carrot, chopped
1 celery stick, chopped
1 leek, white part only, sliced and
    rinsed
1 onion, sliced
125ml/4fl oz/½ cup dry red wine
1.5l/52fl oz/6 cups Game Stock
    (see page 11) or ready-made stock

400g/14oz tinned chopped tomatoes
1 tbsp tomato purée
1 bay leaf
a pinch of sugar
55g/2oz/¼ cup pearl barley
400g/14oz boneless, skinless cooked
    pheasant and/or partridge meat,
    finely shredded
salt and freshly ground black pepper
chopped chives, to serve

1   Put the lardons in a saucepan and fry over a medium heat for 3–5 minutes, stirring, until they begin to crisp and the fat runs. Remove them from the pan and set aside.
2   Add the oil to the fat remaining in the pan and heat over a medium heat. Add the carrot, celery, leek and onion and fry, stirring occasionally, for 3–5 minutes until the leek and vegetables are softened but not coloured. Stir in the wine and cook for 5–6 minutes until almost evaporated. Add the stock, tomatoes, tomato purée, bay leaf and sugar and season with salt and pepper. Cover and bring to the boil, then reduce the heat and simmer for 20 minutes.
3   Strain the stock, pressing down on the vegetables to extract as much flavour as possible, then return it to the pan. Add the barley, cover and return to the boil. Reduce the heat and simmer for 30–40 minutes until tender. Discard the bay leaf.
4   Add the pheasant to the soup and simmer for 2–3 minutes to heat through. Adjust the salt and pepper, if necessary, then serve sprinkled with the lardons and chives.

132 Roast Pheasant & Lentil Soup

PREPARATION TIME 20 minutes, plus roasting the pheasant and making the shallots
COOKING TIME 50 minutes

280g/10oz/1⅓ cups dried Puy or other
    green lentils, rinsed
2 large garlic cloves, chopped
1 leek, chopped and rinsed
1 red onion, chopped
1 tsp juniper berries and 1 bay leaf
    tied together in a piece of muslin
400g/14oz boneless, skinless roast
    pheasant, shredded

any leftover pheasant gravy
    (optional)
4 tbsp crème fraîche or soured cream
salt and freshly ground black pepper
Crisp-Fried Shallots (see page 15),
    to serve
chopped parsley leaves, to serve

1   Put the lentils, garlic, leek, onion, spice bundle and 1.75l/60fl oz/6⅔ cups water in a saucepan over a high heat. Cover and bring to the boil. Skim, then reduce the heat and simmer for 30–40 minutes until the lentils are very soft. Drain, reserving the cooking liquid and discarding the spice bundle.
2   Put a small amount of the cooking liquid in a small saucepan over a medium heat. Add the pheasant and simmer to warm through.
3   Meanwhile, blend the lentils with 500ml/17fl oz/2 cups of the cooking liquid until smooth, then season with salt and pepper. Work the soup through a sieve into a bowl, rubbing back and forth with a spoon and scraping the bottom of the sieve.
4   Return the soup to the pan and slowly stir in the gravy, if using, and enough of the remaining cooking liquid to achieve the preferred consistency. (Any leftover cooking liquid can be used in other recipes or frozen for up to six months.) Stir in the crème fraîche, then adjust the salt and pepper, if necessary. Use a slotted spoon to transfer the pheasant to the soup. Serve sprinkled with the shallots and parsley.

133 Oxtail Soup with Barley

PREPARATION TIME 20 minutes, plus overnight chilling (optional) **COOKING TIME** 4 hours

30g/1oz butter

2 tbsp sunflower or olive oil, plus extra as needed

1kg/2lb 4oz oxtail, cut into large pieces (ask the butcher to do this)

3 celery sticks, chopped, with the leaves reserved

2 carrots, peeled and chopped

2 onions, chopped

4 garlic cloves, finely chopped

1 bouquet garni made with the reserved celery leaves, 1 bay leaf and several parsley and thyme sprigs tied together

85g/3oz/heaped ⅓ cup pearl barley

Worcestershire sauce, to taste

4 tbsp finely chopped parsley leaves

salt and freshly ground black pepper

1   This soup is best made a day before serving, so it can be chilled overnight and the excess fat easily removed. Melt the butter with the oil in a large saucepan over a medium heat. Working in batches, fry the oxtail for 2–3 minutes until browned on both sides, then transfer it to a plate. Add extra oil to the pan between batches, as necessary.

2   Pour off all but 1½ tablespoons of the fat from the pan. Add the celery, carrots and onions and fry, stirring, for 2 minutes. Add the garlic and fry for 1–3 minutes until the onions are softened. Return the oxtail and any accumulated juices to the pan, add 2.5l/88fl oz/10 cups water and season with salt and pepper. Cover and bring to the boil, then skim and add the bouquet garni. Reduce the heat and simmer, covered, for 2½–3 hours until the meat is falling off the bones. Remove the meat and bones from the pan and set aside until cool enough to handle.

3   Strain the soup into a clean pan, discarding the vegetables, and skim. Alternatively, leave the soup to cool completely, then cover and chill overnight for easier removal of the fat. (If you are chilling the soup overnight, spoon a little of it over the meat, cover with cling film and chill until required.)

4   Add the barley, cover and bring to the boil. Reduce the heat and simmer for 30–40 minutes until tender.

5   Meanwhile, remove any skin and all the gristle from the meat and discard, along with the bones. Shred the meat, return it to the pan and reheat. Stir in the Worcestershire sauce and parsley. Adjust the salt and pepper, if necessary, and serve.

CHAPTER 3

POULTRY SOUPS

The delicate flavours of chicken and turkey give cooks

an almost blank canvas for creating delicious soups bursting

with myriad flavours. Thai Red Curry Chicken Soup and

African-Style Chicken & Vegetable Soup, for example,

have big, bold tastes, while Chicken Soup with Matzo Balls

and Scottish Cock-a-Leekie are more subtle and comforting.

The recipe for Chinese Egg-Drop Soup lets you recreate

a restaurant favourite at home, and for anyone watching their

weight, Mexican Poultry & Avocado Broth offers the exciting

flavours of the country's cuisine without the traditional calories.

Chicken Noodle Soup is a universal cure-all for everything

from the common cold to general malaise, and here there's

also a Goji Berry & Garlic Flu Buster, made with rich chicken

stock, which combines the restorative qualities of chicken soup

with the health benefits of two superfoods.

Soups aren't just for everyday eating, though. Jerusalem

Artichoke Soup with Duck Confit, for example, is simple but

impressive for dinner parties, too.

CHICKEN NOODLE SOUP (SEE PAGE 88)

134 Chicken Noodle Soup

PREPARATION TIME 15 minutes, plus making the stock and cooking the chicken
COOKING TIME 35 minutes

1.25l/44fl oz/5 cups Rich Chicken
   Stock (see page 10)
500g/1lb 2oz skinless chicken
   drumsticks and/or thighs,
   or 400g/14oz chicken from making
   the stock, cut into bite-sized pieces
2 carrots, peeled and sliced

2 celery sticks, sliced
1 leek, thinly sliced and rinsed
225g/8oz thin egg noodles
   or spaghetti
4 tbsp finely chopped parsley leaves
salt and freshly ground black pepper

1　If using raw chicken, put the stock in a saucepan, add the raw chicken and season with salt and pepper. Cover and bring to just below the boil. Skim, then reduce the heat and simmer, covered, for 10–15 minutes for thighs and 15–20 minutes for drumsticks until the chicken is cooked through and the juices run clear when you cut a piece. Remove the chicken from the stock and set aside until cool enough to handle. Meanwhile, bring a separate large pan of salted water to the boil.

2　Add the carrots, celery and leek to the stock and return to the boil. Reduce the heat and simmer for 10–12 minutes until tender.

3　Meanwhile, add the noodles to the boiling water and cook for 10 minutes, or according to the packet instructions, until tender. Drain, rinse under cold running water and set aside.

4　Cut the chicken meat from the bones and into bite-sized pieces. Add the freshly cooked or leftover chicken to the soup, stir in the noodles and simmer gently to reheat. Adjust the salt and pepper, if necessary, stir in the parsley and serve.

135 Mexican Chicken Noodle Soup

PREPARATION TIME 35 minutes, plus making the stock and cooking the chicken
COOKING TIME 25 minutes

1 dried chipotle chilli pepper
2 tbsp garlic-flavoured olive oil
1 red onion, finely chopped
1 red pepper, deseeded and diced
100g/3½oz very thin egg noodles,
   such as vermicelli, broken into
   bite-sized pieces
1 tsp ground cumin
1 tsp dried thyme leaves

1.25l/44fl oz/5 cups Chicken Stock
   (see page 11) or ready-made stock
200ml/7fl oz/scant 1 cup passata
a pinch of soft light brown sugar
400g/14oz boneless, skinless cooked
   chicken
salt and freshly ground black pepper
chopped coriander leaves, to serve
hot pepper sauce, to serve
tortilla chips, to serve (optional)

1　Put the chipotle pepper in a bowl, cover with warm water and leave to soak for 20 minutes until tender, then drain, deseed and chop.

2　Heat half the oil in a saucepan. Add the onion and red pepper and fry, stirring occasionally, for 3–5 minutes until the onion is softened but not coloured. Add the remaining oil to the pan and heat. Add the noodles and fry for 2–3 minutes until they just start to brown. Add the chipotle, cumin and thyme and stir for 30 seconds until aromatic. Watch closely so the noodles do not overbrown and the spices do not burn.

3　Stir in the stock, passata and sugar and season with salt and pepper. Cover and bring to the boil, then boil, uncovered, for 3–5 minutes until the noodles and pepper are tender. Stir in the chicken and warm through, and adjust the salt and pepper, if necessary. Serve sprinkled with coriander and with hot pepper sauce and tortilla chips, if you like, on the side. If reheating this soup, add a little extra stock, if necessary, to thin it.

136 Chicken Soup with Matzo Balls

PREPARATION TIME 25 minutes, plus 2 hours chilling and making the stock
COOKING TIME 1¼ hour

1.25l/44fl oz/5 cups Rich Chicken
   Stock (see page 10)
1 large carrot, peeled and sliced
1 leek, halved lengthways,
   sliced and rinsed
115g/4oz savoy cabbage, shredded
salt and freshly ground black pepper
chopped parsley leaves, to serve

MATZO BALLS
2 large eggs
30g/1oz butter, at room temperature
100g/3½oz/1 cup ground almonds
100g/3½oz/1 cup medium ground
   matzo meal
4–5 tbsp Rich Chicken Stock
   (see page 10) or ready-made stock
olive oil, if required (optional)

1 To make the matzo balls, put the eggs in a large bowl and beat with an electric mixer or a wooden spoon for 2–3 minutes until very thick and pale and they hold a 'ribbon' on the surface when the mixer is lifted. Beat in the butter, almonds and matzo meal and season with salt and pepper. Gradually add the stock until the mixture is quite thick and sticky. Cover with cling film and chill for 2 hours.

2 Bring a large saucepan of water to the boil. Using a wet spoon, divide the matzo ball mixture into 24 equal portions. Use wet hands to roll each portion into a ball. Drop the balls into the water and, just before the water returns to the boil, reduce the heat to low. Simmer for 45 minutes until the matzo balls are cooked through when you cut one open. Gently drain and set aside. If making in advance, rub the balls lightly with oil to prevent them from sticking together.

3 Put the stock in a saucepan. Cover and bring to just below the boil. Add the carrot and leek and season with salt and pepper. Simmer, covered, for 10 minutes, then gently stir in the matzo balls and cabbage and simmer for another 5 minutes until they are heated through and the carrots are very tender. Adjust the salt and pepper, if necessary, and serve sprinkled with parsley.

137 Chicken, Fennel & Saffron Soup

PREPARATION TIME 10 minutes, plus making the stock   COOKING TIME 30 minutes

1 tbsp olive or hemp oil
280g/10oz fennel bulbs, quartered
   lengthways and sliced, with the
   fronds reserved to serve
2 large garlic cloves, finely chopped
1 tsp fennel seeds

1.25l/44fl oz/5 cups Chicken Stock
   (see page 11) or ready-made stock
500g/1lb 2oz skinless chicken thighs
1 bay leaf
a large pinch of saffron threads
salt and freshly ground black pepper

1 Heat the oil in a saucepan over a medium heat. Add the fennel and fry, stirring occasionally, for 2 minutes. Add the garlic and fry for 1–3 minutes until the fennel is softened but not coloured. Add the fennel seeds and stir for 30 seconds. Watch closely so they do not burn.

2 Add the stock and chicken. Cover and bring to the boil. Skim, then add the bay leaf and saffron and season with salt and pepper. Reduce the heat and simmer, covered, for 10–15 minutes until the chicken is cooked through and the juices run clear when you cut a piece. Remove the chicken from the soup and set aside until cool enough to handle.

3 Cut the chicken into bite-sized pieces, return it to the soup and reheat. Discard the bay leaf and adjust the salt and pepper, if necessary. Serve sprinkled with the fennel fronds.

138 Scottish Cock-a-Leekie

PREPARATION TIME 10 minutes, plus making the stock   **COOKING TIME** 40 minutes

2 leeks
30g/1oz butter
1.4l/48fl oz/5½ cups Chicken Stock
   (see page 11) or ready-made stock
500g/1lb 2oz skinless chicken thighs

1 bouquet garni made with 1 bay
   leaf, several parsley sprigs and
   1 thyme sprig tied together
6 prunes, stoned and halved
chopped parsley leaves, to serve

1   To prepare the leeks, trim them and separate the white and green parts. Slice the
    white parts thickly, then rinse and set aside. Quarter the green parts lengthways
    and finely shred, then rinse and set aside.
2   Melt the butter in a saucepan over a medium heat. Add the white part of the leeks
    and fry, stirring occasionally, for 5–8 minutes until just starting to turn golden.
    Add the stock and chicken, cover and bring to just below the boil. Skim, then add
    the bouquet garni and reduce the heat to low. Simmer, covered, for 10–15 minutes
    until the chicken is cooked through and the juices run clear when you cut a piece.
    Remove the chicken from the soup and set aside until cool enough to handle.
3   Add the prunes and green parts of the leeks to the soup and simmer, uncovered,
    for 5–10 minutes until the prunes are tender. Discard the bouquet garni.
4   Cut the chicken from the bones into bite-sized pieces, return it to the soup and
    reheat. Adjust the salt and pepper, if necessary, then serve sprinkled with parsley.

139 Malay-Style Chicken Soup

PREPARATION TIME 25 minutes, plus making the stock   COOKING TIME 45 minutes

1.4l/48fl oz/5½ cups Chicken Stock
(see page 11) or ready-made stock
1cm/½in piece of galangal,
peeled and sliced
1cm/½in piece of root ginger,
peeled and sliced
2 garlic cloves, crushed
2 shallots, sliced
1 bird's-eye chilli, deseeded
(optional) and sliced
1 lemongrass stalk, coarsely
chopped, with outer leaves
removed

1 floury potato, peeled and chopped
500g/1lb 2oz skinless chicken thighs
140g/5oz pumpkin, peeled, deseeded
and cut into bite-sized pieces
100g/3½oz green beans, cut into
bite-sized pieces
200ml/7fl oz/scant 1 cup coconut milk
2 tbsp lime juice, or to taste
1 tbsp fish sauce, or to taste
salt and freshly ground black pepper
chopped coriander leaves, to serve
finely shredded spring onions,
to serve

1 Put the stock, galangal, ginger, garlic, shallots, chilli, lemongrass and potato in a saucepan. Cover and bring to the boil, skimming as necessary. Boil, partially covered, for 15 minutes until the potato is very tender. Strain into a large bowl, pressing down on the potato to push as much as possible through the sieve, then return the stock to the pan. Discard the flavourings.

2 Add the chicken, pumpkin and green beans and season with pepper. Cover and bring to the boil. Reduce the heat and simmer for 10–15 minutes until the chicken is cooked through and the juices run clear when you cut a piece. Remove the chicken from the soup and set aside until cool enough to handle.

3 Cut the chicken from the bones and slice, then return it to the soup. Add the coconut milk, lime juice and fish sauce and simmer over a very low heat, stirring, for 2–3 minutes. Adjust the salt and pepper and add more lime juice or fish sauce, if necessary. Serve sprinkled with coriander and spring onions.

140 Japanese-Style Curried Chicken Soup

PREPARATION TIME 25 minutes, plus making the stock and toasting the seeds
COOKING TIME 35 minutes

1 tart apple, peeled, cored
and chopped
1 tbsp lemon juice
2 garlic cloves, chopped
2.5cm/1in piece of root ginger,
peeled and chopped
200g/7oz tinned mango in light
syrup, drained
1 onion, chopped
½ tbsp Worcestershire Sauce,
or to taste
30g/1oz butter

2 tbsp plain white or wholemeal flour
2 tsp curry powder
1l/35fl oz/4 cups Rich Chicken Stock
(see page 10) or ready-made stock
500g/1lb 2oz skinless chicken thighs
1 carrot, peeled, halved lengthways
and thinly sliced
salt and freshly ground black pepper
black sesame seeds, to serve
toasted white sesame seeds
(see page 9), to serve

1 Toss the apple and lemon juice together in a deep bowl or blender, then add the garlic, ginger, mango, onion and Worcestershire sauce. Blend until the mixture forms a paste but is not completely puréed, then set aside.

2 Melt the butter in a saucepan over a medium heat. Stir in the apple paste, then sprinkle in the flour and curry powder and stir for 2 minutes. Slowly add the stock, stirring continuously to prevent lumps from forming. Add the chicken and season with pepper. Cover and bring to the boil, then skim and reduce the heat. Simmer, covered, for 10–15 minutes until the chicken is cooked through and the juices run clear when you cut a piece. Remove the chicken from the soup and set aside until cool enough to handle.

3 Add the carrot to the soup, increase the heat to medium and simmer for 10–12 minutes until tender. Meanwhile, cut the chicken from the bones into thin pieces, return it to the pan and warm through. Adjust the salt and pepper and add more Worcestershire Sauce, if necessary, then serve sprinkled with sesame seeds.

141 Provençal-Style Chicken Soup

PREPARATION TIME 15 minutes, plus making the stock and croûtes
COOKING TIME 25 minutes

1 tbsp extra-virgin olive oil, plus
   extra to serve
1 red onion, finely chopped
4 garlic cloves, very finely chopped
670ml/23fl oz/scant 2⅔ cups passata
500ml/17fl oz/2 cups Chicken Stock
   (see page 11) or ready-made stock
500g/1lb 2oz skinless chicken thighs
1 courgette, halved lengthways
   and sliced

1 bouquet garni made with 1 piece
   of celery stick, 1 bay leaf, several
   parsley and thyme sprigs and
   1 rosemary sprig tied together
salt and freshly ground black pepper
chopped parsley leaves, to serve
1 recipe quantity Goat's Cheese
   Croûtes (see page 14), to serve

1   Heat the oil in a saucepan over a medium heat. Add the onion and fry for 2 minutes. Add the garlic and fry for 1–3 minutes until the onion is softened but not browned. Add the passata, stock and chicken. Cover and bring to the boil, then skim.

2   Add the courgette and bouquet garni and season with salt and pepper. Reduce the heat and simmer, covered, for 10–15 minutes until the chicken is cooked through and the juices run clear when you cut a piece. Remove the chicken from the soup and set aside until cool enough to handle, then discard the bouquet garni.

3   Cut the chicken from the bones into bite-sized pieces, return it to the soup and reheat. Adjust the salt and pepper, if necessary, then serve drizzled with oil, sprinkled with parsley and with croûtes on the side.

142 Curried Chicken & Tomato Soup

PREPARATION TIME 10 minutes, plus making the stock and seeds and preparing
the tomatoes   COOKING TIME 35 minutes

600ml/21fl oz/scant 2½ cups
   Chicken Stock (see page 11)
   or ready-made stock
400ml/14fl oz/scant 1⅔ cups
   coconut milk
2 lemongrass stalks, cut into 3 pieces,
   with outer leaves removed
2.5cm/1in piece of root ginger,
   peeled and smashed in one piece

1 tbsp Madras curry paste
500g/1lb 2oz skinless chicken thighs
2 large tomatoes, peeled (see page 9),
   deseeded and chopped
salt and freshly ground black pepper
Spiced Seeds (see page 15), to serve
chopped coriander leaves, to serve
mini poppadoms, warm, to serve

1   Put the stock, coconut milk, lemongrass, ginger and curry paste in a saucepan over a high heat. Stir until the paste dissolves, then season with salt and pepper. Cover and bring to the boil, then reduce the heat and simmer for 10 minutes. Add the chicken, cover and return to the boil.

2   Skim, then reduce the heat and simmer, covered, for 10 minutes. Stir in the tomatoes and simmer, covered, for another 3–5 minutes until the chicken is cooked through and the juices run clear when you cut a piece. Remove the chicken and set aside until cool enough to handle. Discard the lemongrass and ginger.

3   Cut the chicken from the bones into bite-sized pieces, return it to the soup and reheat, if necessary. Adjust the salt and pepper, if necessary, then serve sprinkled with seeds and coriander and with poppadoms on the side.

143 Mexican-Style Chicken Soup

PREPARATION TIME 15 minutes, plus making the stock   COOKING TIME 35 minutes

1½ tbsp sunflower oil
1 large onion, chopped
2 red or green peppers, deseeded
   and diced
2 garlic cloves, chopped
1 tsp ancho chilli powder, or to taste
875ml/30fl oz/3½ cups Chicken Stock
   (see page 11) or ready-made stock
400g/14oz boneless, skinless
   chicken breasts

400g/14oz/2⅔ cups frozen
   sweetcorn kernels
200g/7oz tinned kidney beans,
   drained and rinsed
salt and freshly ground black pepper
chopped coriander leaves, to serve
lime wedges, to serve
tortilla chips, to serve (optional)

1   Heat the oil in a large saucepan over a medium heat. Add the onion and peppers
    and fry, stirring occasionally, for 2 minutes. Stir in the garlic and fry for 1–3 minutes
    until the onion is softened but not coloured. Add the chilli powder and stir for
    30 seconds. Watch closely so it does not burn.
2   Add the stock and chicken and season with salt and pepper, then cover and bring
    to the boil. Skim, reduce the heat and simmer, covered, for 12–15 minutes until the
    chicken is cooked through and the juices run clear when you cut a piece. Remove
    the chicken from the soup and set aside until cool enough to handle.
3   Add the sweetcorn kernels to the soup and boil for 3–5 minutes until tender. Thinly
    slice the chicken breasts, return them to the soup, add the kidney beans and reheat
    until both are warm. Adjust the salt and pepper, if necessary, then serve sprinkled
    with coriander and with lime wedges for squeezing over and tortilla chips on the
    side, if you like.

144 Chicken & Chickpea Soup

PREPARATION TIME 10 minutes, plus overnight soaking and cooking the chickpeas
(optional), making the stock and toasting the seeds   COOKING TIME 35 minutes

200g/7oz/scant 1 cup dried chickpeas
   or 400g/14oz tinned chickpeas,
   drained and rinsed
1 tbsp garlic-flavoured olive oil
1 leek, sliced and rinsed
1½ tsp ground cumin
a pinch of chilli flakes, or to taste
a pinch of turmeric

1.4l/48fl oz/5½ cups Chicken Stock
   (see page 11) or ready-made stock
500g/1lb 2oz skinless chicken thighs
1 large handful of baby spinach
   leaves
salt and freshly ground black pepper
toasted sesame seeds (see page 9),
   to serve
chopped coriander leaves, to serve

1   If using dried chickpeas, put them in a bowl, cover with water and leave to soak
    overnight, then drain. Transfer to a saucepan and add 1.5l/53fl oz/6 cups water.
    Cover and bring to the boil, then reduce the heat and simmer, covered,
    for 50 minutes–1 hour, then drain.
2   Heat the oil in a saucepan over a medium heat. Add the leek and fry, stirring
    occasionally, for 3–5 minutes until softened but not coloured. Stir in the cumin,
    chilli flakes and turmeric and fry for 30 seconds. Watch closely so the spices
    do not burn. Add the stock and chicken and season with salt and pepper. Cover and
    bring to the boil, then skim.
3   Reduce the heat and simmer, covered, for 10–15 minutes until the chicken
    is cooked through and the juices run clear when you cut a piece. Remove the
    chicken from the stock and set aside until cool enough to handle.
4   Add the spinach and half the chickpeas to the pan and simmer for 3–5 minutes until
    the spinach wilts. Blend the soup until smooth, then add the remaining chickpeas
    and return to the simmer.
5   Cut the chicken from the bones into bite-sized pieces, return it to the soup and
    warm through. Adjust the salt and pepper, if necessary, then serve sprinkled with
    sesame seeds and coriander.

145 Chicken, Pepper & Rice Soup

PREPARATION TIME 15 minutes, plus making the stock and rice
COOKING TIME 30 minutes

1 tbsp garlic-flavoured olive oil
1 onion, finely chopped
1.25l/44fl oz/5 cups Chicken Stock
  (see page 11) or ready-made stock
500g/1lb 2oz skinless chicken thighs
1 green pepper, deseeded and
  finely chopped
1 red pepper, deseeded and
  finely chopped

a pinch of chilli flakes, or to taste
  (optional)
85g/3oz/scant ½ cup frozen
  sweetcorn kernels
200g/7oz/1 cup long-grain rice,
  cooked
salt and freshly ground black pepper
chopped coriander or parsley leaves,
  to serve

1   Heat the oil in a saucepan over a medium heat. Add the onion and fry, stirring
    occasionally, for 3–5 minutes until softened but not coloured. Add the stock and
    chicken and season with salt and pepper. Cover and bring to the boil. Skim, then
    reduce the heat and simmer, covered, for 5 minutes.
2   Add the peppers and chilli flakes, if using, and simmer, covered, for another
    5–10 minutes until the peppers are tender and the chicken is cooked through and
    the juices run clear when you cut a piece. Remove the chicken from the soup and
    set aside until cool enough to handle.
3   Add the sweetcorn kernels to the pan, bring to a slow boil and boil for 3–5 minutes
    until tender. Cut the chicken from the bones into bite-sized pieces, return it to the
    soup with the rice and heat through. Adjust the salt and pepper, if necessary, then
    serve sprinkled with coriander.

146 African-Style Chicken & Vegetable Soup

PREPARATION TIME 20 minutes, plus making the stock   COOKING TIME 40 minutes

1½ tbsp groundnut or sunflower oil
1 large onion, chopped
950ml/32fl oz/scant 4 cups
  Chicken Stock (see page 11)
  or ready-made stock
500g/1lb 2oz skinless chicken thighs
140g/5oz/heaped ½ cup natural
  chunky peanut butter
400g/14oz tinned chopped tomatoes

a pinch of chilli flakes, or to taste
140g/5oz pumpkin, peeled, deseeded
  and cut into bite-sized pieces
55g/2oz white cabbage, cored and
  thinly sliced
55g/2oz green beans, chopped
1 carrot, peeled and sliced
salt and freshly ground black pepper
chopped coriander leaves, to serve

1   Heat the oil in a saucepan over a medium heat. Add the onion and fry, stirring
    occasionally, for 3–5 minutes until softened but not coloured. Add the stock and
    chicken and season with salt and pepper. Cover and bring to the boil, then skim.
    Add the peanut butter, stirring until it dissolves, then add the tomatoes and chilli
    flakes, if using. Reduce the heat and simmer, covered, for 10–15 minutes until the
    chicken is cooked through and the juices run clear when you cut a piece. Remove
    the chicken from the soup and set aside until cool enough to handle.
2   Add the pumpkin, cabbage, green beans and carrot to the pan and return to the
    boil. Reduce the heat and simmer, uncovered, for 10–12 minutes until the
    vegetables are tender.
3   Cut the chicken from the bones into bite-sized pieces, return it to the soup
    and heat through. Adjust the salt and pepper, if necessary, then serve sprinkled
    with coriander.

147 Thai Red Curry Chicken Soup

PREPARATION TIME 15 minutes, plus making the chillies   **COOKING TIME** 30 minutes

2 tbsp sunflower oil
2 large shallots, sliced
1 tbsp red curry paste
500g/1lb 2oz skinless chicken thighs
400ml/14fl oz/scant 1⅔ cups
   coconut milk
2.5cm/1in piece of root ginger,
   peeled and sliced

4 kaffir lime leaves, torn
lime juice, to taste (optional)
palm sugar or soft light brown sugar,
   to taste (optional)
chopped coriander leaves, to serve
Chillies in Vinegar (see page 15),
   to serve
lime wedges, to serve (optional)

1   Measure 1l/35fl oz/4 cups water into a large measuring jug and set aside.
2   Heat the oil in a large wok with a lid or a saucepan over a high heat. Add the
    shallots and curry paste, reduce the heat to medium and stir-fry for 2 minutes.
    Very slowly stir in 200ml/7fl oz/scant 1 cup of the water and stir for 1–2 minutes
    until the fat forms bubbles on the surface. Add the chicken and fry, turning
    occasionally, for 5 minutes, gradually stirring in a little more of the measured water
    if the curry paste looks like it will burn. Slowly add the coconut milk, ginger, lime
    leaves and remaining water, then cover and bring to the boil.
3   Reduce the heat and simmer for 10–15 minutes until the chicken is cooked through
    and the juices run clear when you cut a piece. Remove the chicken from the soup
    and set aside until cool enough to handle.
4   Cut the chicken from the bones into bite-sized pieces and return it to the soup.
    Stir in the lime juice and palm sugar to temper the heat of the curry paste, if you
    like, and reheat the soup. Serve sprinkled with coriander, topped with chillies and
    with lime wedges for squeezing over, if you like.

148 Middle Eastern-Spiced Chicken & Rice Soup

PREPARATION TIME 15 minutes, plus making the stock   COOKING TIME 50 minutes

1.4l/48fl oz/5½ cups Chicken Stock
   (see page 11) or ready-made stock
500g/1lb 2oz skinless chicken thighs
1 large carrot, cut in several pieces
1 onion, unpeeled and halved
1 tsp ground coriander
1 tsp ground cumin

several mint sprigs, tied together
100g/3½oz/½ cup long-grain rice
salt and freshly ground black pepper
1 tsp finely chopped mint leaves for
   each bowl, to serve
lemon wedges, to serve

1 Put the stock in a saucepan over a medium heat. Add the chicken, carrot, onion, coriander, cumin and mint sprigs and season with salt and pepper. Cover and bring to the boil, then skim. Reduce the heat and simmer, covered, for 15–20 minutes until the chicken is cooked through and the juices run clear when you cut a piece. Remove the chicken, carrot, onion and mint sprigs from the stock. Set the chicken aside until cool enough to handle and discard the vegetables.
2 Cover the stock and return to the boil. Stir in the rice, reduce the heat and simmer, covered, for 15–20 minutes until the rice is tender. Skim as necessary. Meanwhile, cut the chicken from the bones into bite-sized pieces, return it to the soup and reheat. Adjust the salt and pepper, if necessary.
3 Put a teaspoon of chopped mint in each bowl, ladle the soup over it and serve with lemon wedges for squeezing over. If reheating this soup, add a little extra stock to thin it.

149 Creamy Chicken & Mushroom Soup

PREPARATION TIME 15 minutes, plus making the stock   COOKING TIME 40 minutes

1l/35fl oz/4 cups Chicken Stock
   (see page 11) or ready-made stock
500g/1lb 2oz skinless chicken thighs
1 bouquet garni made with 1 bay
   leaf, several parsley sprigs and
   1 thyme sprig tied together
30g/1oz butter
1 tbsp olive or hemp oil

1 leek, halved lengthways, thinly
   sliced and rinsed
4 large portobello mushrooms,
   trimmed and sliced
4 tbsp plain white or wholemeal flour
125ml/4fl oz/½ cup single cream
2 tbsp sweet sherry
salt and freshly ground black pepper
chopped parsley leaves, to serve

1 Put the stock and chicken in a saucepan and season with salt and pepper. Cover and bring to just below the boil. Skim, then reduce the heat, add the bouquet garni and simmer, covered, for 10–15 minutes until the chicken is cooked through and the juices run clear if you cut a piece. Remove the chicken from the stock and set aside until cool enough to handle. Discard the bouquet garni.
2 Cut the chicken from the bones into bite-sized pieces and set aside.
3 Meanwhile, melt the butter with the oil in another saucepan over a medium heat. Add the leek and fry, stirring occasionally, for 3 minutes. Add the mushrooms, season with salt and fry for 5–8 minutes until the mushrooms are softened and give off their juices. Sprinkle in the flour and cook, stirring, for 2 minutes. Slowly add enough of the stock to achieve the preferred consistency, stirring continuously to prevent lumps from forming.
4 Bring the soup to the boil, stirring, then reduce the heat to low and stir in the cream and sherry. Add the chicken and simmer until warmed through, then skim and adjust the salt and pepper, if necessary. Serve sprinkled with parsley. If you reheat this soup, do not boil it.

150 'Velvet' Chicken & Edamame Soup

PREPARATION TIME 25 minutes, plus making the stock   COOKING TIME 20 minutes

400g/14oz boneless chicken thighs
1.4l/48fl oz/5½ cups Rich
   Chicken Stock (see page 10)
   or ready-made stock
4cm/1½in piece of root ginger,
   peeled and grated
1 thin slice of galangal, peeled and
   smashed in one piece

100g/3½oz frozen shelled edamame
   soya beans
½ tsp salt
100g/3½oz tinned water chestnuts,
   drained, rinsed and finely chopped
3 spring onions, thinly sliced on the
   diagonal
2 tsp light soy sauce, or to taste

1 Up to 2 hours in advance, prepare the chicken. Put the chicken, skin-side down, on a chopping board and use the flat side of a cleaver or large chef's knife to pound it several times to flatten. Next, use the flat edge along the top of the cleaver or knife to pound the meat until it looks like it has been minced, then use the sharp edge of the knife to scrape the meat away from the skin. Discard the skin. Finely chop the meat, occasionally adding 1 teaspoon cold water until it becomes almost white and fluffy. (You can add up to 3 tablespoons cold water.) Cover and chill until required. Alternatively, skin and very thinly slice the thighs.

2 When ready to cook, bring a small saucepan of water to the boil for the edamame. Put the stock in a separate saucepan, cover and bring to just below the boil. Add the ginger and galangal to the stock, reduce the heat to low, and simmer while you cook the edamame.

3 Add the edamame and salt to the boiling water and boil for 5 minutes until tender. Drain and immediately rinse under cold running water to stop the cooking.

4 Add the chicken, edamame, water chestnuts and spring onions to the stock and simmer for 2–3 minutes until the chicken is cooked through. Discard the galangal. Stir in the soy sauce, adding extra to taste, if you like, then serve.

151 Sweet-and-Sour Chicken Soup

PREPARATION TIME 15 minutes, plus making the stock, chillies and garlic
COOKING TIME 50 minutes

1.4l/48fl oz/5½ cups Rich
   Chicken Stock (see page 10)
   or ready-made stock
1cm/½in piece of root ginger,
   peeled and sliced
2 garlic cloves, halved
5 Thai basil leaves, plus extra
   to serve
1 tbsp sunflower oil
3 shallots, finely chopped

500g/1lb 2oz skinless chicken thighs
1½ tbsp fish sauce, or to taste
1 tbsp lime juice, or to taste
2 tsp palm sugar or soft light brown
   sugar, or to taste
salt and freshly ground black pepper
Chillies in Vinegar (see page 15),
   to serve
Crisp-Fried Garlic (see page 15),
   to serve

1 Put the stock, ginger, garlic and basil in a saucepan, cover and bring to the boil. Reduce the heat and simmer for 20 minutes, then strain into a bowl and set aside.

2 Heat the oil in the rinsed-out and dried saucepan. Add the shallots and fry for 3–5 minutes until softened but not coloured. Add the stock and chicken. Cover and bring to the boil, then skim and stir in the fish sauce, lime juice and sugar. Reduce the heat and simmer, covered, for 10–15 minutes until the chicken is cooked through and the juices run clear when you cut a piece. Remove the chicken from the soup and set aside until cool enough to handle.

3 Cut the chicken from the bones into bite-sized pieces, return it to the soup and warm through. Adjust the salt and pepper and add extra fish sauce, lime juice or sugar, if you like. Serve with the chillies in vinegar and fried garlic on the side.

152 Cream of Chicken Soup with Tarragon & Lemon

PREPARATION TIME 15 minutes, plus making the stock   **COOKING TIME** 30 minutes

1l/35fl oz/4 cups Rich Chicken Stock
  (see page 10) or ready-made stock
500g/1lb 2oz skinless chicken thighs
4 tarragon sprigs, plus extra leaves,
  chopped, to serve
1 bay leaf
1 leek, chopped and rinsed

30g/1oz butter
1 tbsp sunflower oil
2 shallots, finely chopped
4 tbsp plain white flour
125ml/4fl oz/½ cup double cream
finely grated zest of 1 lemon
salt and ground white pepper

1 Put the stock and chicken in a saucepan and season with salt and white pepper.
   Cover and bring to the boil, then skim. Add the tarragon, bay leaf and leek, reduce
   the heat and simmer, covered, for 10–15 minutes until the chicken is cooked
   through and the juices run clear when you cut a piece. Remove the chicken from
   the stock and set aside until cool enough to handle. Strain the stock and set aside.

2 Melt the butter with the oil in another saucepan. Add the shallots and fry, stirring
   occasionally, for 3–5 minutes until softened but not coloured. Sprinkle in the flour
   and stir for 2 minutes, then slowly add the stock, stirring continuously to prevent
   lumps from forming. Leave to simmer while you prepare the chicken.

3 Cut the chicken from the bones into thin pieces and return it to the soup. Stir in the
   cream and lemon zest and reheat. Adjust the salt and pepper, if necessary, then
   serve sprinkled with tarragon.

153 Chicken & Purple Broccoli Soup

PREPARATION TIME 20 minutes, plus making the stock   COOKING TIME 40 minutes

1.25l/44fl oz/5 cups Chicken Stock (see page 11) or ready-made stock
1 large garlic clove, finely chopped
1 onion, grated
1 bouquet garni made with 1 piece of celery stick with its leaves, 1 bay leaf and several parsley and thyme sprigs tied together
1 red pepper, deseeded and chopped

400g/14oz/2⅔ cups frozen sweetcorn kernels
400g/14oz boneless, skinless chicken breasts, thinly sliced
175g/6oz purple sprouting broccoli, or ordinary broccoli, cut into bite-sized pieces
2 tbsp chopped mixed herbs, such as chives, dill, parsley and/or tarragon
salt and freshly ground black pepper

1 Put the stock, garlic, onion and bouquet garni in a saucepan, cover and bring to just below the boil. Reduce the heat and simmer for 10 minutes. Add the red pepper and sweetcorn kernels and simmer, covered, for 3 minutes, then stir in the chicken and season with salt and pepper. Simmer, covered, for 5 minutes, then add the broccoli and simmer, uncovered, for 5 minutes. Discard the bouquet garni.

2 Stir in the herbs and simmer for 3–5 minutes until the chicken is cooked through and the broccoli is tender. Adjust the salt and pepper, if necessary, and serve.

154 Chicken & Pumpkin Broth

PREPARATION TIME 15 minutes, plus making the stock   COOKING TIME 35 minutes

1.4l/48fl oz/5½ cups Chicken Stock (see page 11) or ready-made stock
6 garlic cloves, peeled but left whole
1 bouquet garni made with 1 piece of celery stick with its leaves, 1 bay leaf and several parsley and thyme sprigs tied together

500g/1lb 2oz skinless chicken pieces, such as drumsticks and thighs
250g/9oz pumpkin, peeled, deseeded and diced
55g/2oz green beans, chopped
55g/2oz/heaped ⅓ cup frozen peas
2 tbsp chopped parsley leaves
salt and freshly ground black pepper

1 Put the stock, garlic and bouquet garni in a saucepan. Cover and bring to the boil. Boil for 10 minutes, then reduce the heat to medium, add the chicken and season with salt and pepper. Cover and return to the boil, then skim. Add the pumpkin, reduce the heat and simmer, covered, for 10 minutes.

2 Add the beans and peas and simmer for 5–8 minutes until the vegetables are tender, and the chicken is cooked through and the juices run clear when you cut a piece. Remove the chicken from the soup and set aside until cool enough to handle. Discard the bouquet garni and garlic.

3 Cut the chicken from the bones into bite-sized pieces and return it to the soup. Stir in the parsley and adjust the salt and pepper, if necessary, then serve.

155 Chicken, Leek & Tarragon Soup

PREPARATION TIME 10 minutes, plus making the stock   COOKING TIME 30 minutes

1½ tbsp olive or hemp oil
280g/10oz leeks, halved lengthways, sliced and rinsed
500g/1lb 2oz skinless chicken thighs

1.25l/44fl oz/5 cups Chicken Stock (see page 11) or ready-made stock
1½ tbsp chopped tarragon leaves
salt and freshly ground black pepper

1 Heat the oil in a saucepan over a medium heat. Stir in the leeks, reduce the heat to low and cook, covered, for 8–10 minutes until tender. Add the chicken and stock and season with salt and pepper. Cover and bring to the boil, then skim and reduce the heat to low. Stir in the tarragon and simmer, covered, for 12–15 minutes until the chicken is cooked through and the juices run clear when you cut a piece. Remove the chicken from the soup and set aside until cool enough to handle.

2 Cut the chicken from the bones into bite-sized pieces, return it to the soup and heat through. Adjust the salt and pepper, if necessary, then serve.

156 Chicken & Sweetcorn Soup

PREPARATION TIME 10 minutes, plus making the stock   **COOKING TIME** 25 minutes

2 tbsp arrowroot
1l/35fl oz/4 cups Rich Chicken Stock
   (see page 10) or ready-made stock
400g/14oz boneless, skinless
   chicken breasts
400g/14oz tinned creamed sweetcorn

½ tsp caster sugar
1 egg, beaten
salt and freshly ground black pepper
2 spring onions, finely chopped,
   to serve

1   Put the arrowroot and 3 tablespoons cold water in a small heatproof bowl and mix until smooth, then set aside.
2   Put the stock and chicken in a saucepan and season with salt and pepper. Cover and bring to the boil, then reduce the heat and simmer for 10–12 minutes until the chicken is cooked through and the juices run clear when you cut a piece. Remove the chicken from the stock and set aside until cool enough to handle.
3   Add the sweetcorn and sugar to the pan. Stir a ladleful of the hot stock into the arrowroot mixture, then stir this mixture into the pan. Return to the boil, then boil for 2–3 minutes until the soup thickens slightly.
4   Meanwhile, shred the chicken, return it to the soup and reduce the heat to low. Slowly add the egg, stirring quickly with a fork until it sets in small pieces – the quicker you stir, the finer the pieces will be. Adjust the salt and pepper, if necessary, then serve sprinkled with the spring onions. If you reheat the soup, do not boil it or the eggs will scramble.

157 Thai Green Curry Chicken & Bean Soup

PREPARATION TIME 15 minutes   COOKING TIME 40 minutes

2 tbsp sunflower oil
1 tbsp green curry paste
250g/9oz skinless chicken thighs
1 tbsp fish sauce
225g/8oz green beans, chopped
1 spring onion, chopped

lime juice, to taste (optional)
palm sugar or soft light brown sugar,
   to taste
Thai basil leaves, shredded, to serve
lime wedges, to serve

1 Measure 1.25l/44fl oz/5 cups water and set aside. Heat the oil in a large wok with a lid over a high heat. Add the curry paste, reduce the heat and stir for 2 minutes. Slowly add 250ml/9fl oz/1 cup of the water and stir until the fat forms bubbles.
2 Add the chicken and fry, turning occasionally, for 5 minutes, stirring in a little more of the measured water if the paste looks like it will burn. Add the remaining water and the fish sauce and bring to the boil, then simmer, covered, for 10 minutes. Add the beans and spring onion and simmer, uncovered, for 5–10 minutes until the chicken is cooked through. Remove the chicken and set aside.
3 Cut the chicken into bite-sized pieces and return it to the soup. Stir in the lime juice and/or palm sugar to temper the heat of the curry paste, if you like. Serve sprinkled with Thai basil and with lime wedges for squeezing over.

158 Chicken & Spring Vegetable Soup

PREPARATION TIME 15 minutes, plus making the stock and cooking the chicken
COOKING TIME 25 minutes

1 tbsp butter
1 tbsp garlic-flavoured olive oil
2 celery sticks, finely chopped
1 onion, very finely chopped
1l/35fl oz/4 cups Vegetable Stock
   (see page 12) or ready-made stock
5 new potatoes, diced
55g/2oz asparagus tips
55g/2oz shelled broad beans

55g/2oz/⅓ cup frozen peas
400g/14oz boneless, skinless
   cooked chicken
1 tbsp finely chopped mint leaves
1 tbsp finely chopped parsley leaves
salt and freshly ground black pepper
pesto, to serve
freshly grated Parmesan cheese,
   to serve

1 Melt the butter with the oil in a saucepan over a medium heat. Add the celery and onion and fry, stirring occasionally, for 3–5 minutes until the onion is softened. Add the stock and potatoes and season with salt and pepper. Cover and bring to the boil, then reduce the heat and simmer for 10 minutes. Add the asparagus, beans and peas and simmer for 2–3 minutes until the vegetables are tender.
2 Stir in the chicken and warm through. Add the mint and parsley and adjust the salt and pepper, if necessary. Serve topped with pesto and Parmesan cheese.

159 Chicken & Asian Mushroom Soup

PREPARATION TIME 15 minutes, plus making the stock   COOKING TIME 45 minutes

1.4l/48fl oz/5½ cups Chicken Stock
   (see page 11) or ready-made stock
400g/14oz honshimeji or shiitake
   mushrooms, stalks removed and
   reserved and caps thinly sliced
4 tbsp chopped root ginger,
2 large garlic cloves, chopped

2 star anise
1 thin slice of galangal, smashed
400g/14oz boneless, skinless chicken,
   thinly sliced
light soy sauce, to taste
2 spring onions, sliced, to serve
toasted sesame oil, to serve

1 Put the stock, mushroom stalks, ginger, garlic, star anise and galangal in a saucepan, cover and bring to the boil. Reduce the heat and simmer for 30 minutes, then strain the stock and return it to the pan. Return to the boil.
2 Add the chicken and mushroom caps and simmer for 4–5 minutes until the chicken is cooked through. Season with soy sauce.
3 Serve topped with the spring onions and drizzled with sesame oil.

160 Courgette & Pea Chicken Soup

PREPARATION TIME 15 minutes, plus cooking the chicken and making the stock and shallots   COOKING TIME 25 minutes

1½ tbsp olive or hemp oil
1 carrot, peeled and sliced
1 celery stick, thinly sliced
1 onion, finely chopped
670ml/23fl oz/2⅔ cups passata
625ml/21½fl oz/2½ cups
   Chicken Stock (see page 10)
   or ready-made stock

1 courgette, sliced
1 tsp dried thyme leaves
½ tsp caster sugar
400g/14oz cooked chicken, shredded
85g/3oz/½ cup frozen peas
salt and freshly ground black pepper
Crisp-Fried Shallots (see page 15),
   to serve

1 Heat the oil in a saucepan over a medium heat. Add the carrot, celery and onion and fry, stirring, for 3–5 minutes until the onion is softened. Add the passata and stock and season with salt and pepper. Cover and bring to the boil, then stir in the courgettes, thyme and sugar. Reduce the heat and simmer, covered, for 5 minutes.

2 Add the chicken and peas and simmer, uncovered, for 3–5 minutes until the peas are tender. Adjust the salt and pepper, if necessary, and serve with the shallots.

161 Sunday Night Chicken & Ham Soup

PREPARATION TIME 15 minutes, plus making the stock and cooking the chicken
COOKING TIME 35 minutes

1.4l/44fl oz/5½ cups Chicken Stock
   (see page 11) or ready-made stock
1 bouquet garni made with 1 bay leaf
   and several parsley and thyme
   sprigs tied together
100g/3½oz/½ cup long-grain rice

4 garlic cloves, halved
4 sun-dried tomatoes in oil, chopped
200g/7oz cooked chicken, diced
200g/7oz cooked ham, diced
salt and freshly ground black pepper

1 Put the stock, bouquet garni, rice, garlic and sun-dried tomatoes in a saucepan and season with salt and pepper. Cover and bring to the boil, then skim.

2 Reduce the heat to low. Simmer, covered, for 10–15 minutes until the rice is tender. Add the chicken and ham and heat through. Discard the bouquet garni and garlic and adjust the salt and pepper, if necessary, and serve.

162 Colombian Chicken & Corn Soup

PREPARATION TIME 15 minutes, plus making the stock   COOKING TIME 40 minutes

1½ tbsp sunflower oil
1 large onion, finely chopped
2 tsp dried oregano
500g/1lb 2oz skinless chicken thighs
1.25l/44fl oz/5 cups Chicken Stock
   (see page 11) or ready-made stock
1 floury potato, peeled and grated
1 waxy potato, peeled and diced

3 sweetcorn cobs, husked and each
   cut into 2 or 3 pieces
salt and freshly ground black pepper
2 avocados, to serve
1 tbsp lemon juice, to serve
chopped coriander leaves, to serve
3 tbsp capers, rinsed, to serve
double cream, to serve

1 Heat the oil in a saucepan over a medium heat. Add the onion and fry, stirring, for 3–5 minutes until softened. Stir in the oregano, chicken, stock and grated potato and season with salt and pepper. Cover and bring to the boil, then reduce the heat and simmer for 10–15 minutes until the chicken is cooked through. Remove the chicken from the pan and set aside until cool enough to handle.

2 Add the diced potato and sweetcorn to the pan, cover and return to the boil. Reduce the heat and simmer for 10–12 minutes until the vegetables are tender.

3 Meanwhile, peel, deseed and chop the avocados and toss with the lemon juice, then set aside. Cut the chicken into bite-sized pieces, return it to the soup and heat through. Adjust the salt and pepper, if necessary. Divide the sweetcorn pieces into bowls and ladle the soup over them. Serve sprinkled with coriander and with the avocado, capers and cream on the side.

163 Chicken Mulligatawny Soup

PREPARATION TIME 20 minutes, plus making the stock and cooking the chicken and rice (optional) **COOKING TIME** 35 minutes

1 tbsp groundnut or sunflower oil
1 apple, peeled, cored and chopped
1 carrot, peeled and chopped
1 celery stick, thinly sliced
1 onion, finely chopped
1 green or red pepper, deseeded
  and chopped
1 tbsp plain white or wholemeal flour
1 tsp curry powder
½ tsp mustard powder

1.25l/44fl oz/5 cups Rich
  Chicken Stock (see page 10)
  or ready-made stock
400g/14oz boneless, skinless cooked
  chicken, cut into bite-sized pieces
salt and freshly ground black pepper
cooked white or brown basmati rice,
  hot, to serve (optional)
chopped coriander or parsley leaves,
  to serve

1   Heat the oil in a saucepan over a medium heat. Add the apple, carrot, celery, onion and pepper and fry, stirring occasionally, for 3–5 minutes until the vegetables are softened. Sprinkle in the flour, curry powder and mustard and stir for 2 minutes. Slowly add the stock, stirring continuously to prevent lumps from forming.
2   Season with salt and pepper, cover and bring to the boil. Reduce the heat and simmer for 20 minutes until the apple breaks down, the vegetables are tender and the soup has thickened slightly. Add the chicken and heat through, then adjust the salt and pepper, if necessary.
3   Put a portion of hot rice, if using, in each bowl. Ladle the soup over it, sprinkle with coriander and serve.

164 Roast Chicken Soup

PREPARATION TIME 10 minutes, plus making the stock and roasting the chicken
COOKING TIME 30 minutes

1 tbsp olive or hemp oil
2 carrots, peeled and diced
1 leek, halved lengthways, thinly
   sliced and rinsed
1.25l/44fl oz/5 cups Chicken Stock
   (see page 11) or ready-made stock
1 bay leaf

2 tbsp chicken gravy (optional)
85g/3oz/heaped ½ cup frozen
   sweetcorn kernels
400g/14oz boneless, skinless roast
   chicken, cut into bite-sized pieces
salt and freshly ground black pepper

1 Heat the oil in a saucepan over a medium heat. Add the carrot and leek and fry, stirring occasionally, for 3–5 minutes until the leek is softened but not coloured. Stir in the stock, bay leaf and gravy, if using, and season with salt and pepper, then cover and bring to the boil. Reduce the heat to low, add the sweetcorn and simmer, covered, for 10–15 minutes until the carrots are tender.
2 Stir in the chicken and simmer for 3–5 minutes to warm through. Discard the bay leaf, adjust the salt and pepper, if necessary, and serve.

165 Chicken & Barley Soup

PREPARATION TIME 20 minutes, plus making the stock and cooking the chicken
COOKING TIME 50 minutes

1 tbsp sunflower oil
1 celery stick, chopped
1 onion, finely chopped
2 garlic cloves, finely chopped
½ tsp turmeric
1.25l/44fl oz/5 cups Chicken Stock
   (see page 11) or ready-made stock
55g/2oz/¼ cup pearl barley
2 bay leaves

250g/9oz mixed root vegetables,
   such as carrot, potato, sweet
   potato, swede and turnip,
   or pumpkin, peeled and diced
400g/14oz boneless, skinless cooked
   chicken, diced
1 courgette, coarsely grated
salt and freshly ground black pepper
chopped parsley leaves, to serve

1 Heat the oil in a saucepan over a medium heat. Add the celery and onion and fry, stirring occasionally, for 2 minutes. Stir in the garlic and fry for 1–3 minutes until the onion is softened but not coloured. Stir in the turmeric, then add the stock and season with salt and pepper. Cover and bring to the boil. Skim, then stir in the barley and bay leaves, cover and return to the boil.
2 Reduce the heat and simmer for 20 minutes. Stir in the vegetables and simmer for another 10–20 minutes until the barley is tender. Stir in the chicken and courgette and warm through. Discard the bay leaves and adjust the salt and pepper, if necessary, then serve sprinkled with parsley.

166 Soothing Lemon Thyme & Garlic Broth

PREPARATION TIME 5 minutes, plus at least 15 minutes infusing and making the stock
COOKING TIME 15 minutes

1.5l/52fl oz/6 cups Rich Chicken Stock
   (see page 10) or ready-made stock
8 large garlic cloves, sliced

1 bunch of lemon thyme, about
   30g/1oz, tied together
salt and freshly ground black pepper
   (optional)

1 Put the stock, garlic and lemon thyme in a saucepan, cover and bring to the boil. Uncover and boil for 5 minutes to reduce slightly, then turn off the heat, cover and leave to infuse for at least 15 minutes, or up to several hours, depending on how strongly flavoured you want the soup.
2 Strain the soup, then return it to the pan and reheat. Season with salt and pepper, if you like, but it should be well flavoured as it is, then serve.

167 Greek Lemon & Egg Soup With Orzo

PREPARATION TIME 5 minutes, plus making the stock   COOKING TIME 25 minutes

1.25l/44fl oz/5 cups Chicken Stock
  (see page 11) or ready-made stock
½ tsp salt, plus extra to season
115g/4oz/heaped ½ cup orzo

2 eggs
6 tbsp lemon juice
freshly ground black pepper
chopped parsley leaves, to serve

1   Put the stock and salt in a saucepan, cover and bring to the boil. Stir in the orzo and
    boil for 15–17 minutes, or according to the packet instructions, stirring frequently,
    until tender, then reduce the heat to low.
2   Beat the eggs and lemon juice in a heatproof bowl with a ladleful of the hot stock.
    Remove the pan from the heat and whisk the egg mixture into the soup. Season
    with salt and pepper and serve sprinkled with parsley. If you reheat the soup,
    do not boil it or the eggs will scramble.

168 Chicken Liver & Sweet Onion Soup

PREPARATION TIME 15 minutes, plus making the stock   COOKING TIME 35 minutes

1 tbsp butter
3 tbsp olive or hemp oil
2 large onions, finely chopped
1 tsp caster sugar
200g/7oz chicken livers, trimmed and
  patted dry

1 sage sprig
1.25l/44fl oz/5 cups Chicken Stock
  (see page 11) or ready-made stock
55g/2oz/½ cup small pasta shapes
2 tbsp chopped parsley leaves
salt and freshly ground black pepper

1   Melt the butter with half the oil in a saucepan over a medium heat. Add the onions
    and fry, stirring, for 3–5 minutes until softened. Reduce the heat to very low
    (use a heat diffuser if you have one), stir in the sugar and fry, stirring frequently,
    for 10–15 minutes until the onions are caramelized. Remove them and set aside.
2   Heat the remaining oil with the fat remaining in the pan over a medium heat.
    Add the chicken livers and fry, stirring, for 3–5 minutes until cooked through and
    firm. Remove the chicken livers from the pan and chop.
3   Put the sage and stock in the rinsed-out saucepan and season with salt and pepper.
    Cover and bring to the boil. Add the pasta and boil, uncovered, for 4–6 minutes,
    or according to the packet instructions, until al dente. Discard the sage and add
    the livers, onions and parsley. Warm through, adjust the salt and pepper,
    if necessary, and serve.

169 Chinese Egg-Drop Soup

PREPARATION TIME 10 minutes, plus making the stock   COOKING TIME 25 minutes

1.4l/48fl oz/5½ cups Chicken Stock
  (see page 11) or ready-made stock
5cm/2in piece of root ginger, sliced
3 spring onions, chopped
1 thin slice of galangal, crushed
1 tbsp light soy sauce

2 tbsp arrowroot
2 eggs
1½ tsp toasted sesame oil
salt and ground white pepper
chopped chives, to serve

1   Put the stock, ginger, spring onions and galangal in a saucepan, cover and bring
    to the boil. Boil for 10 minutes to reduce slightly, then strain the stock and return
    it to the pan. Add the soy sauce, cover and return to the boil. Put the arrowroot and
    3 tablespoons cold water in a small heatproof bowl and mix until smooth.
2   Stir a ladleful of the hot stock into the arrowroot mixture. Reduce the heat to low,
    then stir the arrowroot mixture into the pan and simmer for 2–3 minutes until the
    soup thickens slightly. Season with salt and white pepper.
3   Meanwhile, beat the eggs and sesame oil together in a small bowl until blended
    but not frothy. Remove the soup from the heat and pour the egg mixture
    in a steady stream into the centre with one hand while beating continuously
    in a circular motion with a chopstick or fork in the other hand until long, thin strands
    of egg form. Serve immediately, sprinkled with chives.

170 Roasted Pepper, Garlic & Egg Soup

PREPARATION TIME 10 minutes, plus making the stock and croûtes
COOKING TIME 15 minutes

6 tbsp fruity extra-virgin olive oil,
  plus extra for drizzling
1 large garlic bulb, cloves peeled and
  smashed in one piece
1.5l/52fl oz/6 cups Rich Chicken Stock
  (see page 10) or ready-made stock
2 roasted peppers in olive oil,
  drained and chopped

a pinch of saffron threads
a pinch of smoked or sweet paprika
1 recipe quantity Croûtes
  (see page 14)
1 egg for each bowl, at room
  temperature
salt and freshly ground black pepper
chopped parsley leaves, to serve

1   Heat the oil in a saucepan over a medium heat. Add the garlic, reduce the heat
    to low and stir for 30 seconds just until golden brown. Watch closely so it doesn't
    burn. Immediately add the stock, cover and bring to the boil. Skim, if necessary,
    then stir in the peppers, saffron and paprika and season with salt and pepper.
    Boil for 5 minutes until reduced slightly.
2   Put 1 croûte in each bowl and drizzle generously with oil. Gently crack 1 egg over
    each croûte, taking care not to break the yolks.
3   Divide the peppers into the bowls, then ladle the boiling soup over them. At this
    point you can either let the stock lightly poach the eggs or beat each egg with
    a fork so it lightly scrambles. Sprinkle with parsley and serve.

171 Chicken & Parsley Dumpling Soup

PREPARATION TIME 10 minutes, plus making the stock and dumplings
COOKING TIME 45 minutes

1.4l/48fl oz/5½ cups Chicken Stock
  (see page 11) or ready-made stock
2 garlic cloves, halved
1 leek, thinly sliced and rinsed
400g/14oz boneless, skinless chicken
  thighs, cut into thin strips

140g/5oz/scant 1 cup frozen peas
1 recipe quantity Parsley Dumplings
  (see page 13)
salt and freshly ground black pepper
chopped parsley leaves, to serve

1   Put the stock, garlic and leek in a saucepan over a high heat. Cover and bring to just
    below the boil. Reduce the heat and simmer for 20 minutes. Strain the stock.
2   Discard the garlic. Return the soup to the pan, add the chicken and peas and
    season with salt and pepper. Bring the soup to just below the boil. Skim, then
    reduce the heat and simmer, covered, for 10–12 minutes until the chicken
    is cooked through. Add the dumplings and simmer to reheat.
3   Adjust the salt and pepper, if necessary, then serve sprinkled with parsley.

172 Chicken & Leek Broth

PREPARATION TIME 5 minutes, plus making the stock   COOKING TIME 25 minutes

1 tbsp garlic-flavoured olive oil
2 leeks, thinly sliced and rinsed
1.25l/44fl oz/5 cups Rich
  Chicken Stock (see page 10)
  or ready-made stock

500g/1lb 2oz skinless chicken thighs
1 large bay leaf, torn
salt and freshly ground black pepper
chopped chives, to serve

1   Heat the oil in a saucepan over a medium heat. Add the leeks and fry, stirring,
    for 2 minutes. Add the garlic and fry for 1–3 minutes until the leeks are softened.
2   Add the stock and chicken. Cover and bring to the boil. Skim, then add the bay leaf
    and season with salt and pepper. Reduce the heat and simmer, covered,
    for 10–15 minutes until the chicken is cooked through. Remove the chicken from
    the pan and set aside until cool enough to handle.
3   Cut the chicken from the bones into bite-sized pieces, return it to the soup and
    reheat. Remove the bay leaf and adjust the salt and pepper, if necessary. Serve
    sprinkled with the chives.

173 Roman Egg Soup

PREPARATION TIME 5 minutes, plus making the stock   **COOKING TIME** 10 minutes

1.25l/44fl oz/5 cups Chicken Stock
(see page 11) or ready-made stock
2 eggs
100g/3½oz freshly grated
Parmesan cheese

2 tbsp very finely chopped
parsley leaves
2 tbsp lemon juice
salt and freshly ground black pepper

1   Bring the stock to just below the boil in a large saucepan over a high heat, then
reduce the heat to low.
2   Beat the eggs, Parmesan cheese and parsley together in a bowl. Slowly pour this
mixture into the simmering stock, whisking continuously and quickly with a fork
until the eggs set in small pieces – the quicker you whisk the finer the pieces will
be. Stir in the lemon juice, season with salt and pepper and serve immediately.
If you reheat the soup, do not boil it or the eggs will scramble.

174 Mexican Poultry & Avocado Broth

PREPARATION TIME 20 minutes, plus making the stock and preparing the tomato
COOKING TIME 30 minutes

1.4l/48fl oz/5½ cups Chicken Stock
(see page 11) or ready-made stock
4 garlic cloves, finely chopped
2 jalapeño chillies, deseeded
(optional) and sliced
400g/14oz boneless, skinless chicken
or turkey breasts, thinly sliced

1 large tomato, peeled (see page 9),
deseeded and diced
1 avocado
½ tbsp lime juice, plus extra to taste
salt and freshly ground black pepper
shredded coriander leaves, to serve
hot pepper sauce, to serve
tortilla chips, to serve

1   Put the stock, garlic and chillies in a saucepan, cover and bring to the boil. Boil for
10 minutes, then add the chicken and season with salt and pepper. Cover and
return to the boil. Skim, then reduce the heat and simmer for 10–12 minutes until
the chicken is cooked through and the juices run clear when you cut a piece.
2   Meanwhile, peel the avocado, discard the stone and chop. Put the flesh in a bowl,
toss with the lime juice and divide it into serving bowls, then set aside.
3   Stir the tomato into the soup and warm through. Taste and add a little lime juice,
if you like. Adjust the salt and pepper, if necessary, then ladle the soup over the
avocado and sprinkle with coriander. Serve with hot pepper sauce and tortilla chips.

175 Turkey & Orzo Soup

PREPARATION TIME 15 minutes, plus making the stock and cooking the turkey
COOKING TIME 30 minutes

1½ tbsp garlic-flavoured olive oil
1 red onion, finely chopped
1 carrot, peeled and finely chopped
1.25l/44fl oz/5 cups Turkey Stock
(see page 11) or ready-made stock
140g/5oz/scant ⅔ cup orzo

125g/4½oz spinach leaves, chopped
100g/3½oz boneless, skinless cooked
turkey, diced
salt and freshly ground black pepper
chopped parsley leaves, to serve

1   Heat the oil in a saucepan over a medium heat. Add the onion and fry, stirring
occasionally, for 3–5 minutes until softened but not coloured. Stir in the carrot,
then add the stock and season with salt and pepper. Cover and bring to the boil.
2   Add the orzo. Boil, uncovered, for 15–17 minutes, or according to the packet
instructions, until tender. Two minutes before the end of this cooking time, stir in
the spinach and turkey and warm through. Adjust the salt and pepper, if necessary,
then serve sprinkled with parsley.

176 Goji Berry & Garlic Flu Buster

PREPARATION TIME 15 minutes, plus making the stock   **COOKING TIME** 35 minutes

1.5l/52fl oz/6 cups Rich Chicken Stock
(see page 10) or Chicken Stock
(see page 11)
1 large garlic bulb, separated into
cloves
2 leeks, halved lengthways, sliced
and rinsed
1cm/½in piece of root ginger, peeled
and grated

a pinch of chilli flakes, or to taste
grated zest of 1 lemon
2 tbsp medium rolled oats
1 tbsp clear honey
2–4 tbsp lemon juice
2 tbsp dried goji berries
1 large handful of watercress leaves,
slightly torn
chopped chives, to serve

1   Put the stock and garlic in a saucepan, cover and bring to the boil. Boil for
15 minutes until the garlic is very tender. Use a fork to mash the garlic against the
sides of the pan, then stir in the leeks, ginger, chilli flakes, lemon zest and oats.
Reduce the heat and simmer, covered, for 8–10 minutes until thickened slightly
and the oats are tender.

2   Stir in the honey and 1 tablespoon of the lemon juice, then add the remaining
juice to taste. Stir in the goji berries and watercress and simmer, uncovered,
for 1 minute until the berries are softened. Serve sprinkled with chives.

177 Turkey & Rice Soup

PREPARATION TIME 10 minutes, plus making the stock and cooking the turkey
COOKING TIME 35 minutes

1.4l/48fl oz/5½ cups Turkey Stock
 (see page 11) or ready-made stock
2 celery sticks, halved
a pinch of chilli flakes, or to taste
85g/3oz/heaped ⅓ cup long-grain
 white rice
100g/3½oz/⅔ cup frozen
 sweetcorn kernels

140g/5oz savoy cabbage, cored
 and shredded
200g/7oz boneless, skinless cooked
 turkey, diced
1 roasted red pepper in olive oil,
 drained and finely chopped
2 tbsp chopped parsley leaves
salt and freshly ground black pepper

1 Put the stock, celery and chilli flakes in a saucepan and season with salt and
   pepper. Cover, bring to the boil and boil for 10 minutes, then discard the celery.
2 Cover and return the stock to the boil. Add the rice and boil, uncovered,
   for 10 minutes. Stir in the sweetcorn and cabbage and continue boiling for
   5 minutes until the rice is tender. Stir in the turkey, red pepper and parsley and
   warm through. Adjust the salt and pepper, if necessary, and serve.

178 Turkey Meatball & Rice Soup

PREPARATION TIME 30 minutes, plus 30 minutes chilling and making the stock
COOKING TIME 50 minutes

85g/3oz/heaped ⅓ cup basmati rice,
 rinsed until the water runs clear
400g/14oz minced turkey thigh meat
2 shallots, very finely chopped
2 tbsp finely chopped parsley leaves
2 tsp dried thyme leaves
½ tsp ground coriander
½ tsp ground cumin
finely grated zest of 1 lemon
a pinch of cayenne pepper
1 tbsp olive or hemp oil

1 onion, quartered and thinly sliced
1.75l/60fl oz/6⅔ cups Vegetable Stock
 (see page 12) or ready-made stock,
 plus extra as needed
1 leek, halved lengthways, sliced
 and rinsed
½ tbsp dried mint leaves
¼ tsp turmeric
salt and freshly ground black pepper
chopped coriander leaves, to serve

1 Put the rice in a bowl, cover with water and leave to soak until required.
2 Put the turkey, shallots, parsley, thyme, ground coriander, cumin, lemon zest and
   cayenne pepper in a bowl. Season with salt and pepper and mix well with wet
   hands. (Fry a small piece, then taste to test the seasoning, if you like.) Divide the
   mixture into 36 equal portions and roll into meatballs. Put them on a plate, cover
   with cling film and chill for at least 30 minutes. (The meatballs can be made
   up to a day ahead.)
3 Heat the oil in a saucepan over a medium heat. Add the onion, reduce the heat
   to low and cook, covered, for 8–10 minutes, stirring occasionally, until the onion
   turns golden brown. Watch closely so it does not burn. Add half the stock and
   bring to a slow boil. Working in batches, if necessary, gently boil the meatballs
   for 2 minutes. Skim, then add the remaining stock.
4 Drain the rice and add it to the soup, along with the leek, mint and turmeric.
   Season with salt and pepper, then cover and bring to the boil. Uncover and boil for
   20–25 minutes until the rice is tender. If too much stock evaporates, stir in a little
   extra stock or water. Adjust the salt and pepper, if necessary, and serve sprinkled
   with coriander leaves.

179 Onion, Tomato & Chicken Soup

PREPARATION TIME 10 minutes, plus making the stock and croûtes and cooking the chicken **COOKING TIME** 1¼ hours

3 tbsp olive or hemp oil
55g/2oz unsmoked lardons
650g/1lb 7oz onions, thinly sliced
875ml/30fl oz/3½ cups Chicken Stock (see page 11) or ready-made stock
400g/14oz tinned chopped tomatoes
1 red chilli, deseeded (optional) and chopped

85g/3oz boneless, skinless cooked chicken, thinly sliced
salt and freshly ground black pepper
1 recipe quantity Garlic Croûtes (see page 14), to serve
basil leaves, torn, to serve
freshly grated Parmesan cheese, to serve

1 Heat the oil in a saucepan over a medium heat. Add the lardons and fry for 3–5 minutes until they are beginning to crisp but are not browned. Stir in the onions, reduce the heat to very low (use a heat diffuser if you have one) and cook for 45 minutes, stirring occasionally, until the onions are very soft. Watch closely so they do not brown.
2 Add the stock, tomatoes and chilli and season with salt and pepper. Cover and bring to the boil, then reduce the heat and simmer for 20 minutes until the flavours are blended. Add the chicken and warm through. Adjust the salt and pepper, if necessary.
3 Divide the croûtes into bowls and ladle the soup over them. Sprinkle with basil leaves and serve with Parmesan cheese on the side.

180 Duck in Ginger Broth

PREPARATION TIME 25 minutes **COOKING TIME** 1¼ hours

7.5cm/3in piece of root ginger, peeled and sliced
4 coriander sprigs, roots and stalks coarsely chopped, with the leaves reserved to serve
2 carrots, peeled and thickly sliced, plus an extra ½ carrot, peeled and cut into matchsticks
2 large garlic cloves, chopped
2 star anise
1 large onion, unpeeled and halved

1 large leek, half thickly sliced and rinsed, and the rest cut into matchsticks and rinsed
400g/14oz boneless, skinless duck breasts
4 shiitake mushroom caps, thinly sliced
2 Chinese cabbage leaves, rolled and thinly sliced
2 spring onions, sliced on the diagonal
light soy sauce, to taste

1 Put the ginger, coriander, sliced carrots, garlic, star anise, onion, sliced leek and 1.5l/52fl oz/6 cups water in a large saucepan. Cover and bring to the boil, then boil, uncovered, for 10 minutes to reduce slightly.
2 Reduce the heat to low. Add the duck and slowly return the liquid to just below the boil, skimming as necessary. Just before the liquid boils, reduce the heat to very low (use a heat diffuser if you have one) and simmer, covered, for 40–45 minutes until the duck is very tender. Remove the duck from the soup and set aside until cool enough to handle.
3 Strain the stock into a bowl and discard the flavourings. Return the stock to the washed pan, cover and return to the boil. Thinly slice the duck and set aside.
4 Reduce the heat to a simmer, then add the carrot and leek matchsticks, mushrooms, cabbage and spring onions and simmer for 5–8 minutes until they are all tender. Return the duck to the pan and reheat. Season with soy sauce and serve sprinkled with coriander leaves.

181 Jerusalem Artichoke Soup with Duck Confit

PREPARATION TIME 20 minutes **COOKING TIME** 50 minutes

800g/1lb 12oz Jerusalem artichokes,
  unpeeled but well scrubbed
3 lemon slices
30g/1oz butter
1 large onion, finely chopped
500ml/17fl oz/2 cups whole milk
400g/14oz duck confit, skin and
  bones removed and meat finely
  shredded, with a little of the
  surrounding fat reserved

150ml/5fl oz/scant ⅔ cup single
  cream
1½ tbsp lemon juice
salt and ground white pepper
finely shredded watercress leaves,
  to serve

1   Put the artichokes, lemon slices and 750ml/26fl oz/3 cups water in a saucepan,
    adding extra water, if needed to cover the artichokes. Cover and bring to the boil,
    then reduce the heat and simmer for 20–25 minutes until the artichokes are tender
    but still holding their shape. Drain, reserving 600ml/21fl oz/scant 2½ cups of the
    cooking liquid, and set the artichokes aside until cool enough to handle.
2   Use your fingers to peel the artichokes, then mash them with a fork and set aside.
3   Melt the butter in the washed and dried pan over a medium heat. Add the onion and
    fry, stirring occasionally, for 3–5 minutes until softened. Stir in the artichokes, milk
    and reserved cooking liquid and season with salt and white pepper. Cover and bring
    to just below the boil, then reduce the heat and simmer for 5 minutes. Meanwhile,
    heat the duck with a little of its fat in a small frying pan over medium heat.
4   Blend the soup until smooth and reheat, if necessary. Stir in the cream and
    1 tablespoon of the lemon juice, then adjust the salt and pepper and add extra lemon
    juice, if necessary. Serve sprinkled with watercress and topped with the duck confit.

CHAPTER 4

SEAFOOD SOUPS

Seafood soups can range from simple to extravagant, but they all have an essential common feature: for optimum results they must be made with the freshest, best-quality fish and shellfish.

This chapter contains recipes for many familiar fish – cod, haddock, monkfish and salmon – but also includes soups using some of the lesser-known varieties that can help promote seafood sustainability. Recipes like Hake & Mixed Herb Soup, Pollock Quenelle Soup and Tilapia & Coriander Soup satisfy your palate as well as your conscience and your budget. For an even more purse-friendly treat, try Prawn Bisque. If you plan ahead and remember to freeze the prawn shells and heads from other recipes, this rich, sophisticated soup is almost free to make.

Here, too, you will find a selection of delicious seafood recipes from around the world, from creamy North American soup-stews, such as the ever popular New England and Manhattan clam chowders, to Irish Oyster Soup, Scandinavian Salmon & Prawn Soup and ultra-stylish Japanese Scallop Soup.

NEW ENGLAND CLAM CHOWDER (SEE PAGE 114)

182 New England Clam Chowder

PREPARATION TIME 20 minutes   COOKING TIME 45 minutes

55g/2oz unsmoked streaky bacon, rinds removed, if necessary, and diced
30g/1oz butter
2 celery sticks, finely chopped
2 onions, finely chopped
1 tbsp plain white flour
625ml/21½fl oz/2½ cups whole milk

400g/14oz floury potatoes, peeled and diced
48 live littleneck clams, rinsed and soaked in cold water to cover
2 tsp dried thyme leaves
625ml/21½fl oz/2½ cups single cream
salt and freshly ground black pepper
cayenne pepper, to serve
oyster crackers, to serve (optional)

1   Put the bacon in a saucepan over a high heat and fry, stirring, for 5–8 minutes until it crisps and gives off its fat. Remove it from the pan and set aside.
2   Melt the butter in the fat remaining in the pan. Stir in the celery and onions, cover, reduce the heat to low and cook for 8–10 minutes until softened but not coloured. Increase the heat to medium, sprinkle in the flour and stir for 2 minutes, then slowly add the milk, stirring continuously to prevent lumps from forming. Add the potatoes and season with salt and pepper. Bring to just below the boil, cover and simmer for 15–20 minutes until the potatoes are tender.
3   Meanwhile, discard any clams with broken shells or open ones that do not close when tapped. Shuck the clams over a bowl to catch the juices. Discard the shells and chop the clams, then stir them with the juices, thyme and bacon into the soup.
4   Cover and simmer for 1 minute. Stir in the cream and simmer for 1–2 minutes until the clams are cooked through. Adjust the salt and pepper, if necessary, then serve sprinkled with cayenne pepper and with oyster crackers on the side, if you like.

183 Manhattan Clam Chowder

PREPARATION TIME 10 minutes   COOKING TIME 40 minutes

280g/10oz tinned or bottled clams, drained and juices reserved
85g/3oz streaky bacon, rinds removed, if necessary, and diced
15g/½oz butter
2 onions, finely chopped
1 tbsp plain white or wholemeal flour
800g/1lb 12oz tinned chopped tomatoes

2 waxy potatoes, peeled and diced
1 red pepper, deseeded and diced
1 tbsp tomato purée
1 tsp caster sugar
lemon juice, to taste
salt and freshly ground black pepper
chopped parsley leaves or dill, to serve

1   Add enough water to the reserved clam juice to make 500ml/17fl oz/2 cups liquid, if necessary, then set aside.
2   Put the bacon in a saucepan over a high heat and fry, stirring, for 5–8 minutes until it crisps and gives off its fat. Remove it from the pan and set aside. Reduce the heat to medium and melt the butter with the fat remaining in the pan. Add the onions and fry, stirring occasionally, for 3–5 minutes until softened but not coloured. Sprinkle in the flour and stir for 2 minutes, then slowly add the clam liquid, stirring continuously to prevent lumps from forming.
3   Add the tomatoes, potatoes, pepper, tomato purée and sugar and season with salt and pepper. Bring to the boil, then reduce the heat and simmer, covered, for 15–20 minutes until the potatoes are tender. Stir in the clams and bacon and simmer for 2 minutes to warm through. Add lemon juice and adjust the salt and pepper, if necessary, then serve sprinkled with parsley.

184 Salt Cod Soup

PREPARATION TIME 20 minutes, plus 24 hours soaking   **COOKING TIME** 40 minutes

225g/8oz salt cod
1 bay leaf
2 lemon slices
2 leeks, thinly sliced and rinsed
2 large garlic cloves, finely chopped
1 floury potato, peeled and diced

a pinch of saffron threads
1 large roasted red pepper in olive
   oil, drained and chopped
salt and freshly ground black pepper
lemon wedges, to serve
extra-virgin olive oil, to serve

1   Put the salt cod in a bowl, cover with cold water and leave to soak for 24 hours, changing the water several times, then drain.
2   Put the cod and 625ml/21½fl oz/2½ cups water in a frying pan, cover and bring to the boil. Skim, then add the bay leaf and lemon slices. Reduce the heat and simmer, covered, for 10–15 minutes until the fish flakes easily.
3   Remove the fish from the pan and set aside. Strain the liquid through a muslin-lined sieve into a saucepan. Add the leeks, garlic, potato, saffron and another 600ml/21fl oz/ scant 2½ cups water. Cover and return to the boil, then reduce the heat and simmer for 15–18 minutes until the potatoes are starting to fall apart.
4   Meanwhile, flake the cod, discarding all skin and bones. Return it to the soup, add the roasted pepper and heat through. Adjust the salt and pepper, if necessary, but remember the cod might still be very salty. Serve with lemon wedges for squeezing over and extra-virgin olive oil for drizzling at the table.

185 Spicy Tomato & Crab Soup

PREPARATION TIME 10 minutes, plus making the stock and flavoured oil
COOKING TIME 25 minutes

800ml/28fl oz/scant 3½ cups passata
500ml/17fl oz/2 cups Fish Stock
   (see page 11) or ready-made stock
1 bay leaf
1 tbsp lemon juice
1 tbsp tomato purée
1 tsp caster sugar
finely grated zest of ½ lemon

a pinch of chilli flakes, or to taste
1 crab shell (optional; ask the
   fishmonger for this)
400g/14oz shelled white crabmeat,
   picked over and flaked
salt and freshly ground black pepper
1 recipe quantity Crushed Basil Oil
   (see page 15), to serve

1   Put the passata, stock, bay leaf, lemon juice, tomato purée, sugar, lemon zest, chilli flakes and crab shell, if using, in a saucepan and season with salt and pepper. Cover and bring to the boil, then reduce the heat and simmer for 10 minutes. Discard the bay leaf and crab shell, if used, and blend the soup until smooth.
2   Stir the crabmeat into the soup and simmer for 3 minutes until cooked through. Adjust the salt and pepper, if necessary, then serve with basil oil.

186 Smoked Eel & Kale Soup

PREPARATION TIME 15 minutes, plus making the stock   **COOKING TIME** 35 minutes

1.4l/48fl oz/5½ cups Fish Stock
   (see page 11) or ready-made stock
400g/14oz curly kale, stalks removed,
   leaves chopped and rinsed
1 leek, halved lengthways,
   thinly sliced and rinsed
1 tbsp chopped dill

1 long strip of lemon zest,
   all bitter white pith removed
a pinch of chilli flakes, or to taste
450g/1lb smoked eel or mackerel,
   skinned, boned and coarsely flaked
salt and freshly ground black pepper

1   Put the stock, kale, leek, dill, lemon zest and chilli flakes in a saucepan and season with salt and pepper. Cover and bring to the boil, then reduce the heat and simmer for 25 minutes until the kale is very tender.
2   Add the eel and warm through. Adjust the salt and pepper, if necessary, and serve.

187 Crab & Asparagus Soup

PREPARATION TIME 10 minutes, plus making the stock   **COOKING TIME** 25 minutes

2 tbsp arrowroot

1.25l/44fl oz/5 cups Chicken Stock
(see page 11) or ready-made stock

1 tbsp fish sauce

½ teaspoon salt, plus extra to season

350g/12oz asparagus, woody ends
removed and the stalks cut into
bite-sized pieces, with the tips
reserved

1 egg

175g/6oz shelled white crabmeat,
thawed if frozen, picked over
and flaked

ground white pepper

toasted sesame oil, to drizzle

1   Put the arrowroot and 2 tablespoons of the stock in a bowl and mix until smooth,
then set aside. Put the remaining stock in a saucepan over a medium heat and bring
to the simmer. Pour the arrowroot mixture into the stock, whisking continuously,
then bring to just below the boil, stirring. Stir in the fish sauce and salt, reduce
the heat and simmer for 2–3 minutes, stirring, until the soup thickens slightly.

2   Add the asparagus stalks and simmer for 3 minutes, then add the asparagus tips
and simmer for another 3–5 minutes until all the asparagus is tender but still has
a little bite. Return the soup to the boil.

3   Meanwhile, beat the egg in a heatproof bowl, add a ladleful of the hot stock and
whisk together.

4   Remove the pan from the heat and pour the egg mixture in a steady stream into
the centre of the soup with one hand while beating continuously in a circular
motion with a chopstick or fork in the other hand until long, thin strands of egg
form. Stir in the crab and cook over a very low heat for 2–3 minutes until the crab
meat is cooked through. Season with salt and white pepper and serve immediately
drizzled with sesame oil.

188 Rich Crab Soup with Dill Croûtons

PREPARATION TIME 25 minutes, plus making the stock and croûtons
COOKING TIME 35 minutes

1.4l/48fl oz/5½ cups Fish Stock
  (see page 11) or ready-made stock
6 tbsp dry white wine
1 bay leaf
crab shells (ask the fishmonger
  for these)
30g/1oz butter
½ tbsp olive or hemp oil
1 carrot, peeled and finely diced
1 celery stick, very finely chopped
1 onion, finely chopped
1 large garlic clove, finely chopped

4 tbsp plain white flour
2 tbsp tomato purée
1 tbsp chopped parsley leaves
several thyme sprigs, tied together
2 tbsp brandy
140g/5oz shelled brown crabmeat,
  thawed if frozen and picked over
250g/9oz shelled white crabmeat,
  thawed if frozen and picked over
salt and freshly ground black pepper
1 recipe quantity Dill Croûtons
  (see page 14), hot, to serve

1. Put the stock, wine, bay leaf and crab shells in a saucepan. Cover and bring to the boil. Reduce the heat and simmer for 10 minutes, then strain, set the stock aside and discard the flavourings.
2. Meanwhile, melt the butter with the oil in another saucepan. Add the carrot, celery and onion and fry, stirring occasionally, for 2 minutes. Add the garlic and fry for 1–3 minutes until the onion is softened but not coloured, then sprinkle in the flour and stir for 2 minutes. Stir in the tomato purée, parsley and thyme and season with salt and pepper. Slowly add the stock, stirring continuously to prevent lumps from forming.
3. Add the brandy, cover and return to the boil, then cook, uncovered, for 4–6 minutes. Stir in the brown crabmeat and simmer for 2 minutes. Discard the thyme sprigs. Blend the soup until smooth, then add the white crabmeat and simmer for 2–3 minutes until the crab is cooked through. Adjust the salt and pepper, if necessary, and serve sprinkled with croûtons.

189 Shellfish Chowder with Herbs

PREPARATION TIME 30 minutes   COOKING TIME 35 minutes

24 live clams or cockles, soaked
  in cold water to cover
24 live mussels, scrubbed, with
  'beards' removed and soaked
  in cold water to cover
2 garlic cloves, coarsely chopped
1 leek, sliced and rinsed
3 carrots, peeled and finely diced
2 shallots, finely chopped

280g/10oz potatoes, peeled
  and chopped
200ml/7fl oz/scant 1 cup whole milk
1 tbsp chopped chives
1 tbsp chopped parsley leaves,
  plus extra to serve
½ tbsp thyme leaves
salt and freshly ground black pepper

1. Discard any clams or mussels with broken shells or open ones that do not close when tapped. Put the clams, mussels, garlic and leek in a saucepan with at least 1l/35fl oz/4 cups water to cover over a high heat. Cook, covered, for 3–5 minutes, shaking the pan frequently, until all the shells open. Strain the cooking liquid through a muslin-lined sieve into a large bowl and set aside. Discard the flavourings. When the clams and mussels are cool enough to handle, discard any that remain closed. Remove the flesh from the shells and set aside.
2. Meanwhile, put the carrots, shallots, potatoes and 1l/35fl oz/4 cups of the reserved cooking liquid in the rinsed-out saucepan and season with salt and pepper. Cover and bring to the boil. Reduce the heat and simmer for 10–12 minutes until the vegetables are tender.
3. Add the milk, chives, parsley and thyme and simmer, covered, for 10 minutes, but do not boil. Stir in the clams and mussels and gently reheat. Adjust the salt and pepper, if necessary, then serve sprinkled with parsley. If you reheat the soup, do not boil it.

190 Smoked Haddock & Sweet Potato Chowder

PREPARATION TIME 10 minutes, plus making the stock   COOKING TIME 35 minutes

2 streaky bacon rashers, rinds
   removed and meat chopped
½ tbsp sunflower oil
1 onion, finely chopped
2 tbsp plain white flour
420ml/14½fl oz/1⅔ cups Fish Stock
   (see page 11) or ready-made stock
1 large sweet potato, peeled and
   finely diced

400g/14oz undyed smoked haddock
240ml/8fl oz/scant 1 cup whole milk
170ml/5½fl oz/⅔ cup single cream
freshly grated nutmeg, to taste
cayenne pepper, to taste
salt and ground white pepper
chopped parsley leaves, to serve

1   Put the bacon in a saucepan over a high heat and fry for 3 minutes. Remove from the pan and set aside. Add the oil and onion to the pan and fry for 3–5 minutes until the onion is softened. Sprinkle in the flour and stir for 2 minutes, then add the stock, stirring continuously.

2   Add the sweet potatoes and season with white pepper. Cover and bring to the boil, then reduce the heat and simmer for 3–5 minutes until the potato is just soft.

3   Calculate the haddock's cooking time at 10 minutes per 2.5cm/1in of thickness. Add the fish, flesh-side down, and the milk and simmer until the flesh flakes easily. Remove the fish and set aside. Simmer until the potatoes are tender. Do not boil.

4   Skin and bone the fish, then flake it into the soup. Add the bacon, cream, nutmeg and cayenne pepper, then season with salt and return to just below the boil. Adjust the pepper, if necessary, and serve sprinkled with parsley.

191 Scottish Cullen Skink

PREPARATION TIME 15 minutes   COOKING TIME 50 minutes

400g/14oz finnan haddock or other
   cold-smoked haddock
1 onion, chopped
700g/1lb 9oz floury potatoes,
   peeled and coarsely chopped

¼ teaspoon salt
30g/1oz butter
625ml/21½fl oz/2½ cups whole milk
freshly ground black pepper

1   Calculate the fish's cooking time at 10 minutes per 2.5cm/1in of thickness. Put the haddock and at least 875ml/30fl oz/3½ cups water in a large frying pan and bring to just below the boil, skimming as necessary. Reduce the heat to low, add the onion and simmer, covered, for the calculated time until the fish flakes. Remove the fish and set aside. Strain the cooking liquid and reserve; discard the onion. Remove the skin and any bones from the fish, reserving the bones and discarding the skin. Flake the fish into a bowl, cover with a little of the reserved cooking liquid and set aside.

2   Return the bones and remaining cooking liquid to the pan and simmer, covered, while you cook the potatoes.

3   Meanwhile, put the potatoes and salt in a saucepan with water to cover. Cover and bring to the boil, then boil, uncovered, for 15–20 minutes until the potatoes are tender. Drain, then return them to the pan. Add the butter and a ladleful of the simmering cooking liquid and mash until smooth. Pour in the milk and slowly stir in enough of the cooking liquid, without any bones, to achieve the preferred consistency. Add the flaked fish to the soup and reheat, then adjust the salt and pepper, if necessary, and serve.

192 Mackerel in Chilli-Lime Broth

PREPARATION TIME 10 minutes, plus making the stock   COOKING TIME 25 minutes

1.4l/48fl oz/5½ cups Fish Stock
    (see page 11) or ready-made stock
6 kaffir lime leaves, lightly crushed
2.5cm/1in piece of root ginger,
    peeled and grated
1 red chilli, deseeded and sliced
2 tbsp light soy sauce

1 tbsp fish sauce
400g/14oz mackerel fillets
finely grated zest of 1 lime
freshly ground black pepper
shiso leaves or coriander leaves,
    to serve
lime wedges, to serve

1   Put the stock, lime leaves, ginger, chilli, soy sauce and fish sauce in a saucepan.
    Cover and bring to the boil, then reduce the heat and simmer for 10 minutes.
    Add the mackerel and simmer, covered, for 2–3 minutes until the fillets flake easily.
    Remove the mackerel from the pan and remove the skin.
2   Flake the fish into the soup, add the lime zest and season with pepper. Serve
    topped with shiso leaves and with lime wedges for squeezing over.

193 Mackerel & Fennel Soup

PREPARATION TIME 15 minutes, plus making the stock and preparing the tomatoes
COOKING TIME 30 minutes

2 tbsp chilli-flavoured olive oil
2 fennel bulbs, sliced
2 large garlic cloves, finely chopped
½ tsp fennel seeds
1.4l/48fl oz/5½ cups Fish Stock
    (see page 11) or ready-made stock
2 bay leaves
½ tbsp dried dill

2 large tomatoes, peeled
    (see page 9), deseeded and diced
1 tbsp tomato purée
a pinch of sugar
400g/14oz mackerel fillets, cut into
    thin strips
salt and freshly ground black pepper

1   Heat the oil in a saucepan over a medium heat. Add the fennel and fry, stirring,
    for 2 minutes. Stir in the garlic and fry for 1–3 minutes until the fennel is softened.
    Add the seeds and stir for 30 seconds. Add the stock and bay leaves and season
    with salt and pepper.
2   Bring to the boil, then simmer for 5 minutes. Stir in the dill, tomatoes, tomato purée
    and sugar and simmer for 5 minutes. Add the mackerel and simmer, uncovered,
    for 2–3 minutes until it flakes easily. Discard the bay leaves, adjust the salt and
    pepper, if necessary, and serve.

194 White Fish Soup

PREPARATION TIME 15 minutes, plus making the stock and preparing the tomatoes
COOKING TIME 40 minutes

15g/½oz butter
1 tbsp olive oil
1 large onion, finely chopped
2 large garlic cloves, finely chopped
4 large tomatoes, peeled
    (see page 9), deseeded and diced
1 long strip of orange zest, all bitter
    white pith removed

4 tbsp dry white wine
1.4l/48fl oz/5½ cups Fish Stock
    (see page 11) or ready-made stock
400g/14oz boneless, skinless cod,
    cusk, pollock or other white fish,
    cut into large chunks
2 tbsp shredded basil leaves
salt and freshly ground black pepper

1   Melt the butter with the oil in a saucepan over a medium heat. Add the onion and
    fry, stirring, for 2 minutes. Add the garlic and fry for 1–3 minutes until the onion
    is softened. Stir in the tomatoes, orange zest and wine and cook for 2–4 minutes
    until the wine evaporates. Add the stock and season with salt and pepper, then
    cover and bring to the boil. Skim, then simmer, covered, for 10 minutes.
2   Add the fish and simmer, covered, for 4–7 minutes. Stir in the basil and simmer for
    another 1 minute until the fish is cooked through and the flesh flakes easily. Discard
    the zest and adjust the salt and pepper, if necessary, then serve.

195 Aegean Red Mullet Soup

PREPARATION TIME 20 minutes, plus preparing the tomatoes
COOKING TIME 30 minutes

1½ tbsp olive oil
3 garlic cloves, finely chopped
1 leek, halved lengthways,
   sliced and rinsed
1 carrot, peeled and finely chopped
1 celery stick, finely chopped
1 fennel bulb, thinly sliced
1 tbsp aniseed-flavoured spirit,
   such as Pernod
450g/1lb red mullet, heads removed,
   gutted, scaled, rinsed and cut into
   serving pieces on the bone

2 large tomatoes, grated
   (see page 9)
1 bay leaf
2 tbsp orange juice
1 tbsp tomato purée
grated zest of 1 orange
a pinch of saffron threads
a small pinch of chilli flakes
2 tbsp chopped parsley leaves
salt and freshly ground black pepper

1   Heat the oil in a saucepan over a medium heat. Stir in the garlic, leek, carrot, celery
    and fennel, then reduce the heat to low and cook, covered, for 8–10 minutes until
    softened but not coloured. Add the aniseed spirit, increase the heat to high and
    cook for 30 seconds–1 minute until evaporated.
2   Add the fish and 1.25l/44fl oz/5 cups water and season with salt and pepper.
    Cover and bring to just below the boil, then skim. Stir in the tomatoes, bay leaf,
    orange juice, tomato purée, orange zest, saffron and chilli flakes. Reduce the heat
    and simmer, covered, for 8–10 minutes until the fish flakes easily. Stir in the parsley
    and adjust the salt and pepper, if necessary, then serve.

196 New England Seafood Chowder

PREPARATION TIME 20 minutes   COOKING TIME 40 minutes

500g/1lb 2oz mixed boneless,
skinless fish, such as haddock,
halibut and scrod
2 lemon slices
15g/½oz butter
1 tbsp sunflower oil
1 carrot, peeled and grated
1 celery stick, finely chopped

1 onion, finely chopped
1 floury potato, peeled and
finely chopped
625ml/21½fl oz/2½ cups whole milk
4 tbsp evaporated milk
½ tbsp chopped dill
salt and freshly ground black pepper
sweet paprika, to serve

1   Calculate the cooking time for the fish at 10 minutes per 2.5cm/1in thickness. Put the fish, lemon and 975ml/33fl oz/scant 4 cups water in a large frying pan and season with salt and pepper. Cover and slowly bring to just below the boil. Skim, then reduce the heat and simmer, covered, for the calculated time until the fish flakes easily. Add the fish in stages if necessary, starting with the thickest pieces. Remove the fish, set aside and cover. Strain and reserve the cooking liquid.
2   Melt the butter with the oil in a saucepan over a medium heat. Add the carrot, celery, onion and potato and fry, stirring occasionally, for 3–5 minutes until the onion is softened but not coloured. Stir in the milk, evaporated milk and 500ml/17fl oz/2 cups of the reserved cooking liquid, then cover and bring to just below the boil. Reduce the heat and simmer for 10–12 minutes until the potato is tender. Meanwhile, remove the skin and any bones from the fish.
3   Flake the fish into the soup and heat through. Add the dill, adjust the salt and pepper, if necessary, and serve sprinkled with paprika.

197 Soupe de Poissons

PREPARATION TIME 30 minutes, plus making the stock, croûtes and rouille
COOKING TIME 1 hour

3 tbsp olive oil
2 onions, sliced
4 garlic cloves, chopped
4 large tomatoes, chopped
6 tbsp long-grain white rice
900g/2lb mixed fish, such as grey
mullet, haddock and monkfish,
heads removed, gutted, scaled and
trimmed but not boned
250g/9oz large raw prawns, peeled
and deveined, with the heads and
shells reserved
4 tbsp dry white wine
1.25l/44fl oz/5 cups Fish Stock
(see page 11) or ready-made stock

1 bouquet garni made with 1 piece
of celery stick with its leaves, 1 bay
leaf and several parsley and thyme
sprigs tied together
1 long strip of orange zest, all bitter
white pith removed
a pinch of saffron threads
3 tbsp tomato purée
salt and freshly ground black pepper
1 recipe quantity Croûtes
(see page 14), hot, to serve
40g/1½oz Gruyère cheese, grated,
to serve
1 recipe quantity Rouille
(see page 14), to serve

1   Heat the oil in a large saucepan over a medium heat. Add the onions and fry, stirring occasionally, for 3–5 minutes until softened but not coloured. Add the garlic and tomatoes and fry for 3 minutes, then add the rice, fish and prawns, including the heads and shells. Stir in the wine and cook for 30 seconds–1 minute until evaporated. Add the stock and season with salt and pepper.
2   Cover and bring to the boil, then skim. Stir in the bouquet garni, orange zest, saffron and tomato purée. Reduce the heat and simmer, covered, for 30–45 minutes until the fish comes off the bones and is starting to fall apart.
3   Discard the bouquet garni and blend the soup, including the bones and prawn trimmings. Work the soup through a sieve into a bowl, pressing down with a spoon to extract as much flavour as possible. Rub back and forth with a spoon and scrape the bottom of the sieve. Return the soup to the rinsed-out pan and reheat. Adjust the salt and pepper, if necessary.
4   Divide the croûtes into bowls and top with the cheese. Ladle the soup into the bowls and serve immediately with the rouille for stirring in at the table.

198 Prawn Bisque

PREPARATION TIME 15 minutes, plus making the stock   COOKING TIME 50 minutes

40g/1½oz butter
1 tbsp olive or hemp oil
2 shallots, finely chopped
1 carrot, peeled and chopped
1 celery stick, thinly sliced
heads and shells from 600g/1lb 5oz
    raw prawns, with 12 of the prawns
    deveined and reserved
    (the remaining prawns can
    be frozen to use in other recipes)
2 tbsp brandy
400g/14oz tinned chopped tomatoes

4 tbsp dry vermouth
1 tbsp tomato purée
1.4l/48fl oz/5½ cups Fish Stock
    (see page 11) or ready-made stock
6 tbsp long-grain white rice
1 bay leaf
a pinch of chilli flakes, or to taste
½ tbsp salt, plus extra to season
1–2 tbsp lemon juice, to taste
1 tbsp chopped dill, to serve
freshly ground black pepper
lemon wedges, to serve

1   Melt 30g/1oz of the butter with the oil in a saucepan over a medium heat. Add the
    shallots, carrot and celery and fry, stirring occasionally, for 8–10 minutes until the
    shallots are light golden brown. Add the prawn shells and heads and pound them
    into the vegetables with a wooden spoon. Add the brandy, cook for 2–4 minutes
    until evaporated, then add the tomatoes, vermouth and tomato purée. Bring to the
    boil and boil for 1–2 minutes, then add the stock, rice and bay leaf, cover and return
    to the boil. Skim, add the chilli flakes and season with salt and pepper. Reduce the
    heat and simmer, covered, for 15–18 minutes until the rice is tender.
2   Meanwhile, bring a small saucepan of water to the boil and add the salt. Reduce
    the heat to low, add the prawns and simmer for 2–3 minutes until they turn pink
    and curl. Drain, cut in half lengthways and set aside.
3   Blend the soup until smooth, then work it through a sieve into a bowl, rubbing back
    and forth with a spoon and scraping the bottom of the sieve. Return the soup
    to the rinsed-out pan, add the lemon juice and reheat.
4   Melt the remaining butter in the small pan. Add the prawns and dill and toss
    together just to warm through. Do not overcook or the prawns will toughen. Adjust
    the salt and pepper and add extra lemon juice, if necessary. Divide the prawns into
    bowls, ladle the soup over them and serve with lemon wedges for squeezing over.

199 Haddock Chowder with Spinach

PREPARATION TIME 20 minutes   COOKING TIME 45 minutes

400g/14oz haddock or cod fillet
500ml/17fl oz/ 2 cups whole milk
2 bay leaves
30g/1oz butter
1 celery stick, finely chopped
1 onion, diced
1 red pepper, deseeded and diced
85g/3oz new waxy potatoes, diced

125ml/4fl oz/½ cup double cream
½ tbsp dried dill
freshly grated nutmeg, to taste
1 large handful of baby spinach
    leaves
salt and freshly ground black pepper
finely grated lemon zest, to serve
chopped parsley leaves, to serve

1   Calculate the haddock's cooking time at 10 minutes per 2.5cm/1in of thickness.
    Put the haddock, milk, bay leaves and enough water to cover the fish in a frying pan
    over a medium-high heat and season with salt and pepper. Cover and bring to just
    below the boil. Reduce the heat and simmer for the calculated time until the flesh
    turns opaque and flakes easily. Remove the fish from the pan and set aside.
    Discard the bay leaves and reserve the cooking liquid.
2   Melt the butter in a saucepan over a medium heat. Stir in the celery, onion, pepper
    and potatoes and fry, stirring occasionally, for 3–5 minutes until the vegetables are
    softened but not coloured. Add 800ml/28fl oz/scant 3½ cups of the reserved
    cooking liquid, cover and bring to the boil. Reduce the heat and simmer for
    10–12 minutes until the potatoes are tender. Stir in the cream, dill and nutmeg and
    return to just below the boil. Add the spinach and simmer for 2–3 minutes until
    it has wilted. Meanwhile, remove the skin and any bones from the fish.
3   Flake the fish into the soup and warm through. Adjust the salt and pepper,
    if necessary, then serve sprinkled with lemon zest and parsley.

200 Brazilian Fish Soup

PREPARATION TIME 20 minutes, plus making the stock and preparing the tomatoes
COOKING TIME 35 minutes

1½ tbsp groundnut or sunflower oil
1 onion, chopped
1 green pepper, deseeded and
    chopped
1 red pepper, deseeded and chopped
2 large garlic cloves, chopped
1 thick red chilli, deseeded (optional)
    and chopped
1l/35fl oz/4 cups Fish Stock
    (see page 11) or ready-made stock

2 tomatoes, peeled (see page 9),
    deseeded and chopped
1 tbsp tomato purée
200ml/7fl oz/scant 1 cup coconut milk
450g/1lb boneless, skinless firm fish,
    such as hake or swordfish
1 tbsp dendê (red palm oil)
    or olive oil
salt and freshly ground black pepper
chopped coriander leaves, to serve

1 Heat the oil in a saucepan over a medium heat. Add the onion and peppers and fry,
   stirring, for 2 minutes. Stir in the garlic and chilli and fry for 1–3 minutes until the
   onion is softened but not coloured. Add the stock, tomatoes and tomato purée and
   season with salt and pepper. Cover and bring to the boil, then reduce the heat
   to low, stir in the coconut milk and simmer, covered, for 10 minutes. Meanwhile,
   calculate the fish's cooking time at 10 minutes per 2.5cm/1in of thickness.
2 Add the hake to the soup and simmer for the calculated time until it is cooked
   through and flakes easily. Adjust the salt and pepper, if necessary, then stir in the
   palm oil. Serve sprinkled with coriander.

201 Hake & Mixed Herb Soup

PREPARATION TIME 10 minutes, plus making the stock and preparing the tomatoes
COOKING TIME 35 minutes

1 tbsp olive or hemp oil
1 large shallot, sliced
170ml/5½fl oz/⅔ cup dry white wine
500g/1lb 2oz hake or cod steaks
1l/35fl oz/4 cups Fish Stock
    (see page 11) or ready-made stock
2 tomatoes, grated (see page 9)
1½ tbsp tomato purée

4 spring onions, thinly sliced
    on the diagonal
2 tbsp finely chopped parsley leaves
1 tbsp chopped chives
salt and freshly ground black pepper
basil leaves, torn, to serve
extra-virgin olive oil, to serve

1 Heat the oil in a saucepan over a medium heat. Add the shallot and fry, stirring
   occasionally, for 3–5 minutes until softened. Stir in the wine and cook for
   5–6 minutes until almost evaporated. Meanwhile, calculate the hake's cooking time
   at 10 minutes per 2.5cm/1in of thickness and set aside.
2 Add the stock to the pan and season with salt and pepper. Cover and bring to the
   boil, then reduce the heat to low and add the hake, tomatoes and tomato purée.
   Simmer, covered, for the calculated cooking time until the hake flesh flakes easily.
   Remove the hake from the soup and set aside. Add the spring onions to the pan
   and simmer while you discard the hake skin and any bones. Flake the fish into the
   soup and stir in the parsley and chives. Adjust the salt and pepper, if necessary,
   and serve sprinkled with basil and drizzled with extra-virgin olive oil.

North Sea Haddock & Pea Soup

PREPARATION TIME 10 minutes, plus making the stock   **COOKING TIME** 30 minutes

750ml/26fl oz/3 cups Fish Stock
   (see page 11) or ready-made stock
400ml/14fl oz/scant 1⅔ cups
   double cream
2 large garlic cloves, finely chopped
1 bay leaf

finely grated zest of ½ lemon
a pinch of ground cardamom
400g/14oz haddock fillet
200g/7oz/1¼ cups frozen peas
salt and freshly ground black pepper
smoked paprika, to serve

1   Put the stock, cream, garlic, bay leaf, lemon zest and cardamom in a saucepan and
    season with salt and pepper. Cover and bring to the boil, then reduce the heat and
    simmer for 10 minutes.
2   Calculate the haddock's cooking time at 10 minutes per 2.5cm/1in of thickness.
    Add the haddock and simmer, covered, for the calculated time until it is cooked
    through and flakes easily. Five minutes before the end of the calculated cooking
    time, add the peas and simmer, uncovered. Remove the haddock and set aside
    until cool enough to handle. Discard the bay leaf.
3   Bring the soup to the boil and boil for 1–2 minutes until the peas are very soft. Use
    a slotted spoon to transfer half the peas to a bowl. Blend the soup until smooth,
    and rub it through a sieve for an even smoother texture, if you like. Return the peas
    to the pan. Remove the skin and any small bones from the fish and flake it into
    large pieces into the soup. Reheat and adjust the salt and pepper, if necessary.
    Serve very lightly sprinkled with paprika.

203 Mackerel & Shiitake Miso Soup

PREPARATION TIME 10 minutes, plus making the dashi   COOKING TIME 20 minutes

1 recipe quantity Dashi (see page 12)
  or 1.25l/44fl oz/5 cups prepared
  instant dashi
4 tbsp dark miso paste
5 shiitake mushroom caps, sliced

7.5cm/3in piece of daikon, peeled
  and grated, or 2 radishes, grated
5 mackerel fillets, cut into bite-sized
  pieces
light soy sauce, to taste
1 watercress leaf per bowl, to serve

1 Put the dashi in a saucepan, cover and bring to the boil. As soon as it boils,
   reduce the heat and simmer, uncovered.
2 Put the miso paste in an heatproof bowl and slowly stir in a ladleful or two of the
   hot dashi to form a thin paste, then stir the paste into the dashi. Do not allow
   the soup to boil from this point. Add the mushrooms and daikon and simmer for
   3 minutes, then add the mackerel and soy sauce. Simmer for 4–6 minutes until
   the fish flakes easily. Serve immediately, topped with the watercress leaves.

204 Hoki Soup with Pesto

PREPARATION TIME 10 minutes, plus making the stock   COOKING TIME 40 minutes

2 tbsp garlic-flavoured olive oil
1 fennel bulb, chopped
4 large garlic cloves
125ml/4fl oz/½ cup dry white wine
625ml/21½fl oz/2½ cups Fish Stock
  (see page 11) or ready-made stock

670ml/23fl oz/2⅔ cups passata
finely grated zest of 1 lemon
400g/14oz hoki or cod fillet
lemon juice, to taste
salt and freshly ground black pepper
pesto, to serve

1 Heat the oil in a saucepan over a medium heat. Add the fennel and fry, stirring
   occasionally, for 3–5 minutes until softened but not coloured. Add the garlic and fry
   for 1 minute. Stir in the wine and cook for 5–6 minutes until almost evaporated,
   then add the stock, passata and lemon zest and season with salt and pepper. Cover
   and bring to the boil. Reduce the heat and simmer for 10 minutes. Meanwhile,
   calculate the hoki's cooking time at 10 minutes per 2.5cm/1in of thickness.
2 Add the fish and simmer for the calculated cooking time until it is cooked through
   and flakes easily, then remove it from the pan. When it is cool enough to handle,
   remove the skin and any bones. Flake the fish into the soup, reheat and add the
   lemon juice. Adjust the salt and pepper, if necessary, then serve topped with pesto.

205 Mediterranean Swordfish Soup

PREPARATION TIME 15 minutes, plus making the stock   COOKING TIME 40 minutes

3 tbsp olive oil
1 celery stick, very finely chopped
1 onion, very finely chopped
2 large garlic cloves, crushed
400g/14oz tinned chopped tomatoes
250ml/9fl oz/1 cup dry white wine
1 tbsp brined or salted capers, rinsed

1.25l/44fl oz/5 cups Fish Stock
  (see page 11) or ready-made stock
2 tbsp lemon juice
1 tsp dried oregano leaves
1 tsp dried thyme leaves
500g/1lb 2oz swordfish steaks
salt and freshly ground black pepper

1 Heat the oil in a saucepan over a medium heat. Add the celery and onion and fry,
   stirring occasionally, for 2 minutes. Stir in the garlic and fry for 1–3 minutes until
   the onion is softened but not coloured, then add the tomatoes, wine and capers
   and cook for 8 minutes, stirring to break up the tomatoes.
2 Add the stock, lemon juice, oregano and thyme and season with salt and pepper.
   Cover and bring to the boil, then reduce the heat and simmer for 10 minutes.
3 Calculate the swordfish's cooking time at 10 minutes per 2.5cm/1in of thickness,
   then add it to the soup and simmer, covered, for the calculated time until the
   swordfish flakes easily. Adjust the salt and pepper, if necessary. Remove the fish
   from the soup and discard any skin or bones, then flake or cut into large pieces.
   Divide the swordfish into bowls, ladle the soup over it and serve immediately.

206 Pollock Quenelle Soup

PREPARATION TIME 30 minutes, plus making the stock   COOKING TIME 30 minutes

1.4l/48fl oz/5½ cups Fish Stock
(see page 11) or ready-made stock
200g/7oz fennel, sliced
4 dill sprigs, leaves finely chopped,
stalks lightly crushed and both
kept separate
2 tbsp tomato purée
1 tbsp coriander seeds, lightly
crushed
1 long strip of lemon zest, all bitter
white pith removed

a pinch of caster sugar
350g/12oz pollock, carp or pike fillets,
skinned with any small bones
removed
1 large egg white, chilled
2–4 tbsp double cream
1 tsp lemon juice
2 tbsp very finely chopped parsley
leaves, plus extra to serve
4 tbsp crème fraîche or soured cream
salt and ground white pepper

1   Put the stock, fennel, half the dill leaves and all the stalks, tomato purée, coriander
seeds, lemon zest and sugar in a frying pan and season with salt and white pepper.
Cover and bring to the boil. Reduce the heat and simmer for 5 minutes, then
remove from the heat and set aside, covered.

2   To make the quenelles, blend the pollock in a blender or food processor until
it forms a smooth, thick paste. Add the egg white and blend again until well mixed,
then add 2 tablespoons of the cream and blend. The paste will be softer but should
still hold its shape. Slowly beat in the remaining cream but take care that the paste
doesn't become too thin. Add the lemon juice, season with salt and white pepper
and blend again, then stir in the parsley and remaining dill. Use 2 wet tablespoons
to shape the mixture into 12 quenelles, or long, egg-shaped ovals, and set aside
on a plate. Alternatively, roll the mixture into 12 balls with wet hands.

3   Strain the stock, then return it to the pan and bring to the simmer. Do not boil.
Gently lower the quenelles into the stock and poach for 10 minutes, rolling them
over after 5 minutes. Stir in the crème fraîche and warm through, then adjust the
salt and pepper, if necessary. Divide the quenelles into bowls, ladle the soup over
them and serve sprinkled with parsley.

207 Whiting & Anchovy Soup

PREPARATION TIME 15 minutes, plus making the stock   COOKING TIME 35 minutes

15g/½oz butter
1 tbsp olive or hemp oil
2 shallots, chopped
1.25l/44fl oz/5 cups Fish Stock
(see page 11) or ready-made stock
280g/10oz floury potatoes, peeled
and diced
2 bay leaves
1 long strip of lemon zest, all bitter
white pith removed

½ tsp dried thyme leaves
½ tsp dried marjoram leaves
400g/14oz boneless, skinless whiting
or haddock, cut into large chunks
4 anchovy fillets in oil, drained
and chopped
2 tbsp chopped parsley leaves
salt and freshly ground black pepper

1   Melt the butter with the oil in a saucepan over a medium heat. Add the shallots
and fry, stirring occasionally, for 5 minutes until softened but not coloured.
Add the stock, potatoes, bay leaves, lemon zest, thyme and marjoram, then cover
and bring to the boil. Reduce the heat and simmer for 10 minutes. Meanwhile,
calculate the whiting's cooking time at 10 minutes per 2.5cm/1in of thickness.

2   Add the whiting to the soup and simmer for the calculated time until it is cooked
through and flakes easily and the potatoes are tender. Remove the whiting from
the pan if it is cooked before the potatoes. Stir in the anchovies and parsley,
then return the whiting to the pan, if necessary. Season with salt and pepper,
but remember the anchovies will have been salty. Serve immediately.

208 Saffron-Scented Mussel Soup

PREPARATION TIME 30 minutes, plus making the stock   COOKING TIME 45 minutes

1l/35fl oz/4 cups Fish Stock
   (see page 11) or ready-made stock
a large pinch of saffron threads
1.25kg/2lb 12oz live mussels,
   scrubbed, with 'beards' removed
   and soaked in cold water to cover
3 tbsp olive or hemp oil
2 large garlic cloves, finely chopped
1 carrot, peeled and diced
1 celery stick, thinly sliced
1 fennel bulb, sliced

1 leek, halved lengthways,
   sliced and rinsed
150ml/5fl oz/scant ⅔ cup dry
   white wine
1 bouquet garni made with 1 bay
   leaf, 1 parsley sprig, 1 rosemary
   sprig and 1 thyme sprig tied
   together
lemon juice, to taste
salt and freshly ground black pepper

1   Put the stock and saffron in a saucepan, cover and bring to the boil, then remove from the heat and set aside, covered, for the flavours to blend.
2   Discard any cracked mussels or open ones that do not close when tapped. Put the mussels and 250ml/9fl oz/1 cup water in another saucepan and cook, covered, over a medium heat for 5–8 minutes, shaking the pan frequently, until they all open. Strain the cooking liquid through a muslin-lined sieve, then add it to the saffron-flavoured stock. Set the mussels aside until cool enough to handle, then discard any that are still closed. Remove the mussels from the shells and set aside.
3   Meanwhile, heat the oil in the rinsed-out pan over a medium heat. Add the garlic, carrot, celery, fennel and leek and fry, stirring, for 2 minutes. Reduce the heat to low and cook, covered, for 8–10 minutes, stirring occasionally, until all the vegetables are softened but not coloured. Add the stock, white wine and bouquet garni and season with salt. Cover and bring to the boil, then reduce the heat and simmer for 5 minutes.
4   Discard the bouquet garni and stir the mussels into the soup to warm through – take care not to overcook or they will toughen. Adjust the salt and pepper and add lemon juice, if necessary, then serve.

209 Mussel & Basil Soup

PREPARATION TIME 25 minutes, plus making the stock   COOKING TIME 30 minutes

4 tbsp garlic-flavoured olive oil
3 celery sticks, thinly sliced, with the
   leaves reserved
1 large onion, finely chopped
1 green pepper, deseeded and finely
   chopped
625ml/21½fl oz/2½ cups Fish Stock
   (see page 11) or ready-made stock
500ml/17fl oz/2 cups dry white wine
400g/14oz tinned chopped plum
   tomatoes

1 tbsp tomato purée
1 bouquet garni made with the
   reserved celery leaves, 1 bay leaf
   and several parsley sprigs tied
   together
½ tsp caster sugar
1.25kg/2lb 12oz live mussels,
   scrubbed, with 'beards' removed
   and soaked in cold water to cover
1 large handful of basil leaves, torn
salt and freshly ground black pepper

1   Heat the oil in large saucepan over a high heat. Add the celery, onion and green pepper and fry, stirring, for 3–5 minutes until softened. Add the stock, wine, tomatoes, tomato purée, bouquet garni and sugar and season with salt and pepper. Cover and bring to the boil, then boil, partially covered, for 10 minutes to reduce slightly.
2   Discard any cracked mussels or open ones that do not close when tapped. Reduce the heat to low, add the mussels to the pan and simmer, covered, for 5–8 minutes, shaking the pan frequently, until they all open. Strain the soup through a large muslin-lined colander and return it to the pan. Discard any mussels that remain closed, then set the rest aside until cool enough to handle.
3   Reserve a few mussels in their shells for decorating the bowls. Remove the remaining mussels from the shells and add them to the soup. Simmer gently just long enough to warm the mussels through – take care not to overcook or they will toughen. Adjust the salt and pepper, if necessary, then sprinkle the basil into the soup. Serve immediately, topped with the mussels in their shells.

210 Golden Monkfish Soup

PREPARATION TIME 25 minutes, plus making the stock   COOKING TIME 45 minutes

15g/½oz butter
1 tbsp olive or hemp oil
1 carrot, peeled and finely diced
1 leek, halved lengthways, thinly
   sliced and rinsed
1 onion, finely diced
150ml/5fl oz/scant ⅔ cup dry sherry
1l/35fl oz/4 cups Fish Stock
   (see page 11) or ready-made stock
5 tbsp long-grain white rice
a large pinch of saffron threads

450g/1lb monkfish tail or other white
   fish, thin membrane removed,
   central bone cut out, if necessary,
   and flesh cut into bite-sized chunks
finely grated zest of 1 lemon
salt and ground white pepper
1 roasted red pepper in olive oil,
   drained and very finely chopped,
   to serve
chopped dill, to serve

1   Melt the butter with the oil in a saucepan over a medium heat. Stir in the carrot,
    leek and onion and fry, stirring frequently, for 3–5 minutes until the leek and onion
    are softened but not coloured. Stir in the sherry and cook for 5–6 minutes until
    almost evaporated. Add the stock, rice and saffron and season with salt and white
    pepper. Cover and bring to the boil, then reduce the heat and simmer for
    10–15 minutes until the rice is tender. Meanwhile, calculate the monkfish's
    cooking time at 10 minutes per 2.5cm/1in of thickness.
2   Add the monkfish and lemon zest and simmer for the calculated time until the
    monkfish is cooked through and breaks into large flakes easily. Remove the fish
    from the pan, cover and keep warm. Blend the soup until smooth. Rub the soup
    through a sieve for an even smoother texture, if you like.
3   Return the monkfish to the soup and warm through. Adjust the salt and pepper,
    if necessary, and serve sprinkled with the roasted pepper and dill.

211 Tuna Escabeche Soup

PREPARATION TIME 20 minutes, plus making the soup and at least 24 hours marinating
COOKING TIME 20 minutes

1 recipe quantity Slow-Cooked
   Tomato & Orange Soup
   (see page 40)
salt and freshly ground black pepper
finely chopped parsley leaves,
   to serve

TUNA ESCABECHE
250ml/9fl oz/1 cup olive oil
400g/14oz tuna steaks, about
   2cm/¾in thick
1 red onion, finely chopped
250ml/9fl oz/1 cup red wine vinegar
1 large bay leaf
1 large carrot, peeled and chopped
2 large garlic cloves, finely chopped
a pinch of chilli flakes, or to taste
1 tbsp coriander seeds, lightly
   crushed

1   At least one day and up to five days before you plan to serve, make the tuna
    escabeche. Heat 2 tablespoons of the oil in a frying pan over a medium heat.
    Add the tuna and fry for 2 minutes on each side until medium-rare. Remove the
    tuna from the pan and drain on kitchen paper, then set side.
2   Add the remaining oil to the pan and heat over a medium heat. Add the onion and
    fry, stirring, for 3–5 minutes until softened but not coloured. Reduce the heat
    to very low (use a heat diffuser if you have one) and add the vinegar, bay leaf,
    carrot, garlic, chilli flakes and coriander seeds and season with salt and pepper.
    Simmer for 10 minutes, watching closely so none of the ingredients brown.
3   Meanwhile, flake the tuna into a non-reactive bowl, add the oil and vegetable
    mixture and very gently mix together, taking care not to break up the tuna too
    much. Leave to cool completely, then cover and chill until required.
4   When ready to serve, reheat the soup and adjust the salt and pepper, if necessary.
    Remove the tuna from the escabeche mixture, making sure you don't include the
    bay leaf or any of the coriander seeds, and divide it into bowls. Ladle the hot soup
    over it, sprinkle with parsley and serve.

212 Irish Oyster Soup

PREPARATION TIME 20 minutes   COOKING TIME 30 minutes

12 live oysters
up to 1.25l/44fl oz/5 cups whole milk
55g/2oz butter
1 tbsp olive or hemp oil
2 leeks, halved lengthways, thinly
    sliced and rinsed
1 celery stick, finely chopped

1 large garlic clove, finely chopped
2 tbsp plain white flour
2 bay leaves
2 tbsp chopped parsley leaves,
    plus extra to serve
salt and ground white pepper
smoked or sweet paprika, to serve

1 Shuck the oysters over a bowl to catch the juices, then cut each one into
   2 or 3 pieces and set aside. Strain the juices through a muslin-lined sieve into
   a measuring jug. Add enough milk to make 1.25l/44fl oz/5 cups, then set aside.
2 Melt the butter with the oil in a saucepan over a medium heat. Stir in the leeks and
   celery and cook, covered, for 7 minutes, stirring occasionally. Add the garlic and stir
   for 1–3 minutes until the vegetables are softened and light golden brown, then
   sprinkle in the flour and cook, stirring, for 2 minutes. Slowly add in the milk mixture,
   stirring continuously to prevent lumps from forming.
3 Add the bay leaves and parsley and bring to just below the boil, then reduce
   the heat and simmer, covered, for 5 minutes. Add the oysters and simmer for
   2–3 minutes until cooked through – take care not to overcook them or they will
   toughen. Discard the bay leaves and season with salt and white pepper, then
   serve sprinkled with parsley and paprika.

213 Caribbean Callaloo

PREPARATION TIME 15 minutes, plus making the stock   COOKING TIME 40 minutes

15g/½oz butter
2 tbsp sunflower or groundnut oil
1 large onion, chopped
2 garlic cloves, finely chopped
600g/1lb 5oz callaloo greens
    or spinach leaves, chopped
1.25l/44fl oz/5 cups Chicken Stock
    (see page 11) or ready-made stock

800ml/28fl oz/scant 3½ cups coconut
    milk
400g/14oz floury potatoes, peeled
    and chopped
350g/12oz shelled white crabmeat
salt and freshly ground black pepper
hot or sweet paprika, to serve
hot pepper sauce, to serve

1 Melt the butter with the oil in a saucepan over a medium heat. Add the onion and
   fry, stirring, for 2 minutes. Stir in the garlic and fry for 1–3 minutes until the onion
   is softened. Add the greens and stir for 5 minutes until they wilt, then remove
   them from the pan and set aside. Add the stock, coconut milk and potatoes to the
   pan and season with salt and pepper. Cover and bring to the boil, then reduce the
   heat and simmer, partially covered, for 10–12 minutes until the potatoes are tender.
2 Return the greens to the pan and simmer, uncovered, for 5–8 minutes until they
   are tender. Stir in the crabmeat and simmer for 3 minutes until cooked, then adjust
   the salt and pepper, if necessary. Serve sprinkled with paprika and with hot pepper
   sauce on the side.

214 Oyster & Salmon Soup

PREPARATION TIME 20 minutes, plus making the stock   COOKING TIME 35 minutes

12 live oysters
1.75l/60fl oz/6⅔ cups Fish Stock
   (see page 11) or ready-made stock
400g/14oz skinless salmon fillet,
   any small bones removed,
   and cut into bite-sized pieces
12 raw large prawns, peeled
   and deveined
40g/1½oz butter

1 shallot, finely chopped
200ml/7fl oz/scant 1 cup dry
   vermouth or dry white wine
150ml/5fl oz/scant ⅔ cup
   double cream
2 tbsp chopped mixed herbs, such
   as chervil, chives, dill and parsley
lemon juice, to taste
salt and freshly ground black pepper

1   Shuck the oysters over a bowl to catch the juices, then set aside. Put the juices
    and fish stock in a saucepan and bring to the simmer over a medium heat. Add the
    salmon and simmer for 1 minute, then add the oysters and prawns and simmer for
    another 2–3 minutes until the oysters are cooked through and the prawns turn pink
    and curl. Watch closely so the oysters and prawns do not overcook and toughen.
    Remove the seafood from the pan, cover with a little of the cooking liquid and set
    aside. Strain the cooking liquid through a muslin-lined sieve and set aside.
2   Melt 30g/1oz of the butter in the rinsed-out pan. Add the shallot and fry, stirring
    occasionally, for 5 minutes until softened but not coloured. Stir in the vermouth
    and cook for 6–8 minutes until almost evaporated. Add the cooking liquid and
    bring to the boil, then boil until reduced by half. Stir in the cream and boil until
    reduced by half again.
3   Reduce the heat to low and stir in the remaining butter. Return the seafood to the
    pan and simmer to warm through. Stir in the herbs, add lemon juice to taste and
    season with salt and pepper, then serve.

215 Prawn & Orzo Soup

PREPARATION TIME 25 minutes, plus making the stock   COOKING TIME 30 minutes

24 large raw prawns, peeled and
   deveined, with heads and shells
   reserved
1.4l/48fl oz/5½ cups Fish Stock
   (see page 11) or ready-made stock
4 tbsp dry vermouth
2 large garlic cloves, crushed
2 large tomatoes, chopped
1 bay leaf
1 celery stick, chopped

1 tsp marjoram leaves or ½ tsp dried
   marjoram
1 large handful of basil leaves,
   chopped
pared zest of 1 lemon
a pinch of chilli flakes, or to taste
¼ tsp salt, plus extra to season
85g/3oz/½ cup orzo
freshly ground black pepper
lemon-flavoured olive oil, to serve

1   Put the prawn heads and shells, stock, vermouth, garlic, tomatoes, bay leaf, celery,
    marjoram, half the basil, lemon zest, chilli flakes and salt in a large saucepan and
    season with pepper. Cover and bring to the boil. Reduce the heat and simmer for
    10 minutes, then strain, pressing down on the flavourings and rubbing back and
    forth to extract as much flavour as possible. Discard the flavourings, return the
    stock to the pan, cover and set aside.
2   Meanwhile, bring a saucepan of salted water to the boil. Add the orzo and boil for
    15–18 minutes, or according to the packet instructions, until al dente.
3   Shortly before the orzo is finished cooking, return the stock to the simmer, add the
    prawns and cook for 2–3 minutes until they turn pink and curl. If the orzo still isn't
    finished cooking, remove the prawns and set aside so they do not become tough.
4   Drain the orzo, then add it to the soup with the remaining basil and the prawns.
    Adjust the salt and pepper, if necessary, but remember the stock has already
    been salted. Serve drizzled with lemon olive oil.

216 Prawn Ball Soup

PREPARATION TIME 30 minutes, plus making the dashi   **COOKING TIME** 25 minutes

1 recipe quantity Dashi (see page 12)
   or 1.25l/44fl oz/5 cups prepared
   instant dashi
400g/14oz raw prawns, peeled,
   deveined and finely chopped,
   with heads and shells reserved
1 small egg, beaten

1 tbsp cornflour
2 tsp salt
1 tsp sesame oil
coriander leaves or baby shiso
   leaves, to serve
julienned zest of 1 lemon, to serve

1   Put the prawns in a bowl and use your fingers to gradually incorporate the egg
    to make a sticky paste – you might not need all the egg. Sprinkle in the cornflour,
    mix again and shape into a loose ball, which will be a moist, paste-like mixture.
    'Throw' this ball against the inside of the bowl several times to soften the mixture
    and help it stick together more, then cover and chill for at least 15 minutes.

2   Meanwhile, put the dashi and prawn heads and shells in a saucepan. Cover and
    bring to just below the boil, then reduce the heat to very low (use a heat diffuser
    if you have one) and simmer while you prepare the prawn balls. Do not boil.

3   Divide the salt between two saucepans of water, cover and bring to the boil. Put the
    prawn ball on a plate and sprinkle with the sesame oil, letting the excess slide onto
    the plate – this helps make it easy to roll the mixture into balls without it sticking
    to your fingers. Divide the mixture into 36 equal portions and roll them into balls.

4   Divide the prawn balls between the two pans of slowly boiling water and boil for
    1½–2 minutes until they float to the surface. Remove from the water and set aside.

5   Strain the dashi into one of the rinsed-out pans and return to just below the boil.
    Immediately reduce the heat to low, add the prawn balls and warm through.
    Divide the prawn balls into bowls, ladle the soup over them and serve topped
    with coriander and lemon zest.

217 Thai Hot-and-Sour Soup with Prawns

PREPARATION TIME 20 minutes   COOKING TIME 20 minutes

4 lemongrass stalks, cut into 3 pieces
    and lightly crushed, with outer
    leaves removed
4 coriander sprigs, including roots
    and stalks, cut in half, plus extra
    chopped leaves to serve
6 kaffir lime leaves, torn
12 button mushrooms, sliced

1 tsp salt
24 large raw prawns,
    peeled and deveined
3 tbsp lime juice
2 tbsp fish sauce
1–2 bird's-eye chillies, deseeded
    (optional) and diagonally sliced
lime wedges, to serve

1   Bring 1.25l/44fl oz/5 cups water to the boil in a saucepan. Add the lemongrass,
    coriander, lime leaves, mushrooms and salt and boil, covered, for 5 minutes.
2   Reduce the heat to low, add the prawns and simmer for 2–3 minutes until they turn
    pink and curl. Immediately stir in the lime juice, fish sauce and chillies. Discard the
    lemongrass and coriander. Serve sprinkled with coriander leaves and with lime
    wedges for squeezing over.

218 Scottish Poached Salmon & Cabbage Soup

PREPARATION TIME 20 minutes, plus making the stock and cooking the salmon
COOKING TIME 35 minutes

15g/½oz butter
1 tbsp olive or hemp oil
1 leek, halved lengthways, thinly
    sliced and rinsed
1.25l/44fl oz/5 cups Fish Stock
    (see page 11) or ready-made stock
1 carrot, peeled and diced
1 potato, peeled and diced

55g/2oz savoy cabbage,
    finely shredded
400g/14oz boneless, skinless
    poached salmon, all fat removed
    and flaked
salt and freshly ground black pepper
chopped dill, to serve

1   Melt the butter with the oil in a saucepan over a medium heat. Add the leek and
    fry, stirring occasionally, for 3–5 minutes until softened but not coloured. Add the
    stock, carrot and potato and season with salt and pepper.
2   Cover and bring to the boil, then reduce the heat and simmer for 10–12 minutes
    until the potatoes are tender. Add the cabbage and simmer, uncovered,
    for 5 minutes. Stir in the salmon and simmer for 2–3 minutes until it is warmed
    through and the cabbage is tender. Adjust the salt and pepper, if necessary,
    then serve sprinkled with dill.

219 Vietnamese-Style Scallop & Prawn Soup

PREPARATION TIME 20 minutes, plus making the stock   COOKING TIME 25 minutes

1 small handful of bean sprouts
1.4l/48fl oz/5½ cups Fish Stock
    (see page 11) or ready-made stock
12 button mushrooms, trimmed and
    quartered
1 lemongrass stalk, crushed and cut
    in half, with outer leaves removed

1 tbsp fish sauce, or to taste
1 tbsp lime juice, or to taste
1 long red chilli, deseeded (optional)
    and thinly sliced
250g/9oz shelled raw queen scallops
250g/9oz large raw prawns, peeled
    and deveined

1   Put the bean sprouts in a bowl, cover with cold water and set aside. Put the stock,
    mushrooms, lemongrass, fish sauce, lime juice and chilli in a saucepan. Cover and
    bring to the boil, then boil, partially covered, for 10 minutes to reduce slightly.
    Reduce the heat to low.
2   Add the scallops and prawns and simmer for 2–3 minutes until the prawns turn
    pink and curl and the scallops are cooked through when you cut one open. Add
    more fish sauce and lime juice, if necessary. Drain the bean sprouts and add them
    to the soup to warm through, then serve.

220 Cream of Smoked Trout Soup

PREPARATION TIME 20 minutes, plus making the stock and toasting the seeds
COOKING TIME 30 minutes

250ml/9fl oz/1 cup whole milk
2 parsley sprigs, stalks crushed
1 bay leaf
875ml/30fl oz/3½ cups Fish Stock
 (see page 11) or ready-made stock
400g/14oz skinless hot-smoked trout
 fillets with all small bones
 removed

1 large onion, chopped
1 large sweet potato, peeled
 and diced
salt and freshly ground black pepper
toasted white sesame seeds
 (see page 9)
black sesame seeds, to serve
chives, to serve

1   Put the milk, parsley and bay leaf in a small saucepan and bring to just below the
    boil. Cover and set aside to infuse.
2   Put the stock, trout, onion and sweet potato in another saucepan and season with
    salt and pepper. Cover and bring to just below the boil, then reduce the heat and
    simmer for 10–12 minutes until the potato is tender. Remove about one-quarter
    of the trout and set aside.
3   Blend the soup until smooth. Slowly strain in enough of the infused milk to achieve
    the preferred consistency. Adjust the salt and pepper, if necessary, but remember
    the trout might be salty. Divide the soup into bowls and flake the reserved trout
    over it. Serve sprinkled with sesame seeds and chives.

221 Elegant Japanese Scallop Soup

PREPARATION TIME 5 minutes, plus making the dashi   COOKING TIME 10 minutes

1 recipe quantity Dashi (see page 12)
   or 1.25l/44fl oz/5 cups prepared
   instant dashi
4 tsp soy sauce
2 tsp sake or dry sherry
½ tsp salt, plus extra to season

1 large shelled queen scallop for
   each bowl, coral removed and
   reserved and each scallop cut
   into 3 equal horizontal slices
shiso or coriander leaves, to serve
grated yuzu or lemon zest, to serve

1 Put the dashi, soy sauce, sake and salt in a saucepan. Cover and bring to just below
   the boil. Reduce the heat and simmer for 1 minute. Adjust the salt, if necessary.
2 Arrange the scallop slices and coral in bowls and ladle the soup over them. Add
   a shiso leaf to each, sprinkle with yuzu zest and serve.

222 Tilapia & Coriander Soup

PREPARATION TIME 15 minutes, plus making the stock and preparing the tomato
COOKING TIME 25 minutes

2 tbsp groundnut or sunflower oil
1 large red onion, chopped
2 large garlic cloves, finely chopped
1 celery stick, thinly sliced
1 large tomato, peeled (see page 9),
   deseeded and chopped
400g/14oz black tilapia or haddock
   fillets, any bones removed and fish
   cut into bite-sized pieces (no need
   to skin as the skin is edible)

1l/35fl oz/4 cups Fish Stock
   (see page 11) or ready-made stock
2 tbsp fish sauce, or to taste
a pinch of sugar
1 handful of coriander leaves,
   coarsely torn
freshly ground black pepper

1 Heat the oil in a saucepan over a medium heat. Add the onion and cook, stirring,
   for 2 minutes. Add the garlic and cook, stirring, for 1–3 minutes until the onion
   is softened but not browned. Add the celery and tomato and cook for another
   3–5 minutes until the tomato is soft.
2 Add the tilapia and gently stir for 1 minute until the flesh turns white. Add the
   stock, fish sauce and sugar and season with pepper. Cover, bring to the boil, then
   reduce the heat and simmer for 3–5 minutes until the fish is cooked through and
   flakes easily. Stir in the coriander, then adjust the fish sauce and pepper,
   if necessary, and serve.

223 Lightly Spiced Scallop & Spinach Soup

PREPARATION TIME 15 minutes, plus making the stock   COOKING TIME 15 minutes

2 tsp sunflower oil
2 large garlic cloves, finely chopped
1 green chilli, deseeded (optional)
   and finely chopped
2.5cm/1in piece of root ginger,
   peeled and finely chopped
2 tsp dried curry leaves
750ml/26fl oz/3 cups coconut milk

625ml/21½fl oz/2½ cups Fish Stock
   (see page 11) or ready-made stock
400g/14oz shelled bay scallops,
   rinsed
2 large handfuls of baby spinach
   leaves
salt and freshly ground black pepper
lemon wedges, to serve

1 Heat the oil in a saucepan over a medium heat. Add the garlic, chilli, ginger and
   curry leaves and stir for 30 seconds until fragrant. Watch closely so the garlic
   and ginger do not brown. Add the coconut milk and stock and season with salt
   and pepper, then bring to the boil, uncovered.
2 Reduce the heat to low, add the scallops and spinach and simmer for 3–4 minutes
   until the scallops are cooked through when you cut one open. Adjust the salt and
   pepper, if necessary, and serve with lemon wedges on the side for squeezing over.

224 Scandinavian Salmon & Prawn Soup

PREPARATION TIME 20 minutes, plus making the stock and preparing the tomato
COOKING TIME 30 minutes

15g/½oz butter
1 tbsp sunflower oil
½ leek, halved lengthways, thinly
    sliced and rinsed
1 floury potato, peeled and chopped
1 large ripe tomato, peeled (see page
    9), deseeded and finely chopped
400g/14oz skinless salmon fillet, any
    small bones removed

1l/35fl oz/4 cups Fish Stock
    (see page 11) or ready-made stock
1 bay leaf
a pinch of cayenne pepper
a pinch of ground cardamom
250g/9oz medium raw prawns,
    peeled and deveined
3 tbsp chopped dill
salt and freshly ground black pepper

1 Melt the butter with the oil in a saucepan over a medium heat. Stir in the leek,
   potato and tomato, reduce the heat to low and cook, covered, for 10 minutes until
   the vegetables are softened but not coloured. Meanwhile, calculate the salmon's
   cooking time at 10 minutes per 2.5cm/1in of thickness.
2 Add the stock, bay leaf, cayenne pepper and cardamom and season with salt and
   pepper. Cover and bring to the boil. Reduce the heat to low, add the salmon and
   simmer, covered, for 3 minutes less than the calculated time.
3 Stir in the prawns and simmer for 2–3 minutes until they turn pink and curl and the
   salmon flakes easily. If the prawns are cooked before the salmon remove them
   from the pan and set aside. Discard the bay leaf, then stir in the dill and return
   the prawns, if necessary. Adjust the salt and pepper, if necessary, and serve.

225 Spiced Halibut & Sweet Potato Soup

PREPARATION TIME 25 minutes, plus making the stock   COOKING TIME 35 minutes

15g/½oz butter
1 tbsp olive oil
1 celery stick, thinly sliced
1 leek, halved lengthways, thinly
    sliced and rinsed
1 onion, finely chopped
1 green pepper, deseeded and finely
    chopped
1 sweet potato, peeled and diced
2 garlic cloves, crushed
1 tsp ground coriander
1 tsp fennel seeds

½ tsp ground cumin
a large pinch of saffron threads
a pinch of chilli flakes, or to taste
875ml/30fl oz/3½ cups Fish Stock
    (see page 11) or ready-made stock
4 tbsp dry white wine
1 long pared strip of orange zest,
    all bitter white pith removed
400g/14oz skinless halibut steaks
12 large raw prawns, peeled
    and deveined
salt and freshly ground black pepper

1 Melt the butter with the oil in a saucepan over a medium heat. Add the celery, leek,
   onion, green pepper and sweet potato and fry, stirring occasionally, for 2 minutes.
   Add the garlic, coriander, fennel seeds, cumin, saffron and chilli flakes and stir for
   30 seconds. Watch closely so the spices do not burn.
2 Add the stock, wine and orange zest and season with salt and pepper, then cover
   and bring to the boil. Reduce the heat and simmer for 10 minutes to blend the
   flavours. Meanwhile, calculate the halibut's cooking time at 10 minutes
   per 2.5cm/1in of thickness.
3 Add the halibut steaks to the pan and simmer, covered, for 3 minutes less than
   the calculated time. Add the prawns and simmer for 2–3 minutes until the halibut
   is cooked through and flakes easily and the prawns turn pink and curl. If the prawns
   are cooked before the halibut remove them from the pan and set aside. Adjust the
   salt and pepper, if necessary.
4 Remove the halibut from the soup. Divide the prawns into bowls, then ladle the
   soup over them. Flake the halibut over each portion and serve.

CHAPTER 5

PASTA, PULSE & GRAIN SOUPS

With a well-stocked store cupboard, the recipes in this chapter can give you a taste of delicious, satisfying soups from around the world. A variety of pasta shapes, pulses and grains are paired with a colourful mix of vegetables in most recipes. This is your visual clue that these soups not only taste great but are good for you, too. Many of them fit in the category of 'comfort food', ideal for fighting off the chill on dreary grey days. Greeks swear by Greek Lentil & Garlic Soup with loads of garlic and onions to keep colds at bay, and Chickpea & Pasta Soup and Winter Minestrone are two more of the appetizing and hearty winter warmers you'll find here.

Rice is a popular storecupboard staple. You might be in the habit of only cooking long-grain rice, such as basmati, but why not try something new with Red Rice & Wild Rocket Soup or Beef & Wild Rice Soup? Or be even more adventurous and use one of the often overlooked grains, such as spelt, quinoa and millet – they make fantastic soups, and this chapter includes recipes for all of them.

WINTER MINESTRONE (SEE PAGE 142)

226 Chickpea & Pasta Soup

PREPARATION TIME 15 minutes, plus soaking the chickpeas overnight, making the flavoured oil (optional) and preparing the tomatoes **COOKING TIME** 2¼ hours

200g/7oz/scant 1 cup dried chickpeas
2 large bay leaves
2 carrots, cut in half
2 celery sticks, cut in half
2 large garlic cloves, smashed
2 onions, halved
2 rosemary sprigs
100g/3½oz/heaped ½ cup tubetti
  or other small soup pasta

2 large, juicy tomatoes, grated
  (see page 9)
salt and freshly ground black pepper
1 recipe quantity Crushed Basil Oil
  (see page 15) or extra-virgin
  olive oil, to serve
freshly grated Parmesan cheese,
  to serve

1 Put the chickpeas in a bowl, cover with water and leave to soak overnight, then drain. Transfer to a saucepan and add 1.75l/60fl oz/6⅔ cups water. Cover and bring to the boil. Skim, if necessary, then add the bay leaves, carrots, celery, garlic, onions and rosemary. Reduce the heat and simmer, covered, for 1½–2 hours until the chickpeas are tender.
2 Strain the cooking liquid into a bowl. Discard the flavourings and set the chickpeas aside. Skim the liquid, then blend half the chickpeas and 1.5l/52fl oz/6 cups of the cooking liquid until smooth and return the mixture to the pan.
3 Add the pasta and tomatoes and season with salt and pepper. Cover and bring to the boil, then boil, uncovered, for 10–12 minutes, or according to the packet instructions, until the pasta is al dente. Stir occasionally to prevent the pasta from sticking to the base of the pan. Stir in the remaining chickpeas and warm through. Adjust the salt and pepper, if necessary, and serve drizzled with oil and with cheese.

227 Broccoli, Orecchiette & Anchovy Soup

PREPARATION TIME 15 minutes, plus making the stock and crisps
COOKING TIME 35 minutes

1 tbsp extra-virgin olive oil, plus
  extra to serve
1 onion, finely chopped
2 large garlic cloves, chopped
2 tinned anchovy fillets, drained
  and chopped
670ml/23fl oz/2⅔ cups passata
625ml/21½fl oz/2½ cups
  Vegetable Stock (see page 12)
  or ready-made stock

280g/10oz broccoli, cut into small
  florets and stalks thinly sliced
a pinch of chilli flakes (optional)
55g/2oz/⅔ cup orecchiette
salt and freshly ground black pepper
freshly grated Parmesan cheese,
  to serve
1 recipe quantity Parmesan Crisps
  (see page 51), to serve (optional)

1 Heat the oil in a saucepan over a medium heat. Add the onion and fry, stirring, for 2 minutes. Add the garlic and anchovies and stir for 1–3 minutes until the onion is softened and the anchovies break down. Add the passata, stock, broccoli stalks and chilli flakes, if using, and season with pepper. Cover and bring to the boil, then reduce the heat and simmer for 5 minutes.
2 Uncover and increase the heat to a slow boil. Add the broccoli florets and orecchiette and boil for 12–15 minutes, or according to the packet instructions, until the pasta and the florets are tender. Adjust the pepper, if necessary, and season with salt, but remember the anchovies will have been very salty so you might not need any. Serve with cheese, olive oil and Parmesan crisps, if you like, on the side.

228 Thai Wonton Soup

PREPARATION TIME 25 minutes, plus making the stock   COOKING TIME 30 minutes

1.25l/44fl oz/5 cups Rich Chicken Stock
(see page 10) or ready-made stock
4 leaves Chinese cabbage,
thinly sliced
salt and freshly ground black pepper
1 spring onion, finely chopped,
to serve

THAI WONTONS
85g/3oz finely minced pork
55g/2oz small peeled raw prawns,
very finely chopped
½ tbsp finely chopped coriander
leaves, plus 24 small whole leaves
½ tsp sweet soy sauce
½ tsp cornflour
½ tsp sesame oil, plus extra as needed
24 wonton wrappers, thawed if frozen
1 small egg yolk, beaten

1   To make the wontons, put the pork, prawns, chopped coriander and soy sauce
in a bowl and use your fingers to mix together. Sprinkle in the cornflour, mix again
and shape into a ball. Put the ball on a plate and sprinkle with the sesame oil to help
make it easier to roll into balls. Divide and roll the mixture into 24 equal balls.
2   Bring a large saucepan of water to the boil. Meanwhile, position 1 wonton wrapper
in a diamond shape on a work surface and put 1 coriander leaf in the centre, then
top with 1 ball of the filling. Fold the bottom corner of the wrapper over the filling
to make a triangle. Seal the edges with the egg yolk, then fold both side points over
the filling and seal. Repeat with the remaining wontons.
3   Working in batches to avoid overcrowding the pan, boil the wontons until they float
to the surface, then cook for another 1 minute to make sure the filling is cooked
through. Remove with a slotted spoon and set aside. If not using immediately,
sprinkle with sesame oil to prevent them from sticking together.
4   Bring the stock to the boil. Add the cabbage and boil for 1–2 minutes until tender.
Reduce the heat to low, add the wontons to just warm through, then season with
salt and pepper. Divide the wontons and cabbage into bowls, add the stock and
serve sprinkled with the spring onion.

229 Green Tea Noodle Soup

PREPARATION TIME 20 minutes, plus making the stock and toasting the seeds
COOKING TIME 35 minutes

1.25l/44fl oz/5 cups Rich Chicken
Stock (see page 10)
2 large garlic cloves, finely chopped
1cm/½in piece of root ginger, peeled
and smashed in one piece
5mm/¼in piece of galangal, peeled
and smashed in one piece
½ tbsp light soy sauce, or to taste
½ tbsp mirin
140g/5oz green tea noodles
2 tsp toasted sesame oil

400g/14oz boneless, skinless chicken
thighs, cut into thin strips
5 shiitake mushroom caps, sliced
6 tbsp frozen sweetcorn kernels
2 spring onions, finely shredded
salt and freshly ground black pepper
finely shredded mint leaves, to serve
black sesame seeds, to serve
white sesame seeds, toasted
(see page 9), to serve

1   Put the stock, garlic, ginger, galangal, soy sauce and mirin in a saucepan. Cover and
bring to the boil. Reduce the heat and simmer for 10 minutes.
2   Meanwhile, bring another saucepan of water to the boil. Add the noodles, return
to the boil and boil for 6 minutes, or according to the packet instructions, until
tender. Drain, rinse under cold running water and drain again. Toss with the sesame
oil and set aside.
3   Discard the ginger and galangal. Add the chicken, cover and bring to just below
the boil. Skim, then add the mushrooms, reduce the heat and simmer, covered,
for 5 minutes. Add the sweetcorn and spring onions and simmer for 3–5 minutes
until the chicken is cooked through and the juices run clear when you cut a piece.
Add the noodles and warm through. Adjust the salt and pepper and add extra soy
sauce, if necessary. Serve sprinkled with mint leaves and sesame seeds.

Orzo Primavera Soup

PREPARATION TIME 15 minutes, plus making the stock   **COOKING TIME** 40 minutes

1.4l/48fl oz/5½ cups Vegetable Stock (see page 12) or ready-made stock
1 bouquet garni made with 1 piece of celery stick with its leaves, 1 rosemary sprig and several parsley and thyme sprigs tied together
1 young carrot, diced
1 young turnip, peeled and diced
100g/3½oz/heaped ½ cup orzo
80g/2¾oz green beans, chopped
80g/2¾oz/½ cup frozen peas
1 tsp finely grated lemon zest
2 tbsp chopped parsley leaves
salt and freshly ground black pepper

1 Put the stock and bouquet garni in a saucepan over a high heat and season with salt and pepper. Cover and bring to the boil, then reduce the heat and simmer for 10 minutes.

2 Return the stock to the boil, add the carrot and turnip and boil for 2 minutes. Stir in the orzo and boil for 11 minutes, then add the green beans and peas and boil for 4–6 minutes until the orzo and vegetables are tender. Discard the bouquet garni. Stir in the lemon zest and adjust the salt and pepper, if necessary. Stir in the parsley and serve.

231 Buckwheat Noodle Soup with Nori

PREPARATION TIME 5 minutes   COOKING TIME 20 minutes

140g/5oz buckwheat noodles
1 recipe quantity Dashi,
    Vegetarian Dashi (see page 12)
    or 1.25l/44fl oz/5 cups prepared
    instant dashi
6 tbsp soy sauce, or to taste

2 tbsp caster sugar
2 tbsp mirin or sweet sherry
2 tsp salt, plus extra to season
½ sheet nori, finely shredded or torn,
    to serve
wasabi paste, to serve

1   You need a large saucepan for the noodles because they foam up during cooking.
    Fill it three-quarters of the way with water, cover and bring to the boil. Set aside
    a bowl of cold water. Add the noodles to the boiling water and return to the boil.
    As soon as the liquid foams and rises, add a ladleful of the cold water. Return the
    water to just below the boil, then reduce the heat and simmer the noodles for
    2–5 minutes, or according to the packet instructions, until tender. Drain, rinse
    immediately in cold water and set aside.
2   Meanwhile, in a separate saucepan, mix together the dashi, soy sauce, sugar, mirin
    and salt, stirring to dissolve the sugar. Bring to just below the boil, then turn off the
    heat and keep warm if the noodles haven't finished cooking. Adjust the seasoning,
    adding extra soy sauce or salt, if necessary. Divide the noodles and soup into
    bowls, sprinkle with the nori and serve with wasabi paste.

232 Pasta & Potato Soup

PREPARATION TIME 20 minutes   COOKING TIME 45 minutes

3 tbsp extra-virgin olive oil,
    plus extra to serve
1 carrot, peeled and diced
1 celery stick, finely chopped,
    with the leaves reserved
1 onion, diced
1 bouquet garni made with 1 bay
    leaf, the celery leaves and several
    parsley and thyme sprigs tied
    together

280g/10oz floury potatoes,
    peeled and diced
1 Parmesan or pecorino cheese rind,
    about 7.5 x 5cm/3 x 2in, or 1 heel
    of Parma ham (see page 9)
100g/3½oz/⅔ cup dried macaroni
55g/2oz/½ cup freshly grated
    Parmesan cheese
salt and freshly ground black pepper
chopped parsley leaves, to serve

1   Heat the oil in a saucepan over a medium heat. Add the carrot, celery and onion
    and fry, stirring occasionally, for 3–5 minutes until softened.
2   Add the bouquet garni, potatoes, cheese rind and 1.4l/48fl oz/5½ cups water and
    season with salt and pepper, but remember the rind is salty. Cover and bring to the
    boil. Reduce the heat and simmer for 15–20 minutes until all the vegetables are
    very tender, then discard the bouquet garni and cheese rind.
3   Blend the soup until semi-smooth with small pieces of carrot and potato remaining.
    Add the pasta to the soup and return it to the boil, then boil, uncovered, for
    10–12 minutes until just al dente. Stir frequently to prevent the pasta from sticking
    to the base of the pan. Stir in half the cheese and adjust the salt and pepper,
    if necessary, but remember the cheese is salty. Serve with extra oil and cheese.

233 Mediterranean Minestrone

PREPARATION TIME 20 minutes, plus overnight soaking and cooking the beans and preparing the tomatoes COOKING TIME 45 minutes

100g/3½oz/½ cup dried haricot beans
3 tbsp fruity extra-virgin olive oil, plus extra to serve
1 onion, finely chopped
1 leek, thinly sliced and rinsed
1 carrot, peeled and diced
2 new potatoes, peeled and diced
4 thyme sprigs
1 piece of Parmesan cheese rind, about 7.5 x 5cm/3 x 2in
55g/2oz thin French beans, cut into bite-sized pieces

1 courgette, diced
2 beefsteak tomatoes, peeled (see page 9), deseeded and chopped
1 tbsp tomato purée
85g/3oz vermicelli, broken into bite-sized pieces
½ tsp caster sugar (optional)
salt and freshly ground black pepper
pesto, to serve
freshly grated Parmesan cheese, to serve

1 Put the beans in a bowl, cover with water and leave to soak overnight, then drain. Transfer to a saucepan, add 1.5l/53fl oz/6 cups water, cover and bring to the boil. Reduce the heat and simmer, covered, for 50 minutes–1 hour until almost tender, then drain.

2 Heat the oil in a saucepan over a low heat. Stir in the onion and leek and fry, covered, for 10–12 minutes until softened. Stir in the carrot, potatoes, thyme and cheese rind. Season with salt and pepper, but remember the cheese rind will be salty. Add 1.5l/48fl oz/5½ cups water and bring to the boil. Skim, then reduce the heat and simmer, covered, for 10 minutes. Discard the cheese rind.

3 Stir in the haricot beans, French beans, courgette, tomatoes, tomato purée, vermicelli and sugar, if using. Return to the boil, then boil, uncovered, for 10–15 minutes until the beans are tender and the pasta is al dente. Stir frequently to prevent the pasta from sticking to the base of the pan. Adjust the salt and pepper, if necessary, and serve immediately with the pesto, cheese and olive oil.

234 Winter Minestrone

PREPARATION TIME 20 minutes, plus overnight soaking and cooking the beans
COOKING TIME 45 minutes

100g/3½oz/½ cup dried cannellini beans
140g/5oz pancetta, skinned, if necessary, and chopped
1 large onion, finely chopped
4 large garlic cloves, chopped
100g/3½oz white cabbage, finely shredded
1 carrot, peeled, halved lengthways and sliced

1 courgette, halved lengthways and sliced
1 floury potato, peeled and chopped
1 Parmesan cheese rind, about 7.5 x 5cm/3 x 2in (see page 9)
110g/3¾oz/½ cup Arborio rice
salt and freshly ground black pepper
extra-virgin olive oil, to serve
freshly grated Parmesan cheese, to serve (optional)

1 Put the beans in a bowl, cover with water and leave to soak overnight, then drain. Transfer to a saucepan, add 1.5l/53fl oz/6 cups water, cover and bring to the boil. Reduce the heat and simmer, covered, for 50 minutes–1 hour until almost tender, then drain.

2 Put the pancetta in a saucepan over a medium-high heat and fry, stirring, until the fat runs. Add the onion and fry, stirring, for 5–8 minutes until softened and turning golden. Add the garlic, cabbage, carrot, courgette and potato and stir for 1–2 minutes. Add the cheese rind and 1.5l/52fl oz/6 cups water.

3 Cover and bring to the boil. Season with salt and pepper but remember the rind is salty. Reduce the heat and simmer, covered, for 10 minutes. Stir in the cooked dried beans and rice, return the soup to the boil, uncovered, then reduce the heat slightly and slowly boil for 10–15 minutes until the beans and rice are tender. Discard the cheese rind, then adjust the salt and pepper, if necessary. Serve with oil and cheese, if using.

235 Alphabet Soup

PREPARATION TIME 5 minutes, plus making the stock   COOKING TIME 15 minutes

700ml/24fl oz/scant 3 cups
  Vegetable Stock (see page 12)
  or ready-made stock
670ml/23fl oz/2⅔ cups passata
200g/7oz/heaped 1 cup small pasta
  letters or other small soup pasta

150g/5½oz/1 cup frozen
  sweetcorn kernels
salt and freshly ground black pepper
chopped parsley leaves, to serve
freshly grated Parmesan cheese,
  to serve

1   Put the stock and passata in a saucepan. Cover and bring to the boil. Add the pasta
    and sweetcorn and season with salt and pepper. Return to the boil, then boil,
    uncovered, for 3–5 minutes until the pasta is al dente and the sweetcorn is tender.
2   Adjust the salt and pepper, if necessary. Serve sprinkled with parsley and cheese.

236 Very Garlicky Pasta & Cavolo Nero Soup

PREPARATION TIME 10 minutes, plus making the stock   COOKING TIME 30 minutes

1 tbsp fruity extra-virgin olive oil,
  plus extra to serve
1 red onion, finely chopped
4 large garlic cloves, chopped
1.5l/52fl oz/6 cups Vegetable Stock
  (see page 12) or ready-made stock

100g/3½oz cavolo nero or savoy
  cabbage, leaves shredded
175g/6oz/1 cup tubetti or other
  small soup pasta
a pinch of chilli flakes, or to taste
salt and freshly ground black pepper

1   Heat the oil in a saucepan over a medium heat. Add the onion and fry, stirring,
    for 2 minutes. Add the garlic and fry for 1–3 minutes until the onion is softened.
    Stir in the stock, cavolo nero and chilli flakes and season with salt and pepper.
    Cover and bring to the boil. Uncover and reduce the heat to a slow boil, then boil
    for 8–10 minutes until the cavolo nero is very tender.
2   Add the pasta for the final 4–6 minutes, or according to the packet instructions,
    and cook until it is al dente. Adjust the salt and pepper, if necessary. Serve with
    olive oil on the side for drizzling.

237 Cuban Black Bean Soup

PREPARATION TIME 5 minutes   COOKING TIME 2½ hours

350g/12oz/1⅔ cups dried black beans
140g/5oz smoked lardons
1 long green chilli, deseeded
  (optional) and sliced
2 tbsp ground cumin
1 tbsp ground coriander
4 tbsp olive or hemp oil
4 tbsp white distilled vinegar
salt and freshly ground black pepper

TO SERVE
1 avocado
1 tbsp lemon juice
shredded coriander leaves
tortilla chips
soured cream
lime wedges

1   Put the beans in a saucepan and add enough water to cover by 7.5cm/3in.
    Cover, bring to the boil, and boil for 10 minutes, then drain and set aside.
2   Meanwhile, put the lardons in another large saucepan and fry, stirring,
    for 2–4 minutes until they brown and crisp. Stir in the chilli, then add the beans and
    2.5l/87fl oz/10 cups water. Cover and bring to the boil, then reduce the heat and
    simmer for 1 hour.
3   Stir in the cumin, ground coriander, olive oil and vinegar and simmer, covered,
    for 45 minutes to 1 hour, stirring occasionally and topping up the water,
    if necessary, until the beans are tender and the soup has thickened. If the soup
    is too thin, simmer for 15 minutes uncovered.
4   Just before serving, peel, stone and dice the avocado and toss it with the lemon
    juice. Season the soup with salt and pepper and serve topped with coriander leaves
    and with the avocado, tortilla chips, soured cream and lime wedges on the side.

238 Black-Eyed Bean & Rice Soup

PREPARATION TIME 10 minutes, plus soaking the beans overnight and making the stock
COOKING TIME 55 minutes

200g/7oz/1 cup dried
   black-eyed beans
1l/35fl oz/4 cups Vegetable Stock
   (see page 12) or ready-made stock
500ml/17fl oz/2 cups passata
2 large garlic cloves, finely chopped
1 celery stick, thinly sliced, with the
   leaves reserved and torn to serve

1 bouquet garni made with 1 bay leaf
   and several parsley and thyme
   sprigs tied together
a pinch of chilli flakes, or to taste
100g/3½oz/½ cup white or brown
   long-grain rice
salt and freshly ground black pepper
chopped parsley leaves, to serve

1   Put the beans in a bowl, cover with water and leave to soak overnight, then drain.
2   Put the beans, stock, passata, garlic, celery, bouquet garni and chilli flakes, if using, in a saucepan. Cover and bring to the boil, then boil for 10 minutes. Reduce the heat and simmer for 20 minutes.
3   Add the rice, season with salt and pepper and increase the heat to a slow boil. Boil, uncovered, for 10–20 minutes, depending on the type of rice, stirring often to prevent the rice from sticking to the base of the pan, until the beans and rice are tender. Discard the bouquet garni and adjust the salt and pepper, if necessary, then serve sprinkled with the parsley and celery leaves. If reheating this soup, add a little extra stock, if necessary, to thin it.

239 Borlotti Bean & Fennel Soup

PREPARATION TIME 10 minutes, plus overnight soaking and cooking the beans (optional) and making the stock   COOKING TIME 50 minutes

200g/7oz/1 cup dried borlotti beans
   or 400g/14oz tinned borlotti beans,
   drained and rinsed
1½ tbsp garlic-flavoured olive oil
300g/10oz fennel, thinly sliced
1 shallot, chopped
1.25l/44fl oz/5 cups Vegetable Stock
   (see page 12) or ready-made stock
400g/14oz tinned chopped tomatoes

1 Parmesan or Cheddar cheese rind,
   about 7.5 x 5cm/3 x 2in
   (see page 9)
1 tbsp tomato purée
½ tsp caster sugar
2 handfuls of baby spinach leaves
freshly grated nutmeg, to taste
salt and freshly ground black pepper
chopped parsley leaves, to serve

1   If using dried beans, put them in a bowl, cover with water and leave to soak overnight, then drain. Transfer to a saucepan, add 1.5l/53fl oz/6 cups water, cover and bring to the boil. Reduce the heat and simmer, covered, for 50 minutes–1 hour, then drain.
2   Heat the oil in a saucepan over a medium heat. Add the fennel and shallot and fry, stirring occasionally, for 5–8 minutes until softened and golden. Stir in the stock, tomatoes, cheese rind, tomato purée and sugar. Season with salt and pepper, but remember the rind is salty. Cover and bring to the boil, then reduce the heat and simmer for 30 minutes.
3   Stir in the beans and simmer for 3 minutes to warm through. Add the spinach and simmer for 1–2 minutes until it wilts. Discard the cheese rind, add the nutmeg and adjust the salt and pepper, if necessary. Serve sprinkled with parsley.

240 Halloween Bean Soup

PREPARATION TIME 15 minutes, plus overnight soaking and cooking the beans (optional), making the stock and toasting the seeds **COOKING TIME** 1½ hours

110g/3¾oz/½ cup dried black beans
    or 200g/7oz tinned black beans,
    drained and rinsed
1 tbsp hemp or olive oil
1 large red onion, quartered and
    thinly sliced
2 large garlic cloves, chopped
1.25l/44fl oz/5 cups Vegetable Stock
    (see page 12) or ready-made stock
2 bay leaves
a pinch of chilli flakes, or to taste

1 Parmesan or Cheddar cheese rind,
    about 7.5 x 5cm/3 x 2in
    (see page 9; optional)
400g/14oz pumpkin, peeled,
    deseeded and chopped
2 handfuls of baby spinach leaves
salt and freshly ground black pepper
white sesame seeds, toasted
    (see page 9), to serve
black sesame seeds, to serve
chopped parsley leaves, to serve

1   If using dried beans, put them in a bowl, cover with water and leave to soak
    overnight, then drain. Transfer to a saucepan, add 1.5l/53fl oz/6 cups water, cover
    and bring to the boil. Reduce the heat and simmer, covered, for 50 minutes–1 hour,
    then drain.

2   Heat the oil in a saucepan over a medium heat. Add the onion and fry, stirring,
    for 2 minutes. Add the garlic and stir for 1–3 minutes until the onion is softened.
    Add the stock, bay leaves, chilli flakes and cheese rind, if using, and season with
    salt and pepper. Cover and bring to the boil. Add the pumpkin, reduce the heat
    to medium and simmer for 5–8 minutes until tender.

3   Add the beans and heat through for 3 minutes. Stir in the spinach and simmer for
    1–2 minutes until it wilts. Discard the cheese rind, if used. Adjust the salt and
    pepper, if necessary, and serve sprinkled with sesame seeds and parsley.

241 Country-Style Bean & Vegetable Soup

PREPARATION TIME 25 minutes, plus soaking the beans overnight and making the stock
COOKING TIME 1¼ hours

200g/7oz/1 cup dried cannellini beans
30g/1oz smoked lardons
2 tbsp sunflower oil
2 celery sticks, thinly sliced, with the
 leaves reserved
2 large garlic cloves, finely chopped
2 shallots, peeled and diced
1 carrot, peeled and diced
½ turnip, peeled and diced
1.25l/44fl oz/5 cups Chicken Stock
 (see page 11) or ready-made stock

1 bouquet garni made with the celery
 leaves, 1 bay leaf and several
 parsley and thyme sprigs tied
 together
280g/10oz white cabbage, cored
 and chopped
salt and freshly ground black pepper
finely chopped parsley leaves,
 to serve

1 Put the beans in a bowl, cover with water and leave to soak overnight, then drain.
2 Heat a saucepan over a medium-high heat. Add the lardons and fry, stirring,
 for 30 seconds–1 minute until their fat runs. Add the oil and reduce the heat
 to medium. Stir in the celery, garlic, shallots, carrot and turnip and fry, stirring
 occasionally, for 5–8 minutes until softened but not coloured.
3 Add the beans, stock and bouquet garni, adding water, if necessary, so the
 vegetables are covered. Cover and bring to the boil. Skim, reduce the heat and
 simmer, covered, for 45 minutes.
4 Stir in the cabbage and season with salt and pepper. Cover and simmer for
 5–15 minutes until the beans are tender. Discard the bouquet garni and adjust
 the salt and pepper, if necessary. Serve sprinkled with parsley.

242 Nicola's Bean & Onion Soup

PREPARATION TIME 15 minutes, plus soaking the beans overnight, making the stock
and 1½ hours soaking the onions   COOKING TIME 1¼ hours

100g/3½oz/½ cup dried borlotti beans
500g/1lb 2oz onions, chopped
1 tbsp extra-virgin olive oil, plus
 extra to serve
1 large carrot, peeled and quartered
1 celery stick, cut into large chunks

several sage sprigs, tied together
1.25l/44fl oz/5 cups Vegetable Stock
 (see page 12) or ready-made stock
2 bay leaves
salt and freshly ground black pepper

1 Put the beans in a bowl, cover with water and leave to soak overnight, then drain.
2 Put the onions in a large bowl, cover with water and leave to soak for 1½ hours.
 Meanwhile, put the beans and enough water to generously cover in a saucepan.
 Cover and bring to the boil. Add the oil, carrots, celery and sage, then reduce the
 heat and simmer, covered, for 50 minutes–1 hour until the beans are tender. Strain
 the beans, discard the flavourings and set the cooking liquid aside.
3 Drain the onions and use your hands to squeeze out and discard the juices. Put the
 onions, stock and bay leaves in another saucepan and season with salt and pepper.
 Cover and bring to the boil, boil for 5 minutes, then strain into a bowl and reserve
 both the onions and cooking liquid. Discard the bay leaves and return the onions
 and half the cooking liquid to the pan.
4 Blend the onions until smooth, then stir in enough of the remaining cooking liquid
 to achieve the preferred consistency. Rub the soup through a sieve for an even
 smoother texture, if you like. Adjust the salt and pepper, if necessary. Ladle the
 onion soup into bowls, spoon the beans over them and drizzle with oil. Serve with
 extra oil for adding at the table.

243 Winter Bean & Mushroom Soup

PREPARATION TIME 10 minutes, plus making the stock   COOKING TIME 40 minutes

1½ tbsp olive or hemp oil
1 onion, chopped
2 garlic cloves
400g/14oz portobello mushrooms,
   trimmed and sliced
625ml/21½fl oz/2½ cups
   Vegetable Stock (see page 12)
   or ready-made stock

400g/14oz tinned chopped tomatoes
a pinch of sugar
2 tsp dried rosemary
400g/14oz tinned cannellini or haricot
   beans, drained and rinsed
salt and freshly ground black pepper
chopped parsley leaves, to serve

1   Heat the oil in a saucepan over a medium heat. Add the onion and fry, stirring,
    for 2 minutes. Stir in the garlic and fry for 1–3 minutes until the onions are
    softened. Add the mushrooms, season with salt and stir for 5–8 minutes until they
    give off their juices. Stir in the stock, tomatoes and sugar and season with salt and
    pepper. Cover and bring to the boil, then stir in the rosemary.
2   Reduce the heat and simmer, covered, for 15 minutes. Add the beans and warm
    through. Adjust the salt and pepper, if necessary, then serve sprinkled with parsley.

244 White Chilli Soup

PREPARATION TIME 15 minutes, plus making the stock and cooking the chicken
COOKING TIME 20 minutes

1½ tbsp olive oil
1 onion, chopped
2 large garlic cloves
1 green chilli, deseeded and chopped
1 tsp dried oregano
½ tsp dried thyme leaves
½ tsp ground cumin
¼ tsp cayenne pepper, or to taste

750ml/26fl oz/3 cups Chicken Stock
   (see page 11) or ready-made stock
800g/1lb 12oz tinned cannellini
   beans, drained and rinsed
350g/12oz boneless, skinless cooked
   chicken, cut into bite-sized pieces
salt and freshly ground black pepper
chopped parsley leaves, to serve

1   Heat the oil in a saucepan over a medium heat. Add the onion and fry, stirring,
    for 2 minutes. Add the garlic and chilli and stir for 1–3 minutes until the onion
    is softened. Add the oregano, thyme, cumin and cayenne and stir for 30 seconds.
    Watch closely so the spices do not burn. Add the stock, season with salt and
    pepper, then cover and bring to the boil.
2   Add the beans and chicken. Reduce the heat and simmer, covered, for 3–5 minutes
    to heat through. Adjust the salt and pepper, if necessary, then serve sprinkled
    with parsley.

245 Oat Soup with Carrot & Swede

PREPARATION TIME 20 minutes, plus making the stock   COOKING TIME 45 minutes

30g/1oz butter
1 tbsp olive or hemp oil
2 carrots, peeled and finely diced
1 leek, halved lengthways,
   sliced and rinsed
1 onion, finely chopped
80g/3oz swede, peeled and
   finely diced

1.25l/44fl oz/5 cups Vegetable Stock
   (see page 12) or ready-made stock
55g/2oz/heaped ½ cup fine rolled oats
1 bay leaf
150ml/5fl oz/scant ⅔ cup milk
freshly grated nutmeg, to taste
salt and freshly ground black pepper
chopped parsley leaves, to serve

1   Melt the butter with the oil in a saucepan over a medium heat. Add the carrots, leek,
    onion and swede and fry, stirring, for 3–5 minutes until the vegetables are softened.
    Stir in the stock, oats and bay leaf and season well with salt and pepper.
2   Bring to the boil, stirring, then reduce the heat and simmer, covered, for 25–30
    minutes, stirring occasionally, until thickened and the vegetables are tender. Stir in
    the milk, season with nutmeg and reheat without boiling. Adjust the salt and pepper,
    if necessary, and serve sprinkled with parsley. If you reheat the soup, do not boil it.

Green & White Bean Soup

PREPARATION TIME 20 minutes, plus soaking the beans overnight and making the stock
COOKING TIME 1½ hours

200g/7oz/1 cup dried butter beans
2 tbsp fruity extra-virgin olive oil,
  plus extra to serve
4 large garlic cloves, finely chopped
1 leek, thinly sliced and rinsed
1 onion, chopped
1.4l/48fl oz/5½ cups Vegetable Stock
  (see page 12) or ready-made stock
1 small handful of sage and ½ celery
  stick with its leaves, tied together

1 heel of Parma ham (see page 9;
  optional)
¼ head savoy cabbage,
  cored and shredded
85g/3oz green beans, chopped
85g/3oz/½ cup shelled broad beans,
  peeled if not young and tender
1 handful of baby spinach leaves
salt and freshly ground black pepper
pesto, to serve (optional)

1 Put the butter beans in a bowl, cover with water and leave to soak overnight,
  then drain.
2 Heat the oil in a saucepan over a medium heat. Stir in the garlic, leek and onion,
  reduce the heat to low and cook, covered, for 10–12 minutes, stirring occasionally,
  until softened but not coloured. Stir in the butter beans and stock, cover and bring
  to the boil. Skim, then reduce the heat, stir in the sage and ham heel, if using,
  and simmer, covered, for 40–60 minutes until tender.
3 Remove the ham heel and set aside until cool enough to handle. Add the
  cabbage, green beans and broad beans to the pan and simmer, uncovered,
  for 10–12 minutes until all the beans are tender. Stir in the spinach and simmer
  for another 1 minute until the leaves wilt.
4 Remove the meat from the ham heel, shred it into small pieces and set aside.
  Season the soup with salt and pepper, but remember the ham heel will have
  been salty. Serve with the ham sprinkled over the top, if used. Add a dollop
  of pesto to each portion and serve with olive oil on the side for drizzling.

247 Persian Lentil & Squash Soup

PREPARATION TIME 10 minutes, plus making the stock   COOKING TIME 45 minutes

4 tbsp olive or hemp oil
1 large onion, chopped
2 large garlic cloves, crushed
1 tsp turmeric
1.4l/48fl oz/5½ cups Vegetable Stock
   (see page 12) or ready-made stock

250g/9oz/1⅓ cups dried green lentils,
   rinsed
1 tsp cornflour
350g/12oz butternut squash, peeled
   and cut into bite-sized cubes
salt and freshly ground black pepper
shredded mint leaves, to serve

1 Heat the oil in a saucepan. Add the onion and fry, stirring, for 2 minutes. Add the
   garlic and fry for 1–3 minutes until the onion is softened. Stir in the turmeric, then
   add the stock and lentils, cover and bring to the boil. Reduce the heat and simmer
   for 15 minutes. Meanwhile, put the cornflour and 1 tablespoon cold water
   in a small bowl and mix until smooth.
2 Stir the cornflour mixture and squash into the soup and season with salt and
   pepper. Cover and return to the boil, then reduce the heat and simmer for
   12–15 minutes until the lentils and squash are tender and the soup thickens
   slightly. Adjust the salt and pepper, if necessary, and serve sprinkled with mint.

248 Butter Bean Soup with Carrots & Bacon

PREPARATION TIME 15 minutes, plus soaking the beans overnight and making the stock
COOKING TIME 1¼ hours

200g/7oz/1 cup dried butter beans
4 tbsp olive or hemp oil
several thyme sprigs, tied together
1 bay leaf
1 small carrot, grated
1 large onion, chopped
290ml/10fl oz/generous 1 cup milk

400ml/14fl oz/1½ cup Chicken Stock
   (see page 11) or ready-made stock,
   plus extra as needed
3 rashers streaky bacon
salt and freshly ground black pepper
chopped chives, to serve

1 Put the beans in a bowl, cover with water and leave to soak overnight, then drain.
2 Put the beans and water to cover generously in a large saucepan. Cover and bring
   to the boil, then skim. Reduce the heat, add the olive oil and thyme and simmer,
   covered, for 35 minutes. Strain the beans, reserving the cooking liquid, and discard
   the thyme. Return the beans to the pan, add the bay leaf, carrot, onion, milk and
   stock and season with salt and pepper. Bring to just below the boil, then reduce
   the heat and simmer for 15–25 minutes until the beans are tender.
3 Meanwhile, preheat the grill to high, then grill the bacon for 5 minutes, turning
   once, until crisp. Chop and set aside.
4 Discard the bay leaf and blend one-third of the soup until smooth. Work the mixture
   through a sieve back into the pan, using a spoon, then stir well. If the soup is too
   thick, add a little of the reserved cooking liquid. Adjust the salt and pepper,
   if necessary, and serve sprinkled with the bacon and chives.

249 Italian Tortellini Soup

PREPARATION TIME 5 minutes, plus making the stock   COOKING TIME 20 minutes

1.4l/48fl oz/5½ cups any homemade
   stock (see pages 10–13)
   or ready-made stock
500g/1lb 2oz fresh or dried tortellini,
   with your favourite filling

salt and freshly ground black pepper
freshly grated Parmesan cheese,
   to serve
fruity extra-virgin olive oil, to serve

1 Bring the stock to the boil in a covered saucepan over a high heat. Add the pasta
   and season with salt and pepper. Return to the boil, then boil for about 2 minutes
   for fresh or 10–12 minutes for dried pasta, or according to the packet instructions,
   until the pasta is al dente and rises to the surface.
2 Serve sprinkled with Parmesan and with olive oil for drizzling over.

250 Puréed Kidney Bean Soup

PREPARATION TIME 15 minutes, plus soaking the beans overnight and making the stock
COOKING TIME 2½ hours

210g/7½oz/1 cup dried
  red kidney beans
1.5l/52fl oz/6 cups Vegetable Stock
  (see page 12) or ready-made stock
15g/½oz butter
1 tbsp olive or hemp oil
2 celery sticks, chopped
1 carrot, peeled and chopped
1 onion, chopped

4 garlic cloves, chopped
½ tsp ground coriander
½ tsp ground cumin
a pinch of cayenne pepper,
  or to taste
1 bay leaf
salt and freshly ground black pepper
Greek-style yogurt, to serve
chopped chives, to serve

1 Put the beans in a bowl, cover with water and leave to soak overnight, then drain.
2 Put the beans and stock in a saucepan. Cover, bring to the boil and boil for
    10 minutes, then skim.
3 Meanwhile, melt the butter with the oil in another saucepan over a medium heat.
    Add the celery, carrot and onion and fry, stirring, for 2 minutes. Add the garlic and
    stir for 1–3 minutes until the onion is softened. Add the coriander, cumin and
    cayenne and fry for 30 seconds. Watch closely so the spices do not burn.
4 Add the stock and beans to the vegetables and add the bay leaf. Cover and return
    to the boil. Skim the surface again. Reduce the heat and simmer for 1½–2 hours
    until the beans are very tender.
5 Discard the bay leaf, then blend the soup until smooth. Season with salt and pepper
    and serve topped with yogurt and sprinkled with chives.

251 Broad Bean & Spinach Soup

PREPARATION TIME 20 minutes, plus overnight soaking and cooking the beans (optional)
and making the stock **COOKING TIME** 30 minutes

200g/7oz/1⅓ cups dried broad beans
  or 400g/14oz tinned broad beans,
  drained and rinsed
1½ tbsp olive or hemp oil
2 shallots, chopped
2 large garlic cloves, chopped
½–1 tbsp smoked paprika
2 tsp ground cumin
2 tsp ground coriander

1.4l/48fl oz/5½ cups Vegetable Stock
  (see page 12) or ready-made stock
400g/14oz tinned chopped tomatoes
140g/5oz spinach, any thick stalks
  removed, and leaves thinly sliced
salt and freshly ground black pepper
ground sumac, to serve
chopped coriander leaves, to serve

1 If using dried beans, put them in a bowl, cover with water and leave to soak
    overnight, then drain. Transfer to a saucepan and add 1.5l/53fl oz/6 cups water.
    Cover and bring to the boil, reduce the heat and simmer, covered, for 50 minutes–
    1 hour, then drain.
2 Heat the oil in a saucepan over a medium heat. Add the shallots and fry, stirring,
    for 2 minutes. Stir in the garlic and fry for 1–3 minutes until the shallots are
    softened but not coloured. Add the paprika, cumin and ground coriander and stir
    for 30 seconds. Watch closely so the spices do not burn.
3 Add the stock and tomatoes and season with salt and pepper. Cover and bring
    to the boil. Reduce the heat and simmer for 10 minutes for the flavours to blend.
    Meanwhile, if you have cooked dried beans, remove the thick outer skins.
4 Stir the beans and spinach into the pan and simmer for 2–3 minutes until the beans
    are hot and the spinach wilts. Adjust the salt and pepper, if necessary, then serve
    sprinkled with sumac and coriander leaves.

252 The Italian Doctor's Bean & Spaghetti Soup

PREPARATION TIME 15 minutes, plus soaking the beans overnight
COOKING TIME 1½ hours

200g/7oz/1 cup dried butter beans
1 carrot, peeled
1 celery stick, broken in half
1 onion, peeled and quartered
15g/½oz sage, tied together
4 tbsp extra-virgin olive oil, plus
    extra to serve

100g/3½oz spaghetti, broken into
    small pieces
salt and freshly ground black pepper
freshly grated Parmesan cheese,
    to serve

1   Put the beans in a bowl, cover with water and leave to soak overnight, then drain.
2   Put the beans, carrot, celery, onion, sage, oil and 2l/70fl oz/8 cups water in a
    saucepan. Cover and bring to the boil. Reduce the heat and simmer for 1¼ hours,
    stirring occasionally, until the beans are almost tender, then strain, reserving the
    cooking liquid. Discard the carrot, celery and sage and blend the onion and one-third
    of the beans until smooth. Return the mixture to the pan and stir in the remaining
    beans and 1.4l/48fl oz/5½ cups of the cooking liquid. Season with salt and pepper.
3   Bring to the boil, stirring occasionally. Stir in the spaghetti and boil for 8–10 minutes,
    or according to the packet instructions, until the pasta is al dente and the beans are
    tender. Stir frequently to prevent the spaghetti from sticking to the base of the pan.
    Adjust the salt and pepper, if necessary, then serve drizzled with olive oil and with
    cheese on the side.

253 Chickpea & Chorizo Soup

PREPARATION TIME 15 minutes, plus overnight soaking and cooking the chickpeas
(optional) and making the stock   COOKING TIME 1½ hours

220g/7¾oz/1 cup dried chickpeas
    or 400g/14oz tinned chickpeas,
    drained and rinsed
1 tbsp olive oil
100g/3½oz chorizo, casing removed
    and chopped
1 celery stick, finely chopped
4 large garlic cloves, finely chopped

1 red onion, finely chopped
400g/14oz tinned chopped tomatoes
1 tbsp tomato purée
½ tsp caster sugar
1l/35fl oz/4 cups Chicken Stock
    (see page 11) or ready-made stock
salt and freshly ground black pepper
fruity extra-virgin olive oil, to serve

1   If using dried chickpeas, put them in a bowl, cover with water and leave to soak
    overnight, then drain. Transfer to a saucepan, add 1.5l/53fl oz/6 cups water, cover
    and bring to the boil. Reduce the heat and simmer, covered, for 50 minutes–1 hour
    until almost tender, then drain.
2   Heat the oil in a saucepan over a medium heat. Add the chorizo and fry, stirring, for
    2–3 minutes until the fat starts to run. Remove from the pan and set aside. Stir the
    celery, garlic and onion into the fat remaining in the pan, reduce the heat to low and
    cook, covered, for 8–10 minutes until the onion and celery are softened. Stir in the
    chickpeas, tomatoes, tomato purée and sugar.
3   Add the stock and season with salt and pepper. Cover and bring to the boil. Skim,
    then reduce the heat to low and simmer, covered, for 10 minutes.
4   Blend half of the soup until smooth. Stir this mixture back into the pan, add the
    chorizo and reheat. Adjust the salt and pepper, if necessary, and serve drizzled
    with fruity olive oil.

Syrian Red Lentil & Lamb Soup

PREPARATION TIME 10 minutes, plus making the stock   **COOKING TIME** 1¼ hours

1.25l/44fl oz/5 cups Vegetable Stock
  (see page 12) or water
650g/1lb 7oz lamb shoulder chops
250g/9oz/1 cup split red lentils, rinsed
  and picked over
1 carrot, peeled and chopped
1 onion, peeled and finely chopped
1 tsp dried mint leaves
½ tsp ground coriander

½ tsp ground cumin
½ tsp chilli powder
a pinch of saffron threads
salt and freshly ground black pepper
chopped coriander or parsley leaves,
  to serve
lemon wedges, to serve
hot pepper sauce, to serve (optional)

1 Put the stock, lamb, lentils, carrot, onion, mint, ground coriander, cumin, chilli
   powder and saffron in a saucepan. Cover and bring to the boil. Reduce the heat
   to very low (use a heat diffuser if you have one) and simmer for 1–1¼ hours until
   the lamb is tender and the lentils have fallen apart.
2 Remove the lamb and bones from the soup and set aside until cool enough to
   handle. Skim the soup, if necessary. Cut the meat from the bones into bite-sized
   pieces and return it to the soup. Stir well and season with salt and pepper.
3 Serve sprinkled with coriander leaves and with lemon wedges for squeezing over
   and hot pepper sauce for adding at the table, if you like.

255 Mexican Bean Soup

PREPARATION TIME 15 minutes, plus overnight soaking and cooking the beans, 30 minutes soaking the chilli and making the stock   COOKING TIME 1 hour

100g/3½oz/scant ½ cup dried red
  kidney beans
100g/3½oz/1 cup dried pinto beans
1 dried chipotle chilli
1 tbsp sunflower oil
1 onion, chopped
2 large garlic cloves, finely chopped
1 tsp ground cumin
950ml/32fl oz/scant 4 cups
  Vegetable Stock (see page 12)
  or ready-made stock

400g/14oz tinned chopped tomatoes
½ tbsp dried oregano
a pinch of caster sugar
200g/7oz/1⅓ cups frozen sweetcorn
  kernels
salt and freshly ground black pepper
soured cream, to serve
chopped coriander leaves,
  to serve
tortilla chips, to serve

1   Put the kidney and pinto beans in a bowl, cover with water and leave to soak overnight, then drain. Transfer to a saucepan and add 1.5l/53fl oz/6 cups water. Cover, bring to the boil over a high heat, and boil for 10 minutes. Reduce the heat and simmer, covered, for 1 hour, then drain.

2   Put the chipotle chilli and at least 250ml/9fl oz/1 cup boiling water in a heatproof bowl and leave to soak for 30 minutes until tender, then strain, reserving 200ml/7fl oz/scant 1 cup of the water. Deseed the chilli, if you like, then finely chop and set aside.

3   Heat the oil in a saucepan over a medium heat. Add the onion and fry, stirring, for 2 minutes. Add the garlic and fry for 1–3 minutes until the onion is softened. Add the cumin and stir for 30 seconds until it is aromatic. Watch closely so it does not burn. Stir in the reserved soaking liquid, beans, chilli, stock, tomatoes, oregano and sugar and season with salt and pepper. Cover and bring to the boil, then reduce the heat and simmer for 40–50 minutes until the beans are tender.

4   Blend about one-third of the soup until smooth. Return this mixture to the soup, add the sweetcorn and boil for 3–5 minutes until tender. Adjust the salt and pepper, if necessary, and serve topped with soured cream and coriander and with tortilla chips on the side.

256 Red Lentil, Coconut & Spinach Soup

PREPARATION TIME 20 minutes, plus making the stock and seeds
COOKING TIME 55 minutes

2 tbsp groundnut or sunflower oil
1 large onion, chopped
1 large garlic clove, chopped
2.5cm/1in piece of root ginger,
  peeled and grated
1 red chilli, deseeded and chopped
1 tsp ground coriander
1 tsp ground cumin
½ tsp turmeric
1l/35fl oz/4 cups Vegetable Stock
  (see page 12) or ready-made stock

100g/3½oz/heaped ⅓ cup split red
  lentils, rinsed
400g/14oz tinned chopped tomatoes
½ tsp caster sugar
200ml/7fl oz/scant 1 cup coconut milk
2 handfuls of baby spinach leaves,
  chopped
salt and freshly ground black pepper
Spiced Seeds (see page 15), to serve
chopped coriander leaves, to serve

1   Heat the oil in a saucepan over a medium heat. Add the onion and fry, stirring, for 2 minutes. Add the garlic, ginger and chilli and stir for 1–3 minutes until the onion is softened. Add the ground coriander, cumin and turmeric and stir for 30 seconds. Watch closely so the spices do not burn. Add the stock, lentils, tomatoes and sugar. Cover and bring to the boil, then reduce the heat and simmer for 20 minutes.

2   Stir in the coconut milk and season with salt and pepper, then simmer, covered, for 10–20 minutes until the lentils are very tender. Add the spinach and simmer for 2–3 minutes until it wilts. Adjust the salt and pepper, if necessary, and serve sprinkled with the seeds and chopped coriander.

257 South Indian Lentil & Tomato Soup

PREPARATION TIME 15 minutes, plus making the chilli bon-bon (optional)
COOKING TIME 50 minutes

6 large garlic cloves, chopped
1 long red chilli, deseeded and
  thinly sliced
1½ tbsp sunflower or groundnut oil
1 large onion, finely chopped
3 tbsp split red lentils, rinsed
800g/1lb 12oz tinned chopped
  tomatoes

1 tbsp tomato purée
2 tbsp tamarind paste
¼ tsp black mustard seeds
¼ tsp fenugreek seeds
4 curry leaves
a pinch of ground asafoetida
salt and freshly ground black pepper
Chilli Bon-Bon, to serve (optional)

1 Put the garlic and chilli in a mortar and pound until a paste forms, then set aside.
2 Heat 1 tablespoon of the oil in a saucepan over a medium heat. Add the onion and
  fry, stirring, for 3–5 minutes until softened but not coloured. Add the garlic-chilli
  paste and stir for 30 seconds until aromatic. Watch closely so the paste does not
  burn. Stir in the lentils, tomatoes, tomato purée and 1.4l/48fl oz/5½ cups water,
  then cover and bring to the boil.
3 Add the tamarind paste and stir until it dissolves. Reduce the heat and simmer,
  covered, for 30–40 minutes until the lentils are tender. Season with salt and
  pepper, if necessary. Strain the soup for an even smoother texture, if you like.
4 Before serving, heat the remaining oil in a small frying pan over a high heat.
  Add the mustard seeds and stir for about 30 seconds until they pop. Stir in the
  fenugreek seeds, curry leaves and asafoetida, then pour this mixture over the soup.
  Serve with chilli bon-bon on the side.

258 Yellow Lentil Soup

PREPARATION TIME 15 minutes, plus making the stock COOKING TIME 40 minutes

30g/1oz ghee or butter
1 tbsp groundnut or sunflower oil
1 onion, finely chopped
1cm/½in piece of root ginger,
  peeled and grated
6 green cardamom pods, lightly
  crushed
1 tsp turmeric
½ tsp ground coriander
½ tsp cumin seeds
a pinch of ground asafoetida
a pinch of chilli powder, or to taste

100g/3½oz/⅓ cup split yellow lentils
  (toor dal), rinsed
1.5l/52 fl oz/6 cups Vegetable Stock
  (see page 12) or water
2 coriander sprigs, leaves and stalks,
  chopped, plus extra torn leaves
  to serve
lemon juice, to taste
salt and freshly ground black pepper
natural yogurt, to serve (optional)
garam masala, to serve

1 Melt the ghee with the oil in a saucepan over a medium heat. Add the onion and fry,
  stirring occasionally, for 3–5 minutes until softened but not coloured. Add the ginger,
  cardamom, turmeric, ground coriander, cumin seeds, asafoetida and chilli powder
  and stir for 30 seconds until aromatic. Watch closely so the spices do not burn.
2 Add the lentils, stock and coriander leaves and stalks. Cover and bring to the boil,
  then reduce the heat and simmer for 20–25 minutes until the lentils are very tender
  and starting to fall apart. Use a slotted spoon to fish out and discard the cardamom
  pods, then blend the soup to the preferred consistency. Add lemon juice and
  season with salt and pepper. Serve topped with yogurt and sprinkled with garam
  masala and coriander leaves.

259 Sour Green Lentil Soup

PREPARATION TIME 10 minutes, plus making the stock   COOKING TIME 50 minutes

1 tbsp groundnut or sunflower oil
1 large onion, finely chopped
2 garlic cloves, finely chopped
1 tsp ground coriander
1 tsp ground cumin
¼ tsp chilli flakes, or to taste
½ tsp cinnamon
1.25l/44fl oz/5 cups Vegetable Stock
   (see page 12) or ready-made stock

400g/14oz tinned chopped tomatoes
100g/3½oz/½ cup dried green lentils,
   rinsed
2 tbsp tamarind paste
2 tbsp tomato purée
1 tsp caster sugar
salt and freshly ground black pepper
chopped coriander leaves, to serve

1   Heat the oil in a saucepan over a high heat. Add the onion and fry, stirring,
    for 2 minutes. Add the garlic and fry for 1–3 minutes until the onion is softened but
    not coloured. Add the ground coriander, cumin, chilli flakes and cinnamon and stir
    for 30 seconds. Watch closely so the spices do not burn.
2   Add the stock, tomatoes, lentils, tamarind paste, tomato purée and sugar. Cover
    and bring to the boil, then reduce the heat and simmer for 30–40 minutes until
    the lentils are tender. Season with salt and pepper and serve sprinkled with
    chopped coriander.

260 Puy Lentil & Fennel Soup

PREPARATION TIME 15 minutes, plus making the stock   COOKING TIME 40 minutes

2 tbsp olive or hemp oil
1 celery stick, sliced
400g/14oz fennel, quartered
   lengthways and sliced, with the
   fronds reserved
1 shallot, finely chopped
4 large garlic cloves, finely chopped
1.4l/48fl oz/5½ cups Vegetable Stock
   (see page 12) or ready-made stock

100g/3½oz/½ cup dried Puy lentils,
   rinsed
½ tbsp dried dill
2 bay leaves
1 large handful of rocket leaves
salt and freshly ground black pepper
freshly grated Parmesan or pecorino
   cheese, to serve (optional)

1   Heat the oil in a saucepan over a medium heat. Add the celery, fennel and shallot
    and fry, stirring, for 2 minutes. Add the garlic and fry for 1–3 minutes until the
    vegetables are softened but not coloured. Add the stock, lentils, dill and bay leaves,
    then cover and bring to the boil. Reduce the heat and simmer for 20–30 minutes
    until the lentils are tender.
2   Discard the bay leaves and season with salt and pepper. Stir in the rocket leaves
    and simmer, uncovered, for 2–3 minutes until they have wilted. Serve with cheese
    for sprinkling over, if you like.

261 Starry Night Soup with Spinach

PREPARATION TIME 5 minutes, plus making the stock   COOKING TIME 15 minutes

1.4l/48fl oz/5½ cups any homemade
   stock (see pages 10–13)
200g/7oz/1⅓ cups stelline or other
   small soup pasta
a small pinch of chilli flakes

2 large handfuls of baby spinach
   leaves
salt and freshly ground black pepper
fruity extra-virgin olive oil, to serve
freshly grated Parmesan cheese,
   to serve

1   Put the stock in a saucepan and season with salt and pepper. Cover and bring
    to the boil. Add the pasta and chilli flakes and return to the boil, then boil
    for 2 minutes.
2   Stir in the spinach and boil for 1–3 minutes until the pasta is al dente. Adjust the
    salt and pepper, if necessary. Serve immediately, sprinkled with Parmesan and
    drizzled with oil.

262 Thai Chicken & Jasmine Rice Soup

PREPARATION TIME 10 minutes, plus making the chillies and garlic
COOKING TIME 30 minutes

2 coriander sprigs, including roots,
    stalks and leaves, coarsely
    chopped, plus extra leaves to serve
1cm/½in piece of galangal, peeled
    and smashed in one piece
1cm/½in piece of root ginger, peeled
    and smashed in one piece
500g/1lb 2oz skinned chicken thighs

175g/6oz/heaped ¾ cup jasmine rice,
    rinsed with cold water and drained
1 tsp salt
Chillies in Vinegar (see page 15),
    to serve
Crisp-Fried Garlic (see page 15),
    to serve
fish sauce, to serve

1   Put the coriander, galangal, ginger and 1.25l/44fl oz/5 cups water in a saucepan.
    Cover and bring to the boil. Add the chicken, cover and return to the boil. Skim,
    then reduce the heat and simmer for 15–20 minutes until the chicken is cooked
    through and the juices run clear when you cut a piece. Remove the chicken and set
    aside until cool enough to handle. Discard the coriander stalks, galangal and ginger
    and keep the soup simmering.
2   Meanwhile, put the rice and salt in another saucepan and cover with enough water
    to come up to the first joint in your finger from the top of the rice. Bring to the boil,
    uncovered. As soon as the water boils, reduce the heat and simmer, covered,
    for 6–10 minutes until the rice is tender and has absorbed most of the liquid. Turn
    off the heat, immediately stir in 4 ladlefuls of the chicken cooking liquid and leave
    the rice to stand, uncovered, until the soup is ready. If the rice dries out and holes
    appear on the surface, add more of the cooking liquid.
3   Cut the chicken from the bones into bite-sized pieces and return it to the soup.
    Divide the rice into bowls and ladle the soup over it. Serve sprinkled with coriander
    and with the chillies, fried garlic and fish sauce on the side.

263 Lentil & Sausage Soup

PREPARATION TIME 20 minutes, plus making the stock   COOKING TIME 55 minutes

55g/2oz thick smoked lardons
1 carrot, peeled and finely chopped
1 celery stick, finely chopped
2 shallots, finely chopped
½ leek, thinly sliced and rinsed
1 tsp dried thyme leaves
½ tsp ground cumin
a pinch of ground cloves
1.25l/44fl oz/5 cups Vegetable Stock
    (see page 12) or ready-made stock
280g/10oz/scant 1½ cups dried Puy
    or other green lentils, rinsed

1 bay leaf
2 tbsp garlic-flavoured olive oil
3 pork sausages, such as Toulouse
    or Italian sweet
1 large roasted red pepper in olive
    oil, drained and chopped
salt and freshly ground black pepper
chopped parsley leaves, to serve
balsamic or red wine vinegar,
    to serve

1   Heat a large saucepan over a medium-high heat. Add the lardons and fry, stirring,
    for 5–7 minutes until they are lightly coloured and starting to give off their fat. Stir in
    the carrot, celery, shallots and leek and cover. Reduce the heat to low and cook for
    10–12 minutes until lightly browned. Stir in the thyme, cumin and cloves. Add the
    stock, lentils and bay leaf. Cover and bring to the boil. Reduce the heat and simmer
    for 10 minutes.
2   Meanwhile, heat the oil in a small frying pan over a high heat. Add the sausages
    and fry, turning occasionally, until browned all over. Transfer the sausages to the
    pan with the lentils and simmer, covered, for 15–20 minutes until the lentils are
    tender and the sausages are cooked through. Remove the sausages and slice
    diagonally, then return to the pan, add the red pepper and heat through. Discard the
    bay leaf. Season with salt and pepper, then serve sprinkled with parsley and with
    vinegar on the side.

264 # Red Rice & Wild Rocket Soup

PREPARATION TIME 10 minutes, plus making the stock   **COOKING TIME** 55 minutes

1.5l/52fl oz/6 cups Vegetable Stock
  (see page 12) or ready-made stock
4 large garlic cloves, crushed
1 tsp fennel seeds
1½ tbsp olive or hemp oil, plus extra
  to serve (optional)
2 shallots, halved lengthways and
  thinly sliced

100g/3½oz/½ cup red rice
1 tsp dried thyme leaves
2 large handfuls of wild rocket
  leaves, rinsed and torn
salt and freshly ground black pepper
French bread, to serve

1 Put the stock, garlic and fennel seeds in a saucepan. Cover and bring to the boil, then boil slowly for 10 minutes to blend the flavours. Strain the stock, discarding the garlic and seeds, and set aside.

2 Heat the oil in a saucepan over a medium heat. Add the shallots and fry, stirring occasionally, for 3–5 minutes until softened but not coloured. Stir in the rice, then add the stock and thyme and season with salt and pepper. Cover and bring to the boil. Reduce the heat and simmer for 20–25 minutes, or according to the packet instructions, until the rice is tender but chewy.

3 Add the rocket and simmer, uncovered, for 2–3 minutes until wilted. Adjust the salt and pepper, if necessary, and serve with French bread.

265 Brown Lentil Soup

PREPARATION TIME 15 minutes, plus making the stock and seeds
COOKING TIME 1 hour

2 tbsp garlic-flavoured olive oil
1 carrot, diced
1 celery stick, finely chopped
1 onion, finely chopped
1 turnip, finely chopped
1.25l/44fl oz/5 cups Vegetable Stock
   (see page 12) or ready-made stock

200g/7oz/heaped 1 cup dried brown
   lentils, rinsed
1 rosemary sprig
salt and freshly ground black pepper
Spiced Seeds (see page 15), to serve
chopped coriander leaves, to serve

1   Heat the oil in a saucepan over a medium heat. Add the carrot, celery, onion and turnip, reduce the heat to low and cook for 8–10 minutes, stirring occasionally, until the vegetables are softened but not coloured.

2   Add the stock, lentils and rosemary. Cover and bring to the boil. Reduce the heat and simmer for 35–40 minutes until the lentils are tender. Discard the rosemary sprig and season with salt and pepper. Serve sprinkled with seeds and coriander.

266 Canadian Yellow Pea Soup

PREPARATION TIME 15 minutes, plus making the stock and flavoured oil
COOKING TIME 1½ hours

2 tbsp olive or sunflower oil
1 carrot, peeled and very finely diced
1 celery stick, very finely chopped
1 onion, very finely chopped
1.6l/55½fl oz/6½ cups Chicken Stock
   (see page 11) or ready-made stock

200g/9oz/scant 1 cup yellow split
   peas, rinsed
2 bay leaves
200g/7oz smoked ham, shredded
salt and freshly ground black pepper
1 recipe quantity Paprika & Lemon
   Oil (see page 26), to serve

1   Heat the olive oil in a large saucepan over a medium heat. Stir in the carrot, celery and onion, reduce the heat to low and cook, covered, for 8–10 minutes, stirring occasionally, until softened but not coloured.

2   Add the stock, split peas and bay leaves, cover and bring to the boil. Reduce the heat to very low (use a heat diffuser if you have one) and simmer, stirring occasionally, for 1¼–1½ hours until the peas are very tender. Stir in the ham and heat through. Discard the bay leaves. Season with salt and pepper, but remember the ham might be salty. Serve drizzled with the paprika oil.

267 Split Pea & Apple Soup

PREPARATION TIME 15 minutes   COOKING TIME 2 hours

2 sweet cooking apples, peeled,
   quartered, cored and chopped
1 tbsp lemon juice
2 tbsp sunflower oil
2 leeks, sliced and rinsed
200g/7oz/scant 1 cup green split
   peas, rinsed

1.5l/52fl oz/6 cups Vegetable Stock
   (see page 12) or ready-made stock
1 tsp ground ginger
lemon juice, to taste
125ml/4fl oz/½ cup double cream
salt and freshly ground black pepper

1   Toss the apples and lemon juice together in a bowl and set aside.

2   Heat the oil in a saucepan over a medium heat. Add the leeks and fry, stirring occasionally, for 3–5 minutes until softened but not coloured. Stir in the split peas and stock, cover and bring to the boil. Skim, if necessary, then reduce the heat and simmer, covered, for 1¼ hours.

3   Add the apples and simmer, covered, for 15–30 minutes until the split peas are very tender. Season with salt and pepper, then blend the soup until smooth. Stir in the ginger and add lemon juice to taste. Stir in the cream and reheat the soup, if necessary. Adjust the salt and pepper, if necessary, and serve. If reheating this soup, add a little extra stock, if necessary, to thin it.

268 Split Pea & Ham Soup

PREPARATION TIME 15 minutes, plus making the flavoured oil   **COOKING TIME** 2 hours

2 tbsp sunflower oil
2 celery sticks, finely chopped
1 carrot, peeled and finely chopped
1 onion, finely chopped
1 cooked unsmoked gammon bone
    with any meat that is left on it
200g/7oz/scant 1 cup green split
    peas, rinsed

2 bay leaves
½ tbsp dried thyme leaves
350g/12oz cooked ham in one thick
    piece, shredded or finely diced
caster sugar, to taste (optional)
salt and freshly ground black pepper
1 recipe quantity Crushed Mint Oil
    (see page 15), to serve

1   Heat the oil in a large saucepan over a medium heat. Stir in the celery, carrot and
    onion, reduce the heat to low, cover and cook, stirring occasionally, for 8–10 minutes
    until softened but not coloured.
2   Add the gammon bone and split peas to the pan and stir in 1.6l/56fl oz/
    scant 6½ cups water. Cover and bring to the boil. Skim, if necessary. Stir in the bay
    leaves and thyme, reduce the heat to very low (use a heat diffuser if you have one)
    and simmer, covered, stirring frequently, for 1½–2 hours, until the split peas are very
    tender and have thickened the soup and any meat is coming away from the bone.
3   Remove the bone from the pan and set aside. When it is cool enough to handle,
    shred any meat that might have been on it. Return the meat to the soup, add
    the ham and reheat. Adjust the salt and pepper, if necessary, but remember the
    gammon bone will have been salty so you might only need pepper; if the soup
    is too salty, stir in a little sugar. Serve drizzled with the mint oil.

269 Black Lentil & Cauliflower Soup

PREPARATION TIME 20 minutes, plus making the stock and preparing the tomatoes
COOKING TIME 1¼ hours

1.5l/52fl oz/6 cups Vegetable Stock
(see page 12) or ready-made stock
140g/5oz/heaped ½ cup split black
lentils (urad dal), rinsed
4 coriander sprigs, leaves and stalks
chopped, plus extra chopped
leaves to serve
seeds from 6 green cardamom pods,
3 cloves, 3 sliced garlic cloves,
1 bay leaf, ½ cinnamon stick and
1 tsp lightly crushed coriander
seeds, tied together in muslin

1cm/½in piece of root ginger,
peeled and grated
1 tbsp groundnut or sunflower oil
1 onion, finely chopped
2 garlic cloves, crushed
1 tsp cumin seeds
a pinch of chilli flakes, or to taste
2 large tomatoes, grated (see page 9)
280g/10oz cauliflower, cut into florets
salt and freshly ground black pepper

1 Put the stock, lentils, coriander, spice bundle and ginger in a saucepan. Cover and bring to the boil, then reduce the heat and simmer for 35–40 minutes until the lentils are very soft.
2 Meanwhile, heat the oil in another saucepan over a medium heat. Add the onion and fry, stirring, for 2 minutes. Add the garlic and fry for 1–3 minutes until the onion is softened. Add the cumin seeds and chilli flakes and stir for 30 seconds until aromatic. Watch closely so the seeds do not burn. Stir in the tomatoes.
3 Remove two-thirds of the lentils from the soup and set aside. Discard the spice bundle. Add the tomato and onion mixture to the pan with the lentils and blend until smooth. Season with salt and pepper, then return the soup to the boil, skimming as necessary. Add the cauliflower and gently boil, uncovered, for 10–12 minutes until the florets are tender but still hold their shape. Return the reserved lentils to the pan and heat through. Adjust the salt and pepper, if necessary, and serve sprinkled with coriander leaves.

270 Rice & Purple Broccoli Soup

PREPARATION TIME 10 minutes, plus making the stock   COOKING TIME 35 minutes

55g/2oz lardons
1 tbsp olive oil
1 onion, finely chopped
1 garlic clove, crushed
140g/5oz/⅔ cup Arborio rice

1.5l/52fl oz/6 cups Chicken Stock
(see page 11) or ready-made stock
115g/4oz small purple or green
broccoli florets
2 thyme sprigs
salt and freshly ground black pepper

1 This soup is best served just after making and not left to stand, or it will become too thick. Put the lardons in a saucepan over a medium heat and fry, stirring, for 3–5 minutes until they begin to crisp and the fat runs. Remove them from the pan and set aside. Add the oil to the fat remaining in the pan and heat. Add the onion and fry, stirring, for 2 minutes. Add the garlic and fry for 1–3 minutes until the onion is softened but not coloured. Add the rice and stir for 1 minute.
2 Add a ladleful of the stock and stir until it is absorbed. Stir in the remaining stock, cover and bring to the boil, then reduce the heat to low. Add the broccoli and thyme and season with salt and pepper.
3 Simmer, uncovered, for 15–18 minutes until the rice is tender, stirring occasionally to prevent it from sticking to the base of the pan. Add the lardons and discard the thyme sprigs. Adjust the salt and pepper, if necessary, and serve immediately.

271 Creamed Barley Soup

PREPARATION TIME 15 minutes, plus making the stock and toasting the seeds
COOKING TIME 50 minutes

1½ tbsp olive or hemp oil
1 large onion, sliced
3 garlic cloves, finely chopped
110g/3¾oz/½ cup pearl barley
1.4l/48fl oz/5½ cups Vegetable Stock
  (see page 12) or ready-made stock
140g/5oz pumpkin, peeled, deseeded
  and finely chopped

1 leek, sliced and rinsed
4 tbsp natural yogurt (optional)
salt and freshly ground black pepper
pumpkin seeds, toasted (see page 9),
  to serve
chopped coriander leaves, to serve

1   Heat the oil in a saucepan over a medium heat. Add the onion and fry, stirring
    occasionally, for 2 minutes. Add the garlic and fry for 1–3 minutes until the onion
    is softened but not coloured.
2   Stir in the barley and stock. Cover and bring to the boil. Skim. Stir in the pumpkin
    and leek, reduce the heat and simmer, covered, for 30–40 minutes until the barley
    is very tender, then season with salt and pepper. Blend half the soup for an even
    smoother texture, if you like.
3   Stir in the yogurt, if using, and adjust the salt and pepper, if necessary. Serve
    immediately, sprinkled with seeds and coriander.

272 Egyptian Brown Lentil & Greens Soup

PREPARATION TIME 15 minutes, plus making the stock and dukkah
COOKING TIME 45 minutes

1 tbsp garlic-flavoured olive oil
1 onion, chopped
2 large garlic cloves, finely chopped
1.4l/48fl oz/5½ cups Vegetable Stock
  (see page 12) or ready-made stock
200g/7oz/heaped 1 cup dried brown
  lentils, rinsed

280g/10oz greens, such as curly kale
  or mustard greens, thick stalks
  removed and leaves chopped
1 handful of coriander leaves,
  chopped
2–4 tbsp lemon juice
salt and freshly ground black pepper
Dukkah (see page 15), to serve

1   Heat the oil in a saucepan over a medium heat. Add the onion and fry, stirring,
    for 2 minutes. Add the garlic and fry for 1–3 minutes until the onion is softened but
    not coloured. Add the stock and lentils, cover and bring to the boil, then reduce the
    heat and simmer for 15 minutes.
2   Add the greens, coriander and 2 tablespoons of the lemon juice and simmer for
    15–20 minutes until the lentils are tender. Season with salt and pepper, adding
    extra lemon juice, if you like. Serve sprinkled with dukkah.

273 Greek Lentil & Garlic Soup

PREPARATION TIME 10 minutes, plus making the stock   COOKING TIME 55 minutes

2 tbsp olive or hemp oil
8 garlic cloves, crushed
2 onions, chopped
400g/14oz tinned chopped tomatoes
250g/9oz/1 cup split red lentils, rinsed
1l/35fl oz/4 cups Chicken Stock
  (see page 11) or ready-made stock

1 bay leaf
1 tbsp tomato purée
1 tsp caster sugar
salt and freshly ground black pepper
finely chopped coriander or mint
  leaves, to serve
red wine vinegar, to serve

1   Heat the oil in a large saucepan over a medium heat. Stir in the garlic and onions,
    reduce the heat to low and cook, covered, for 10–12 minutes until softened. Stir in
    the tomatoes, lentils, stock, bay leaf, tomato purée and sugar. Season with pepper.
2   Cover and bring to the boil. Reduce the heat to very low (use a heat diffuser if you
    have one) and simmer for 30–40 minutes until the lentils are tender, then season
    with salt and pepper. Serve sprinkled with coriander and with vinegar on the side.

274 Rice & Courgette Soup

PREPARATION TIME 15 minutes, plus making the stock and croûtes
COOKING TIME 45 minutes

2 tbsp olive or hemp oil
1 large onion, finely chopped
280g/10oz courgettes, halved
 lengthways and sliced
1.5l/52fl oz/6 cups Vegetable Stock
 (see page 12) or ready-made stock
1 tbsp tomato purée
2 garlic cloves, finely chopped
2 tbsp chopped parsley leaves

1 bay leaf
85g/3oz/scant ½ cup long-grain
 white rice
salt and freshly ground black pepper
1 small handful of basil leaves, torn,
 to serve
1 recipe quantity Goat's Cheese
 Croûtes (see page 14), to serve

1 This soup is best made just before serving because its vibrant green colour dulls
   on standing. It also thickens on standing and will need extra stock stirred in
   if reheated. Heat the oil in a saucepan over a medium heat. Add the onion and fry,
   stirring occasionally, for 3 minutes. Add the courgettes and fry for 3 minutes until
   the skins turn bright green and the onions are softened.
2 Stir in the stock, tomato purée, garlic, parsley and bay leaf and season with salt and
   pepper. Cover and bring to the boil, then reduce the heat and simmer, covered, for
   10–15 minutes until the courgettes are very soft. Discard the bay leaf and blend the
   soup to the preferred consistency. Stir in the rice and return the soup to the boil,
   then boil, uncovered, for 10–15 minutes until the rice is tender, stirring frequently
   to prevent it from sticking to the base of the pan. Adjust the salt and pepper,
   if necessary, and serve immediately, sprinkled with basil and with cheese croûtes.

275 Wild Rice & Mushroom Soup

PREPARATION TIME 15 minutes, plus 30 minutes soaking the mushrooms and making
the stock   COOKING TIME 1 hour

30g/1oz dried porcini mushrooms
15g/½oz butter
1 tbsp olive or hemp oil
1 celery stick, finely chopped
1 onion, finely diced
250g/9oz portobello or chestnut
 mushrooms, trimmed and sliced
500ml/17fl oz/2 cups Vegetable Stock
 (see page 12) or ready-made stock

200g/7oz/1 cup wild rice
1 tbsp chopped tarragon
 or ½ tbsp dried
½ tbsp Worcestershire Sauce
salt and freshly ground black pepper
2 spring onions, finely chopped,
 to serve

1 Put the porcini mushrooms and 750ml/26fl oz/3 cups boiling water in a heatproof
   bowl and leave to soak for 30 minutes until tender. Strain through a muslin-lined
   sieve and reserve the liquid. Squeeze the mushrooms dry and trim the stalks,
   if necessary, then thinly slice the caps and stalks and set aside.
2 Melt the butter with the oil in a saucepan over a medium heat. Add the celery and
   onion and fry, stirring occasionally, for 3–5 minutes until softened but not coloured.
   Stir in the porcini and portobello mushrooms, season with salt and fry, stirring
   occasionally, for 5–8 minutes until they give off their juices. Add the stock and wild
   rice and season with pepper. Cover and bring to the boil.
3 Stir in the tarragon, reduce the heat and simmer, covered, for 35–40 minutes until
   the rice is tender. Stir in the Worcestershire sauce and adjust the salt and pepper,
   if necessary, but it is unlikely to need salt. Serve sprinkled with the spring onions.

276 Wild Mushroom Risotto Soup

PREPARATION TIME 10 minutes, plus making the stock   **COOKING TIME** 1 hour

30g/1oz dried porcini mushrooms
15g/½oz dried morel mushrooms
1.25l/44fl oz/5 cups Vegetable Stock
   (see page 12) or ready-made stock,
   plus extra as needed
5 tbsp olive oil
2 tbsp finely chopped parsley leaves
1 large onion, finely chopped

2 garlic cloves, very finely chopped
140g/5oz/⅔ cup Arborio rice
4 tbsp dry red wine
55g/2oz freshly grated Parmesan
   cheese, plus extra to serve
1 tbsp butter
salt and freshly ground black pepper
basil leaves, to serve

1   Put both mushrooms and the stock in a saucepan and season lightly with salt. Cover and bring to the boil, then reduce the heat and simmer for 15 minutes until the mushrooms are tender. Strain through a muslin-lined sieve, then set the liquid aside in a covered saucepan over a low heat. Rinse the mushrooms, then squeeze them dry, trim the base of the stalks and thinly slice the caps and stalks.

2   Heat 2 tablespoons of the oil in a frying pan over a medium heat. Add the mushrooms, season lightly with salt and stir for 5–8 minutes until they give off their juices. Stir in the parsley and season with pepper, then transfer to a bowl and set aside.

3   Heat the remaining oil in the wiped-out frying pan over a medium heat. Add the onion and fry, stirring, for 2 minutes. Stir in the garlic and fry for 1–3 minutes until the onion is softened. Add the rice and stir until the grains are coated. Add the wine and cook for 2–4 minutes until it is absorbed, then add a ladleful of the stock and stir until it is absorbed. Continue adding stock, ladleful by ladleful, for 15–20 minutes, stirring, until the rice is tender. The texture should be 'soupy' and not as thick as a conventional risotto, so stir in extra stock, if necessary.

4   Add the mushrooms, cheese and butter and stir until the cheese melts. Adjust the salt and pepper, if necessary, but remember the mushrooms have already been salted and the cheese is salty. Serve sprinkled with basil and cheese.

277 Venetian Rice & Pea Soup

PREPARATION TIME 10 minutes, plus making the stock   **COOKING TIME** 35 minutes

85g/3oz butter
1 tbsp extra-virgin olive oil,
   plus extra to serve
1 shallot, finely chopped
85g/3oz pancetta, skin removed,
   if necessary, and chopped
5 tbsp dry vermouth or
   dry white wine

200g/7oz/scant 1 cup Arborio rice
1.25l/44fl oz/5 cups Chicken Stock
   (see page 11) or ready-made stock,
   plus extra as needed
140g/5oz/1 cup frozen peas
55g/2oz freshly grated Parmesan
   cheese, plus extra to serve
salt and freshly ground black pepper

1   Melt 55g/2oz of the butter with the oil in a saucepan over a medium heat. Add the shallot and fry, stirring, for 2 minutes. Stir in the pancetta and fry for 1–3 minutes until the shallot is softened but not coloured. Add the vermouth and simmer for 4–6 minutes until almost evaporated.

2   Add the rice and stir until coated. Stir in the stock and season with salt and pepper. Bring to the boil, stirring occasionally, then reduce the heat and simmer for 10 minutes, stirring. Add the peas and stir for 5–10 minutes until the rice is tender but not overcooked and the peas are tender. The texture should be 'soupy' and not as thick as a conventional risotto, so stir in extra stock, if necessary. Stir in the remaining butter and the cheese and adjust the salt and pepper, if necessary, but remember the cheese is salty. Serve with olive oil and cheese on the side.

Mixed Grain & Red Lentil Soup

PREPARATION TIME 10 minutes, plus making the stock and preparing the tomatoes
COOKING TIME 50 minutes

1 tbsp olive or hemp oil
1 large onion, finely chopped
2 large garlic cloves, chopped
1.4l/48fl oz/5½ cups Vegetable Stock
  (see page 12) or ready-made stock
4 tbsp split red lentils, rinsed
2 tbsp bulgar wheat
2 tbsp long-grain white rice

3 tomatoes, grated (see page 9)
1 tbsp dried mint, plus extra to serve
2 tbsp tomato purée
½ tbsp hot or sweet paprika,
  or to taste
½ tsp cayenne pepper, or to taste
salt and freshly ground black pepper
extra-virgin olive oil, to serve

1 Heat the oil in a saucepan over a medium heat. Add the onion and fry, stirring,
   for 2 minutes. Add the garlic and fry for 1–3 minutes until the onion is softened but
   not coloured. Add the stock, lentils, bulgar wheat, rice, tomatoes, mint, tomato
   purée, paprika and cayenne. Cover and bring to the boil, then reduce the heat and
   simmer for 30–40 minutes until the lentils, wheat and rice are all tender. Stir
   occasionally to prevent the grains from sticking to the base of the pan.
2 Blend half of the soup until smooth. Return the mixture to the pan, stir well and
   season with salt and pepper. Serve sprinkled with mint and drizzled with olive oil.

279 Moroccan Vegetable & Couscous Soup

PREPARATION TIME 20 minutes, plus making the stock and dukkah
COOKING TIME 20 minutes

1½ tbsp olive or hemp oil
1 red onion, chopped
2 large garlic cloves, crushed
1 tsp ground coriander
1 tsp ground cumin
1 tsp turmeric
2 tsp harissa paste, or to taste
1.25l/44fl oz/5 cups Vegetable Stock
  (see page 12) or ready-made stock
225g/8oz pumpkin, peeled, deseeded
  and chopped

1 courgette, quartered lengthways
  and sliced
1 red pepper, deseeded and sliced
85g/3oz/scant ½ cup couscous
1 tbsp butter
salt and freshly ground black pepper
Dukkah (see page 15), to serve
shredded coriander leaves, to serve
hot pepper sauce, to serve

1 Heat the oil in a saucepan over a medium heat. Add the onion and fry, stirring occasionally, for 2 minutes. Add the garlic and fry for 1–3 minutes until the onion is softened. Stir in the ground coriander, cumin and turmeric and fry for 30 seconds. Watch closely so the spices do not burn.
2 Stir in the harissa paste, then add the stock, pumpkin, courgette and red pepper and season with salt and pepper. Cover and bring to the boil. Reduce the heat and simmer for 10–15 minutes until all the vegetables are tender. Adjust the salt and pepper, if necessary.
3 Meanwhile, put the couscous and butter in an heatproof bowl, season with salt and pepper and add enough boiling water to cover by 2.5cm/1in. Cover with a clean, folded tea towel and set aside for 10 minutes, or according to the packet instructions, until the water is absorbed and the grains are tender. Pour off any excess water, if necessary, then fluff with a fork. Divide the couscous into bowls and ladle the soup over it. Sprinkle with the dukkah and coriander leaves and serve with hot pepper sauce.

280 Mushroom & Millet Soup

PREPARATION TIME 20 minutes, plus making the stock   COOKING TIME 40 minutes

1½ tbsp garlic-flavoured olive oil
100g/3½oz/½ cup millet
1 leek, thinly sliced and rinsed
2 large garlic cloves, chopped
500g/1lb 2oz chestnut or button
  mushrooms, trimmed and sliced
1.25l/44fl oz/5 cups Beef Stock
  (see page 10) or ready-made stock

2 carrots, peeled, halved lengthways
  and sliced
1 bay leaf
2 tsp dried marjoram
15g/½oz parsley, leaves finely
  chopped and stalks tied together
  and crushed
salt and freshly ground black pepper

1 Heat 1 tablespoon of the oil in a saucepan over a medium heat. Add the millet and stir for 1–2 minutes until it gives off a toasted aroma and just starts to brown. Watch closely so it does not burn. Immediately transfer it to a bowl and set aside.
2 Heat the remaining oil in the pan. Add the leek and fry, stirring occasionally, for 2 minutes, then add the garlic and fry for 1–3 minutes until the leek is softened but not coloured. Add the mushrooms, season with salt and fry, stirring occasionally, for 5–8 minutes until the mushrooms give off their juices.
3 Return the millet to the pan. Add the stock, carrots, bay leaf, marjoram and parsley stalks and season with salt and pepper. Cover and bring to the boil, then reduce the heat and simmer for 15–20 minutes until the millet is tender. Discard the bay leaf and parsley stalks and stir in the parsley leaves. Adjust the salt and pepper, if necessary, and serve.

281 Turkish Chickpea Soup

PREPARATION TIME 15 minutes, plus soaking the chickpeas overnight and making the stock   COOKING TIME 2 hours

220g/7¾oz/1 cup dried chickpeas
2 tbsp garlic-flavoured olive oil,
   plus extra to serve
1 large onion, finely chopped
2 large garlic cloves, chopped
½ tsp ground coriander
½ tsp ground cumin
a pinch of chilli flakes, or to taste

1.25l/44fl oz/5 cups Vegetable Stock
   (see page 12) or ready-made stock
400g/14oz tinned chopped tomatoes
salt and freshly ground black pepper
ground sumac, to serve
feta cheese, crumbled, to serve
chopped coriander leaves, to serve

1   Put the chickpeas in a bowl, cover with water and leave to soak overnight, then drain.
2   Heat the oil in a saucepan over a medium heat. Add the onion and fry, stirring, for 2 minutes. Add the garlic and stir for 1–3 minutes until the onion is softened. Add the coriander, cumin and chilli flakes and stir for 30 seconds. Watch closely so the spices do not burn. Stir in the stock, tomatoes and chickpeas, cover and bring to the boil, then reduce the heat and simmer for 1½–2 hours, stirring occasionally and topping up with water, if necessary, until the chickpeas are very tender. Season with salt and pepper.
3   Blend about one-third of the soup until smooth. Stir this mixture back into the pan, adjust the salt and pepper, if necessary, and serve sprinkled with sumac, feta and coriander.

282 Hearty Barley & Mushroom Soup

PREPARATION TIME 15 minutes, plus 30 minutes soaking the mushrooms and making the stock   COOKING TIME 1 hour

15g/½oz dried porcini mushrooms
55g/2oz smoked lardons
1 tbsp olive or hemp oil, as needed
1 large red onion, finely chopped
2 garlic cloves, chopped
400g/14oz chestnut or portobello
   mushrooms, trimmed and
   chopped

1l/35fl oz/4 cups Beef Stock
   (see page 10) or ready-made stock
55g/2oz/¼ cup pearl barley
1 tbsp dried oregano or sage
½ tbsp Worcestershire sauce
salt and freshly ground black pepper
chopped parsley leaves, to serve

1   Put the porcini mushrooms in a heatproof bowl, cover with 250ml/9fl oz/1 cup hot water and leave to soak for 30 minutes until tender. Strain the mushrooms through a muslin-lined sieve and reserve the liquid. Squeeze the mushrooms dry, then trim off the base of the stalks, chop the stalks and caps and set aside.
2   Put the lardons in a saucepan over a medium heat and fry, stirring, for 3–5 minutes until they begin to crisp and the fat runs. Remove them from the pan and set aside.
3   Add as much oil as necessary to the fat remaining in the pan to make about 1 tablespoon and heat. Add the onion and fry, stirring, for 2 minutes, then add the garlic and fry for 1–3 minutes until the onion is softened but not coloured. Add the chestnut mushrooms, season with salt and stir for 5–8 minutes until the mushrooms give off their liquid. Add the porcini mushrooms, soaking liquid, stock, barley and oregano.
4   Cover and bring to the boil, then reduce the heat and simmer for 30–40 minutes until the barley is tender. Add the Worcestershire sauce and adjust the salt and pepper, if necessary, but remember the mushrooms have already been salted. Serve immediately, sprinkled with parsley.

283 Spelt & Pinto Bean Soup

PREPARATION TIME 15 minutes, plus overnight soaking and cooking the beans
COOKING TIME 1½ hours

100g/3½oz/½ cup dried pinto beans
1½ tbsp olive or hemp oil,
    plus extra to serve
1 carrot, peeled and finely chopped
½ celery stick, finely chopped
½ onion, finely chopped
2 large garlic cloves, finely chopped

400g/14oz tinned chopped tomatoes
1 small handful of thyme,
    tied together
1½ tsp dried sage
55g/2oz/scant ⅓ cup spelt
salt and freshly ground black pepper
chopped parsley leaves, to serve

1   Put the beans in a bowl, cover with water and leave to soak overnight, then drain.
    Transfer to a saucepan and add 1.5l/53fl oz/6 cups water. Cover and bring to the
    boil, then reduce the heat and simmer, covered, for 50 minutes–1 hour. Drain.
2   Heat the oil in a saucepan over a medium heat. Add the carrot, celery and onion
    and fry, stirring occasionally, for 2 minutes. Add the garlic and fry for 1–3 minutes
    until the onion is softened but not coloured, then stir in the beans, tomatoes,
    thyme, sage and 1.4l/48fl oz/5½ cups water. Cover and bring to the boil, then
    reduce the heat and simmer for 30 minutes.
3   Add the spelt and return the soup to the boil, stirring. Reduce the heat and simmer,
    covered, for 35–45 minutes until the beans and spelt are tender. Discard the thyme
    sprigs and season with salt and pepper, if necessary. Serve sprinkled with parsley
    and with oil on the side for drizzling. If reheating this soup, add a little extra stock,
    if necessary, to thin it.

284 Quinoa Soup with Tomatoes & Broccoli

PREPARATION TIME 15 minutes, plus making the stock and gremolata and preparing
the tomatoes   **COOKING TIME** 35 minutes

1 tbsp hemp or olive oil
1 onion, finely chopped
4 large garlic cloves, very finely
    chopped
670ml/23fl oz/2⅔ cups passata
875ml/30fl oz/3½ cups Vegetable
    Stock (see page 12)
    or ready-made stock

4 large tomatoes, peeled
    (see page 9), deseeded
    and chopped
¼ head broccoli, cut into small florets
150g/5½oz/¾ cup quinoa, rinsed
salt and freshly ground black pepper
1 recipe quantity Gremolata
    (see page 198), to serve

1   Heat the oil in a saucepan over a medium heat. Add the onion and fry, stirring
    occasionally, for 2 minutes. Add the garlic and fry for 1–3 minutes until the onion
    is softened but not coloured, then stir in the passata and 625ml/21½fl oz/2½ cups
    of the stock and season with salt and pepper.
2   Cover and bring to the boil, then reduce the heat and simmer for 10 minutes.
    Stir in the tomatoes and broccoli and simmer, uncovered, for 10–15 minutes
    until the broccoli is tender.
3   Meanwhile, put the quinoa and remaining stock in a separate saucepan, cover
    and bring to the boil. Reduce the heat and simmer for 15–20 minutes until the
    grains are tender and most of the liquid is absorbed. Drain.
4   Stir the quinoa into the soup and adjust the salt and pepper, if necessary.
    Serve topped with gremolata.

285 Buckwheat & Vegetable Soup

PREPARATION TIME 10 minutes, plus making the stock and shallots
COOKING TIME 20 minutes

1.4l/48fl oz/5½ cups Beef Stock
  (see page 10) or ready-made stock
250g/9oz cauliflower, cut into small
  florets and the stalks thinly sliced
2 carrots, peeled and thinly sliced
1 bouquet garni made with 1 piece
  of celery stick with its leaves and
  1 rosemary sprig tied together

55g/2oz/¼ cup buckwheat groats
salt and freshly ground black pepper
Crisp-Fried Shallots (see page 15),
  to serve
chopped parsley leaves,
  to serve

1 Put the stock, cauliflower stalks, carrots and bouquet garni in a saucepan and
   season with salt and pepper. Cover and bring to the boil. Add the buckwheat
   and cauliflower florets, then reduce the heat and simmer, covered, for 5 minutes.
   Remove the pan from the heat and leave to stand, covered, for 2–3 minutes until
   the buckwheat and vegetables are tender. Discard the bouquet garni.
2 Adjust the salt and pepper, if necessary. Serve sprinkled with shallots and parsley.

286 Kasha & Tomato Soup

PREPARATION TIME 10 minutes, plus making the stock and pumpkin seeds
and preparing the tomatoes   COOKING TIME 30 minutes

1½ tbsp olive or hemp oil
1 large onion, chopped
4 large garlic cloves, finely chopped
670ml/23fl oz/2⅔ cups passata
750ml/26fl oz/3 cups Vegetable Stock
  (see page 12) or ready-made stock
15g/½oz thyme sprigs, tied together

55g/2oz/¼ cup kasha
  (toasted buckwheat)
2 tomatoes, grated (see page 9)
salt and freshly ground black pepper
chopped parsley leaves, to serve
Roasted Pumpkin Seeds
  (see page 15) to serve

1 Heat the oil in a saucepan over a medium heat. Add the onion and fry, stirring,
   for 2 minutes. Add the garlic and fry for 1–3 minutes until the onion is softened,
   then add the passata, stock and thyme and season with salt and pepper. Cover and
   bring to the boil, then reduce the heat and simmer for 10 minutes. Stir in the kasha.
2 Simmer, covered, for 5 minutes. Remove from the heat, stir in the tomatoes and
   leave to stand, covered, for 2–3 minutes until the kasha is tender. Discard the
   thyme and adjust the salt and pepper, if necessary. Serve sprinkled with parsley
   and seeds. If reheating this soup, add a little extra stock, if necessary, to thin it.

287 Fragrant Mung Bean Soup

PREPARATION TIME 15 minutes, plus soaking the beans overnight, making the stock
and seeds and preparing the tomato   COOKING TIME 55 minutes

100g/3½oz/½ cup dried mung beans
1 tbsp olive or hemp oil
1 large onion, finely chopped
3 large garlic cloves, finely chopped
1 tsp Chinese five-spice powder
1.25l/44fl oz/5 cups Vegetable Stock
  (see page 12) or ready-made stock

1 carrot, peeled and finely diced
1 large tomato, peeled (see page 9),
  deseeded and diced
salt and freshly ground black pepper
shredded coriander leaves, to serve
Spiced Seeds (see page 15),
  to serve (optional)

1 Put the beans in a bowl, cover with water and leave to soak overnight, then drain.
2 Heat the oil in a saucepan over a medium heat. Add the onion and fry, stirring, for
   2 minutes, then add the garlic and fry for 1–3 minutes until the onion is softened.
   Add the five-spice powder and stir for 30 seconds. Watch closely so it does not
   burn. Add the beans and stock, cover and bring to the boil, then boil for 10 minutes.
3 Add the carrot and tomato, reduce the heat and simmer, covered,
   for 25–30 minutes until the mung beans are tender. Season with salt and pepper,
   then serve sprinkled with coriander leaves and spiced seeds, if using.

288 # Wild Mushroom & Toasted Spelt Soup

PREPARATION TIME 15 minutes, plus 30 minutes soaking the mushrooms and making the stock   **COOKING TIME** 1 hour

30g/1oz dried porcini mushrooms
2 tbsp olive or hemp oil
85g/3oz/scant ½ cup spelt
15g/½oz butter
1 celery stick, finely chopped, with the leaves reserved
1 large red onion, finely chopped
400g/14oz mixed wild mushrooms, such as chanterelles, horns of plenty and oysters, trimmed, if necessary, and coarsely chopped
2 large garlic cloves, chopped

1l/35fl oz/4 cups Beef Stock (see page 10) or ready-made stock
1 bouquet garni made with the celery leaves, 1 bay leaf and several parsley and thyme sprigs tied together
1 large waxy potato, diced
1 small handful of dill, finely chopped
salt and freshly ground black pepper
soured cream or smetana, to serve (optional)

1   Put the porcini mushrooms and at least 200ml/7fl oz/scant 1 cup boiling water in a heatproof bowl and leave to soak for 30 minutes until tender. Strain through a muslin-lined sieve and set the liquid aside. Squeeze the mushrooms and trim the stalks, if necessary, then thinly slice the caps and stalks and set aside.

2   Heat 1 tablespoon of the oil in a saucepan over a high heat. Add the spelt and stir for 2–3 minutes until it gives off a toasted aroma. Immediately transfer to a bowl and set aside.

3   Melt the butter with the remaining oil in the pan over a medium heat. Add the celery and onion and fry, stirring, for 2 minutes. Stir in the wild mushrooms and garlic, season with salt and fry for 5–8 minutes, stirring occasionally, until the mushrooms soften and give off their liquid.

4   Stir in the spelt and fry for 2 minutes, then add the stock, bouquet garni, porcini mushrooms and reserved soaking liquid and season with salt and pepper. Cover and bring to the boil. Reduce the heat and simmer for 20 minutes, then stir in the potato and simmer for 15–20 minutes until the spelt and potato are tender. Stir in the dill and adjust the salt and pepper, if necessary. Serve with sour cream, if using.

CHAPTER 6

BIG BOWL SOUPS

A big bowl of steaming soup makes a fantastic one-pot meal, ideal when you want simple meals for friends or for eating in front of the TV. All the meat-based and vegetarian soups in this chapter contain a mix of protein and starch with plenty of vegetables, so you don't have to spend time preparing lots of side dishes. These are the recipes to turn to for easy cooking.

Restaurant favourites, such as Teriyaki Salmon Ramen and Prawn Laksa, are here, along with slow-cooked winter warmers like Beef & Vegetable Hotpot and Winter Vegetable Soup with Quinoa. Lamb Shank & Butter Bean Soup and Borscht are two examples of soups that can be made a day in advance and reheated just before serving, for even easier entertaining when friends are coming round.

For filling vegetarian meals, try Buddha's Delight, Vegetable Jungle Curry with Noodles and Yogurt Soup with Chickpea Dumplings. The inspiration for these soups comes from predominately vegetarian cultures, so you are guaranteed a satisfying meal in a bowl.

TERIYAKI SALMON RAMEN (SEE PAGE 187)

289 Italian Wedding Soup

PREPARATION TIME 35 minutes, plus 30 minutes chilling and making the stock
COOKING TIME 1¼ hour

1.75l/60fl oz/6⅔ cups Beef Stock
   (see page 10) or ready-made stock
1 Parmesan cheese rind, about
   7.5 x 5cm/3 x 2in (see page 9)
1 Parma ham heel (see page 9)
1 bay leaf
2 tbsp fruity extra-virgin olive oil,
   plus extra to serve
2 celery sticks, finely chopped
1 onion, finely chopped
2 garlic cloves, chopped
250g/9oz escarole or curly kale,
   thick stalks removed and
   leaves chopped
100g/3½oz spinach, chopped
salt and freshly ground black pepper
freshly grated Parmesan cheese,
   to serve

VEAL MEATBALLS
55g/2oz/heaped ½ cup dried
   breadcrumbs
4 tbsp milk
800g/1lb 12oz minced veal
5 garlic cloves, finely chopped
4 spring onions, very finely chopped
40g/1½oz parsley leaves,
   very finely chopped
3 tbsp very finely chopped dill
85g/3oz Parmesan cheese,
   finely grated
2 eggs, beaten
olive oil, for frying

1 The meatballs can be made up to 1 day in advance. Put the breadcrumbs and milk in a bowl and leave to soak. Meanwhile, line a baking tray or two plates that will fit in your refrigerator with greaseproof paper. Put the veal, garlic, spring onions, parsley, dill and cheese in a large bowl, add the breadcrumb mixture and season with salt and pepper. Add the egg little by little and work it into the mixture with your fingers. Fry a small amount of the mixture to test for seasoning. With wet hands, divide the mixture into 12 equal portions, then divide each portion into 6 equal portions to make a total of 72. Roll into meatballs and put them on the baking tray. Cover with cling film and chill for at least 30 minutes.

2 Meanwhile, put the stock, cheese rind, ham heel and bay leaf in a saucepan. Cover and bring to the boil, then reduce the heat to very low (use a heat diffuser if you have one) and simmer while you fry the meatballs.

3 To fry the meatballs, heat one or two large frying pans over a high heat until a splash of water 'dances' on the surface. Add a thin layer of olive oil, reduce the heat to medium and add as many meatballs as will fit without overcrowding the pan. Fry the meatballs, turning gently, for 5–8 minutes until golden brown. Drain on kitchen paper and set aside until required. (At this point they can be left to cool completely and chilled for up to 24 hours.)

4 To finish making the soup, heat the olive oil in another large saucepan over a medium heat. Stir in the celery, onion and garlic, reduce the heat to low and cook, covered, for 10–12 minutes until softened but not coloured. Add the stock, along with the cheese rind, ham heel and bay leaf, cover and bring to the boil. Add the escarole and spinach, reduce the heat and simmer, covered, for 30 minutes.

5 Gently add the meatballs and simmer for another 5 minutes until warmed through. Season with salt and pepper, but remember the cheese rind and ham heel will have been salty.

6 Discard the cheese rind, ham heel and bay leaf. Divide the meatballs and greens into bowls and ladle the soup over them. Serve immediately with olive oil and grated Parmesan cheese on the side.

290 Tuscan 'Twice-Cooked' Vegetable & Bean Soup

PREPARATION TIME 10 minutes, plus making the minestrone a day in advance
and making the croûtes   COOKING TIME 55 minutes

2 garlic cloves, halved
2 recipe quantities Winter
   Minestrone (see page 142),
   made through step 3 with cavolo
   nero or savoy cabbage instead
   of white cabbage

2 recipe quantities Garlic Croûtes
   (see page 14)
extra-virgin olive oil, to drizzle
1 red onion, thinly sliced

1   Preheat the oven to 190°C/375°F/gas 5. Rub the inside of an ovenproof casserole
    dish with the garlic cloves, pressing down firmly, then discard the garlic. Put half
    the soup in the casserole, top with enough of the croûtes to cover and drizzle with
    oil. Repeat the layers, then sprinkle the onion over the top and drizzle with more oil.
2   Bake, uncovered, for 45 minutes–1 hour until the onion is tender. Serve straight
    from the casserole dish with any remaining croûtes on the side.

291 Carl's Mulligatawny Soup

PREPARATION TIME 20 minutes, plus making the stock, rice and chilli bon-bon (optional)
and overnight chilling (optional)   COOKING TIME 35 minutes

30g/1oz butter
1 tbsp sunflower or groundnut oil
2 carrots, chopped
2 celery sticks, chopped
1 onion, chopped
2 tsp Madras curry powder
1 tsp ground coriander
a pinch of chilli powder (optional)
1 large sweet cooking apple, peeled,
   cored and chopped
400g/14oz tinned chopped tomatoes
salt and freshly ground black pepper
400g/14 oz cooked long-grain brown
   rice, hot, to serve
chopped coriander leaves, to serve
Chilli Bon-Bon (see page 15),
   to serve (optional)

LAMB STOCK
3 lamb shanks
5 bay leaves
3 garlic cloves, chopped
2 celery sticks, with their leaves,
   chopped
1 large carrot, chopped
1 onion, chopped
1 tsp coriander seeds, lightly crushed
1 tsp black peppercorns,
   lightly crushed

1   The stock can be made up to 2 days in advance. Put the lamb in a large saucepan
    and cover with water. Cover and bring to the boil. Skim, then add the bay leaves,
    garlic, celery, carrot, onion, coriander seeds and peppercorns. Reduce the heat
    to very low (use a heat diffuser if you have one) and simmer, covered,
    for 1½–2 hours until the lamb is very tender and coming away from the bones.
    Strain the stock, set the lamb aside until cool enough to handle and discard the rest
    of the flavourings. Skim the fat from the surface of the stock. (Alternatively, leave
    the stock to cool completely, then cover and chill overnight. The fat can then
    be lifted off.) Set aside 1.75l/60fl oz/6⅔ cups of the stock. (Any leftovers can
    be frozen for up to 3 months to use in other soups.) Remove the meat from the
    bones and shred, then cover and chill until required.
2   Melt the butter with the oil in the washed-out and dried saucepan. Add the carrots,
    celery and onion and fry, stirring, for 3–5 minutes until the onion is softened.
    Add the curry powder, ground coriander and chilli powder, if using, and stir for
    30 seconds. Watch closely so the spices do not burn. Stir in the apple, then add
    the reserved stock and tomatoes and season with salt and pepper. Cover and
    bring to the boil, then reduce the heat and simmer for 20 minutes.
3   Blend the soup, then add the lamb and warm through. Adjust the salt and pepper,
    if necessary. Serve over hot rice, sprinkled with chopped coriander, and with Chilli
    Bon-Bon on the side, if you like.

292 Slow-Cooked Pork & Bean Soup

PREPARATION TIME 15 minutes, plus soaking the beans overnight and making the stock
COOKING TIME 2 hours

280g/10oz/1⅓ cup dried
   cannellini beans
1.75l/60fl oz/6⅔ cups Vegetable Stock
   (see page 12) or ready-made stock
3 carrots, peeled and chopped
2 celery sticks, chopped, with the
   leaves reserved
2 large onions, chopped

1 bouquet garni made with the
   celery leaves, 2 bay leaves and
   a small handful of parsley sprigs
   tied together
4 tbsp tomato purée
1½ tbsp dried thyme
1.25kg/2lb 12oz pork belly
salt and freshly ground black pepper
chopped parsley leaves, to serve
hot pepper sauce, to serve

1 Put the beans in a bowl, cover with water and leave to soak overnight, then drain. Transfer to a saucepan, add 1.5l/53fl oz/6 cups water, cover and bring to the boil. Reduce the heat and simmer, covered, for 50 minutes–1 hour, then drain.
2 Put the stock, carrots, celery, onions, bouquet garni, tomato purée, thyme and pork in a saucepan. Cover and bring to the boil. Skim, then reduce the heat to low (use a heat diffuser if you have one) and simmer, covered, for 30 minutes.
3 Stir in the beans and return the soup to the boil. Skim, then reduce the heat and simmer for another 1–1¼ hours until the pork and beans are both very tender. Remove the pork from the pan and set aside until cool enough to handle. Discard the bouquet garni.
4 Trim and discard the rind and excess fat from the pork and shred the meat into bite-sized pieces. Return it to the soup and reheat, if necessary. Season with salt and pepper and serve sprinkled with parsley and with hot pepper sauce on the side.

293 Chicken Gumbo Soup

PREPARATION TIME 20 minutes, plus making the stock and rice
COOKING TIME 1½ hours

55g/2oz butter
2 tbsp sunflower oil
4 tbsp plain white flour
4 garlic cloves, finely chopped
1 large onion, finely chopped
1 green pepper, deseeded
   and chopped
1 red pepper, deseeded and chopped
1 celery stick, thinly sliced
1.5l/52fl oz/6 cups Chicken Stock
   (see page 11) or ready-made stock
200g/7oz okra, chopped

2 bay leaves
2 tbsp chopped parsley
1 tsp dried thyme leaves
800g/1lb 12oz tinned
   chopped tomatoes
½ tsp caster sugar
cayenne pepper, to taste
1kg/2lb 4oz skinless chicken thighs
salt and freshly ground black pepper
400g/14oz cooked long-grain rice,
   hot, to serve
hot pepper sauce, to serve

1 First, make a roux: melt the butter with the oil in a saucepan over a low heat (use a heat diffuser if you have one). Sprinkle in the flour and cook, stirring, for 15–20 minutes until it turns a deep golden brown. Watch closely because when the roux starts to brown it will colour very quickly.
2 Add the garlic, onion, peppers and celery and stir for 5–8 minutes until the onion is softened. Add half the stock, stirring continuously to prevent lumps from forming. Add the remaining stock, okra, bay leaves, parsley, thyme, tomatoes, sugar and cayenne pepper and season with salt and pepper. Cover and bring to the boil, then reduce the heat and simmer for 45 minutes. The okra will make the soup glutinous.
3 Add the chicken, cover and bring to the boil, then skim. Reduce the heat and simmer for 10–15 minutes until the chicken is cooked through and the juices run clear when you cut a piece. Remove the chicken and set aside until cool enough to handle, then cut the meat from the bones into bite-sized pieces and return it to the soup. Discard the bay leaves. Reheat, adjust the salt and pepper, if necessary, and serve over the rice with the hot pepper sauce.

294 Smoky Mixed Bean & Sausage Soup

PREPARATION TIME 15 minutes, plus making the stock   COOKING TIME 1 hour

55g/2oz smoked lardons, chopped
1 tbsp sunflower or olive oil
2 onions, chopped
1 celery stick, finely chopped
2 tsp smoked paprika
1.75l/60fl oz/6 cups Beef Stock
(see page 10) or ready-made stock
5 smoked frankfurters, cut into
bite-sized pieces
1 large carrot, peeled and sliced

1 bay leaf
1 tbsp dried thyme leaves
2 tsp caraway seeds
½ tsp cinnamon
200g/7oz tinned pinto beans, drained
and rinsed
400g/14oz tinned cannellini beans,
drained and rinsed
1 tbsp red-wine vinegar, or to taste
salt and freshly ground black pepper

1   Put the lardons in a saucepan over a high heat and fry, stirring, for 3–5 minutes until
they start to crisp and give off their fat. Remove them from the pan and set aside.
2   Add the oil to the pan and heat over a medium heat. Add the onion and celery and
fry, stirring, for 3–5 minutes until the onion is softened. Add the paprika and stir for
30 seconds. Add the stock, frankfurters, carrot, bay leaf, thyme, caraway seeds and
cinnamon and season with salt and pepper. Cover and bring to the boil, then reduce
the heat and simmer for 30 minutes.
3   Add the beans and simmer for 10 minutes. Discard the bay leaf and stir in the
vinegar. Adjust the salt and pepper and add extra vinegar, if necessary, then serve.

295 Thai Duck Soup with Noodles

PREPARATION TIME 20 minutes, plus 30 minutes marinating   COOKING TIME 1½ hours

½ duck, about 1.1kg/2lb 7oz,
chopped into large pieces
2 tbsp sunflower oil, plus extra
for frying
1 tbsp light or sweet soy sauce
1 tsp salt, plus extra to season
4 garlic cloves, chopped
6 coriander sprigs, including the
roots and leaves, 4 left whole and
2 coarsely chopped, plus 4 roots,
left whole
150g/5½oz bean sprouts

2 carrots, peeled and sliced
1 celery stick, sliced
1 onion, peeled and cut in half
2 tsp Chinese five-spice powder
1 tbsp palm sugar or soft light
brown sugar
250g/9oz medium-width ready-to-eat
rice noodles
1 tsp sesame oil
1 tsp fish sauce
freshly ground black pepper

1   Put the duck in a large bowl. Add the sunflower oil, soy sauce, salt, garlic and
chopped coriander sprigs and rub everything together. Leave to marinate at room
temperature for 30 minutes. Put the bean sprouts in a bowl, cover with cold water
and set aside.
2   Put the carrots, celery, onion, whole coriander sprigs and 2l/70fl oz/8 cups water
in a saucepan. Cover and bring to the boil, then reduce the heat and simmer.
3   Heat enough oil to cover the base of a large wok over a high heat. Add the
five-spice powder, coriander roots and sugar, reduce the heat to low and stir
for 30 seconds. If the spice powder looks like it is about to burn, immediately
add a ladleful of water from the simmering pan.
4   Add the duck and marinade and fry over a medium heat, turning occasionally,
for 15 minutes, then transfer the duck and liquid in the wok to the simmering pan.
Season with salt and pepper, but remember the duck is already salted. Bring
to the boil and skim. Reduce the heat to very low and simmer, partially covered,
for 40 minutes–1 hour until the duck is very tender.
5   Remove the duck and set aside. Strain the broth, return it to the pan and keep hot.
6   Just before serving, put the noodles in a heatproof bowl and cover with boiling
water for 30 seconds. Drain and transfer to a bowl. Add the sesame oil and fish
sauce and toss well, then set aside. Drain the bean sprouts.
7   Cut the duck into bite-sized pieces, discarding the skin and bones. Divide the
noodles, bean sprouts and duck into bowls, ladle the broth over them and serve.

Vietnamese Beef & Noodle Soup

PREPARATION TIME 20 minutes, plus making the stock   **COOKING TIME** 20 minutes

1 small handful of bean sprouts
1.75l/60fl oz/6⅔ cups Beef Stock
  (see page 10)
4cm/1½in piece of root ginger,
  peeled and thinly sliced
4 star anise
1 cinnamon stick
seeds from 4 green cardamom pods
1 tbsp fish sauce, or to taste
1 red pepper, halved, deseeded and
  very thinly sliced

500g/1lb 2oz medium-width
  ready-to-eat rice noodles
600g/1lb 5oz beef sirloin, rump
  or topside, in one piece, very thinly
  sliced against the grain

TO SERVE
lime wedges
1 handful of mint leaves
1 handful of coriander leaves
2 spring onions, thinly sliced
thinly sliced red chillies

1   Put the bean sprouts in a bowl, cover with cold water and set aside. Put the stock, ginger, star anise, cinnamon stick, cardamom seeds and fish sauce in a large saucepan. Cover and bring to the boil, then reduce the heat and simmer for 10 minutes. Add the red pepper for the final 3 minutes of simmering to soften them.

2   Just before serving, use a slotted spoon to scoop the spices out of the stock and discard, then bring the stock to the boil. Put the noodles in a heatproof bowl, cover with boiling water and leave to soak for 15–30 seconds to warm through. Drain and divide into serving bowls, then divide the beef into the bowls.

3   Drain the bean sprouts and add them to the bowls. Ladle the boiling stock and red peppers over and serve immediately with lime wedges and small bowls of mint, coriander, spring onions and chillies on the side.

297 Hot & Sour Pork Soup with Noodles

PREPARATION TIME 20 minutes, plus marinating the pork and making the stock, chillies and garlic   COOKING TIME 20 minutes

750g/1lb 10oz pork fillet,
   very thinly sliced
4 tsp sesame oil
2 tsp soy sauce
4 coriander sprigs, leaves and stalks,
   finely chopped
1.75l/60fl oz/6⅔ cups Vegetable Stock
   (see page 12) or ready-made stock
6 kaffir lime leaves
3 large garlic cloves, crushed
2 lemongrass stalks, thickly sliced,
   with outer leaves removed
3 tbsp lime juice
3 tbsp fish sauce

500g/1lb 2oz ready-to-eat
   rice noodles
1 tsp toasted sesame oil
salt and freshly ground black pepper

TO SERVE
4 spring onions, thinly sliced
2 carrots, very thinly sliced
2 celery sticks, very thinly sliced
2 handfuls of baby spinach leaves
lime wedges
Chillies in Vinegar (see page 15)
Crisp-Fried Garlic (see page 15)

1   Put the pork, sesame oil, soy sauce and coriander in a bowl and mix well. Season with salt and pepper, mix again and leave to marinate at room temperature.
2   Put the stock, lime leaves, garlic, lemongrass, lime juice and fish sauce in a saucepan and season with salt and pepper. Cover and bring to the boil, then boil for 5 minutes.
3   Meanwhile, prepare the bowls for serving. Divide the spring onions, carrots, celery and spinach into serving bowls and set aside.
4   Uncover the stock and reduce the heat to a gentle simmer. Add the noodles and simmer for 30 seconds to warm through, then use tongs or chopsticks to transfer them to a large bowl. Toss with the toasted sesame oil so they don't stick together, then divide them into the bowls and set aside.
5   Add the pork to the stock and cook for 3–5 minutes until cooked through when you cut a piece. Skim and adjust the salt and pepper, if necessary, then divide the pork into the bowls. Ladle the stock over. Serve topped with a lime wedge and chillies in vinegar and fried garlic on the side.

298 Beef & Vegetable Hotpot

PREPARATION TIME 20 minutes, plus making the stock and cooking the beef
COOKING TIME 45 minutes

2l/70fl oz/8 cups Beef Stock
   (see page 10) or ready-made stock
400g/14oz tinned chopped tomatoes
10 black peppercorns, lightly crushed
4 garlic cloves, chopped
2 bay leaves
2 leeks, coarsely chopped and rinsed
1 bouquet garni made with 1 piece
   of celery stick with its leaves, 1 bay
   leaf and several parsley and thyme
   sprigs tied together

5 new potatoes, sliced
2 carrots, peeled and sliced
1 turnip, peeled and chopped
400g/14oz tinned butter beans,
   drained and rinsed
750g/1lb 10oz boneless cooked beef,
   trimmed and cut into bite-sized
   pieces
100g/3½oz savoy cabbage, shredded
salt and freshly ground black pepper
chopped parsley leaves, to serve

1   Put the stock, tomatoes, peppercorns, garlic, bay leaves and leeks in a saucepan and season with salt and pepper. Cover and bring to the boil. Uncover and boil for 10–15 minutes. Strain the stock, return it to the pan and add the bouquet garni. Add the potatoes, carrots and turnip and season with salt and pepper. Cover and bring to the boil, then reduce the heat and simmer for 10–15 minutes until the potatoes and carrots are tender.
2   Stir in the butter beans, beef and cabbage and simmer for another 5 minutes until warmed through. Discard the bouquet garni. Adjust the salt and pepper, if necessary, then serve sprinkled with parsley.

299 Beef & Tomato Soup

PREPARATION TIME 15 minutes   **COOKING TIME** 2¼ hours

1 bone-in beef shin, about 1.5kg/
3lb 5oz, with the bone cracked
in several places (use a mallet
to do this or ask the butcher)
100g/3½oz boneless beef silverside
or chuck, trimmed and cut into
4cm/1½in cubes
2 garlic cloves, halved
2 onions, unpeeled and halved
1 leek, halved lengthways, chopped
and rinsed

1 bouquet garni made with 1 piece
of celery stick with its leaves, 1 bay
leaf and several parsley and thyme
sprigs tied together
800g/1lb 12oz tinned tomatoes
2 tbsp tomato purée
1 tsp caster sugar
salt and freshly ground black pepper
chopped parsley leaves, to serve

1   Put the beef shin and silverside, garlic, onions, leek and bouquet garni in a large
saucepan. Add enough water to cover the meat and season with salt and pepper.
Cover and bring to the boil. Skim, then reduce the heat to very low (use a heat
diffuser if you have one). Simmer, covered, for 1¾–2 hours until the beef shin
is very tender and almost falling off the bone and the silverside is tender.
2   Add the tomatoes, tomato purée and sugar and simmer, uncovered, for
10 minutes, using a spoon to break up the tomatoes. Remove the shin and cubed
beef from the pan and set aside until cool enough to handle. Strain the soup into
a large bowl, using a spoon to press through as much of the tomatoes as possible,
then return the soup to the pan and simmer, uncovered, for 5 minutes to reduce
slightly. Skim any excess fat from the surface.
3   Remove the shin meat from the bone, then finely shred both types of beef, return
the meat to the soup and reheat. Adjust the salt and pepper, if necessary. Serve
sprinkled with parsley.

300 Lamb Shank & Butter Bean Soup

PREPARATION TIME 15 minutes, plus overnight soaking and cooking the beans
and making the stock and flavoured oil (optional)   **COOKING TIME** 2½ hours

280g/10oz/scant 1½ cups dried
butter beans
3 tbsp garlic-flavoured olive oil
3 lamb shanks, about 1.5kg/3lb 5oz
400g/14oz fennel, chopped
2 large garlic cloves, chopped
625ml/21½fl oz/2½ cups Beef Stock
(see page 10) or ready-made stock
670ml/23fl oz/2⅔ cups passata

1 bouquet garni made with 1 piece
of celery stick with its leaves, 2 bay
leaves, 2 rosemary sprigs and
several parsley and thyme sprigs
tied together
salt and freshly ground black pepper
1 recipe quantity Paprika & Lemon
Oil (see page 24) or extra-virgin
olive oil, to serve

1   Put the beans in a bowl, cover with water and leave to soak overnight, then drain.
Transfer to a saucepan and add 1.5l/53fl oz/6 cups water. Cover and bring to the
boil, then reduce the heat and simmer, covered, for 50 minutes–1 hour, then drain.
2   Heat the oil in a saucepan over a medium heat. Working in batches, if necessary,
fry the lamb shanks until brown on both sides. Remove from the pan and set aside.
Pour off all but 1½ tablespoons of the oil, add the fennel and fry, stirring
occasionally, for 3 minutes. Add the garlic and fry for 1–2 minutes until the fennel
is softened but not coloured, then return the shanks to the pan.
3   Add the stock, passata and enough water to cover the lamb shanks, if necessary.
Cover and bring to the boil, then skim. Add the bouquet garni and season with salt
and pepper. Reduce the heat and simmer, covered, for 1¼ hours.
4   Stir in the beans, cover and return to the boil. Reduce the heat and simmer for
40–50 minutes until the lamb is tender and falling off the bones and the beans
are tender. Remove the shanks and set aside until cool enough to handle.
5   Remove the bones, any fat and sinew from the shanks and cut the meat into
bite-sized pieces. Return it to the soup and reheat. Adjust the salt and pepper,
if necessary, and serve drizzled with the paprika oil.

301 Borscht

PREPARATION TIME 25 minutes, plus making the stock and horseradish cream
COOKING TIME 2½ hours

1kg/2lb 4oz boneless beef silverside,
    brisket or chuck, in one piece,
1.75l/60fl oz/6⅔ cups Beef Stock
    (see page 10) or ready-made stock
4 carrots, peeled and sliced
4 large tomatoes, coarsely chopped
3 celery sticks, sliced, with the
    leaves reserved
2 onions, halved and studded with
    several cloves in each half
2 tbsp tomato purée

1 bouquet garni made with the celery
    leaves, 2 bay leaves, a small
    handful of parsley sprigs and
    several dill sprigs tied together
a pinch of caster sugar
4 large cooked beetroots, peeled and
    coarsely grated
2 bay leaves
2 tbsp red wine vinegar
salt and freshly ground black pepper
1 recipe quantity Horseradish & Dill
    Cream (see page 21), to serve
chopped dill, to serve

1   Put the beef, stock, carrots, tomatoes, celery, onions, tomato purée, bouquet garni
    and sugar in a saucepan and season with salt and pepper. Cover and bring to the
    boil. Skim, then reduce the heat to very low (use a heat diffuser if you have one)
    and simmer, covered, for 2 hours until the meat is tender.
2   Remove the beef from the pan and set aside until cool enough to handle. Strain
    the soup, pressing down to extract as much flavour as possible, then discard the
    flavourings and return the stock to the pan.
3   Remove any sinew from the beef, cut the meat into bite-sized pieces and return
    it to the soup. Add the beetroots, bay leaves and vinegar and simmer, covered,
    for 15 minutes until the beef is very tender. Discard the bay leaves and adjust the
    salt and pepper, if necessary. Serve topped with the horseradish cream and
    sprinkled with dill.

302　Indonesian Chicken & Noodle Soup

PREPARATION TIME 25 minutes, plus making the stock, hard-boiled eggs and shallots
COOKING TIME 35 minutes

1 large handful of bean sprouts
8 shallots, 6 halved and 2 chopped
4 garlic cloves
2 tbsp chopped root ginger
½ tbsp turmeric
2 tbsp groundnut oil
1.75l/60fl oz/6⅔ cups Chicken Stock
　(see page 11) or ready-made stock
1kg/2lb 4oz skinless chicken thighs
6 waxy new potatoes, peeled
　and sliced
140g/5oz white cabbage, shredded

1 lemongrass stalk, crushed,
　with outer leaves removed
2cm/¾in piece of galangal,
　peeled and sliced
1 bird's-eye chilli, deseeded and
　sliced
500g/1lb 2oz ready-to-eat vermicelli
　rice noodles
salt and freshly ground black pepper
3 hard-boiled eggs, sliced, to serve
Crisp-Fried Shallots (see page 15),
　to serve

1　Put the bean sprouts in a bowl, cover with cold water and set aside. Pound the
　　halved shallots, 2 garlic cloves, the ginger and turmeric with a mortar and pestle
　　or use a small food processor and blend until a paste forms, then set aside.
2　Heat the oil in a stockpot over a medium heat. Add the remaining shallots and fry
　　for 2 minutes. Add the remaining garlic and fry for another 1–3 minutes until the
　　shallots are softened. Add the shallot paste and fry for 2–3 minutes until aromatic.
　　Watch closely so it does not burn and add a spoonful of the stock, if necessary.
3　Add the stock and chicken, cover and bring to the boil. Skim, then add the potatoes,
　　cabbage, lemongrass, galangal and chilli and season with salt and pepper. Reduce
　　the heat and simmer, covered, for 15–20 minutes until the chicken is cooked
　　through. Discard the lemongrass and galangal. Remove the chicken from the soup
　　and set aside. Shred or cut the chicken from the bones into bite-sized pieces.
4　Return the chicken to the soup. Drain the bean sprouts and add them to the soup.
　　Warm through, adjusting the salt and pepper, if necessary. Divide the noodles into
　　bowls. Ladle the soup over and serve topped with hard-boiled eggs and shallots.

303　Chicken & Chickpea Tagine Soup

PREPARATION TIME 10 minutes, plus making the stock and toasting the almonds
COOKING TIME 40 minutes

3 tbsp olive or hemp oil
2 large onions, finely chopped
4 large garlic cloves, crushed
750g/1lb 10oz skinless chicken thighs
1.75l/60fl oz/6⅔ cups Chicken Stock
　(see page 11) or ready-made stock
a large pinch of saffron threads
1 bouquet garni made with 1 piece
　of celery stick, 1 bay leaf, and
　several coriander, parsley and
　thyme sprigs tied together
1½ tbsp ground coriander

1½ tbsp ground cumin
1½ tbsp ground ginger
½ tsp harissa paste, or to taste
400g/14oz tinned chickpeas, rinsed
200g/7oz/heaped 1 cup ready-to-eat
　dried apricots
2 preserved lemons, sliced
280g/10oz/1⅓ cups couscous
15g/½oz butter
salt and freshly ground black pepper
toasted flaked almonds (see page 9),
　to serve

1　Heat the oil in a large saucepan over a medium heat. Add the onions and fry,
　　stirring, for 6 minutes. Stir in the garlic and fry for 1–2 minutes until softened.
2　Add the chicken and stock and season with salt and pepper. Cover and bring
　　to the boil, then skim. Stir in the next six ingredients. Reduce the heat and simmer,
　　covered, for 10 minutes. Stir in the chickpeas, apricots and preserved lemons
　　and simmer, covered, for another 10–15 minutes until the chicken is tender.
3　Meanwhile, put the couscous and butter in an heatproof bowl and season with
　　salt and pepper. Add enough boiling water to cover by 1cm/½in and cover.
　　Leave to stand for 10 minutes until the water is absorbed. Fluff with a fork.
4　Remove the chicken from the pan, cut the meat into bite-sized pieces, and return
　　it to the soup. Adjust the salt and pepper and add extra harissa, if necessary. Divide
　　the couscous into bowls and ladle the soup over it. Serve sprinkled with almonds.

304 Chicken & Vegetable Chowder

PREPARATION TIME 25 minutes, plus making the stock, toasting the seeds and making the croûtes (optional) COOKING TIME 40 minutes

1kg/2lb 4oz skinless chicken thighs
1.75l/60fl oz/6⅔ cups Chicken Stock
  (see page 10) or ready-made stock
250g/9oz butternut squash, peeled,
  deseeded and diced
4 waxy new potatoes, sliced
2 carrots, peeled and sliced
2 celery sticks, thinly sliced, with the
  leaves reserved
2 large garlic cloves, finely chopped
1½ tbsp dried tarragon
1 tbsp dried oregano

2 tbsp chopped parsley leaves,
  plus extra to serve
1 bouquet garni made with the
  celery leaves, 1 bay leaf and
  several parsley and thyme sprigs
  tied together
280g/10oz broccoli, cut into florets
200g/7oz/1 cup long-grain rice
125ml/4fl oz/½ cup whole milk
salt and freshly ground black pepper
Cheddar Croûtes (see page 14),
  to serve (optional)

1 Put the chicken and stock in a saucepan and season with salt and pepper. Cover and bring to the boil. Skim, then add the squash, potatoes, carrots, celery, garlic, tarragon, oregano, parsley and bouquet garni. Reduce the heat and simmer, covered, for 15 minutes. Add the broccoli and rice and return to a slow boil.

2 Cook, uncovered, for 10–15 minutes until the chicken is cooked through and the juices run clear when you cut a piece. Stir occasionally to prevent the rice from sticking to the base of the pan. Remove the chicken and set aside until cool enough to handle. Discard the bouquet garni.

3 Cut the chicken from the bones into bite-sized pieces and return it to the soup. Stir in the milk and heat through without boiling. Adjust the salt and pepper, if necessary, and serve sprinkled with parsley and with croûtes on the side, if you like. If you reheat the soup, do not boil it.

305 Japanese Salmon Hotpot

PREPARATION TIME 20 minutes, plus making the dashi COOKING TIME 30 minutes

400g/14oz watercress, any thick
  stalks or yellow leaves removed
280g/10oz thin rice noodles
2l/70fl oz/8 cups Dashi (see page 12)
  or prepared instant dashi
10cm/4in piece of daikon, peeled and
  finely grated
1 red chilli, deseeded and thinly
  sliced

750g/1lb 10oz salmon fillet, small
  bones removed, and fish cut
  across the grain into
  1cm/½in thick slices
12 shiitake mushroom caps
280g/10oz firm tofu, drained and cut
  into 12 cubes
200g/7oz enoki mushrooms,
  stalks trimmed
salt
ponzu dipping sauce, to serve

1 Bring a saucepan of lightly salted water to the boil, and bring another saucepan of unsalted water to the boil. Boil the watercress in the salted water just until the leaves wilt, which will be almost instantly. Drain and immediately rinse under cold running water, then drain again and set aside. Meanwhile, boil the rice noodles in the unsalted water for 6–8 minutes, or according to the packet instructions, until tender. Drain and immediately rinse under cold running water and set aside.

2 Put the dashi in a saucepan, cover and bring to just below the boil. Meanwhile, mix together the daikon and chilli in a small bowl and set aside. Just before the dashi boils, reduce the heat to low, add the salmon and shiitake mushrooms and simmer for 5 minutes or until the salmon is cooked to your liking. One minute before the end of the cooking, add the tofu and enoki mushrooms and simmer until the enoki are tender. Season with salt.

3 Divide the noodles into bowls and top with the salmon. Use a slotted spoon to transfer the watercress, mushrooms and tofu into the bowls. Ladle the dashi over them and serve immediately with small bowls of dipping sauce and the daikon and chilli mixture on the side.

306 Hot, Hot, Hot Caribbean Chicken Soup

PREPARATION TIME 25 minutes, plus making the stock and rice and overnight chilling (optional)   **COOKING TIME** 45 minutes

3 tbsp sunflower oil
1 onion, chopped
2 garlic cloves, crushed
½ tsp ground coriander
½ tsp black mustard seeds
1 Scotch bonnet chilli, left whole
    or chopped, as desired
1.5l/52fl oz/6 cups Chicken Stock
    (see page 11) or ready-made stock
750g/1lb 10oz boneless, skinless
    pieces of chicken, such as breasts,
    drumsticks and thighs
250g/9oz butternut squash, peeled,
    deseeded and cut into bite-sized
    pieces

3 waxy new potatoes, diced
2 bay leaves
½ aubergine, cut into
    bite-sized pieces
400ml/14fl oz/scant 1⅔ cups
    coconut milk
½ tbsp tamarind paste
1 mango, peeled, stoned and diced
1 papaya, peeled, deseeded and
    chopped
juice of 1 lime, plus lime wedges,
    to serve
salt
400g/14 oz cooked long-grain rice,
    hot, to serve

1   This soup is best made a day in advance and chilled so the excess fat can
    be removed. Heat the oil in a large saucepan over a medium heat. Add the onion
    and fry, stirring occasionally, for 7 minutes. Add the garlic and fry for 1–3 minutes
    until the onion is golden brown. Stir in the coriander, mustard seeds and chilli and
    stir for 30 seconds. Watch closely so the spices do not burn.
2   Add the stock, chicken, squash, potatoes, bay leaves and aubergine and season
    with salt. Cover and bring to the boil. Skim, then stir in the coconut milk and
    tamarind paste. Reduce the heat and simmer, covered, for 15–20 minutes until
    the chicken is cooked through and the juices run clear when you cut a piece.
    Remove the chicken from the pan and set aside until cool enough to handle.
3   Skim the fat from the surface of the soup. (At this point, the soup can be left
    to cool completely, then covered and chilled overnight so the excess fat can be
    removed before serving.)
4   Add the mango, papaya and lime juice to the pan and simmer for 5 minutes.
    Cut the chicken into bite-sized pieces and return it to the soup. Adjust the salt,
    if necessary, then discard the bay leaves. Serve immediately over rice and
    with lime wedges for squeezing over.

307 Chinese Chicken Noodle Soup

PREPARATION TIME 15 minutes, plus making the stock   COOKING TIME 20 minutes

1 small handful of bean sprouts
3 tbsp groundnut or sunflower oil
750g/1lb 10oz boneless, skinless
 chicken breasts, thinly shredded
200g/7oz Chinese cabbage, shredded
100g/3½oz tinned bamboo shoots,
 drained and thinly sliced
8 shiitake mushroom caps, sliced
4 spring onions, thinly sliced

1 tsp Chinese five-spice powder
1 tbsp Chinese rice wine
1 tbsp light soy sauce
1.75l/60fl oz/6⅔ cups Chicken Stock
 (see page 11) or ready-made stock
500g/1lb 2oz ready-to-eat Chinese
 egg noodles
salt and freshly ground black pepper
toasted sesame oil, to serve

1 Put the bean sprouts in a bowl, cover with cold water and set aside. Heat a wok
over a high heat. Add 2 tablespoons of the oil, then add the chicken and stir-fry
for 2–3 minutes until it is cooked through. Remove from the wok and set aside.
2 Add the remaining oil to the wok, if necessary, and heat. Add the cabbage,
bamboo shoots, mushrooms, spring onions and five-spice powder and stir-fry for
2–3 minutes until tender. Stir in the rice wine and soy sauce, then add the stock
and bring to the boil, uncovered. Add the chicken, noodles and bean sprouts
to the soup and warm through. Serve sprinkled with sesame oil.

308 Buddha's Delight

PREPARATION TIME 20 minutes, plus 30 minutes soaking the bean curd skins,
mushrooms and lily buds and making the dashi   COOKING TIME 20 minutes

55g/2oz dried bean curd skins
15g/½oz dried lily buds or golden
 flower vegetable
55g/2oz dried wood ear mushrooms
1 small handful of bean sprouts
3 tbsp groundnut or sunflower oil
1cm/½in piece of root ginger,
 peeled and sliced
350g/12oz small broccoli florets
85g/3oz tinned bamboo shoots,
 drained and thinly sliced
85g/3oz tinned or vacuum-packed
 lotus root slices, drained and sliced
85g/3oz tinned water chestnuts,
 drained and sliced
12 baby corn, halved lengthways

1.75l/60fl oz/6⅔ cups Vegetarian
 Dashi (see page 12) or prepared
 instant dashi or ready-made stock
85g/3oz shimeji mushrooms,
 trimmed and sliced
8 shiitake mushroom caps, sliced
6 mangetout, very thinly sliced
 lengthways
2 tbsp Chinese rice wine
1½ tbsp light soy sauce
1 tsp Chinese five-spice powder
3 tbsp arrowroot
140g/5oz fried tofu, cubed
4 spring onions, thinly sliced
55g/2oz ready-to-eat thin
 rice noodles

1 Put the bean curd skins and lily buds in separate heatproof bowls, cover with
boiling water and leave to soak for 30 minutes until tender, then drain. Thinly slice
the bean curd skins and set aside. Tie each lily bud into a knot and set aside. Put
the dried mushrooms and 250ml/9fl oz/1 cup boiling water in a heatproof bowl and
leave to soak for 30 minutes. Strain through a muslin-lined sieve into a bowl and set
the liquid aside. Squeeze the mushrooms, cut off the stalks and slice the caps, then
set aside. Put the bean sprouts in a bowl, cover with cold water and set aside.
2 Heat the oil in a large wok or saucepan over a high heat. Add the ginger and fry
for 1–2 minutes until golden, then remove and discard. Add the broccoli, bamboo
shoots, lotus roots, water chestnuts and baby corn and stir-fry for 2 minutes. Add
the dashi and reserved soaking liquid and bring to the boil, then reduce the heat
to low. Add the bean curd skins, all the mushrooms and the mangetout. Stir in the
rice wine, soy sauce and five-spice powder and simmer, covered, for 2 minutes.
3 Meanwhile, put the arrowroot and 3 tablespoons cold water in a small heatproof
bowl and mix until smooth. Stir in a ladleful of the hot liquid and mix well, then stir
this mixture into the soup and simmer for 2–3 minutes until the soup thickens
slightly. Drain the bean sprouts and add them to the soup with the tofu and spring
onions. Add the noodles and warm through. Serve.

309 Yogurt Soup with Chickpea Dumplings

PREPARATION TIME 15 minutes   COOKING TIME 25 minutes

800g/1lb 12oz/3¼ cups
   Greek-style yogurt
½ tsp white wine vinegar
4 tbsp chickpea flour
2–3 tbsp soft light brown sugar
1 tsp chilli powder
½ tsp ground asafoetida
½ tsp cinnamon
½ tbsp salt
4 tbsp sunflower oil
2 tsp mustard seeds

10 curry leaves or 2 tsp crumbled
   dried curry leaves
2 whole dried chillies
freshly ground black pepper

CHICKPEA DUMPLINGS
125g/4½oz/heaped 1 cup
   chickpea flour
1 tsp salt
½ tsp bicarbonate of soda
groundnut oil, for deep-frying

1 To make the dumplings, mix the chickpea flour, salt and bicarbonate of soda together and make a well in the centre. Add 125–150ml/4–5 fl oz/½–scant ⅔ cup cold water to the well and stir in the flour from the side to make a smooth batter that just falls off the tip of a spoon without lingering. Set aside for 15 minutes.

2 Meanwhile, put the yogurt in a large bowl and beat in the vinegar until smooth. Mix a spoonful of the yogurt mixture into the chickpea flour, then stir it into the yogurt until blended with no lumps. Stir in the sugar, chilli powder, asafoetida, cinnamon and salt. Stir in 1l/35fl oz/4 cups water and set aside.

3 Heat the sunflower oil in a saucepan over a high heat. Add the mustard seeds, curry leaves and chillies and stir for 30 seconds until the seeds pop. Slowly stir in the yogurt mixture and bring to the boil, stirring. Lower the heat and simmer for 15–20 minutes until the soup is the consistency of milk.

4 Meanwhile, fry the dumplings. Heat enough oil for deep-frying in a saucepan over a high heat until it reaches 190°C/375°F or until a cube of bread browns in 30 seconds. Line a plate with kitchen paper. Grease a spoon with a little oil and stir the batter. Working in batches, drop spoonfuls of the batter into the oil. Fry the dumplings for 60–90 seconds until dark golden brown. Remove and drain on the plate. Reheat the oil between batches, if necessary, and keep the finished dumplings warm.

5 Divide the dumplings into bowls, ladle the soup over them and serve.

310 North African Lamb & Chickpea Soup

PREPARATION TIME 15 minutes   COOKING TIME 2¼ hours

2 tbsp olive oil
750g/1lb 10oz boneless lamb
   shoulder, cut into 3 large chunks
2 carrots, peeled and finely chopped
6 large garlic cloves, chopped
2 large red onions, chopped
1 tbsp ras el hanout, or to taste
800g/1lb 12oz tinned chopped
   tomatoes
2 tbsp tomato purée

2 tsp caster sugar
1 handful of coriander leaves,
   chopped, plus extra to serve
400g/14oz tinned chickpeas, rinsed
150g/5½oz/heaped ⅔ cup split red
   lentils, rinsed
a large pinch of saffron threads
200g/7oz fine egg pasta, broken
½ tsp salt, plus extra to season
freshly ground black pepper

1 Heat the oil in a saucepan over a medium heat. Fry the lamb for 2–3 minutes until browned on all sides. Set aside. Add the carrots, garlic and onions to the pan, reduce the heat to low and cook, covered, for 10–12 minutes until the onions are golden brown. Add the ras el hanout and stir for 30 seconds. Stir in the tomatoes, tomato purée, sugar and coriander. Return the lamb and its juices to the pan.

2 Add 2l/70fl oz/8 cups water and bring to the boil. Skim, then simmer, covered, for 1 hour. Add the chickpeas and lentils and simmer for 30–40 minutes until tender. Remove the lamb and set aside. Stir in the saffron, pasta and salt and gently boil, uncovered and stirring occasionally, for 10–15 minutes until the pasta is tender.

3 Discard any remaining fat or sinew from the lamb and cut it into bite-sized pieces. Return it to the soup. Adjust the salt and pepper and serve sprinkled with coriander.

311 Spiced Vegetable Soup with Couscous

PREPARATION TIME 25 minutes, plus making the stock   COOKING TIME 45 minutes

2 tbsp olive oil
2 large onions, finely chopped
4 cloves garlic, chopped
2 tbsp sweet or smoked paprika
1 tsp turmeric
½ tsp cinnamon
1.75l/60fl oz/6⅔ cups Vegetable Stock
    (see page 12) or ready-made stock
450g/1lb butternut squash, peeled,
    deseeded and finely chopped
400g/14oz tinned chopped tomatoes
2 celery sticks, finely chopped

1 carrot, peeled and finely chopped
2 bay leaves
1 red or green jalapeño chilli,
    deseeded and finely chopped
1–2 tbsp tahini
800g/1lb 12oz tinned chickpeas,
    drained and rinsed
280g/10oz/1½ cups couscous
1 tbsp butter
salt and freshly ground black pepper
chopped coriander leaves, to serve

1   Heat the oil in a saucepan over a medium heat. Add the onion and fry, stirring, for 2 minutes. Add the garlic and fry for 1–3 minutes until the onion is softened. Stir in the paprika, turmeric and cinnamon and fry for 30 seconds. Watch closely so the spices do not burn. Add the stock and squash and season with salt and pepper, then cover and bring to the boil.
2   Add the tomatoes, celery, carrot, bay leaves, chilli and tahini. Reduce the heat and simmer, covered, for 25–30 minutes until the vegetables are tender. Add the chickpeas and warm through. Discard the bay leaves and adjust the salt and pepper, if necessary.
3   Meanwhile, put the couscous and butter in an heatproof bowl and season with salt and pepper. Add enough boiling water to cover by 2.5cm/1in and cover with a clean, folded tea towel. Set aside for 10 minutes until the water is absorbed and the grains are tender, then fluff with a fork.
4   Divide the couscous into bowls and ladle the soup and vegetables over it. Serve sprinkled with coriander.

312 Chicken-Udon Hotpot

PREPARATION TIME 10 minutes, plus making the stock   COOKING TIME 35 minutes

2l/70fl oz/8 cups Chicken Stock
    (see page 11) or ready-made stock
750g/1lb 10oz skinless chicken thighs
2 slices of carrot for each bowl
1 shiitake mushroom cap for
    each bowl
400g/14oz baby spinach leaves

3 mangetout for each bowl
500g/1lb 2oz fresh udon noodles
salt and freshly ground black pepper
yuzu powder or grated lemon zest,
    to serve
togarashi seasoning, to serve
    (optional)

1   Put the stock in a saucepan over a high heat. Add the chicken and season with salt and pepper. Cover and bring to just below the boil. Skim, then reduce the heat and simmer, covered, for 15–20 minutes until the chicken is cooked through and the juices run clear when you cut a piece. Remove from the pan and set aside until cool enough to handle. Skim the excess fat from the surface of the stock, then add the carrots and shiitake mushrooms and leave to simmer.
2   Meanwhile, bring a separate saucepan of lightly salted water to the boil and cook the spinach for 30 seconds until it just wilts. Transfer to a colander, using a slotted spoon, and immediately rinse under cold running water, then set aside. Return the water to the boil, add the mangetout and boil for 2–3 minutes until just tender. Drain and immediately rinse under cold running water.
3   Cut the chicken from the bones into bite-sized pieces. Return the stock to just below the boil, add the noodles and simmer for 1–2 minutes, or according to the packet instructions, to warm through.
4   Divide the noodles and spinach into bowls and top each portion with some of the chicken, 3 mangetout, 2 carrot slices and 1 shiitake mushroom. Add the stock and serve sprinkled with yuzu and togarashi, if you like.

313 Iraqi Chicken, Lentil & Rice Soup

PREPARATION TIME 10 minutes, plus making the stock and 1 hour soaking the rice
COOKING TIME 50 minutes

100g/3½oz/½ cup long-grain
  white rice
2 tbsp olive or hemp oil
1 large onion, finely chopped
1 tsp ground coriander
1 tsp ground cumin
¼ tsp turmeric
1.75l/60fl oz/6⅔ cups Chicken Stock
  (see page 11) or ready-made stock

1kg/2lb 4oz skinless chicken thighs
125g/4oz/½ cup split red lentils,
  rinsed
salt and freshly ground black pepper
finely shredded mint leaves, to serve
finely chopped parsley leaves,
  to serve
hot pepper sauce, to serve

1   Put the rice in a bowl, cover with cold water and leave to soak for 1–2 hours, then drain and set aside.

2   Heat the oil in a saucepan over a medium heat. Add the onion and fry for 3–5 minutes until softened, then stir in the coriander, cumin and turmeric and fry for 30 seconds. Watch closely so the spices do not burn. Add the stock and chicken and season with salt and pepper. Cover and bring to the boil. Skim, then stir in the rice and lentils, reduce the heat and simmer, covered, for 30–40 minutes until the lentils are tender. Remove the chicken and set aside until cool enough to handle.

3   Cut the chicken into bite-sized pieces, return it to the soup and heat through. Adjust the salt and pepper, if necessary. Serve sprinkled with mint and parsley and with hot pepper sauce on the side.

314 Danish Cabbage & Meatball Soup

PREPARATION TIME 25 minutes, plus 30 minutes chilling the meatballs and making the stock   COOKING TIME 45 minutes

350g/12oz very finely minced veal
  or a mixture of veal and beef
350g/12oz very finely minced pork
1 large onion, grated
½ tbsp dried thyme leaves
55g/2oz/⅔ cup fresh white
  breadcrumbs
1 egg, beaten
3½ tbsp soda water or milk

40g/1½oz butter
1 tbsp sunflower oil, plus extra
  for frying the meatballs
400g/14oz white cabbage,
  finely shredded
1.75l/60fl oz/6⅔ cups Beef Stock
  (see page 10) or ready-made stock
salt and freshly ground black pepper
chopped parsley leaves, to serve

1   To make the meatballs, line a baking sheet or 2 plates that will fit in your refrigerator with greaseproof paper. Mix the minced meats together in a large bowl. Add the onion, thyme, breadcrumbs, egg and soda water and season with salt and pepper. Mix well with wet hands. Divide the mixture into 6 equal portions, then divide each portion into 9 equal portions to make a total of 54. Roll into meatballs and put on the baking sheet. Cover with cling film and chill for 30 minutes. (At this point they can be chilled for up to 24 hours.)

2   Meanwhile, melt the butter with the oil in a saucepan over a low heat (use a heat diffuser if you have one). Add the cabbage and cook, covered, for 30 minutes, stirring occasionally, until very soft and light brown. Add the stock and season with salt and pepper. Bring to the boil, covered, then reduce the heat to very low and simmer while the meatballs are chilled and cooked.

3   When ready to fry the meatballs, heat one or two large frying pans over a high heat until a splash of water 'dances' on the surface. Add a thin layer of oil, reduce the heat to medium-low and add as many meatballs as will fit without overcrowding the pan. Fry for 5–8 minutes, turning gently, until golden brown. Drain on kitchen paper and set aside until all the meatballs are fried. (At this point they can be left to cool completely and chilled for up to 24 hours.)

4   Gently drop the meatballs into the simmering soup and warm through. Adjust the salt and pepper, if necessary, and serve sprinkled with parsley.

315 Chicken, Leek & Pancetta Risotto Soup

PREPARATION TIME 10 minutes, plus making the stock and cooking the chicken
COOKING TIME 35 minutes

85g/3oz pancetta
2 tbsp olive oil
1 leek, halved lengthways,
    sliced and rinsed
2 large garlic cloves, crushed
280g/10oz/1⅓ cups Arborio rice
150ml/5fl oz/scant ⅔ cup dry
    white wine

2l/70fl oz/8 cups Chicken Stock
    (see page 11) or ready-made stock,
    simmering, plus extra as needed
450g/1lb boneless, skinless cooked
    chicken, thinly shredded
85g/3oz freshly grated Parmesan
    cheese, plus extra to serve
salt and freshly ground black pepper
basil leaves, torn, to serve

1   Put the pancetta in a saucepan over a medium heat and fry, stirring,
    for 3–5 minutes until it begins to crisp and the fat runs. Remove it from the pan and
    set aside. Add the olive oil to the pan and heat. Add the leek and fry for 2 minutes.
    Stir in the garlic and fry for 1–3 minutes until the leek is softened but not coloured.
2   Add the rice and stir until the grains are coated. Add the wine and cook, stirring,
    until absorbed. Add a ladleful of the stock and stir until absorbed. Continue adding
    stock this way, ladleful by ladleful, for 15–20 minutes, stirring, until tender.
3   Add the chicken, cheese and pancetta, then stir in the remaining stock and simmer
    to warm the chicken through. The texture should be 'soupy' and not as thick
    as a conventional risotto, so stir in extra stock, if necessary. Season with salt and
    pepper, but remember the cheese is salty. Serve sprinkled with basil and with
    extra cheese on the side.

316 Teriyaki Salmon Ramen

PREPARATION TIME 15 minutes, plus making the dashi, stock and seeds and at least
30 minutes marinating   COOKING TIME 20 minutes

750g/1lb 10oz salmon fillet,
    small bones removed,
    cut into serving portions
5 tbsp teriyaki sauce
1 tbsp sesame oil
1l/35fl oz/4 cups Dashi (see page 12)
    or prepared instant dashi
1l/35fl oz/4 cups Fish Stock
    (see page 11) or ready-made stock
5cm/2in piece of root ginger, peeled
    and grated
2 large garlic cloves, finely chopped

2 long red chillies, deseeded
    and thinly sliced
5 shiitake mushroom caps, sliced
100g/3½oz pickled preserved
    bamboo shoots
4 tsp toasted sesame oil
500g/1lb 2oz ramen noodles
1 large handful of bean sprouts,
    rinsed
sesame seeds, toasted (see page 9),
    to serve
torn coriander leaves, to serve

1   Put the salmon on a plate, add the teriyaki sauce and rub it all over with your hands.
    Cover and chill for 30 minutes–2 hours. When ready to cook, remove from the
    fridge and heat a frying pan over a high heat until a splash of water 'dances' on the
    surface. Add the sesame oil to the pan and swirl around. Add the salmon, skin-side
    down, and cook for 3 minutes on each side or until cooked to your liking. Remove
    from the pan and set aside.
2   Meanwhile, to cook the noodles, fill a large saucepan three-quarters full of water
    and bring to the boil. Ramen noodles froth up so the pan needs to be very large.
3   Put the dashi and stock in another saucepan and bring to the boil. Reduce the heat
    to low, stir in the ginger, garlic, chillies, mushrooms, bamboo shoots and half the
    toasted sesame oil. Cover and keep warm while the noodles cook.
4   Add the noodles to the boiling water and cook for 4 minutes, or according to the
    packet instructions. For the last minute of the cooking time, add the bean sprouts
    to the other pan to soften slightly. Drain, then divide the noodles into bowls. Divide
    the mushrooms, bamboo shoots and bean sprouts into the bowls, then add the
    salmon pieces. Ladle the soup over and serve sprinkled with the remaining toasted
    sesame oil, sesame seeds and coriander.

317 Winter Vegetable Soup with Quinoa

PREPARATION TIME 20 minutes, plus making the stock and toasting the seeds
COOKING TIME 50 minutes

2l/70fl oz/8 cups Vegetable Stock
(see page 12) or ready-made stock
6 large garlic cloves, peeled and
thickly sliced
1 bouquet garni made with 1 large
piece of celery stick with its leaves,
2 bay leaves and several parsley
and thyme sprigs tied together
a pinch of chilli flakes, or to taste
280g/10oz sweet potatoes, peeled
and cut into bite-sized pieces
1 large leek, sliced and rinsed

2 green peppers, cored, deseeded
and cut into bite-sized pieces
2 large handfuls of curly kale,
thick stalks removed and
leaves chopped
350g/12oz/1¾ cups quinoa, rinsed
salt and freshly ground black pepper
Chinese chives, chopped, or spring
onions, chopped, to serve
pumpkin seeds, toasted (see page 9),
to serve

1   Put the stock, garlic, bouquet garni and chilli flakes in a saucepan and season
with salt and pepper. Cover and bring to the boil, then boil, partially covered,
for 10 minutes until slightly reduced. Discard the bouquet garni.

2   Add the sweet potato, cover and return to the boil. Boil for 5 minutes, then reduce
the heat, add the leek and peppers and simmer for 10–15 minutes. Stir in the kale
and simmer for 3 minutes until tender. Adjust the salt and pepper, if necessary.

3   Meanwhile, put the quinoa and 750ml/26fl oz/3 cups water in another saucepan,
cover and bring to the boil. Reduce the heat and simmer for 20 minutes until the
grains are tender. Drain and keep warm. Divide the quinoa into bowls, ladle the
soup over it and serve sprinkled with chives and pumpkin seeds.

318 Bouillabaisse

PREPARATION TIME 30 minutes, plus making the stock, croûtes and rouille
COOKING TIME 40 minutes

2 tbsp olive oil
1 fennel, quartered and thinly sliced
1 leek, thinly sliced and rinsed
1 onion, chopped
4 garlic cloves, chopped
4 tbsp aniseed-flavoured spirit
1.25l/44fl oz/5 cups Fish Stock
(see page 11)
500ml/17fl oz/2 cups passata
2 large pinches of saffron threads
12 live mussels, scrubbed, with
'beards' removed and soaked
in cold water

900g/2lb mixed fish, such as sea
bass, halibut, or red or grey mullet,
heads removed, gutted and scaled
and trimmed as necessary, boned
and cut into large chunks
500g/1lb 2oz large raw prawns,
peeled and deveined
salt and freshly ground black pepper
2 recipe quantities Croûtes
(see page 14), to serve
1½ recipe quantities Rouille
(see page 14), to serve

1   Heat the oil in a saucepan over a medium heat. Add the fennel, leek and onion and
fry, stirring, for 2 minutes. Add the garlic and fry for 1–3 minutes until the onion
is softened. Add the spirit and cook for 2–4 minutes until almost evaporated, then
add the stock, passata and saffron and season with salt and pepper. Cover and
bring to the boil. Reduce the heat and simmer for 10 minutes.

2   Meanwhile, calculate the cooking time for the fish at 10 minutes per 2.5cm/1in
of thickness. Discard any mussels with broken shells or open ones that do not
close when tapped. Add the mussels to the pan and cook, covered, for 3–5
minutes, shaking the pan frequently, until all the shells open. Remove the mussels
from the pan and set aside. Discard any closed mussels.

3   Add the fish to the pan and simmer for the calculated time until all the fish
is cooked through and flakes easily. If necessary, add the fish in stages, starting
with the thickest pieces. Three minutes before the end of the calculated cooking
time, add the prawns and cook until they curl and turn pink. Return the mussels
in their shells to the pan and adjust the salt and pepper, if necessary. Serve with
croûtes spread with rouille on the side.

319 Vegetable Jungle Curry with Noodles

PREPARATION TIME 20 minutes, plus making the stock   COOKING TIME 25 minutes

2 tbsp sunflower oil
1–2 tbsp red curry paste
1 tbsp soft light brown sugar
½ tbsp rice vinegar, to taste
1.75l/60fl oz/6⅔ cups Vegetable Stock
  (see page 12) or ready-made stock
350g/12oz butternut squash, peeled,
  deseeded and finely chopped
4 asparagus spears, woody ends
  removed and stalks and tips
  chopped and kept separate
6 kaffir lime leaves, finely shredded

2 carrots, peeled and sliced
1 red onion, quartered and sliced
2 tbsp fish sauce, or to taste
200g/7oz white cabbage,
  cored and sliced
8 cherry tomatoes
2 long red chillies, deseeded
  and sliced
500g/1lb 2oz ready-to-eat
  udon noodles
chopped coriander leaves, to serve

1   Heat the oil in a saucepan over a high heat. Stir in the curry paste, sugar and
    vinegar, then reduce the heat to low and stir-fry for 2 minutes. Watch closely and
    stir in a little stock if the paste begins to brown. Stir in 200ml/7fl oz/scant 1 cup
    of the stock and cook until the fat separates and the surface is shiny.
2   Add the squash, asparagus stalks, lime leaves, carrots, onion and several more
    ladlefuls of the stock so the vegetables are covered. Cover and bring to the boil.
    Reduce the heat and simmer for 5 minutes, then stir in the fish sauce, asparagus
    tips, cabbage, tomatoes, half of the sliced chillies and the remaining stock. Simmer,
    covered, for 5–10 minutes until the vegetables are tender.
3   Add the noodles to the pan and warm through. Add extra fish sauce, if you like.
    Divide the noodles into bowls, ladle the soup over them and serve sprinkled with
    the remaining sliced chilli and coriander leaves.

320 Prawn Laksa

PREPARATION TIME 20 minutes, plus making the stock   COOKING TIME 50 minutes

500ml/17fl oz/2 cups Fish Stock
  (see page 11) or ready-made stock
1kg/2lb 4oz raw large prawns,
  peeled and deveined, with heads
  and shells reserved
½ tsp salt
1 large handful of bean sprouts
12 coriander sprigs, leaves and stalks
  coarsely chopped, plus extra
  chopped leaves to serve
5 large garlic cloves, chopped
1 bird's-eye chilli, deseeded
  (optional) and chopped

1 lemongrass stalk, chopped,
  with outer leaves removed
4cm/1½in piece of root ginger,
  peeled and chopped
2 tbsp shrimp paste
½ tsp turmeric
4 tbsp groundnut or sunflower oil
1l/35fl oz/4 cups coconut milk
1½ tbsp fish sauce, or to taste
1½ tbsp lime juice, or to taste
250g/9oz medium ready-to-eat
  rice noodles

1   Put the stock, prawn heads and shells and salt in a saucepan. Cover and bring
    to the boil, then reduce the heat and simmer for 10 minutes. Put the bean sprouts
    in a bowl, cover with cold water and set aside.
2   Meanwhile, to make the laksa paste, put the coriander, garlic, chilli, lemongrass,
    ginger, shrimp paste and turmeric in a mini food processor and blend until a paste
    forms. Add 3 tablespoons of the oil and blend again, then set aside.
3   Strain the stock through a muslin-lined sieve and set aside. Heat the remaining oil
    in a large saucepan over a high heat. Add the paste and stir-fry for 1–2 minutes until
    fragrant. Watch closely so it doesn't burn and add a little of the simmering stock
    if necessary. Stir in the stock, coconut milk, fish sauce and lime juice and bring
    to the boil, stirring. Cover, reduce the heat to low, and simmer for 20 minutes.
4   Add the prawns and simmer for 2–3 minutes until they curl and turn pink. Drain the
    bean sprouts and add them and the noodles to the soup and cook for 30 seconds
    to warm through. Adjust the fish sauce and lime juice, if necessary. Serve sprinkled
    with coriander.

321 Edamame & Pumpkin Soup with Jasmine Rice

PREPARATION TIME 25 minutes, plus making the rice   **COOKING TIME** 30 minutes

2 tbsp hemp or sunflower oil
1 onion, chopped
2 carrots, peeled and sliced
450g/1lb pumpkin, peeled, deseeded
  and cut into bite-sized pieces
800ml/28fl oz/scant 3½ cups coconut
  milk
125g/4½oz frozen shelled edamame
  soya beans
4 pak choi, quartered lengthways
salt and freshly ground black pepper
280g/10oz/2 cups cooked Thai
  Jasmine Rice (see recipe 262), hot,
  to serve

chopped coriander leaves, to serve
lime wedges, to serve

RED CHILLI PASTE
5 garlic cloves, chopped
2.5cm/1in piece of root ginger,
  peeled and chopped
2 red chillies, deseeded (optional)
  and chopped
2 lemongrass stalks, chopped, with
  outer leaves removed

1   Put all the ingredients for the chilli paste and 2 tablespoons water in a mini food
    processor and process for 20–30 seconds until a thin, coarse paste forms.
2   Heat the oil in a heavy-based stockpot over a high heat. Add the onion and fry,
    stirring occasionally, for 3–5 minutes until softened but not coloured. Add the chilli
    paste and stir for 2–3 minutes until the fat separates around the edge. Add the
    carrots, pumpkin and 1l/35fl oz/4 cups water and season with salt and pepper.
    Cover and bring to the boil, then reduce the heat and simmer for 10 minutes.
3   Add the coconut milk, edamame and pak choi and simmer, uncovered, for 3–5
    minutes until the edamame are tender. Adjust the salt and pepper, if necessary.
4   Divide the rice into bowls and ladle the soup over it. Serve sprinkled with
    chopped coriander and with lime wedges for squeezing over.

322 Posole

PREPARATION TIME 15 minutes, plus overnight soaking and cooking the hominy and making the stock   COOKING TIME 1¾ hours

280g/10oz hominy
  (dried corn kernels)
2l/70fl oz/8 cups Chicken Stock
  (see page 11) or ready-made stock
1kg/2lb 4oz boneless pork shoulder,
  in one piece, rind and fat removed
any available pork bones (optional;
  ask the butcher for these)
2 large onions, unpeeled,
  quartered and each piece
  studded with one clove

4 large garlic cloves, chopped
1 tbsp dried oregano
2 tsp ground cumin
2 green jalapeño chillies, deseeded
  (optional), and sliced
2 tbsp dried thyme leaves
1 tsp dried ancho chilli powder
1 tsp salt, plus extra to season
freshly ground black pepper
1 handful of coriander leaves,
  chopped, to serve

1 Put the hominy in a bowl, cover with water and leave to soak overnight, then drain. Transfer to a saucepan and cover generously with water. Cover and bring to the boil, then reduce the heat and simmer for 4 hours. Drain and set aside.
2 Put the stock, pork, and pork bones, if using, in a saucepan. Cover and bring to the boil. Skim, then add the onions, garlic, oregano and cumin. Reduce the heat and simmer, covered, for 30 minutes.
3 Add the hominy, chillies, thyme, chilli powder and salt. Cover and return to the boil, then reduce the heat and simmer for another 1–1¼ hours until the meat and hominy are very tender. Remove the pork and set aside until cool enough to handle. Discard the onions and bones, if used.
4 Shred the pork, then return it to the pan. Adjust the salt and pepper, if necessary, and serve sprinkled with coriander.

323 Peruvian 'Breakfast' Soup – for Any Time of the Day

PREPARATION TIME 15 minutes, plus making the stock and hard-boiling the eggs
COOKING TIME 45 minutes

1 egg for each bowl
2l/70fl oz/8 cups Rich Chicken Stock
  (see page 10) or ready-made stock
6 garlic cloves, crushed
3 celery sticks, coarsely chopped
4cm/1½in piece of root ginger,
  peeled and coarsely chopped
1kg/2lb 4oz skinless chicken pieces,
  such as breasts and drumsticks

400g/14oz waxy potatoes,
  peeled and chopped
salt and freshly ground black pepper
chopped coriander leaves, to serve
2 roasted red peppers in olive oil,
  drained and sliced, to serve
chopped spring onions, to serve

1 Put the eggs in a saucepan, add enough water to cover by 2.5cm/1in and bring to the boil, then reduce the heat and simmer for 9 minutes. Pour off the hot water, then run cold water over the eggs for 1–2 minutes to stop the cooking. Set aside until cool enough to handle, then peel and set aside.
2 Meanwhile, put the stock, garlic, celery and ginger in a saucepan and season with salt and pepper. Cover and bring to the boil, then boil, uncovered, for 10 minutes until slightly reduced. Discard the flavourings.
3 Add the chicken and potatoes to the pan, cover and bring to the boil. Skim, then reduce the heat and simmer for 15–20 minutes until the potatoes are tender and the chicken is cooked through and the juices run clear when you cut a piece. Remove the chicken from the pan and set aside until cool enough to handle.
4 Cut the chicken from the bones into bite-sized pieces and return to the stock to warm through. Adjust the salt and pepper, if necessary. Cut the hard-boiled eggs in half lengthways and arrange on a plate. Serve the soup sprinkled with coriander and with the peppers, eggs and spring onions on the side.

CHAPTER 7

CHILLED SOUPS

The sweet and savoury soups in this chapter are the key to staying cool in the kitchen when the temperatures are high. These recipes include many vegetarian and vegan soups, as well as a good selection of super-healthy raw soups such as Raw Emerald Soup, Green Cucumber & Chilli Soup and Big Red Raw Soup.

From sunny Spain, Gazpacho and White Garlic and Almond Soup are ideal for summer entertaining, as is Bloody Mary Party Soup. And if rain clouds threaten your catering plans, don't worry: soups like Vichyssoise, Fennel & Apple Soup and Sweet Buttermilk Dessert Soup do double duty as hot soups.

The important thing to remember with all the recipes in this chapter is to taste and adjust the salt and pepper, if necessary, before serving. Chilling soups dulls the flavours and what previously tasted fresh and exciting might need more seasoning after a couple hours in the fridge. Most soups also thicken as they chill and will require a little extra liquid stirred in before serving.

ICED TOMATO & ORANGE SOUP WITH GOAT'S MILK YOGURT SORBET (SEE PAGE 203)

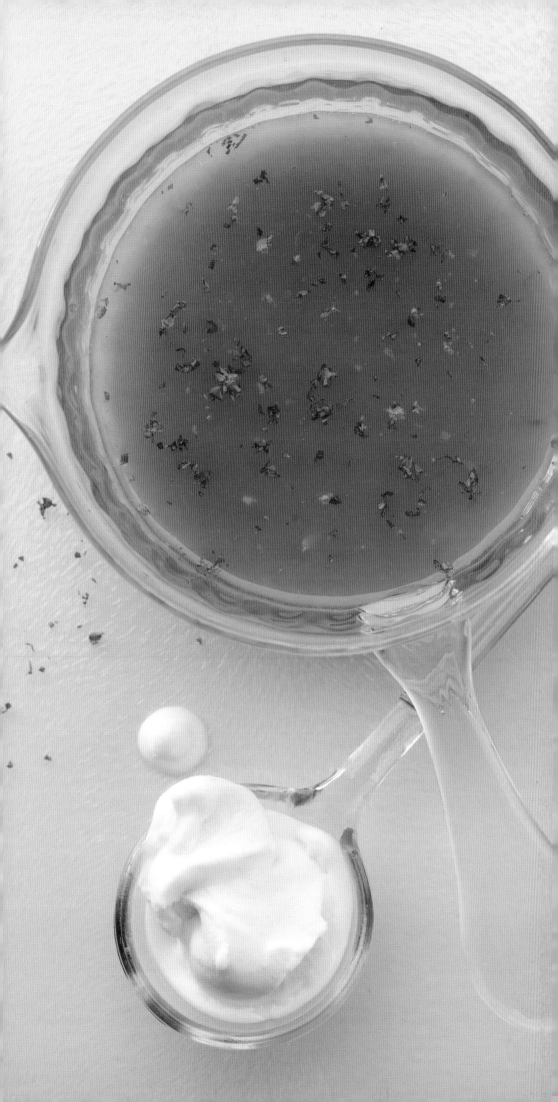

324 Vichyssoise

PREPARATION TIME 15 minutes, plus making the stock, cooling and at least 2 hours chilling   COOKING TIME 40 minutes

55g/2oz butter
900g/2lb leeks, chopped and rinsed
1 onion, sliced
1l/35fl oz/4 cups Vegetable Stock
  (see page 12) or ready-made stock,
  plus extra as needed

250g/9oz floury potatoes,
  peeled and chopped
200ml/7fl oz/scant 1 cup single cream
salt and ground white pepper
chopped chives, to serve

1   Melt the butter in a saucepan over a medium heat. Add the leeks and onion, reduce the heat to low and cook, covered, for 8–10 minutes until softened but not coloured. Add the stock and potatoes and season with salt and white pepper. Cover and bring to the boil, then reduce the heat to very low (use a heat diffuser if you have one) and simmer for 20–25 minutes until the vegetables are very tender.
2   Blend the soup until smooth, then work it through a sieve into a large bowl, rubbing back and forth with a spoon and scraping the bottom of the sieve. Set aside to cool completely, then cover and chill for at least 2 hours.
3   When ready to serve, stir in the cream and a little extra stock if the soup has thickened. Adjust the salt and pepper, if necessary, and serve sprinkled with chives.

325 Consommé & Vegetable Soup

PREPARATION TIME 15 minutes, plus making the consommé, preparing the tomato, cooling and at least 2 hours chilling

1 carrot, peeled and grated
1 courgette, peeled and grated
1 tomato, peeled (see page 9),
  deseeded and finely diced
2 tbsp finely chopped chives
2 tbsp finely chopped
  parsley leaves

1 recipe quantity Beef or Chicken
  Consommé (see page 13)
  or 1.25l/44fl oz/5 cups tinned beef
  or chicken consommé, at room
  temperature
salt and freshly ground black pepper
dry sherry, to serve
1 pomegranate, to serve (optional)

1   Put the carrot, courgette, tomato, chives, parsley and consommé in a bowl, stir well and season very lightly with salt and pepper. Cover and chill for at least 2 hours. The consommé will lightly gel while chilling.
2   When ready to serve, put 1 teaspoon dry sherry in each serving bowl, then ladle in the soup. If you want to garnish with pomegranate seeds, bash the pomegranate with a wooden spoon, then cut it in half. Hold one half over one of the bowls and tap the top with the spoon so the seeds fall over the soup and remove any white pith. Repeat to sprinkle the remaining bowls with pomegranate seeds, then serve.

326 Cherry Tomato & Consommé Soup

PREPARATION TIME 10 minutes, plus making the consommé, flavoured oil and croûtes (optional) and at least 2 hours chilling

1 recipe quantity Chicken Consommé
  (see page 13) or 1.25l/44fl oz/
  5 cups tinned chicken consommé,
  at room temperature
900g/2lb cherry tomatoes, chopped
4 spring onions, finely chopped
2 tbsp tomato purée

a pinch of caster sugar
salt and freshly ground black pepper
1 recipe quantity Crushed Mint Oil
  (see page 15), to serve
1 recipe quantity Goat's Cheese
  Croûtes (see page 14), to serve
  (optional)

1   Put the consommé, tomatoes, spring onions, tomato purée and sugar in a blender and season with salt and pepper. Blend the soup until smooth, then work it through a nylon sieve into a bowl, using a large spoon. Cover and chill for at least 2 hours.
2   When ready to serve, stir well and adjust the salt and pepper, if necessary. Serve drizzled with the oil and with croûtes on the side, if you like.

327 Fennel & Apple Soup

PREPARATION TIME 10 minutes, plus making the stock and seeds, cooling and at least 2 hours chilling   **COOKING TIME** 40 minutes

1½ sweet cooking apples, peeled,
   cored and chopped
1 tbsp lemon juice
1½ tbsp olive or hemp oil
280g/10oz fennel, sliced,
   with the fronds reserved
1 leek, thinly sliced and rinsed
4 tbsp dry vermouth

1.25l/44fl oz/5 cups Vegetable Stock
   (see page 12) or ready-made stock,
   plus extra as needed
apple juice, as needed (optional)
salt and freshly ground black pepper
Crunchy Mixed Seeds (see page 15),
   to serve

1   Toss the apple and lemon juice together in a bowl and set aside.
2   Heat the oil in a saucepan over a medium heat. Stir in the fennel and leek and fry for 2 minutes. Reduce the heat to low and cook, covered, for 8–10 minutes until softened but not coloured. Stir in the vermouth and cook for 2–4 minutes until evaporated, then add the stock and season with salt and pepper. Cover and bring to the boil. Reduce the heat and simmer for 5 minutes.
3   Add the apples and simmer for 8–10 minutes until they are falling apart. Stir in the fennel fronds, then blend the soup until smooth and work it through a sieve into a bowl, rubbing back and forth with a spoon and scraping the bottom of the sieve. Set aside to cool completely.
4   Cover and chill for at least 2 hours. When ready to serve, stir well and add a little extra stock or apple juice if the soup has thickened too much. Adjust the salt and pepper, if necessary, and serve sprinkled with the seeds. This soup also tastes good served hot. After blending, adjust the salt and pepper, if necessary, and serve.

328 Curried Chicken Soup

PREPARATION TIME 20 minutes, plus making the stock and almonds, cooling and at least 2 hours chilling   **COOKING TIME** 40 minutes

1½ tbsp sunflower oil
2 celery sticks, thinly sliced
2 leeks, white parts only, halved
   lengthways, thinly sliced and rinsed
1 large onion, finely chopped
1½ tsp Madras curry powder
1l/35fl oz/4 cups Rich Chicken Stock
   (see page 10) or ready-made stock,
   plus extra as needed

400g/14oz skinless chicken pieces,
   such as drumsticks and thighs
280g/10oz floury potatoes, peeled
   and chopped
1 cooking apple
250ml/9fl oz/1 cup single cream
salt and freshly ground black pepper
toasted flaked almonds (see page 9),
   to serve

1   Heat the oil in a saucepan over a medium heat and add the celery, leeks and onion. Cover, reduce the heat to low and cook, stirring occasionally, for 8–10 minutes until the onion is softened. Add the curry powder and stir for 30 seconds until aromatic. Watch closely so it does not burn.
2   Add the stock, chicken and potatoes and season with salt and pepper. Cover and bring to the boil. Skim, then reduce the heat and simmer, covered, for 15–20 minutes until the chicken is cooked through and the juices run clear when you cut a piece. Remove the chicken and set aside to cool completely. Blend the soup until smooth and set aside to cool completely.
3   Cut the chicken from the bones into bite-sized pieces and return it to the soup. Cover and chill for at least 2 hours.
4   Just before serving, stir a little extra stock into the soup if it has thickened too much. Peel, core and finely chop the apple, then stir it and the cream into the soup. Adjust the salt and pepper, if necessary, and serve sprinkled with toasted almonds.

329 Beetroot Soup

PREPARATION TIME 10 minutes, plus making the consommé, cooling and at least
4 hours chilling   COOKING TIME 30 minutes

1 recipe quantity Beef Consommé
(see page 13) or 1.25l/44fl oz/
5 cups tinned consommé, plus
extra as needed
600g/1lb 5oz beetroot, peeled
and grated

1 onion, halved
2 tbsp lemon juice, or to taste
1 tbsp soft light brown sugar,
or to taste
salt and freshly ground black pepper
chopped dill, to serve

1   Put the consommé, beetroot and onion in a saucepan. Season with salt and pepper,
cover and bring to the boil. Reduce the heat and simmer for 20 minutes, then leave
to cool completely. Once cooled, cover and chill for at least 4 hours.
2   When ready to serve, discard the onion halves. Stir in the lemon juice and sugar
and add a little extra consommé if the soup has thickened. Adjust the salt and
pepper, if necessary, and serve sprinkled with dill.

330 Carrot & Orange Soup

PREPARATION TIME 15 minutes, plus making the stock, cooling and at least
2 hours chilling   COOKING TIME 45 minutes

1½ tbsp olive or hemp oil
350g/12oz carrots, peeled and
coarsely chopped
1 leek, chopped and rinsed
1 large red onion, chopped
875ml/30fl oz/3½ cups Vegetable
Stock (see page 12)
or ready-made stock

4 tbsp orange juice, plus extra
as needed
1 large garlic clove, crushed
1 tsp caster sugar
finely grated zest of 1 orange
a pinch of cayenne pepper
salt and freshly ground black pepper

1   Heat the oil in a saucepan over a medium heat. Add the carrots, leek and onion,
cover and reduce the heat to low. Cook for 10–12 minutes, stirring occasionally,
until the vegetables are softened but not coloured. Add the stock, orange juice,
garlic, sugar, orange zest and cayenne pepper and season with salt and pepper.
Cover and bring to the boil, then reduce the heat and simmer for 20–25 minutes
until the carrots are very tender.
2   Blend the soup until smooth, then work it through a sieve into a bowl, rubbing back
and forth with a spoon and scraping the bottom of the sieve. Set aside to cool
completely, then cover and chill for at least 2 hours.
3   When ready to serve, stir well and add a little extra orange juice if the soup
has thickened. Adjust the salt and pepper, if necessary, and serve.

331 Creamy Courgette Soup

PREPARATION TIME 15 minutes, plus making the stock, cooling and at least
2 hours chilling   COOKING TIME 20 minutes

875ml/30fl oz/3½ cups Vegetable
Stock (see page 12) or ready-made
stock, plus extra as needed
350g/12oz courgettes, sliced
1 onion, chopped

175g/6oz soft garlic-and-herb
cream cheese
salt and ground white pepper
2 tbsp finely chopped parsley leaves,
to serve

1   Put the stock, courgettes and onion in a saucepan. Season with salt and white
pepper, cover and bring to the boil. Reduce the heat and simmer for 8–10 minutes
until the courgettes are very tender, then blend until smooth.
2   Put the cheese in a small bowl, add several spoonfuls of the soup and beat until
smooth. Add this mixture to the soup, stirring until well blended. Set aside and
leave to cool completely, then cover and chill for at least 2 hours.
3   When ready to serve, add a little extra stock if the soup has thickened. Adjust the
salt and pepper, if necessary, and serve sprinkled with parsley.

332 Curried Courgette Soup

PREPARATION TIME 15 minutes, plus making the stock, cooling and at least
2 hours chilling   **COOKING TIME** 25 minutes

1½ tbsp sunflower oil
6 spring onions, chopped
1 large garlic clove, crushed
750g/1lb 10oz courgettes, chopped
2 tsp mild curry powder
400ml/14fl oz/scant 1⅔ cups
   Vegetable Stock (see page 12)
   or ready-made stock, plus extra
   as needed

185g/6½oz/¾ cup Greek-style yogurt
salt and freshly ground black pepper
torn or chopped coriander or mint
   leaves, to serve
mini poppadoms, fried, to serve
   (optional)

1   Heat the oil in a saucepan over a medium heat. Add the spring onions and
    garlic and fry, stirring, for 3 minutes until the spring onions are softened but
    not coloured. Add the courgettes and fry, stirring, for 2–3 minutes until the
    skins turn bright green. Add the curry powder and stir for 30 seconds. Watch
    closely so it does not burn.
2   Add the stock and season with salt and pepper. Cover and bring to the boil,
    then reduce the heat and simmer for 8–10 minutes until the courgettes are
    tender. Blend until smooth, then transfer to a heatproof bowl and set aside
    to cool completely. Once cool, stir in the yogurt, then cover and chill for
    at least 2 hours.
3   When ready to serve, stir well and add a little extra stock if the soup has
    thickened. Adjust the salt and pepper, if necessary, and serve sprinkled with
    coriander and with mini poppadoms on the side, if you like.

333 Courgette & Basil Soup

PREPARATION TIME 15 minutes, plus making the stock, flavoured oil and croûtes
(optional), cooling and at least 2 hours chilling   **COOKING TIME** 30 minutes

1.25l/44fl oz/5 cups Vegetable Stock
   (see page 12) or ready-made stock,
   plus extra as needed
4 garlic cloves, cut in half
400g/14oz tinned chopped tomatoes
½ tsp caster sugar
1 large handful of basil leaves
2 tbsp garlic-flavoured olive oil

1 onion, finely chopped
750g/1lb 10oz courgettes,
   halved lengthways and sliced
salt and freshly ground black pepper
1 recipe quantity Crushed Basil Oil
   (see page 15), to serve
Goat's Cheese Croûtes (see page 14),
   to serve (optional)

1   Put the stock, garlic, tomatoes, sugar and basil in a saucepan and season with
    salt and pepper. Cover and bring to the boil, then boil for 10 minutes.
2   Meanwhile, heat the garlic oil in another saucepan over a medium heat. Add the
    onion and fry, stirring, for 2 minutes. Add the courgettes and fry for 2–3 minutes
    until the skins turn bright green and the onion is softened.
3   Strain the stock into a large heatproof bowl, pressing down on the flavourings
    to extract as much flavour as possible, then discard them. Return the stock
    to the pan, add the courgettes and return to the boil. Reduce the heat to low,
    and simmer, uncovered, for 5–8 minutes until the courgettes are tender. Set
    aside to cool completely, then cover and chill for at least 2 hours.
4   When ready to serve, stir well and add a little extra stock if the soup has
    thickened. Adjust the salt and pepper, if necessary, and serve drizzled with
    basil oil and with croûtes on the side, if you like. This soup also tastes good
    served hot. When the courgettes are tender, adjust the salt and pepper,
    if necessary, and serve.

334 Chargrilled Yellow Pepper Soup

PREPARATION TIME 25 minutes, plus making the stock and chargrilled peppers, cooling and at least 2 hours chilling   COOKING TIME 25 minutes

3 tbsp garlic-flavoured olive oil,
  plus extra to serve
1 onion, finely chopped
5 large yellow peppers, chargrilled
  (see page 9), peeled, deseeded
  and chopped
1 small carrot, peeled and sliced
1 potato, peeled and chopped

1l/35fl oz/4 cups Vegetable Stock
  (see page 12) or ready-made stock,
  plus extra as needed
salt and ground white pepper

GREMOLATA
finely grated zest of 1 lemon
1 garlic clove, very finely chopped
3 tbsp finely chopped parsley leaves

1   Heat the oil in a saucepan over a medium heat. Add the onion and fry, stirring occasionally, for 3–5 minutes until softened but not coloured. Stir in the peppers, carrot and potato, season with salt and white pepper and fry, stirring occasionally, for 5 minutes. Add the stock, cover and bring to the boil. Reduce the heat and simmer for 5–10 minutes until the vegetables are very tender.
2   Blend the soup until smooth, then work it through a sieve into a bowl, rubbing back and forth with a spoon and scraping the bottom of the sieve. Set aside to cool completely, then cover and chill for at least 2 hours.
3   Shortly before serving, mix together all the ingredients for the gremolata in a bowl. (This is best made just before serving, although it will retain its fresh flavour for several hours, if you want to make it in advance.) Stir the soup well and add a little extra stock if it has thickened. Adjust the salt and pepper, if necessary, and serve sprinkled with the gremolata and drizzled with garlic oil.

335 Spanish White Garlic & Almond Soup

PREPARATION TIME 15 minutes, plus at least 2 hours freezing the grapes and chilling the water   COOKING TIME 10 minutes

1 small bunch of seedless white
  grapes, to serve
8 large garlic cloves, peeled but
  left whole
250g/9oz day-old country-style bread,
  crusts removed

4–6 tbsp sherry vinegar
250g/9oz/2½ cups ground almonds
125ml/4fl oz/½ cup extra-virgin olive
  oil, plus extra to serve
salt and ground white pepper

1   At least 2 hours before serving, put the grapes in the freezer and put a jug with 1.2l/40fl oz/4¾ cups water in the fridge to chill. If your refrigerator is large enough, chill the serving bowls as well.
2   Put the garlic cloves in a small saucepan and cover with water. Cover and bring to the boil, then strain into a bowl and set the garlic aside. Tear the bread into a large bowl, sprinkle with the garlic-flavoured water and set aside for 10–12 minutes until softened, then use your hands to squeeze any water from the bread.
3   Blend the bread with the garlic, 4 tablespoons of the vinegar, ground almonds and oil to form a thick paste-like mixture. Season with salt and white pepper. Slowly add the chilled water and continue blending to achieve the preferred consistency. Adjust the salt and pepper and add the remaining sherry vinegar, if you like. At this point, the soup can be served as it is, or covered and chilled until required.
4   When ready to serve, stir well and add extra chilled water if the soup has thickened. Serve with the frozen grapes acting as ice cubes and drizzle with oil.

336 No-Cook Cucumber & Horseradish Soup

PREPARATION TIME 10 minutes, plus making the stock and croûtons and at least
2 hours chilling

250ml/9fl oz/1 cup Vegetable Stock
  (see page 12) or ready-made stock
4 spring onions, chopped
600g/21oz/1lb 5oz cucumbers, peeled
  and deseeded

250ml/9fl oz/1 cup soured cream
1 tbsp grated horseradish, or to taste
salt and ground white pepper
1 recipe quantity Dill Croûtons
  (see page 14), to serve

1 Put the stock and spring onions in a blender and blend. Add the cucumbers,
soured cream and horseradish and blend again. Season with salt and white pepper.
2 Cover and chill for at least 2 hours. When ready to serve, stir well because the
soup will have separated. Adjust the salt and pepper and add extra horseradish,
if necessary. Serve sprinkled with croûtons.

337 Cucumber & Yogurt Soup with Mint

PREPARATION TIME 15 minutes, plus making the stock, cooling and at least
2 hours chilling COOKING TIME 30 minutes

625ml/21½fl oz/2½ cups
  Vegetable Stock (see page 12)
  or ready-made stock
1 shallot, finely chopped
400g/14oz cucumber, peeled,
  deseeded and chopped
2 tbsp mint leaves, plus extra, finely
  shredded, to serve

400g/14oz/scant 1⅔ cups
  Greek-style yogurt
200ml/7fl oz/scant 1 cup buttermilk,
  plus extra as needed
finely grated zest of 1 lemon
a pinch of cayenne pepper
salt and ground white pepper
chopped pistachio nuts, to serve

1 Put the stock and shallot in a saucepan. Cover and bring to the boil, then boil for
10 minutes. Reduce the heat to low, add the cucumber and simmer, covered,
for 10 minutes, then add the mint and blend until smooth. Transfer the soup
to a bowl and set aside to cool completely. Once cool, stir in the yogurt, buttermilk,
lemon zest and cayenne pepper and season with salt and white pepper.
2 Cover and chill for at least 2 hours. When ready to serve, stir well and add a little
extra buttermilk if the soup has thickened. Adjust the salt and pepper, if necessary,
and serve sprinkled with mint and pistachio nuts.

338 Yellow Tomato Soup

PREPARATION TIME 15 minutes, plus cooling and at least 2 hours chilling and making
the flavoured oil COOKING TIME 30 minutes

1½ tbsp olive or hemp oil
1 yellow pepper, deseeded
  and chopped
1 shallot, chopped
500g/1lb 2oz yellow tomatoes,
  chopped
875ml/30fl oz/3½ cups Vegetable
  Stock (see page 12) or ready-made
  stock, plus extra as needed

½ tsp caster sugar
salt and ground white pepper
1 recipe quantity Crushed Basil
  or Mint Oil (see page 15),
  to serve
crumbled feta cheese, to serve

1 Heat the oil in a saucepan over a medium heat. Add the pepper and shallot and fry,
stirring, for 3–5 minutes until the shallot is softened. Add the tomatoes and cook
for 5 minutes. Add the stock and sugar and season with salt and pepper. Cover and
bring to the boil, then reduce the heat and simmer for 10 minutes. Blend the soup.
2 Work the soup through a sieve into a bowl, rubbing back and forth with a spoon.
Set aside to cool completely, then cover and chill for at least 2 hours.
3 When ready to serve, stir well and add a little extra stock if the soup has thickened.
Adjust the salt and pepper, if necessary, and serve drizzled with herb oil and
sprinkled with cheese.

339 Bloody Mary Party Soup

PREPARATION TIME 15 minutes, plus making the stock, cooling and at least
2 hours chilling **COOKING TIME** 30 minutes **MAKES** 14 x 100ml/3½fl oz/
scant ½ cup servings or 4–6 conventional servings

1 tbsp chilli-flavoured olive oil
100g/3½oz carrot, peeled and
   finely chopped
1 celery stick, finely chopped, plus
   extra celery sticks with leaves
   to serve (optional)
1 onion, finely chopped
670ml/23fl oz/2⅔ cups passata, plus
   extra as needed

750ml/26fl oz/3 cups Vegetable Stock
   (see page 12) or ready-made stock,
   plus extra as needed
150ml/5fl oz/scant ⅔ cup vodka
a pinch of chilli flakes, or to taste
lemon juice, to taste
salt and freshly ground black pepper
sweet sherry, to serve
celery salt, to serve
celery seeds, to serve

1   Heat the oil in a saucepan over a medium heat. Stir in the carrot, celery and onion,
reduce the heat to low and cook, covered, for 8–10 minutes, stirring occasionally,
until softened. Stir in the passata, stock, vodka and chilli flakes and season with
salt and pepper. Cover and bring to the boil, then reduce the heat and simmer
for 10 minutes. Add lemon juice to taste, then blend until smooth.

2   Strain the soup through a sieve into a large bowl, rubbing back and forth with
a spoon and scraping the bottom of the sieve. Set aside to cool completely,
then cover and chill for at least 2 hours.

3   When ready to serve, stir the soup and add a little extra passata or stock if it has
thickened. Adjust the salt and pepper, if necessary. Put ½ teaspoon sweet
sherry in fourteen small or four to six regular mugs or glasses. Add the
soup, sprinkle with celery salt and celery seeds, add celery sticks
to act as stirrers, if you like, and serve.

340 Minted Pea Soup

PREPARATION TIME 15 minutes, plus making the stock, cooling and at least
2 hours chilling   COOKING TIME 30 minutes

1½ tbsp olive or hemp oil, plus extra
   to serve
4 spring onions, finely chopped, plus
   extra, thinly sliced on the diagonal,
   to serve
1 floury potato, peeled and finely
   chopped

850ml/29fl oz/3½ cups Vegetable
   Stock (see page 12) or ready-made
   stock, plus extra as needed
600g/1lb 5oz/4 cups frozen peas
30g/1oz mint leaves, plus extra small
   ones to serve
salt and freshly ground black pepper

1   Heat the oil in a saucepan over a medium heat. Add the spring onions and fry,
    stirring, for 3–5 minutes until softened but not coloured. Stir in the potato, then
    add the stock and season with salt and pepper, cover and bring to the boil.
    Reduce the heat and simmer for 10–12 minutes until the potato is tender. Add the
    peas and mint, return to the boil, uncovered, then reduce the heat and simmer for
    3–5 minutes until the peas are tender.
2   Blend the soup. For a smoother texture, work it through a sieve, if you like, rubbing
    back and forth with a spoon and scraping the bottom of the sieve to remove the
    pea skins. Leave to cool completely, then cover and chill for at least 2 hours.
3   When ready to serve, stir well and add extra stock if the soup has thickened. Adjust
    the salt and pepper, if necessary. Serve sprinkled with spring onions and mint
    leaves and drizzled with a little olive oil.

341 Edamame & Pea Soup with Crushed Basil Oil

PREPARATION TIME 10 minutes, plus making the stock and flavoured oil, cooling and
at least 2 hours chilling   COOKING TIME 15 minutes

100g/3½oz frozen shelled edamame
   soya beans
500ml/17fl oz/2 cups Vegetable Stock
   (see page 12) or ready-made stock
finely grated zest of 1 lemon
a pinch of chilli flakes, or to taste
400g/14oz/2⅔ cups frozen peas

400ml/14fl oz/scant 1⅔ cups
   rice milk or almond milk,
   plus extra as needed
½ tbsp lemon juice, plus extra
   to taste
salt and freshly ground black pepper
1 recipe quantity Crushed Basil Oil
   (see page 15), to serve
flax seeds, lightly crushed, to serve

1   Bring a covered saucepan of salted water to the boil. Add the edamame and boil,
    uncovered, for 5 minutes until tender. Drain and immediately rinse under cold
    running water. Set aside.
2   Meanwhile, put the stock, lemon zest and chilli flakes in another saucepan and
    season with salt and pepper. Cover and bring to the boil. Add the peas, reduce the
    heat and simmer, uncovered, for 3–5 minutes until tender, then stir in the rice milk.
3   Blend two-thirds of the pea mixture to the preferred consistency. Rub the mixture
    through a sieve for an even smoother texture, if you like. Return the mixture to
    the pan, stir in the edamame and lemon juice and set the soup aside to cool
    completely, then cover and chill for at least 2 hours.
4   When ready to serve, add a little extra milk if the soup has thickened. Stir well and
    adjust the salt and pepper and add extra lemon juice, if necessary. Serve drizzled
    with basil oil and sprinkled with flax seeds.

342 Gazpacho

PREPARATION TIME 20 minutes, plus preparing the tomatoes, at least 2 hours chilling and making the croûtons

6 large tomatoes, peeled (see page 9), deseeded and chopped
2 red peppers, deseeded and chopped
2 large garlic cloves, coarsely chopped
400g/14oz cucumber, peeled, deseeded and chopped
4 tbsp extra-virgin olive oil, plus extra to serve
tomato juice (optional)
sherry vinegar, to taste
salt and freshly ground black pepper

TO SERVE
1 recipe quantity Garlic Croûtons (see page 14)
2 spring onions, thinly sliced
1 large green pepper, deseeded and finely diced
1 large red pepper, deseeded and finely diced
½ cucumber, peeled, deseeded and finely diced
ice cubes (optional)

1　Blend the tomatoes, peppers, garlic, cucumber and oil to the preferred consistency. Depending on how juicy the tomatoes were, it might be necessary to stir in a little tomato juice to give the soup a more liquid texture. Strain the soup for an even smoother texture, if you like.

2　Season with salt and pepper, add sherry vinegar and blend again. Cover and chill for at least 2 hours.

3　When ready to serve, stir well. Adjust the salt and pepper and add more vinegar, if necessary. Serve with an ice cube added to each portion, if you like, and with the croûtons, spring onions, peppers and cucumber on the side.

343 Chilled Tomato & Yogurt Soup

PREPARATION TIME 15 minutes, plus making the stock and seeds, preparing the tomatoes, cooling and at least 2 hours chilling　COOKING TIME 30 minutes

1½ tbsp fruity extra-virgin olive oil
1 red onion, finely chopped
2 large garlic cloves, chopped
1 tsp dried thyme or mint
½ tsp cinnamon
500ml/17fl oz/2 cups Vegetable Stock (see page 12) or ready-made stock, plus extra as needed
5 tomatoes, grated (see page 9)
2 sun-dried tomatoes in oil, drained and chopped

a pinch of caster sugar
600g/1lb 5oz/scant 2½ cups Greek-style yogurt
salt and freshly ground black pepper
oil from the sun-dried tomatoes or extra-virgin olive oil, to serve
Toasted Pumpkin Seeds (see page 9), to serve
chopped coriander leaves, to serve

1　Heat the oil in a saucepan over a medium heat. Add the onion and fry, stirring, for 2 minutes. Add the garlic and fry, stirring, for 1–3 minutes until the onion is softened but not coloured. Add the thyme and cinnamon and stir for 30 seconds until aromatic. Watch closely so they do not burn.

2　Add the stock, tomatoes, sun-dried tomatoes and sugar and season with salt and pepper. Cover and bring to the boil. Reduce the heat and simmer for 10–15 minutes until the onions are very tender.

3　Blend the soup until smooth, then stir in the yogurt. Set the soup aside to cool completely, then cover and chill for at least 2 hours.

4　When ready to serve, stir well and a little extra stock if the soup has thickened. Adjust the salt and pepper, if necessary, and serve drizzled with oil and sprinkled with seeds and coriander.

344 Iced Tomato & Orange Soup with Goat's Milk Yogurt Sorbet

PREPARATION TIME 5 minutes, plus making, cooling and at least 2 hours chilling the soup and 2 hours freezing the sorbet   COOKING TIME 10 minutes

1 recipe quantity Slow-Cooked
  Tomato & Orange Soup
  (see page 40), chilled for at least
  2 hours
orange juice (optional)
salt and freshly ground black pepper
  (optional)
very finely chopped parsley, to serve

GOAT'S MILK YOGURT SORBET
250g/9oz/1 cup goats' milk yogurt
200g/7oz/scant 1 cup caster sugar
1 tbsp lemon juice

1   To make the sorbet, put the yogurt, sugar, lemon juice and 185ml/6fl oz/¾ cup water in a saucepan over a medium heat and stir until the sugar dissolves. Bring to the boil, then boil, without stirring, for 5 minutes. Brush down the side of the pan with a wet pastry brush, if the mixture splashes the sides, but do not stir.
2   Pour the mixture into a shallow heatproof bowl and set aside to cool completely. Churn the sorbet in an ice-cream maker, following the manufacturer's instructions, then transfer to a freezerproof bowl and freeze until required. Alternatively, put the mixture in the freezer and freeze for 2 hours. Use an electric mixer or fork to beat the semi-frozen mixture, then return it to the freezer. Repeat two more times, then return the sorbet to the freezer until required.
3   Remove the sorbet from the freezer 10 minutes before serving. When ready to serve, stir the soup well and add extra orange juice, if you like. Adjust the salt and pepper, if necessary, and serve immediately with 1 scoop of sorbet per portion, sprinkled with parsley. Any leftover sorbet can be kept frozen for up to 3 months.

345 Big Red Raw Soup

PREPARATION TIME 15 minutes, plus preparing the tomatoes, making the seeds and at least 2 hours chilling

1.25kg/2lb 12oz tomatoes,
  peeled (see page 9), deseeded
  and chopped
450g/1lb carrots, peeled and chopped
2 red peppers, deseeded and
  chopped
125ml/4fl oz/½ cup Vegetable Stock
  (see page 12) or ready-made stock,
  plus extra as needed

tomato juice (optional)
2 tsp caster sugar
finely grated zest of 2 oranges
salt
1 tbsp Greek-style yogurt for each
  bowl, whisked, to serve
Crunchy Mixed Seeds (see page 15),
  to serve

1   Put the tomatoes, carrots, peppers and stock in a blender or food processor and blend until smooth. Working in batches, strain through a nylon sieve, rubbing back and forth with a spoon and scraping the bottom of the sieve. Depending on how juicy the tomatoes are, you might have to add tomato juice to make the soup up to 1.25l/44fl oz/5 cups, or to thin it to the preferred consistency.
2   Stir in the sugar and orange zest and season with salt. Cover and chill for at least 2 hours.
3   When ready to serve, stir well and add a little stock or tomato juice if the soup has thickened. Adjust the salt, if necessary, and serve with a swirl of yogurt and sprinkled with seeds.

346 Raw Emerald Soup with Crushed Basil Oil

PREPARATION TIME 10 minutes, plus making the flavoured oil and stock and 2 hours chilling

3 avocados
2 tbsp lime juice, or to taste
1 tsp olive or hemp oil
400g/14oz baby spinach leaves
875ml/30fl oz/3½ cups Vegetable
  Stock (see page 12) or ready-made
  stock, at room temperature, plus
  extra as needed

3 garlic cloves, crushed
salt and ground white pepper
1 recipe quantity Crushed Basil Oil
  (see page 15), to serve

1 Cut the avocados in half, remove the stones and use a spoon to scoop the flesh
   into a blender. Add the lime juice, oil, spinach, stock and garlic and season with
   salt and white pepper, then blend until smooth. Cover with cling film directly
   resting on the surface of the soup and chill for 2 hours.
2 When ready to serve, stir well and adjust the salt and pepper, if necessary.
   Serve drizzled with basil oil.

347 Fresh Red Detox Soup

PREPARATION TIME 15 minutes, plus at least 2 hours chilling and making the seeds

875ml/30fl oz/3½ cups carrot juice
2 celery sticks, chopped
1 small cooked beetroot, peeled
  and chopped
200g/7oz cucumber, deseeded and
  chopped

½ fennel bulb, chopped
½ tsp celery seeds
orange juice, to taste
Crunchy Mixed Seeds (see page 15),
  to serve

1 Blend the carrot juice, celery, beetroot, cucumber, fennel and celery seed to the
   preferred consistency. Rub the soup through a sieve for an even smoother texture,
   and to remove the fibres from the vegetables, if you like. Cover and chill for at least
   2 hours.
2 When ready to serve, stir in the orange juice. Serve sprinkled with seeds.

348 Green Cucumber & Chilli Soup

PREPARATION TIME 15 minutes, plus 30 minutes standing, making the croûtes (optional)
and at least 2 hours chilling

1 large cucumber, deseeded and
  coarsely chopped
½ tsp salt, plus extra to season
1l/35fl oz/4 cups Vegetable Stock
  (see page 12) or ready-made stock
6 spring onions, chopped
1 handful of coriander leaves, plus
  extra to serve
5 tbsp extra-virgin olive oil, plus
  extra to serve

1 green serrano chilli, deseeded
  (optional) and chopped
1 tsp ground cumin
1 tbsp Chinese rice vinegar,
  or to taste
freshly ground black pepper
flax seeds, lightly crushed, to serve
Goat's Cheese Croûtes (see page 14),
  to serve (optional)

1 Put the cucumber in a sieve, sprinkle with the salt and leave to drain for
   30 minutes, then rinse under cold running water and squeeze dry.
2 Put the cucumber, stock, spring onions, coriander, oil, chilli, cumin and vinegar
   in a blender and blend until well mixed and finely chopped but not puréed. Season
   with salt and pepper. Transfer to a bowl, cover and chill for at least 2 hours.
3 When ready to serve, stir the soup well because it will have separated. Adjust
   the salt and pepper, if necessary, and add extra oil or vinegar, if you like. Serve
   sprinkled with coriander leaves and flax seeds and drizzled with olive oil, and
   with croûtes on the side, if you like.

349 Fennel & Red Pepper Soups

PREPARATION TIME 25 minutes, plus making the stock, cooling and at least
2 hours chilling   **COOKING TIME** 40 minutes

4 tbsp olive oil
2 onions, very finely chopped
2 bulbs fennel, finely chopped, with
   the fronds reserved and chopped
125ml/4fl oz/½ cup Vegetable Stock
   (see page 12) or ready-made stock
2 tbsp lemon juice

1 tsp aniseed-flavoured spirit,
   such as Pernod
2 large red peppers, deseeded
   and diced
a pinch of cayenne pepper
1 tbsp crème fraîche or sour cream
salt and ground white pepper

1   Heat the oil in a saucepan over a medium heat. Add the onions and fry, stirring
    occasionally, for 3–5 minutes until softened. Remove half the onions and set aside.
2   To make the fennel soup, add the fennel to the onion in the pan and cook, stirring,
    for 5 minutes. Add half the stock, the lemon juice, spirit and enough water to cover.
    Season with salt and white pepper. Cover and bring to the boil, then reduce the
    heat and simmer for 12–15 minutes until the fennel is very tender. Blend until
    smooth, then work the soup through a sieve into a bowl. Stir in the crème fraîche
    and set aside to cool completely, then cover and chill for at least 2 hours.
3   Meanwhile, make the red pepper soup. Put the remaining onion in a saucepan and
    reheat. Add the peppers and cook, stirring, for 5 minutes. Add the remaining stock,
    cayenne pepper, enough water to cover, and season with salt. Cover and bring
    to the boil, then reduce the heat and simmer for 12–15 minutes until the peppers
    are very tender. Blend until smooth. Work the soup through a sieve into a bowl.
    Set aside to cool completely, then cover and chill for at least 2 hours.
4   To serve, stir each soup and adjust the salt and pepper, if necessary. Filling one
    soup bowl at a time, put the fennel soup in half the bowl, then add the red pepper
    soup to the other half and use the tip of a knife to swirl decoratively. Alternatively,
    put a metal ring in the middle and fill it with the fennel soup. Spoon the red pepper
    soup around the outside of the ring, then carefully lift the ring. In any case, always
    pour the fennel soup first because it is thicker and will remain in position. Sprinkle
    with the fennel fronds and serve.

350 Avocado & Coconut Soup

PREPARATION TIME 15 minutes, plus making the stock and seeds, cooling and at least 2 hours chilling   COOKING TIME 15 minutes

500g/1lb 2oz avocados
1½ tbsp lime juice, or to taste
1½ tbsp olive or hemp oil
1 leek, sliced and rinsed
875ml/30fl oz/3½ cups Chicken Stock (see page 11) or ready-made stock
finely grated zest of 1 lime

2 tbsp chopped coriander leaves
170ml/5½fl oz/⅔ cup coconut milk
salt and ground white pepper
Spiced Seeds (see page 15), to serve
toasted coconut flakes, to serve
lime wedges, to serve

1   Peel and remove the stones from the avocados, chop the flesh and toss it in a bowl with 1 tablespoon of the lime juice, then set aside.
2   Heat the oil in a saucepan over a medium heat. Add the leek and fry, stirring, for 3–5 minutes until softened. Add the stock, avocados, remaining lime juice and lime zest and season with salt and white pepper. Cover and bring to the boil, then simmer for 2–3 minutes until the avocado is tender. Stir in the coriander leaves and blend the soup until smooth. Transfer to a bowl and set aside to cool, then cover and chill for at least 2 hours.
3   When ready to serve, stir in the coconut milk and adjust the salt and pepper, if necessary, and add extra lime juice, if you like. Serve sprinkled with the seeds and coconut flakes, and with lime wedges for squeezing over.

351 Mexican Corn & Pepper Soup

PREPARATION TIME 15 minutes, plus making the stock, cooling and at least 2 hours chilling   COOKING TIME 1¼ hours

1.4l/48fl oz/5½ cups Vegetable Stock (see page 12) or ready-made stock, plus extra as needed
400g/14oz/2 cups fresh corn kernels, cobs reserved and cut in half
2 yellow peppers
1 large garlic bulb
1 hot or mild chilli, to taste
4 tbsp olive oil, plus extra as needed

1 red onion, finely chopped
1 celery stick, thinly sliced
1 tsp ground coriander
1 tsp ground cumin
salt and freshly ground black pepper
Mexican queso fresco or feta cheese, drained and crumbled, to serve
tortilla chips, to serve
lime wedges, to serve

1   Preheat the oven to 220°C/425°F/gas 7. Put the stock and corn cobs into a saucepan and season with salt. Cover and bring to the boil, then reduce the heat to very low (use a heat diffuser if you have one) and simmer, covered, for 45 minutes.
2   Meanwhile, rub the peppers, garlic and chilli with oil. Put the peppers on the oven rack and roast for 20 minutes. Add the chilli and garlic and roast for another 20–25 minutes until all are lightly charred and the garlic is soft.
3   Transfer the peppers and chilli to a bowl, cover and leave to cool, then peel, deseed and chop the peppers. Deseed the chilli, scrape the flesh from the skin and set aside. Reserve any juices that accumulate in the bowl. When cool enough to handle, separate the garlic into cloves and squeeze the flesh onto a plate.
4   Bring a saucepan of salted water to the boil. Meanwhile, heat the oil in a saucepan over a medium heat. Add the onion and celery and fry, stirring, for 3–5 minutes until softened. Add the coriander and cumin and stir for 30 seconds.
5   Add the peppers, garlic and chilli flesh to the onion mixture, then stir in half the corn kernels, the stock with the corn cobs and any reserved juices. Cover and bring to the boil, then reduce the heat and simmer for 5–7 minutes until the kernels are tender. Meanwhile, put the remaining corn kernels in the pan of boiling water and boil for 3–5 minutes until tender, then drain and set aside.
6   Discard the corn cobs from the large pan and blend the soup until smooth. Add the drained corn kernels to the soup and season with salt and pepper. Transfer to a bowl and set aside to cool completely, then cover and chill for at least 2 hours.
7   When ready to serve, stir well and add stock if the soup has thickened. Adjust the salt and pepper, if necessary, and serve sprinkled with cheese and with tortilla chips on the side and lime wedges for squeezing over.

352 Jewelled Cucumber & Walnut Soup

PREPARATION TIME 15 minutes, plus making the stock, toasting the walnuts, 30 minutes standing and at least 2 hours chilling

280g/10oz cucumber, grated
½ tsp salt, plus extra to season
600g/21fl oz/2½ cups Greek-style
  yogurt, plus extra as needed
600g/21fl oz/2½ cups Vegetable Stock
  (see page 12) or ready-made stock
2 garlic cloves, crushed

85g/3oz/scant ¾ cup walnut halves,
  very lightly toasted (see page 9)
  and finely chopped
2 tbsp finely chopped mint leaves,
  plus extra to serve
ground white pepper
pomegranate syrup, to serve
walnut oil, to serve
1 pomegranate, to serve

1   Put the cucumber in a sieve, sprinkle with the salt and leave to drain for 30 minutes, then rinse under cold running water and pat dry. Transfer the cucumber to a bowl and stir in the stock, yogurt, garlic, walnuts and mint. Season with salt and white pepper, then cover and chill for at least 2 hours.

2   When ready to serve, stir well and add a little extra yogurt if the soup has thickened. Adjust the salt and pepper, if necessary, and divide into bowls. Sprinkle with mint and drizzle with pomegranate syrup and walnut oil. Bash the pomegranate with a wooden spoon, then cut it in half. Hold one half over one of the bowls and tap the top with the spoon so the seeds fall over the soup. Remove any white pith, if necessary. Repeat to sprinkle the remaining bowls with pomegranate seeds, then serve.

353 Lebanese Cucumber Soup

PREPARATION TIME 15 minutes, plus 30 minutes standing, making the stock and prawns and at least 2 hours chilling

350g/12oz cucumber, halved
  lengthways, deseeded and diced
½ tsp salt, plus extra to season
1 egg
2 large garlic cloves, one halved and
  one crushed in one piece
150g/5½oz/⅔ cup Greek yogurt
600ml/21fl oz/scant 2½ cups tomato
  juice, plus extra as needed

600ml/21fl oz/scant 2½ cups
  Vegetable Stock (see page 12)
  or ready-made stock
freshly ground black pepper
12 medium prawns, peeled,
  deveined and cooked, then cut
  in half lengthways, to serve
chopped dill, to serve
extra-virgin olive oil, to serve
hot pepper sauce, to serve (optional)

1 Put the cucumber in a sieve, sprinkle with the salt and leave to drain for 30 minutes, then rinse under cold running water and pat dry. Meanwhile, put the egg in a saucepan, cover with 2.5cm/1in water and bring to the boil, then reduce the heat and simmer for 9 minutes. Pour off the hot water, then run cold water over the egg for 1–2 minutes to stop the cooking. Set aside until cool enough to handle, then peel.

2 Rub the garlic halves over the inside of the bowl you are going to make the soup in, pressing down very firmly to extract as much flavour as possible, then discard. Put the yogurt in the bowl and slowly whisk in the tomato juice until evenly blended, then add the stock and season with salt and pepper. Add the cucumber and crushed garlic, then cover and chill for at least 2 hours.

3 When ready to serve, stir well and adjust the salt and pepper, if necessary. Stir in a little extra tomato juice if the soup has thickened and discard the crushed garlic. Dice the hard-boiled egg. Divide the prawns into bowls and ladle the soup over them. Sprinkle with the hard-boiled egg and dill and serve with oil and hot pepper sauce on the side, if you like.

354 Lemon & Saffron Soup

PREPARATION TIME 10 minutes, plus making the stock, cooling and at least 2 hours chilling   COOKING TIME 45 minutes

1 large lemon, well scrubbed
30g/1oz butter
2 tbsp plain white flour
a large pinch of saffron threads
950ml/32fl oz/scant 4 cups Vegetable
  Stock (see page 12) or ready-made
  stock, plus extra as needed

150ml/5fl oz/scant ⅔ cup crème
  fraîche or soured cream
salt and ground white pepper
finely shredded mint leaves, to serve
goji berries (optional), to serve

1 Put the lemon in a small saucepan and cover generously with water. Cover and bring to the boil, boil for 5 minutes, then drain. Repeat this process three more times. After the fourth time, cut the lemon in half in a soup bowl to capture all the juices and set aside.

2 Melt the butter in a large saucepan over a medium heat. Sprinkle in the flour, add the saffron and stir for 2 minutes. Remove the pan from the heat and slowly pour in the stock, stirring continuously to prevent lumps from forming. Stir in the crème fraîche, then return the soup to the heat and bring to the boil, stirring. Boil for 2 minutes, then remove from the heat and set aside.

3 Use the tip of a knife to remove the seeds from the lemon halves, then chop each half, including the skins. Add the lemon and any accumulated juices to the soup and blend until smooth. Season with salt and white pepper. Set aside to cool completely, then cover and chill for at least 2 hours.

4 When ready to serve, add a little extra stock if the soup has thickened and stir well. Adjust the salt and pepper, if necessary, and serve sprinkled with mint leaves and goji berries, if you like. This soup is also good served hot, sprinkled with mint leaves and chopped pistachio nuts.

355 Rocket Soup with Smoked Salmon

PREPARATION TIME 25 minutes, plus making the stock and flavoured oil, cooling, and at least 2 hours chilling COOKING TIME 35 minutes

1 tbsp olive or hemp oil
200g/7oz fennel, chopped
4 spring onions, chopped
1l/35fl oz/4 cups Chicken Stock
 (see page 11), plus extra as needed
30g/1oz rocket, leaves and stalks
 separated, with the stalks tied
 together and lightly crushed

salt and freshly ground black pepper
55g/2oz smoked salmon, shredded,
 to serve
1 recipe quantity Crushed Mint
 or Basil Oil (see page 15), to serve

1 Heat the oil in a saucepan over a medium heat. Add the fennel and fry, stirring, for 5 minutes. Add the spring onions and fry for 1–2 minutes until softened, then add the stock and season with salt and pepper. Cover and bring to the boil. Reduce the heat and simmer for 15–20 minutes until the fennel is very tender. Add the rocket leaves and stalks and simmer for 1 minute until the leaves have wilted.
2 Discard the stalks and blend the soup until smooth, then work it through a sieve. Leave to cool completely, then cover and chill for at least 2 hours.
3 When ready to serve, add extra stock if the soup has thickened. Stir and adjust the salt and pepper, if necessary. Serve topped with smoked salmon and drizzled with mint oil.

356 Peach & Orange Buttermilk Soup

PREPARATION TIME 15 minutes, plus toasting the almonds and at least 2 hours chilling

750g/1lb 10oz peaches, peeled,
 stoned and chopped
500ml/17fl oz/2 cups buttermilk,
 plus extra as needed
150ml/5fl oz/scant ⅔ cup orange juice
1 tsp clear honey, or to taste

½ tsp almond extract
a small pinch of salt
lemon juice, to taste (optional)
toasted flaked almonds (see page 9),
 to serve

1 Put the peaches, buttermilk, orange juice, honey, almond extract and salt in a blender and blend until smooth. Add lemon juice, if necessary.
2 Cover and chill for at least 2 hours. When ready to serve, add extra buttermilk if the soup has thickened. Stir well, then adjust the salt and add extra honey or lemon juice, if necessary. Serve sprinkled with toasted almonds.

357 Spiced Fruit Salad Soup

PREPARATION TIME 20 minutes, plus at least 1 hour infusing, cooling and at least 2 hours chilling COOKING TIME 10 minutes

500ml/17fl oz/2 cups
 pomegranate juice
500ml/17fl oz/2 cups orange juice
2 tbsp lime juice
finely grated zest of 1 lime
2 star anise
1 cinnamon stick
1 thin slice of root ginger, crushed

200g/7oz cucumber, very finely diced
225g/8oz pineapple, peeled,
 cored and finely diced
1 mango, peeled and finely diced
1 crisp apple, halved, cored
 and diced
2 tbsp finely chopped mint leaves
1 pomegranate, to serve

1 Pour all the juices into a saucepan, cover and bring to the boil. Remove from the heat, add the zest, star anise, cinnamon stick and ginger and leave to stand, covered, for at least 1 hour for the flavours to blend.
2 Transfer the mixture to a bowl and leave to cool completely. Add the cucumber, pineapple, mango, apple and mint leaves. Stir well, cover and chill for at least 2 hours.
3 When ready to serve, stir well. Discard the spices and divide the soup into bowls. Decorate with pomegranate seeds (see recipe 352), then serve.

358 Sweet Buttermilk Dessert Soup

PREPARATION TIME 20 minutes, plus toasting the almonds, 30 minutes soaking, cooling and at least 2 hours chilling   COOKING TIME 7 minutes

55g/2oz/scant ½ cup sultanas
2 tbsp light or dark rum
4 tbsp rice flour
1.25l/44fl oz/5 cups buttermilk
1 cinnamon stick
2 egg yolks
2 tbsp caster sugar, or to taste
finely grated zest of 1 orange,
    plus extra to serve

150ml/5fl oz/scant ⅔ cup double
    cream, lightly whipped
salt
finely grated zest of 1 lemon, to serve
finely grated zest of 1 lime, to serve
toasted flaked almonds (see page 9),
    to serve

1   Put the sultanas in a bowl, cover with the rum and leave to soak for 30 minutes.
2   Drain the sultanas. Put the rice flour in a saucepan and slowly add the buttermilk, stirring to prevent lumps from forming. Add the sultanas and cinnamon stick and season lightly with salt. Heat over a low heat, stirring, for 5–7 minutes until thickened. Remove from the heat, discard the cinnamon stick and set aside.
3   In a large bowl, beat the egg yolks and sugar, using an electric mixer, until thickened and pale and the mixture holds a 'ribbon' on the surface when the beaters are lifted. Slowly beat in the soup, then add extra sugar or salt, if you like. Set aside to cool completely, then stir in the orange zest, cover and chill for at least 2 hours.
4   When ready to serve, stir well. Stir in the whipped cream and serve sprinkled with citrus zests and almonds.

359 Refreshing Honeydew Melon Soup

PREPARATION TIME 15 minutes, plus at least 2 hours chilling

800g/1lb 12oz cucumbers, peeled,
    deseeded and diced
1 honeydew melon, about 1kg/
    2lb 4oz, peeled, deseeded and
    diced
1 large celery stick, strings removed,
    if necessary, and sliced

4 spring onions, white parts only,
    finely chopped
225g/8oz/scant 1 cup Greek-style
    yogurt
white wine vinegar, to taste
3 tbsp thinly sliced mint leaves,
    plus extra to serve
salt and ground white pepper

1   Put the cucumbers, melon, celery, spring onions, yogurt, vinegar and mint in a large bowl or blender. Season with white pepper and mix well. Blend until smooth, then season with salt and extra pepper, if necessary. Cover and chill for at least 2 hours.
2   When ready to serve, stir well and adjust the salt and pepper, if necessary, and add extra vinegar, if you like. Serve sprinkled with mint leaves.

360 Strawberry Soup with Orange Sorbet

PREPARATION TIME 15 minutes, plus at least 1 hour standing and at least 2 hours chilling

1.5kg/3lb 5oz strawberries, hulled
200g/7oz/scant 1 cup sugar, plus
    extra as needed
orange juice (optional)

orange sorbet, to serve
freshly ground black pepper, to serve
finely grated orange zest, to serve
balsamic vinegar, to serve

1   Stir the strawberries and sugar together in a large non-reactive bowl and leave to stand for at least 1 hour until the juices run, then blend until smooth. Strain the liquid through a sieve into a bowl, rubbing back and forth with a spoon. Cover and chill for at least 2 hours.
2   When ready to serve, stir well. Add extra sugar and stir in a little orange juice, if necessary, and divide into bowls. Put 1 scoop of sorbet in each one and sprinkle with pepper and orange zest. Serve immediately, with balsamic vinegar on the side.

361 Green Tea Soup with Coconut Jelly

PREPARATION TIME 15 minutes, plus chilling the coconut jelly, cooling the soup and at least 2 hours chilling   **COOKING TIME** 15 minutes

2 tbsp matcha (green tea powder)	COCONUT JELLY
1.25l/44fl oz/5 cups whole milk	250ml/9fl oz/1 cup coconut milk
1 tbsp caster sugar, or to taste	1 heaped tbsp agar agar flakes
finely grated lime zest, to serve	1 tbsp caster sugar

1   To make the coconut jelly, rinse the inside of a shallow, heatproof 8.5 x 12cm/
3½ x 4½in dish (or use a small ice cube tray), then pour the water out, but do not
dry it, and set aside. Put the coconut milk, agar agar flakes and sugar in a saucepan.
Bring to the simmer over a low heat, without stirring. Once it is simmering, stir
occasionally for 3–5 minutes until the agar agar flakes dissolve completely – put
some of the mixture in a clean spoon and look closely for any specks of agar agar.
Pour the mixture into the prepared dish and set aside to cool completely. Cover and
chill to set while you make the soup. You can speed up the cooling process by
resting the dish inside a larger dish filled with cold water.

2   To make the soup, mix the matcha and a little of the milk together in a small bowl
to make a thin paste, then stir the mixture into the rinsed-out saucepan, along
with the remaining milk and the sugar. Bring to just below the boil and stir until
the sugar has dissolved, then immediately remove the pan from the heat and pour
the soup into a heatproof bowl. Set aside to cool completely, then cover and chill
for at least 2 hours.

3   When ready to serve, run the tip of a round-bladed knife around the edges
of the coconut jelly, then invert it onto a plate, shake well and remove the dish.
Cut the jelly into bite-sized pieces. Stir the soup and add extra sugar, if you like.
Serve topped with the coconut jelly and sprinkled with lime zest.

362 Hungarian Cherry Soup

PREPARATION TIME 15 minutes, plus toasting the almonds, cooling and at least 2 hours chilling **COOKING TIME** 20 minutes

900g/2lb fresh cherries, stoned
250ml/9fl oz/1 cup rosé
   or dry red wine
1 tbsp soft light brown sugar
1 cinnamon stick
pared zest of 1 large lemon,
   all bitter white pith removed
185g/6½oz/¾ cup Greek yogurt,
   smetana or soured cream

1 tsp almond extract
lemon juice, to taste (optional)
salt
2 tbsp cherry brandy or kirsch
   (optional)
toasted flaked almonds (see page 9),
   to serve

1   Put the cherries, wine, sugar, cinnamon stick, lemon zest and 200ml/7fl oz/scant 1 cup water in a saucepan and stir to dissolve the sugar. Cover and bring to just below the boil, then reduce the heat and simmer for 10–12 minutes until the cherries are very tender.

2   Discard the cinnamon stick and lemon zest and blend the soup until smooth. Stir in the yogurt, almond extract, lemon juice and season lightly with salt. Transfer to a bowl and set aside to cool completely, then cover and chill for at least 2 hours.

3   When ready to serve, stir in the brandy, if using. Adjust the salt and add extra lemon juice, if necessary, then serve sprinkled with almond flakes, either as a dessert soup or, as in Hungary, as a first course.

363 Cantaloupe 'Gazpacho'

PREPARATION TIME 15 minutes, plus at least 2 hours chilling

1kg/2lb 4oz cantaloupe, peeled,
deseeded and coarsely chopped
200g/7oz cucumber, peeled,
deseeded and chopped
250g/9oz/1 cup Greek-style yogurt
sherry or balsamic vinegar, to taste

salt and ground white pepper
55g/2oz Serrano or Parma ham,
very thinly sliced, to serve
spring onions, white parts only,
finely chopped, to serve

1   Put the cantaloupe, cucumber and yogurt in a blender and blend until smooth.
Season with salt and white pepper, then cover and chill for at least 2 hours.
2   When ready to serve, stir well, add the vinegar and adjust the salt and pepper,
if necessary. Serve sprinkled with ham and spring onions.

364 Adzuki Bean Soup with Orange Sorbet

PREPARATION TIME 5 minutes, plus overnight soaking, cooling and at least
2 hours chilling   COOKING TIME 1½ hours

220g/7¾oz/1 cup dried adzuki beans
15cm/6in piece of dried kombu
2½ tbsp caster sugar, or to taste

orange sorbet, to serve
finely grated orange zest, to serve
cinnamon, to serve

1   Put the adzuki beans and kombu in a large saucepan and cover generously with
water. Cover and bring to the boil. Boil for 10 minutes, then skim and reduce
the heat to very low (use a heat diffuser if you have one). Simmer, covered, for
1–1¼ hours until the beans are soft enough to mash against the side of the pan.
Strain, discard the kombu and reserve the cooking liquid.
2   Put the beans, sugar and 500ml/17fl oz/2 cups of the reserved cooking liquid
in a bowl and stir until the sugar dissolves. Blend until smooth, then work the
mixture through a sieve into a bowl, rubbing back and forth with a spoon and
scraping the bottom of the sieve. Slowly stir in enough of the reserved cooking
liquid to achieve the preferred consistency. Set the rest of the cooking liquid aside.
Leave the soup to cool completely, then cover and chill for at least 2 hours.
3   About 5 minutes before serving, remove the sorbet from the freezer. When ready
to serve, stir a little of the reserved liquid into the soup if it has thickened too much
and adjust the sugar, if necessary. Divide into bowls, put 1 scoop of sorbet in each
one and serve immediately, sprinkled with orange zest and cinnamon.

365 Watermelon & Strawberry Soup

PREPARATION TIME 20 minutes, plus making the stock, cooling and at least 2 hours
chilling   COOKING TIME 15 minutes

½ tbsp sunflower oil
½ onion, chopped
280g/10oz strawberries, hulled and
coarsely chopped
125ml/4fl oz/½ cup Vegetable Stock
(see page 12) or ready-made stock
a pinch of salt, plus extra to season

1.3kg/3lb watermelon, rind removed,
deseeded and coarsely chopped
½ tbsp orange juice, or to taste
(optional)
feta cheese, crumbled, to serve
very thinly sliced mint leaves,
to serve

1   Heat the oil in a saucepan over a medium heat. Add the onion and fry, stirring,
for 3–5 minutes until softened but not coloured. Add the strawberries, stock and
salt and bring to the boil, then reduce the heat and simmer for 3–4 minutes, stirring,
until the strawberries are soft. Remove from the heat and stir in the watermelon
and the orange juice if the berries aren't at the height of their summer flavour.
2   Blend the soup until smooth, then work it through a sieve into a bowl, rubbing back
and forth with a spoon and scraping the bottom of the sieve. Leave to cool
completely, then cover and chill for at least 2 hours.
3   When ready to serve, stir well. Adjust the salt and add extra orange juice,
if necessary. Serve sprinkled with feta cheese and mint leaves.

Index